REPUBLIC OF WRATH

Also by James A. Morone

*The Devils We Know: Us and Them in
America's Raucous Political Culture*

The Heart of Power: Health and Politics in the Oval Office
(with David Blumenthal)

Hellfire Nation: The Politics of Sin in American History

By the People: Debating American Government
(with Rogan Kersh)

*The Democratic Wish: Popular Participation and the
Limits of American Government*

Health Care Politics and Policy
(edited with Daniel Ehlke)

*Healthy, Wealthy, and Fair:
Health Care and the Good Society*
(edited with Lawrence Jacobs)

*The Politics of Health Care Reform:
Lessons from the Past, Prospects for the Future*
(edited with Gary Belkin)

REPUBLIC OF WRATH

HOW AMERICAN POLITICS TURNED TRIBAL, FROM GEORGE WASHINGTON TO DONALD TRUMP

JAMES A. MORONE

BASIC BOOKS
New York

Basic Books
Hachette Book Group
1290 Avenue of the Americas, New York, NY 10104
www.basicbooks.com

Printed in the United States of America

First Edition: September 2020

Published by Basic Books, an imprint of Perseus Books, LLC, a subsidiary of Hachette Book Group, Inc. The Basic Books name and logo is a trademark of the Hachette Book Group.

The Hachette Speakers Bureau provides a wide range of authors for speaking events. To find out more, go to www.hachettespeakersbureau.com or call (866) 376-6591.

The publisher is not responsible for websites (or their content) that are not owned by the publisher.

Print book interior design by Trish Wilkinson.

Library of Congress Control Number: 2020938784

ISBNs: 978-0-4650-0244-3 (hardcover), 978-1-5416-7453-0 (ebook), 978-1-5416-4619-3 (library ebook)

LSC-C

10 9 8 7 6 5 4 3 2 1

For Rebecca

CONTENTS

Contents

INTRODUCTION

How American Politics Turned Tribal

A merican politics is loud, angry, and bristling with us versus them. The hostility between Republicans and Democrats seems to swell with every election. In 2009, a Republican Congressman shouted "You lie!" at President Barack Obama on national television and raked in almost two million dollars in campaign contributions the following week. Seven years later, candidate Donald Trump screamed "Punch him in the face!" and a delirious white supporter at a campaign rally buffeted a young black man while others shouted racial epithets. Democrats responded to President Trump's election with annual "Not My President" marches. In the House of Representatives, 229 (out of 233) Democrats voted to impeach Trump without a single Republican vote. Republican Party members call Democrats "immoral" and "lazy." Democrats fire back with "closed minded" and "dishonest." On dating apps, people even spurn romance with partners from the opposite party—and that's just as well since six out of ten parents would be unhappy if their children married someone from across the political divide.[1]

But is there anything new in our screaming political divisions? Do they endanger the republic, as many observers fear? Or should we all take a deep breath as American politics runs through just another rowdy stretch? This book scans American history to explain

1

what is different about the passionate present—and how the past might guide us to toward a better future.

Much of what we deplore today is nothing new: nastiness, violence, intolerance, fraud, twisting the election rules, bashing the government, bias in the media, fistfights in Congress, and even a violent coup in North Carolina. We have seen it all before.

But, yes, there is something different about partisanship today, and it centers on two conflicts that each burned hot throughout American history—the long, hard battles that surrounded race and immigration. In every generation, African Americans dared the nation to honor its founding statements—and then braved the violent backlashes. Clashes over slavery, segregation, racial equality, white privilege, and black lives profoundly shaped each twist and turn in the history of partisan politics. Immigrants faced a different set of challenges as they pressed for a place at the American table. Some Americans always seemed to fear the new arrivals— they came from the wrong places, represented inferior races, clung to un-American values, or professed dangerous religions. Spasms of nativism met each immigrant generation. The conflicts over race and immigration touch every aspect of the American story. They reshape the partisan debates because race and immigration create disruptive new answers to the deepest question in American politics: Who are we?

Today the partisan politics enfolding race and immigration have taken a new and unprecedented form. Historically, each of this country's two major political parties defended—and, in turn, disdained—a different group on the margins of power. Nineteenth-century Democrats welcomed European immigrants and thrust ballots into their hands almost before they'd recovered from the sea voyage. But the Democrats were also the party of thumping white supremacy and stridently defended slavery, segregation, and white privileges. On the other side, the conservative party was more enlightened about race but shouted "Fraud!" as the Irish or Sicilian or Jewish immigrants lined up to vote. At times, the parties broke into internal factions and the clash went on within their ranks. But, one way or another, the parties split up the nation's most explosive conflicts by picking different sides in the struggles over race and immigration. Then, beginning in the 1930s, a new alignment began to take shape.

African Americans boldly joined the Democrats—the bastion of white supremacy—and slowly, over decades, became a major force within the party. A second seismic change came from immigration. Between 1970 and 2017, more than sixty million people arrived in the United States, and the number of Americans born abroad leapt from less than one in twenty (in 1970) to almost one in seven people today. By the mid-2000s, most naturalized immigrants had also begun to identify with Democrats. For the first time, black Americans and immigrants were members of the same party.

An unprecedented coalition began to emerge. Democrats assembled African Americans, immigrants, and their liberal supporters. The modern Republican Party gathered people who consider themselves white and native. The most passionate differences ringing through American history are now organized directly into the parties. For the first time, all the so-called minorities are on one side.

The politics grew more treacherous when the US Census Bureau crunched the 2000 census results and made a controversial prediction: the United States would become majority-minority within a generation. White people (who are not Hispanic) would make up 46 percent of the population by 2050 and just 36 percent by 2060. In the past, the parties would have diffused the political impact—each party would have claimed one part of the rising majority. But thanks to the new party alignment, "majority-minority" sounds suspiciously like "majority-Democratic."[2]

Today's party division threatens to turn every difference into a clash of tribes. Policy questions—what to do about health care or taxes or global warming—become caught up in the us-versus-them battles. Both parties are deeply enmeshed in feelings about identity because each draws people who see themselves as fundamentally different from those on the other side. To be sure, Americans argue about many different things—as they always have. But, generation after generation, nothing has ignited political passions like the intertwined issues of race and immigration. And now the parties inject those fervors directly into every political debate.[3]

The history of partisanship reveals four additional twists to the politics of us versus them. The first springs from a curious silence at the very heart of the republic: How should we run elections? The men who wrote the Constitution shrugged off the question and left it to the states. And there, from the start, the majorities ruthlessly changed the rules to their own advantage. During the very first presidential campaign—when two parties each fielded a single candidate (in 1800)—seven out of the sixteen states changed or debated changing the election rules. As parties developed, they grew more brazen about rigging the process. To this day, there is often no neutral arbiter to oversee elections, carve the districts, decide who qualifies to vote, determine registration procedures, specify how votes are cast, count the ballots, or adjudicate disputed returns. There are few rules and almost no guidelines—just political muscle down in the states and towns.

Second, rigging the rules is simplified because, astonishingly, there is no right to vote in the United States. Again, it's up to the states. Take, for example, the Seventeenth Amendment to the Constitution which allegedly gave citizens the right to vote directly for their US senators. Well, not exactly. The amendment extends the ballot to those entitled to vote for the "most numerous branch of the state legislatures"—in 1913, when the amendment was ratified, that meant black voters in New York but not North Carolina, and women in Nevada but not New Jersey. The Seventeenth Amendment is just one example of the long tradition: when it comes to elections, we defer to the states, and the states are not bound by a basic right to vote. The Supreme Court invoked two centuries of jurisprudence after the disputed 2000 election in its *Bush v. Gore* decision: "The individual citizen has no constitutional right to vote for electors of the president of the United States." The fight over who votes and how has kindled ferocious conflicts throughout American history. And the most intense battles have always blazed around African Americans and immigrants.[4]

A third twist emerges from the familiar American resistance to a strong national government. A painful racial history lurks deep in the antigovernment tradition. There was always a white supremacy party ready to fight the feds. Each new national program faced the same anxious filter: Might it give the federal government the authority to someday, somehow, threaten slavery? Or segregation? Or white privilege? To be sure, many Americans opposed federal power in the name of personal freedom and local democracy. But throughout American history, the honorable tradition of resisting the central government in the name of liberty has drawn much of its potency from an alliance with raw racial animosity. We'll see that link in every chapter. To the discomfort of many conservatives, the connection remains robust. An American majority (including 46 percent of whites) considered President Trump a racist three years after he'd been elected. Future Republicans will face the hard job of severing the long historical connection between resisting the national government in the name of freedom and attacking it out of racial hostility.[5]

Finally, sexuality escalates the intensity of each fray. Racially divided societies always construct powerful taboos against interracial sex. If black men marry white women, the carefully fabricated racial differences will collapse. In the United States, the violently enforced sexual taboos came with strict gender controls. Nineteenth-century observers, like Alexis de Tocqueville, commented on the unusually rigid limits imposed on women in America—they were barred from both politics and markets. By the late 1830s, however, women had begun to challenge the restrictions. The gender rights campaign emerged directly from the fight against slavery. Supporters of both racial rights and gender equality traditionally found a home in the same political party. Today, gender coalesces with race and immigration to differentiate the parties. It's an unprecedented configuration: African Americans, immigrants, and women lean to one party, white, native males toward the other.

My focus on American identity—on race, immigration, and gender—is different from most accounts of our partisan history. The usual emphasis is rooted in economics. Most political historians emphasize tariffs and banks, labor and capital, booms and busts, and, most important of all, the rise and fall of inequality. All these issues appear in the pages that follow—the battle between rich and poor, for example, powered the rise of active government and forms the great lost tradition for contemporary Democrats. But as I pored over 220 years of newspapers, speeches, and party platforms, I was constantly struck by the tribal passions that intensified all those other conflicts, mutating from one generation to the next and roaring into our own time.

We begin with the hesitant rise of partisan politics. Americans founded their republic with little thought about how the people (meaning affluent white men) might air their political differences. In fact, we can find the origins of this deep silence in one of the most romantic tales about the young republic—the military coup that did not happen.

————

The ragtag American army had defeated the most powerful empire in the world. Now, in March 1783, they camped in Newburgh, New York, waiting for the peace treaty that would end the American Revolution. But there was no cheer among the troops because Congress, which did not have the power to raise taxes, had not paid them in months. The soldiers were cold, hungry, and impoverished. The officers had turned their blankets into coats, their troops didn't even have blankets. What some of them did have were wives and children begging in the streets. When they mustered out of the military, the officers were facing hardship, poverty, and possibly even debtors' prison.

Wild plans filtered through the camp. An anonymous letter circulated among the officers and called on them to "assume a bolder Tone." Some wanted to head for the western forests and turn their guns against this "country that tramples on your rights, disdains your cries—& insults your distresses." Others thought the army should march on Congress, demand their pay, and perhaps thrust one of their own into power.[6]

The idea that the American Revolution might have ended in a coup sounds fantastic to us today. But that is exactly how revolutions normally end—strong men seize power. Some of General George Washington's officers were ready and willing. The plotters called a secret meeting. "The passions were all inflamed," fretted an anxious Washington when he got wind of the cabal. He issued an order, asserting his authority by changing the date of the meeting. Maybe waiting a few more days would cool things off, he wrote to a member of Congress.

On March 15, hundreds of officers gathered on a windy bluff overlooking the camp in a large building known as the Temple of Virtue. A nervous Washington strode through his mutinous troops to the front of the room and read a meticulously crafted speech. He implored them to back down, cheered them for their valor, and promised to always champion their interests. It was a beautiful speech—so eloquent that it is still read by every cadet at the US Military Academy—but it didn't work. The men remained sullen and unmoved.

Washington then unfolded a letter from a member of Congress promising to win the soldiers their pay. Washington read, haltingly, and then stopped. Reaching into his tunic, he pulled out a new pair of spectacles. The officers had never seen their general wearing glasses. The tall, powerful solider who had taken command eight years ago was getting old—he was now past fifty. "Gentlemen, you must pardon me," muttered Washington, "I have grown gray in your service and now I find myself growing blind." Stagecraft? Perhaps. But seeing their general's infirmity worked like no words could. We know from their letters home that some of these tough, battle-hardened warriors began to weep. That was the end of their rebellion.

The usual moral of the famous story is simple. Good leaders like Washington or his officers do not seek power; they do their job and go home. Washington drew a different lesson: the new nation must have a strong central government—it was the government's weakness that almost led to the coup.[7] Washington squared the circle between abjuring personal power on the one hand and calling for a strong government on the other by denouncing politics. Public officials, he thought, should do the right thing. Nothing excited his wrath more than political parties or democratic societies (as the interest groups were called) trying to bend government toward their own interests. Washington's *Farewell Address*, traditionally read out loud across the country to mark his birthday, is an extended blast against parties and factions. The party spirit, he practically shouted, was a "horrible," "baneful," "frightful despotism" that would wreck our empire of liberty.[8]

The men who wrote the Constitution disagreed on a lot of issues, but they all agreed with Washington about this—political parties were poison. Benjamin Franklin was so fearful of them that he made a strange proposal at the Constitutional Convention. Do not pay people who serve in the executive department because, if we do, political parties will rise up and grasp for the spoils of office. James Madison, the most sophisticated political thinker of them all, identified political faction as "the mortal disease under which popular governments have everywhere perished." John Quincy Adams called parties "a baneful weed" that malicious Europeans had planted in the land of liberty. And as usual, Thomas Jefferson spun the best aphorism: The party spirit, he wrote, was "the last degradation of a free and moral agent. If I could not get to heaven but with a party, I would not go there at all."[9]

There was just one problem with all that high-minded talk. It immediately proved impossible to run a republic without political parties. Americans disagreed about all kinds of things. Should the national government be strong or weak? Should we despise England or France? Where should we put the capital? What should we do about slavery? Or the Irish, French, and Haitian refugees that entered the country with pamphlets full of incendiary ideas? Whether the founders liked them or not, political parties gave the people (which, at the time, meant mainly wealthy white men) their say. Parties lined up popular support behind the politicians who were wrestling over these issues.

Jefferson may indeed have ended up in hell because he and Madison quickly rallied opponents of strong national government into something that looked a lot like a party—complete with a newspaper digging up dirt about the other side (conveniently funded by Jefferson's State Department). Their rivals, led by Alexander Hamilton and John Adams, organized too. And in no time those infernal parties were part of the political scene. Everyone acknowledged that what they were doing was wrong—but, what else could they do? Each side organized a faction because they were convinced their rivals would ruin the republic. Each side believed its passage to the dark side would be temporary. They all expected to return to their nonpartisan ways as soon as they had saved the nation from their irresponsible competitors.

As a result of their nonpartisan illusion, the founding generation left behind no wisdom about partisan politics—and not many rules.

Political parties were not seriously discussed at the Constitutional Convention, were not mentioned in the Constitution, and scarcely appear in *The Federalist Papers* (editorials which explained the Constitution and pushed for ratification in New York). The Constitution shuffled most of the details off to the state governments. There, the majorities schemed up all kinds of ways to keep people away from the ballot box if they were not deserving or not ready or not on our side.[10]

Efforts to bar political rivals from the ballot run through the years: eligibility rules, registration requirements, violence, literacy tests, poll taxes, gerrymanders, barriers for felons, barriers for former felons, shifting ID laws—on and on it rolls through US history, the politics of who votes and how easily. The rigmarole that surrounds voting would rise through the years, especially when it mixed with the creedal politics of race and immigration.[11]

THE VERY FIRST CONTESTED ELECTION, IN 1800, ESTABlished the traditional party attitudes toward race and immigration. President John Adams, who had succeeded George Washington, was running for reelection with the Federalist Party against Thomas Jefferson and the Democratic-Republicans.*

---

*A word about party names: The Jeffersonians generally referred to themselves as Republicans. Later, they came to be called Democrats, the same name by which the party is known today. Historians have tidied things up by calling the Jeffersonians "Democratic-Republicans," though the party members did not use the term themselves. On the other side, the Federalist Party soon vanished, and most members (and their attitudes) drifted into the Whig Party, in the 1830s, and, from there, to the Republicans, in the mid-1850s. Of course, the nineteenth-century parties look very different than their twenty-first-century counterparts, but by the election of 1856, the two major parties were the Democrats and the Republicans.

President Adams and the Federalists aspired to a classical, orderly republic where people deferred to their leaders. Instead, they faced a brawling, partisan uproar intensified by refugees who were fired up by the egalitarian ideals of the French Revolution and loudly scorned the president for acting like a king. The Federalists tried to impose order with the Alien Acts, which authorized government officials to deport foreigners without testimony or trial. They also passed a sedition law that established prison sentences for newspaper editors who dared to impugn the government. The blundering legislation, meant to hush political debate, had exactly the opposite effect. The laws became major issues in the boisterous election of 1800. For the next sixty years, the Democrats continued to stand up for immigrants and mocked their rivals for clinging to the "spirit" of the Alien and Sedition Acts (as the Democratic Party platform of 1852 put it), even long after the laws—and the Federalists—had vanished into history.[12]

The clash over the Alien Acts remains infamous to this day. However, the 1800 election also focused on slavery, and on this issue, the parties took very different positions. Now, it was the Federalists who were more tolerant. Throughout the 1790s, Americans had anxiously followed the slave rebellion shaking Saint-Domingue, the French colony in the Caribbean that would later become Haiti. In 1791, the slaves rose up and overthrew their French masters. When the English tried to take advantage of the chaos and seize control of the island, the rebel slaves fought and defeated them (the British forces suffered almost as many casualties in the conflict on Haiti as they had during the American Revolution). After defeating the British, the rebel leader, Toussaint Louverture, proposed a trade alliance to the Adams administration. The administration agreed in 1799, and the fledgling US Navy even went so far as to shell one of Toussaint's rivals. The Democrats, who had been so welcoming to the European refugees, were horrified by an alliance with former slaves. What would happen, asked Jefferson, when Haitian vessels

landed in southern ports with black crews who had won their freedom with guns and knives? American slaves might be inspired to
launch a revolt of their own.

Sure enough, even as voters in some states were casting ballots in
1800, a large and well-organized slave insurrection was discovered
in Virginia. The Democratic-Republican newspapers blamed this
terrifying conspiracy on the Federalists' rash alliance with a nation
of slaves who, as the party members constantly reminded everyone,
had won their liberty by murdering their masters.

A pattern had already emerged. The conservative party (the Federalists, followed by the Whigs and the Republicans) was more tolerant toward African Americans. Over time, they offered a political
home to most black voters, abolitionists, and civil rights activists.
But aliens vexed them. The conservatives continually invented new
ways to keep the newcomers away from politics and power. On
the other side, the Democrats championed European immigrants
(Asians would be a different matter), but they bitterly denounced
efforts to meddle with slavery, states' rights, segregation, or white
supremacy.

THE UNITED STATES FINALLY CAST ASIDE WASHINGTON'S
warnings and built unabashed, all-in mass parties for the white male
masses in the 1820s and 1830s. They hit the political scene with an
arresting claim—parties could calm the rising storm over slavery.
Martin Van Buren—a short, smooth-talking, self-educated, gaudily
dressed, flamboyantly whiskered, political genius from New York—
sold the idea to southern leaders. A proper party, purred Van Buren, would break the northern "clamor against Southern Influence
and African slavery" by channeling political competition into a focus on the plums (or jobs) that would be distributed after election
victories.[13]

The very fear that Benjamin Franklin had voiced at the Constitutional Convention, when he suggested not paying federal officials, now mutated into a way to protect the republic from the slavery debate. The party faithful would follow their party chieftains and fight for the spoils of office instead of relying on such mischievous motives as regional feeling or personal judgment. Americans built their first mass party partially to blunt the great tribal issue of the day. It worked for, roughly, three decades until the slavery question simply got too powerful and broke the parties.

As slavery moved to the center of American politics, each party groped for ways to keep its northern and southern members together. The Democrats managed, for a time, by simply leaving the issue to the states. No one, they insisted, had any right to meddle with the states' control over their "domestic institutions." But the Democrats soon undermined their tidy solution. In the 1840s, they began to proclaim that it was the nation's providential destiny to spread across the entire continent. But each new acre brought with it an inescapable question—would this territory be slave land or free soil? States' rights offered no simple solution, and the party began to strain over the question that it had pushed before the country.[14]

The Whigs never found any answer to the slavery question and when it became the dominant issue, the party cracked into northern and southern factions. Most northern Whigs migrated to the Republican Party—it opposed the spread of slavery but also included a cadre of nativists fearful of immigrants. The new party's attitudes about race and immigration kept getting entangled with one another. For example, after the Civil War, in 1869 a Republican Congress overrode furious Democratic objections and passed the Fifteenth Amendment extending suffrage to black men—at the time, it was a bold and radical move. But Republican efforts to empower black voters in the South clashed with Republican efforts to control immigrants. A forceful version of the Fifteenth Amendment would have directly protected the right of all citizens to vote, but it won only five votes in the Senate. The proposal failed to attract more Republican support because it would have ruled out the literacy tests and poll taxes that Republicans deployed to limit Irish voters in the Northeast. Other senators, from both parties, feared that a powerful voting rights amendment might empower Chinese immigrants in the west. The actual Fifteenth Amendment was more constricted and only forbade states from denying any citizen the right to vote "on account of race, color or previous condition of servitude." The amendment did extend suffrage to black men for decades—an extraordinary achievement. Eventually, however, Democrats won control in Washington and enabled the southern states to use the loopholes in the amendment—literacy tests, poll taxes—to deny black Americans voting rights. Voters in the 1890s were barred not because they were black (forbidden by the Fifteenth Amendment) but because they were not able to pass a literacy test or pay a poll tax or jump the many hurdles that were carefully engineered to keep them from the ballot box (perfectly legal, ruled the Supreme Court at the time).

The decades following the Civil War brings a jolting theme to the surface. While the former slaves struggled to build new lives—gathering churches, uniting families, engaging in politics, seeking to get ahead in the new South—they faced the longest, most sustained terrorism campaign in American history, especially in states and regions that had majority black populations. Over forty violent years, white elites slowly stripped the vote from African Americans and, in some states, vastly limited the democracy altogether. In one typical midterm election, for example, the 2.2 million people in Mississippi (49 percent African American) cast just 35,000 votes—a turnout of just over 1 percent.[15]

By the start of the twentieth century, both parties had turned away from racial rights. The Democrats, based in the South, remained committed to white supremacy. Republicans still claimed to be the party of civil rights and commanded the allegiance of most black Americans but abandoned any real effort at reform. President William Howard Taft, a Republican from Ohio, began his inaugural address (in 1909) by sadly confessing that the black man's friends once thought to give him the vote but that had proved a mistake. Neither party would push civil rights or racial justice.

At the same time, the turn of the twentieth century, the traditional party pattern regarding immigration also broke down. Democrats (long the party of immigrants) and Republicans (the party with a nativist streak) reacted to the largest immigration in American history by each splitting into factions supporting and opposing immigration. After a long debate, the critics won the debate and pushed the golden gates almost shut starting in 1921. In 1907, 1.2 million people had arrived on American shores. A quarter century later, Franklin Roosevelt launched the New Deal as just 23,000 immigrants landed. One of the great conflicts in American history went quiet. Identity issues lost their partisan intensity.

On the national level, both parties abandoned civil rights and, a little more than a decade later, shut down immigration. Social scientists have recently reconstructed metrics of partisanship. With the great identity issues put aside, the partisan brawling steadily declined. To be sure, we will see stinging battles and fundamental changes. But the angriest disagreements were now within the parties rather than between them. Each party had conservative and liberal wings that clashed with one another on a wide range of topics, including the issues of identity, race, and immigration. As a result, the first half of the twentieth century registers on most scales as cheerfully bipartisan.[16]

AT EVERY TURN IN THE AMERICAN STORY, WE'LL SEE HOW African Americans themselves drove national changes. At the start of the twentieth century, blacks altered the political calculus by moving north. They faced discrimination and hard times, but up north they had a powerful weapon—the vote that they had been denied in the South. Some local Democratic bosses did what they had always done with newcomers: they started signing them into the party. As early as the election of 1932, black voters began to drift from Republican to Democrat in significant numbers, and in 1936, during Franklin Roosevelt's first reelection campaign, a majority of black voters ticked the Democratic box.

At first the white newspaper columnists chuckled over the preposterous alliance. The Democratic Party, dominated by southern segregationists, could never be a real political home to African Americans. But black activists proved the pundits wrong as they crowded into that hostile party and slowly became a political force to be reckoned with. By the election of 1948, the last vote of the New Deal era, a roaring Democratic convention beat the white supremacists and narrowly endorsed a bold civil rights plank. The segregationists, who had dominated the party for more than a century, walked out in protest and ran their own candidate, Dixiecrat Strom Thurmond, the governor of South Carolina.

The migration of northern black voters from the Republicans to the Democrats rewrote American politics. The Dixiecrats did not get far in 1948, but the changes in the Democratic Party that precipitated their bolt had seismic consequences. It broke the Democrats' hold on the South. In the election before the rupture, the Democrats had won a whopping 83 percent of the vote in the Deep South, but in the election afterward, they got just 54.7 percent. Southern Democrats responded by looking for new allies. Eventually, the conservative wings of each party—led by southern Democrats and midwestern Republicans—united under the Republican banner. The liberals in both parties drifted to the Democrats.[17]

In popular memory, the political alignment changed in a flash. "There goes the South," President Lyndon Johnson supposedly sighed when he signed the Civil Rights Act of 1964. In reality, the tectonic plates had been rumbling for decades and the changes were slowly taking hold, developing gradually from the first stirrings in 1928 to the visible changes by the 1960s. There is a reason, however, that we remember that election of 1964.

For starters, it fully exposed racial tumult across the country. The pugnacious segregationist George Wallace challenged President Lyndon Johnson for the Democratic nomination with a truculent, resentful, impolite (today we'd say incorrect) campaign. Wallace attacked civil rights as an international plot designed to rob white people of their jobs, their neighborhoods, and their way of life. He repeated his commitment to law and order like a mantra and boasted that if he came across protesters, he'd put a pistol to their heads or run them over in his car. The most often quoted defiance, from his inaugural address as governor of Alabama, hovered over his campaign: "Segregation today . . . segregation tomorrow . . . segregation forever."[18] In his first foray north, in the Wisconsin primary, the segregationist stunned everyone by taking 33 percent of the Democratic primary vote. He followed that shocker by repeating the results in Indiana and almost winning in Maryland. At the time, however, nominations were still controlled by party bosses, and Democratic leaders had no intention of permitting Wallace to get a place on the ticket. But his campaign revealed a disquieting truth: civil rights kindled white anxiety in the North as well as the South. George Wallace always seemed a sideshow in the American political pageant—until Donald Trump rode the same attitudes all the way to the White House.[19]

The election of 1964 marked the emergence of the political parties as we recognize them today. Republican senators had saved the Civil Rights Act—thirty-three (out of thirty-nine) members voted to break the southern filibuster that had gone on and on for some sixty working days. But a single nay cast by Senator Barry Goldwater (R-AZ) eclipsed all those resolute ayes. Less than a month later, conservatives seized control of the Republican convention and nominated Goldwater.[20]

Goldwater preached the antigovernment gospel like no presidential candidate had done in modern times. He had always actively opposed segregation, but during the campaign he stayed mum as segregationists swarmed into his campaign. The handful of black delegates at the Republican convention, including Jacky Robinson, who had broken the color line in baseball, published harrowing stories in the black newspapers about what they had encountered— screams, racial epithets, flying bottles, and threats of violence. "I had a better understanding of how it must have felt to be a Jew in Hitler's Germany," summed up Robinson. In the end, roughly 90 percent of black voters went Democratic. It was the end of the black Republican vote.[21]

Liberal George Romney (R-MI), who had run against Goldwater for the Republican nomination, wrote a long, bitter, private letter to Goldwater, upbraiding the nominee for turning a blind eye to the racial hostility that surrounded his campaign. "Your strategists proposed to make an all-out attempt for the Southern White segregationist vote and to . . . exploit the so-called 'white backlash' in the North," Romney wrote to Goldwater. Convention delegates, continued Romney, received racial "hate literature." And you never said a word. But Republican liberals like George Romney were now vulnerable. They had always counted on northern black voters and, as the black voters turned to the Democrats, the Republican liberals would slowly vanish.[22]

Less than a year after the Democrats won the 1964 election with the party's largest landslide of the twentieth century (61.8 percent of the popular vote), liberal Democrats won a different kind of civil rights reform. The tiny immigration quotas set in the 1920s, they argued, were just another form of discrimination. It was time, said Vice President Hubert Humphrey, to align immigration law with "the spirit of . . . civil rights law." Democrats had supported immigration back to the early nineteenth century. Now they were also the party of civil rights—and, for the first time, placed immigration reform in the same political framework as civil rights.

The proposed reform sailed through Congress, and the United States opened to large-scale immigration for the first time in fifty years. At first, the change seemed insignificant in comparison to the massive expansion of African American rights in the mid-1960s. But it led to the second largest immigration (in proportion to the population) in US history. The parties unwittingly broke a pattern that stretched back to the first campaign. Although it took decades for the partisan lines to clarify, by the 2000s, the Democrats stood for both black rights *and* immigration. Republicans attracted the skeptics.[23]

There were more turns on the road to today's political parties. The most significant came during the 1970s, when two different women's movements helped to redefine both the Republicans and the Democrats. A moral crusade, dominated by churchwomen, rose up to fight against the Equal Rights Amendment (the ERA, which was debated between 1972 and 1979 and would have inserted gender equality into the Constitution) and the Supreme Court ruling in *Roe v. Wade* (the 1973 decision that struck down laws restricting abortion). The women championed traditional gender roles, denounced homosexuality, and warned the nation about an immoral culture that threatened the old-fashioned family. They injected their quest to restore traditional morals into the heart of the modern Republican Party.

At the same time, a new generation of feminists mobilized on the other side of the same issues. They pressed for ratification of the ERA, promoted gender equality, and emphasized women's freedom to control procreation (from birth control to abortion rights). By the end of the decade, the movement began to fight for rights in the gay and lesbian communities. Their views would become central to the modern Democratic Party.

In short, the contemporary parties emerged with an unprecedented division that reflected the fiercest culture conflicts running through American history. On the one side, African Americans, immigrants, and liberal women. On the other, people who see themselves as white, native, and supporters of what they call the traditional family. One consequence can be seen in the membership of the House of Representatives fifty years later: the Democratic Caucus in 2020 was just 39 percent white men and included eighty-nine women. Across the aisle, the Republicans remained 89 percent white men and counted just 13 women. For the first time, the parties reflected all the us-versus-them intensity of the American culture wars.

TODAY, POLARIZATION HAS SPREAD INTO EVERY NOOK AND cranny of American governance. A brief scan of our national institutions suggests the sweeping reach of partisan attitudes—it's us versus them in every direction.

Partisanship swept into Congress in the early 1990s. Republican Congressman Ron Machtley first encountered it over basketball. His family and his friends were back home in Rhode Island, and playing hoops gave Ron a welcome connection to other members. One day, in 1993, a couple of stony-faced colleagues came up to him with a blunt message from a rising new Republican leader, Newt Gingrich of Georgia. "No more basketball. You're playing with Democrats. They are the enemy." The Republicans had languished in the minority for sixty years. The path back to power, believed Gingrich, required discipline and fire. The message to voters would be that Democrats were lax, corrupt, immoral, and wrong for America.[24]

For most of the twentieth century, the members had battled by day and then retired for bourbon and bull sessions at The Hole in The Wall, tucked between the House and Senate chambers. Not anymore. Now, they spend very little time together. Members fly into the capital on Tuesday and leave on Thursday night. Over 110 Republicans, eager to avoid any tincture of Washington, sleep on cots in their offices. It is a government of strangers with little loyalty for or understanding of the institution—much less the other party.

Congress does not work very well because it had evolved, over the generations, into a body that required cooperation between the parties. When members see the strangers from the other party as their mortal enemy, the machinery grinds to a halt. Each party spies the same path to success: block the other, win big, get your way, and finally reap the benefits from a grateful public. Cooperation doesn't figure into the plan.[25]

As Congress bogged down, power filtered to the White House, which began to face new levels of hostility from the rival party. The animosity did not begin with Donald Trump. The previous three previous incumbents all heard chants of "Not my president!" Republicans met Bill Clinton's election, in 1992, with cries of "illegitimate" (he won with just 39 percent of the popular vote in a three-way race). Congressional Republicans took a position that was, at the time, unusually confrontational: they pledged to block his agenda, whatever it turned out to be. Republican President George W. Bush followed Clinton and also faced charges of illegitimacy when he lost the popular vote but grasped the office thanks to the Electoral College—the first president to lose the popular vote since Benjamin Harrison back in 1888.[26]

Barack Obama won two elections by a larger margin than any Democrat in more than sixty years but faced the most unfiltered umbrage in generations. False rumors about him proliferated. He was said to have been born in Kenya (like his father) or in Indonesia (where he had lived as a youngster). Donald Trump raced around the televisions shows, gathering publicity as he broadcast the lie.

"Growing up, no one knew him," he announced on *Good Morning America* in March 2011. "He doesn't have a birth certificate, or if he does, there's something on that certificate that is very bad for him." The White House released Obama's birth certificates—short form, long form—but that did not quiet the skeptics. As his second term came to an end, only one in four Republicans were ready to agree that the president had been born in the United States. The conspiracy gathered intensity from another falsehood. Barack Obama, a practicing Christian, was said to be a Muslim—presumably the "bad thing" he was hiding on that birth certificate. The charges reflected the same deep angst over national identity that has sprung up, again and again, throughout US history. To some Americans, President Obama was the wrong race, the wrong religion, and even the wrong nationality. Many white Americans felt that he just did not seem like one of "us."[27]

Still, when Bill Clinton, George W. Bush, and Barack Obama took office, they all repeated the ritual pledges to reach out to the other side. The rhetorical gestures took on new weight when President Donald Trump, who lost the popular tally by almost three million votes, cast aside the conventional gestures of reconciliation with tweets, rallies, provocations, and executive orders all blazing with hard knuckle us versus them. His followers ardently approved, precisely because everyone else was so offended.

THE COURTS, TOO, HAVE SLID INTO THE PARTISAN VORTEX. One of Trump's first actions as president was to issue an executive order blocking people from six majority Muslim nations from entering the United States. Democrats sued in Hawaii and six weeks later, Justice Derrick Kahala Watson blocked the order from going into effect. But why Hawaii? In December 2018, US District Court Justice Reed O'Connor struck down the Affordable Care Act (or Obamacare) lock, stock, and barrel. He gave Republicans a policy victory that they had failed to win in Congress (though he stayed his own decision). But why a Texas court?[28]

Political scientists call it venue shopping—find a court that leans your way. Partisanship has become an essential feature of the American judicial system, exploding one of the most important myths in American governance. Chief Justice John Roberts neatly summed up the fading ideal at his confirmation hearing: "Judges are like umpires. Umpires don't make the rules; they apply them." Judges, appointed for life, apply the laws and protect individual rights. For a long time, that fiction held. Most Supreme Court justices were appointed with near unanimous votes. But social scientists have shown, in study after study, that since the 1950s, ideology is the most powerful predictor of judicial votes, especially on major cases. Today, the general public has caught on—a full 75 percent agree that "justices sometimes let their ideological views influence their decisions."[29]

The courts were designed to be above the partisan fray. But the partisan wave that engulfs American politics now endangers the courts' role as arbiters of the American rules. We have been here before. Past generations packed the courts (in the 1860s) or threatened to pack them (in the 1930s) when the judiciary and the elected branches grew far out of synch. Now, once again, left-leaning policy wonks buzz with ideas about reorganizing the courts to break the tightening conservative grip on them.

THE BIGGEST CHANGE APPEARS TO LIE IN THE STATES. ONCE they were viewed as "laboratories of democracy," testing all kinds of experimental policies before they went national—social security, women's suffrage, alcohol prohibition, and same-sex marriage to name a few. In many places, the parties worked together once the elections were over. But partisanship has risen in the states too. Today, the state experiments increasingly focus on keeping the other party down.[30]

After Democrats narrowly won statewide office in Wisconsin in 2018, for example, the lame duck Republican legislature stripped the incoming Democratic governor of the authority to interfere with the new work requirements that their party had affixed to food stamps and Medicaid; he could not withdraw the state from a law suit against Obamacare or loosen the voting requirements that they had tightened. Most of these moves were imported from Republican efforts in North Carolina. In Texas, Democrats fled the state in 2003 in an unsuccessful effort to deny Republicans a quorum for their bare-knuckle redistricting plan. In Oregon in 2019, Republicans tried the same trick and went into hiding to deny the Democrats a quorum for their cap-and-trade environmental legislation to curb greenhouse gases. State militia groups pledged to defend the Republicans with arms, if necessary. Threats of violence grew louder and led the police to shut down the legislature as a public safety measure.

Those laboratories of democracy in the states, sum up political scientists Steven Levitsky and Daniel Ziblatt, "are in danger of becoming laboratories of authoritarianism." In truth, the efforts to suppress the other side and even the threats of militia violence are nothing new. We see them throughout American history—especially as immigrants or black voters cast ballots in large numbers. When the ruling powers feared a rising majority-minority, repression often followed. The laboratories of democracy have never been good places to test truculent attitudes about us versus them.[31]

FOR A LONG TIME—BY BOTH DESIGN AND CHANCE—THE parties deflected identity conflicts. In the nineteenth century, each recruited very different kinds of groups. In the early twentieth century, each party divided within itself on matters of race, immigration, and gender. By contrast, today's parties are internally united on all those dimensions and, as a result, zoom them straight into politics. Raise a policy issue, any policy issue, and watch it flow into the clash of identity and culture. Politics has grown so hot because it now boomerangs right back to the primal question: Who are we? To answer "Republican" (much less to shout "Trump") is practically a slur in some neighborhoods. A white male Democrat is practically an oxymoron in others.

How did we get here? What warnings lie buried in the past? Where should we go next? Those were the questions on my mind as I wrote the chapters that follow.

PART I

THE PARTIES RISE

ONE

INTO THE TEMPLE OF LIBERTY ON THE SHOULDERS OF SLAVES

The First Political Campaign (1800)

I n 1800, a slave named Gabriel meticulously plotted a rebellion in Richmond, Virginia. He was a skilled blacksmith whose owner rented him out and pocketed most of the wages. Gabriel stood more than six feet tall and could read and write. He had once bitten off a white overseer's ear but escaped the gallows thanks to a quirky loophole in the legal code—he recited a biblical passage at his trial and was punished, instead, with a brand on his left hand.

Gabriel planned to lead hundreds of slaves into Richmond, waving a flag inscribed "Death or Liberty"—an ironic turn of Patrick Henry's famous American Revolution oration, "Give me liberty or give me death." The rebels would spread through the city and seize guns, money, and food. They would take Governor James Monroe as a hostage and burn the bridge over the James River to foil a counterattack. The rebellion, they hoped, would reverberate across Virginia as thousands of slaves rose up and joined them. Gabriel and his colleagues believed they were the latest wave in an inexorable historical tide. The Americans had thrown off English tyrants, the French had rebelled against an oppressive king, and the slaves in Saint-Domingue (Haiti) had cast aside their masters. Now, the bondsmen and women in Virginia would take their turn and redeem America's promise of liberty.[1]

But luck turned against the rebels. Torrential storms washed out the roads and bridges on August 30, the appointed day. The uprising was deferred, causing two recruits to panic and spill the secret. Once authorities got wind of the plan, all hell broke loose. Governor Monroe hung some 27 black men, and white Virginia buzzed with anxiety.

THE SLAVE REBELLION LOOMED LARGE BECAUSE IT BROKE just as Americans were conducting their first actively contested two party presidential election in 1800. Although only 62,000 men voted (in a total population of 5.3 million), the first campaign taught Americans something important: how to cast off the founders' dream of consensus and settle their differences by voting. President John Adams and the Federalists stood for reelection against Thomas Jefferson and the Democratic-Republicans. The campaign sparked all kinds of debates—including a fierce clash over American identity. Gabriel's rebellion pushed the issue of slavery into the election. The role of refugees in American politics loomed even larger. In multiple ways, the election of 1800 put that enduring question before the protean new republic—Who are we?

The election between Adams and Jefferson was a watershed. It was the first time any nation used an election to change governments, replacing the Federalists with Jefferson's Democratic-Republicans. How did the nation manage this historical campaign? Not terribly well. States unabashedly rigged the voting rules in order to swing the Electoral College their way. And when the votes were cast, the election ended in a dead tie between Jefferson and his vice-presidential candidate, Aaron Burr. The Constitution had not foreseen political parties with their slate of candidates running nationwide and had simply specified that the presidency would go to the person with the most votes, the vice presidency to the runner up. After the tied election, the Federalists brazenly tried to cling to power by cutting a deal with their erstwhile rival, Aaron Burr. Here is another enduring legacy of the first campaign: rising political parties bent the ambiguous voting rules to their own advantage. That urge grows intense when the debate turns to the fundamental matter of American identity—as it did in 1800. As it does today.

——————

JUNE 1790. ALEXANDER HAMILTON WAS FRANTIC. HIS FI-nancial plan had gone down in the House by two votes. Northern representatives, who supported the scheme, were so angry that they threatened to lead their states right out of the union. To let tempers cool, the chamber had suspended business. As Hamilton anxiously paced back and forth in front of President Washington's New York mansion, he bumped into Thomas Jefferson, newly returned from France to take up his role as secretary of state. The suave Jefferson heard Hamilton out and invited him to dinner.

The next night, Hamilton, Jefferson, and James Madison met for what one historian calls "the most celebrated meal in American history." Hamilton pleaded his case. The federal government must stabilize the republic's shaky finances by assuming all the debt that states had run up during the Revolution. It would issue federal bonds, which would give people a safe haven for investment (the major alternative, land speculation, was treacherous and had ruined some of the country's wealthiest men). Madison and Jefferson both hated the idea—Jefferson called it "pabulum to the stock-jobbing herd." Financial speculators had been buying up the apparently worthless state bonds from impoverished veterans for as little as ten cents to the dollar. Now, if Hamilton got his way, the rogues would make a killing. The swindle, insisted Jefferson and Madison, would corrupt our plain, honest republic.[2]

Over the course of the dinner, Hamilton persuaded them. Why? Jefferson later said that he and Madison surrendered because they were worried "about the preservation of the union"—the Constitution was just four years old and it was not yet clear if it would hold. Since Hamilton's "pill would be peculiarly bitter to the Southern States," the three agreed to sweeten it by compromising on another contentious issue: the question of where to locate the nation's capital. Hamilton was pushing for New York, others wanted Philadelphia, and the southerners favored northern Virginia. Half the roll call votes in the first Congress had been about the issue. Now the three men made their bargain. The federal government would assume the states' debts and the national capital would lie just north of Virginia. When the matter came back to the House, two Virginia representatives flipped their votes, and Hamilton's financial program became a reality along with the new capital on the shores of the Potomac.[3]

Jefferson later contended that the political parties sprang out of that bargain—which he called the worst of his life. In reality, the parties were springing up anyway. But Hamilton's financial program helps identify exactly what was at stake as the two parties went public. Their differences stretched beyond economics and touched the definition of friend and foe, how the citizens of a republic ought to behave, and exactly who should count as a voting citizen in the first place. Add it all up and the great debate—out in the open for the first time during the election of 1800—amounted to nothing less than a fight about what kind of nation the United States ought to be.

Hamilton and the Federalists imagined America as a rising mercantile power with a sophisticated financial system, a national bank, and a growing manufacturing sector. The national government would construct roads, dredge rivers, sponsor a national university, and spur American factories with protective tariffs. It was an audacious vision. The new country's cities were still tiny—New York's population was roughly thirty-three thousand, while London and Beijing each counted over a million people. American cities had no smokestacks, no mills, few clocks, and no conception of the modern workday. Merchants routinely drank rum all day long. Nevertheless, Hamilton and his allies (mainly in the North) imagined an ambitious national government steering a thriving economy into the nineteenth century.[4]

Many Federalists also clung to a high Puritan view of leadership. As one of their newspapers explained, the country needed a president "who honestly tells men how wicked they are and that nothing will keep good order but the powerful restraint of a strong government." Good order and strong government were their watchwords. As the Federalists saw it, the people needed to select superior leaders and then defer to them. They blasted anyone who tried, as George Washington had put it, to "counteract" or "awe" (or influence) elected leaders. The Federalists looked down on, well, politics itself. And yet, here they were, just four years after Washington's *Farewell Address*, plunging into the very things they despised—organizing a campaign and scrambling to win over the voters.[5]

The Jeffersonian party response to the Federalist ideas could be summed up in three words: No! No! No! They pictured an agrarian people who tilled their own land and were therefore reliant on no other person—even when the actual tilling was done by slaves. The Democratic-Republicans countered the Federalist call for a strong central government by insisting on a modest one that deferred to the states and citizens. Where the Federalists called for order and deference, the Democratic-Republicans celebrated the voice of the (white, male) people. Unlike their rivals, the Democratic-Republicans could hear the raucous, rough and tumble politics that was rising in the new century.[6]

FOREIGN POLICY OFFERED ANOTHER MIRROR OF THE PARTIES' fears and aspirations for the United States. England and France were at war with one another, and the young republic had to choose which nation to side with. The calculations went deeper than politics and policy. The two nations stood, in the American mind, for opposing principles: English hierarchy and order versus French revolutionary fervor and rights. Which should the young republic respect? Which revile? These were not policy questions so much as existential ones. They reflected the kind of nation the different parties aspired to build.

The Federalists, of course, admired England and feared France. They never tired of pointing out how the bloody mobs of the French Revolution had yielded chaos, blood, and terror. When the Democratic-Republicans talked about equality, liberty, and fraternity, the Federalists denounced them as Jacobins (after the radical French Club) luring America into the same anarchy that roiled the French Revolution.[7]

On the other side, Jefferson and his party thought the Federalists had been dazzled "by the glare of royalty and nobility." The Republican newspapers printed affidavits from men who declared they had overheard Hamilton or Adams or other Federalists secretly confessing their love for monarchy. The Federalists had entirely forgotten our own revolutionary ideals, charged the critics, and the fact that the French had fought by our side when we won our freedom.[8]

AS JOHN ADAMS STEPPED INTO THE PRESIDENCY IN 1787, HE immediately faced a foreign policy crisis. The Federalists had pushed through a treaty with England and, in response, the French began to seize US ships. They took more than three hundred—brazenly grabbing one right outside New York harbor. Whispers of war began to spread. Even former President Washington speculated on whether "the French [would] be so mad as to openly . . . invade these United States."[9]

Adams convened a special session of Congress and rattled the rafters with a fiery speech. The president dispatched a delegation to negotiate peace with France. Some Democratic-Republicans seemed more loyal to their foreign ally than their own Federalist government. Jefferson secretly advised the French counsel how to play Adams and his negotiators (as Hamilton had done earlier, during negotiations with England). This time, the back channeling did not matter because the French foreign minister, Charles-Maurice de Talleyrand-Perigord, coolly humiliated the Americans with his demands. Adams must retract his speech, the Americans must loan the French money, and before any negotiations began, the delegation was strongly encouraged to offer Talleyrand himself a little *doucer*—a bribe. For the cynical Talleyrand, this was business as usual, but the stunned American negotiators rejected his ultimatums and sent an outraged dispatch describing the details back to the president.[10]

Worrying that his own Federalist Party would rush the country into war, Adams buried the report. "There is not more prospect of seeing a French army here as there is in heaven," he grumbled to his secretary of war, James McHenry. When the Republicans discovered that Adams had squelched the report, they assumed he was trying to poison relations with France and blasted him. Adams backed down, published the document, and basked in the uproar that followed.[11]

The details *were* sensational, and the newspapers reprinted all the craven, money-grubbing details. The Federalist press jeered the Democratic-Republicans for admiring the French. "The recent exposure of the corruption and rapacity of the infernal republic [France]," crowed the Federalist *Gazette of the United States*, "has proved to [be] like the shock of some vast explosion." The Jeffersonians were indeed shocked by the revelations. Before releasing the damning report, Adams had delicately suppressed the names of the French negotiators and simply referred to them as X, Y, and Z, and that gave the episode its rather mysterious name, the XYZ Affair.[12]

Suddenly, unexpectedly, Adams and his party became heroes. The roly-poly president had never been a soldier, but now he marched about the capital wearing military regalia. The Federalists swept the midterm election in 1798 and won the largest margins they would ever enjoy in both the House and the Senate. Riding high, the party overreached.

The Federalist Congress established a Navy and authorized "a provisional army" of up to twenty-two thousand soldiers. Their rivals protested. Republics like the United States were supposed to rely on citizen militias—standing armies were for emperors and kings. A foreign visitor described how, suddenly, the cities were full of soldiers "dressed in splendor." Democratic-Republicans saw this as confirmation of the monarchial disease metastasizing in American government.[13]

In short, the disagreement over England and France bluntly reflected the emerging choice that Americans faced. Would the nation emulate England with its stability and harmony or France and Liberté! Égalité! Fraternité! Each alternative alarmed one of America's factions and pushed them to organize like-minded citizens. Americans slowly began to understand that parties and politics enabled the nation to debate questions and resolve disagreements.

Future generations would dream of a bipartisan foreign policy, fearful that the nation could not afford division in the face of its enemies. The young republic was under no such illusion. Far from it—when Americans looked abroad in 1800, they projected their hopes and fears onto other nations. We will run into this theme again and again. Forget about unity at the water's edge. Looking across the seas constantly raised partisan storms back home, stirring dreams about who we could be—or nightmares about what we were becoming.

THE ADMINISTRATION'S NEXT MOVE CAUSED A LOT MORE trouble than the soldiers dressed in splendor. In the years leading up to the election, revolutionary upheaval in Europe sent thousands of émigrés fleeing to the United States. In 1798, for example, Irish revolutionaries who escaped the gallows arrived holding deeply republican (and ferociously anti-English) views.

Federalists saw danger striding down the gangplanks. They believed the French fomented strife in a nation before striking with their military. According to the Federalist *Porcupine's Gazette*, these seemingly desperate refugees entering the young republic were plotting *"to excite a rebellion supported by France."* Even George Washington fretted from his retirement. "A Certain description of men in our Country . . . are sent among us . . . for the express purpose of poisoning the minds of our people and to sow dissensions among them, in order to alienate their affections from the Government."[14]

President Adams was dubious about any French invasion, but he worried about the newcomers. "The continual accession of foreigners," he wrote, "will endanger and destroy our peace, if we know not how to govern them. They will moreover corrupt our elections and tear us to pieces." Examples of those corrupt election practices filled the Federalist press.[15]

For example, the Federalist *Gazette of the United States* reported that "a Jewish tavern owner with a very Jewish name [Israel Israel]" had been elected to the Pennsylvania Senate because "his violent attachment to French principles" appealed to Philadelphia's radical refugees. Mr. Israel was actually an active Methodist but, no matter, the newspaper charged that this Democratic-Republican had swept into office on a wave of illegal refugee votes. Federalist authorities threw out the results and repeated the election in February 1798. This time, announced the *Gazette*, foreign voters would be required "to take out their certificates" and prove they had paid their taxes and were eligible to vote. Mr. Israel narrowly lost the rematch. Even before the turn of the nineteenth century, Americans were fighting about who should vote, what values were dangerous, and—always the deepest question—who was a proper American in the first place.[16]

The English gave the Federalists, who so admired them, a model law to emulate. In 1793, the British Parliament passed the Aliens Act, empowering the crown's authorities to deport French refugees at the first sign of radical politics. In 1798, the Federalist Congress came up with its own version of the policy. Three laws, known collectively as the Alien Acts, were the first controversial effort to regulate newcomers in what would prove to be an immigrant nation.[17]

The first of the new acts required immigrants to wait fourteen years before applying for citizenship—originally, the wait had been two years, and the Washington administration had raised it to five. Some Federalists pushed for "never"—they wanted to forbid foreigners from ever becoming Americans. Their proposal lost out, but it marks the anxiety that would repeatedly burst out from the ranks of the Federalists and their successors, the Whigs and the Republicans.

The second act—the notorious Alien Friend Act—gave the executive branch the power to hunt down aliens it considered dangerous and deport them without any judicial process. Democratic-Republican Congressman Albert Gallatin led the opposition—and for him it was personal. Pennsylvania had elected the Swiss-born Gallatin to the US Senate. Federalists had promptly removed him (on a party line vote, 14–12) because he did not meet the nine-year residency requirement for Senators specified in the Constitution. Two years later, he won election to the House, where he argued vehemently that the Constitution prevented the federal government from exercising any authority over naturalization at all. The Alien Acts, he said, were unfair, unwise, and unconstitutional.

Others offered stronger criticisms. "No man can tell what conduct will avoid suspicion," argued congressman Edward Livingston, a Democratic-Republican from New York, in a speech to his fellow lawmakers. "No indictment; no jury; no trial; no public procedure; no statement of the accusation . . . no counsel for the defense; all is dark, dark, dark." Livingston ended with his most powerful blast: if the executive branch was granted the power to deport aliens, slavers would be able to "hold . . . [their] species of property . . . [only] at the will and pleasure of the president." The act posed a threat, not just to aliens but to the institution of slavery itself. Livingston's argument would be repeated in countless ways. For the Democratic-Republicans and their heirs, every whiff of federal power would be scrutinized for its potential threat to the racial order.[18]

The focus, in 1800, was not on shutting down immigration but protecting republican institutions from the foreign born. The fear of strangers evolves from one generation to the next, and yet the essential political fact remains the same more than two centuries after the Alien Acts. Some Americans embrace immigrants and celebrate the strength and diversity they add to the nation, while others fret along with President John Adams that the strangers "will corrupt our elections and tear us to pieces." More than two centuries after the Alien Acts, a newly elected president would barge onto the national scene and, in his very first act, ban people from Muslim nations for the alleged danger they posed to the homeland and its democratic institutions. While each era was very different, the underlying anxieties alert us to the hard, nativist streak breaking to the surface from generation to generation across American history.

THE FEDERALISTS ALSO TRIED TO QUIET THE PARTISAN din that, they were sure, encouraged the enemy. Former President Washington predicted that if the French invaded, "their operations will commence in the southern quarter," since "they will expect, from the tenor of the debates in Congress to find more friends there." Translation: the South is the regional base of Democratic-Republicans, who endanger the nation with their brash talk.[19]

The Adams administration tried to calm the turbulent politics with the ill-advised Sedition Act of 1789, which made it a crime to "write, print, utter, or publish . . . any false, scandalous, and malicious writing . . . against the government of the United States . . . with intent to . . . bring them into contempt or disrepute or to excite people against them."

What really got under the Federalists' skin was the rising media of the day . . . coruscating partisan newspapers that cheered one party and attacked the other. Newspapers like the *Aurora* (in Philadelphia) and the *New York Argus* took the Democratic-Republican side (and were targeted by the administration), while a larger network of newspapers, led by the *Gazette of the United States*, answered for the Federalists. The inexpensive four-page weeklies freely borrowed from one another—reprinting and embellishing, hooting and refuting. Here's how one editor, secretly funded by Thomas Jefferson, sized up President Adams: "Judge the prattle of a president [who compounds] ignorance and ferocity, deceit and weakness. . . . He has neither the force nor firmness of a man, nor the gentleness and sensibility of a woman." The newspapers published charges, countercharges, rumors, insults, leaked letters, silly ballads, and official documents like the French Constitution or the XYZ dispatches. George Washington himself subscribed to ten.[20]

The Sedition Act only turned the carping editors into heroes— and right in time for the presidential election. But the Alien and Sedition Acts reflected something deeper than partisan calculations. Conservatives were trying to shore up a waning vision. Republics, they believed, ought to put aside self-interest and operate by consensus, honor, and deference. Today, political scientists often condemn the Federalists for violating the First Amendment and maliciously squashing their opponents' free speech. But, from a purely political point of view, they were guilty of a graver sin. They were clinging to ideas that had grown out of date in the vibrant republic.[21]

In the end, the Federalists' effort to suppress dissent backfired— editors who had been indicted under the Sedition Act reported on the proceedings with wicked glee. "The editor can steadfastly assure his reader," wrote the *Aurora*'s William Duane, scribbling dispatches from his own trial, "that neither persecution nor any other peril to which bad men may expose him, can make him swerve from the cause of republicanism."[22] The entire Democratic-Republican press celebrated each brave writer who "stood . . . in the defense of his countrymen and his neighbors." In all, there were seventeen trials, each pictured heroically in the opposition papers.[23]

If the Federalists looked back to a fading ideal, the Democrats looked forward to politics, confrontation, and an aggressive interpretation of states' rights. Two states in particular challenged the government's restrictions on speech. The Kentucky and Virginia Resolutions, secretly written by Thomas Jefferson and James Madison respectively, declared the Alien and Sedition Acts in violation of the Constitution and, in the words of the Kentucky Resolution, "unauthoritative, void, and of no force." Madison's language in Virginia was more cautious—he merely opposed the federal act rather than declaring it void. When the House of Burgesses debated the Virginia Resolution, it quickly became clear that the delegates were primarily concerned with safeguarding the institution of slavery. They decided that an overreaching national government posed the gravest threat of all. It was up to the states, they agreed, to protect slavery against federal power. The Kentucky and Virginia Resolutions enacted a model for standing up to the feds that guided the states' rights position during the slavery debate that rose in the decades ahead.[24]

The Sedition Act seemed, until recently, like the dusty past. But, rising attacks on the media—culminating in yelps of "fake news"—blew the dust right off that history. Adams and the Federalists, riding their brief thermal of wartime popularity, enacted their violations of free speech and due process. They were only the first in a long line. Their blundering efforts at what we would call censorship sends a warning message, blinking down the years to the perilous present.[25]

PERHAPS NO EVENT IN THE 1790S SHOOK THE UNITED States quite like the revolution in Haiti—the only successful slave uprising that ended in the founding of a new state ruled by former slaves. The Haitian Revolution landed directly in the 1800 presidential campaign because, a year before the vote, the Adams administration did something unusually bold. It recognized the rebels.

Saint-Domingue, as Haiti was called at the time, was a lucrative French colony where slavery had been exceptionally cruel—and very profitable. Africans routinely ran for freedom, collecting into small bands in the brush. Owners staged slave hunts and punished runaways by castrating them or burning them alive—violent spectacles designed to terrify the rest of the population into submission. Officials back in France occasionally tried to restrain the vicious excesses, but they were largely ignored on the island.

By 1791, dreams of liberty were rippling out from the French Revolution to Saint-Domingue. The island's authorities frantically tried to staunch their flow. They guarded the piers against abolitionists or their propaganda and banned the planters from freeing any slaves, removing even the thinnest hope of freedom. But black leaders on Saint-Domingue could see that the whites were vastly outnumbered and bitterly divided—between rich and poor, between white planters and mixed-race overseers, and between the French born and the island born. The slave's rebellion finally erupted in August 1791. At least in popular lore, a carefully planned uprising was actually set off by a Vodou ritual dramatically wreathed in lightning and thunder. The rebels burst out across the island's northern plain, burning estates, killing planters, and breaking machines. The white survivors retreated to the northern city of Cap-Français where they watched thick columns of smoke rising from the blazing plantations. They responded to the revolt by massacring free black people, hanging slaves on scaffolds erected in the town square, and racking suspected conspirators on wheels. The rebels met violence with violence.[26]

Over the next decade, Spain, England, and France all tried to conquer the colony and put the slaves back to work. A charismatic leader, Toussaint Louverture, emerged through the long fight. In 1793, Britain dispatched a large army to pluck the island. Some local planters threw aside their French identity and rallied to the invaders, hoping to reimpose slavery. For five horrific years, the English fought to subdue the former slaves. By the time the British gave up, they had sustained something like one hundred thousand casualties and forty thousand dead. They left Saint-Domingue in ruins.

The canny Louverture turned to the United States for help. In a letter to President Adams, he professed to be surprised and disheartened that American ships had stopped trading with his island. By now, the Adams administration had entered into its quasi-naval war with France and embargoed all French colonies. Louverture pretended not to know about all that but casually pointed out that while Saint-Domingue was still technically a French colony, it was quite emphatically no longer under French control. Louverture invited the Adams administration to trade on favorable terms and sent an emissary, Joseph Bunel, to Philadelphia, which served as the American capital while Washington, DC, was under construction. Bunel met with Secretary of State Thomas Pickering, who seized on the idea of an alliance with Louverture as a way to push Saint-Domingue even further from French control and to prevent any prospect of a French invasion from the island.[27]

Bunel had dinner with President Adams to help seal the agreement. For a long time, historians cheered their meal as the first between an American president and a person of color, but more recent analysis reveals that Bunel was a white businessman, though his wife, Marie Esteve, was a black Creole freewoman. We can say that Bunel was the first presidential dinner companion representing a black leader or married to a black partner—and, more important, that the administration was boldly proposing an alliance with a nation governed by former slaves.[28]

In January 1799, the Adams administration moved to resume trading with Saint-Domingue. The proposed legislation, known as "Toussaint's Clause," immediately sparked a fight over race and slavery. The Democratic-Republicans fiercely objected to any deal with former slaves. Representative Albert Gallatin, the Swiss-born rising star from Pennsylvania, stood up in the House and played directly to the slavers' fears. Saint-Domingue, said Gallatin, was "a wholly black nation with a wholly black interest." Its sailors and citizens would "visit the states of South Carolina and Georgia and spread their views among the Negro people there." They would "excite dangerous insurrections." Gallatin kept going, denouncing the country in fearful terms that would ring through the nineteenth century. Haiti was "almost entirely [made up] of slaves just emancipated, of men who received their first education under the lash of the whip, and who have been initiated to liberty only by that series of rapine, pillage and massacre, that have laid waste and deluged that island in blood." No one, continued Gallatin, "wishes more than I do to see an abolition of slavery, when it can be properly effected; but no man would be more unwilling than I to constitute a whole nation of freed slaves . . . and thus to throw so many wild tigers on society." Why, he added, to clinch his argument against trucking with the savages, "the general [Louverture] is black, and his agent here [Bunel] is married to a black woman in this city."[29]

Thanks to the 1798 midterm victory that had followed the XYZ affair, the Federalists had the votes to pass Toussaint's Clause on purely party lines. Jefferson reflected the Democratic-Republican attitude in a sour note to Madison. "We may expect, therefore, black crews, supercargoes & missionaries thence into Southern states. . . . We have to fear it."[30]

With trading reestablished, the Adams administration deployed the newly commissioned Navy to protect American vessels doing business with the island. Eventually, American warships helped Louverture consolidate control of Saint-Domingue by shelling his rival, André Rigaud (who had been attacking American vessels). The navy bombardment tipped the balance in a struggle for control on the island and marked the first time the US Navy intervened in a foreign civil war.

Adams and the Federalists went into the election of 1800 after forging a controversial alliance with men and women who had thrown off slavery. The Federalists, who had been so repressive toward refugees, engineered an enlightened policy toward the liberated slaves in Haiti—over the vehement opposition of the Democrats who kept insisting on the horror of slave insurrection and the danger that the Haitian example posed to the American slavers.[31]

THE DRAMATIC CODA TO THE HAITI STORY CAME AFTER JEF-ferson had won the election of 1800. In 1802, Napoleon Bonaparte cast his eye on the prized French island—and the New World. His covert plan was to retake control of Saint-Domingue, reestablish slavery, and use the island as his staging ground for military campaigns in the new world. As part of his plan, he acquired the vast Louisiana territories (lying west of the Mississippi River) from Spain and dispatched a large army to Saint-Domingue commanded by his brother-in-law, General Charles Victor Emmanuel Leclerc.

President Thomas Jefferson initially pledged to cooperate with the French invasion. "Nothing could be easier," he assured the French representative in Washington, "than to furnish your army and your fleet with everything, and to starve out Toussaint."[32] But the size of the French armada sobered up the administration and Jefferson backed away from his pledge of aid. General Leclerc made things worse by pushing the US envoy off the island and blaming American merchants—whom he dismissed as "Jews"—for having armed Louverture. When the French attacked, they were stunned by the discipline and ferocity of the former slaves—and by their passion for freedom. "These men . . . laugh at death," reported Leclerc, and "it is the same with the women." In fact, women frequently appeared on the list of rebel leaders and were routinely executed. Yellow fever and malaria decimated the French force—Leclerc himself died from disease. The embattled French escalated the savagery by turning to genocide. New slaves, they reasoned, could always be imported from Africa after the island had been pacified. Eventually, the former slaves defeated the French. Saint-Domingue reclaimed its aboriginal name, Haiti, and declared independence in January 1804. Toussaint Louverture, however, did not live to see the victory. He had grown weary from a decade of warfare and Leclerc lured him into putting down his arms, double-crossed him, clapped him in chains, and sailed him to France where he died, freezing in a prison high in the French Alps. A new nation of former slaves survived genocidal wars with all the major European powers—Spain, England, and France.[33]

The unexpected Haitian victory redounded to America's great advantage. By holding off the French, the Haitians thwarted Napoleon's plans for New World conquests. Starved for funds, he sold the French possessions on the American mainland to the United States for $15 million. Jefferson's great achievement—the Louisiana Purchase that doubled the young republic's territory—was made possible by the indomitable rebels in Haiti.

The Haitians accomplished something unprecedented: a group of slaves had liberated themselves and managed to keep their freedom by fighting off the avaricious European empires. Inspired by their example, slaves reached for freedom in Puerto Rico, Venezuela, Grenada, Cuba, Virginia, and beyond. To African Americans, Haiti became a symbol of hope. Abolitionist David Walker was just one of many writers to frame the slaves' triumph as a providential warning to racial oppressors in America.

O my suffering brethren! Read—the history of Hayti and see how they were butchered by the whites. . . . God will indeed deliver you . . . from your deplorable and wretched condition under the Christians of America.[34]

To whites, and especially to slaveholders, Haiti became an island of horrors. As Americans repressed their own slaves, Haiti served as a constant, guilty reminder of the terror and anarchy that beat underneath the slave driver's boot: slave rebellion could happen here.

The debate in 1800 became a template for the ways the two parties wrestled over the people they feared. For the next century, the conservative party (the Federalists and, later, the Whigs and Republicans) would be, by the standards of the day, enlightened on issues of race. But, for the most part, they remained suspicious of immigrants and would try to blunt their dangerous influence. The Democrats, on the other hand, were usually more generous to European immigrants but kept doubling down on white supremacy. Of course, the positions were still hazy and evolving—even the Federalists would not flatly condemn slavery in 1800—but the party divisions between race and immigration would grow right through the nineteenth century.

WHITE RESIDENTS IN CITIES LIKE RICHMOND AND NORFOLK worried about their slaves associating "with French Negroes from Saint-Domingue." Their influence was said to make the American slaves "insolent & troublesome . . . and rife for insurrection."[35]

The slaveholders' worst fears were confirmed by Gabriel's meticulously planned rebellion. News of the slave's plot broke while states were still choosing electors—Gabriel's trial coincided with the day Maryland voted. The newspapers carried all the shocking (often exaggerated) details: over six hundred slaves had been in on the plot, shadowy white Frenchmen were egging them on. But the most terrible aspect of the entire affair—to the anxious slavers—was the rebels' attitude. They did not seem to feel the least bit ashamed or apologetic. "We have as much right to fight for our liberty as any man," declared one conspirator. "I have nothing more to offer," declared another, "than what George Washington would have had to offer had he been taken by the British and put to trial. I have adventured my life in endeavoring to obtain the liberty of my countrymen."[36]

Fearful southerners were quick to connect the horrors of Saint-Domingue to the revolt in Virginia. The Democratic-Republicans offered endless variations of "we told you so." This is what came of "treating with Toussaint in the West Indies," reported the *Herald of Liberty*. The treaty with former slaves had sent its dangerous message. After all, the Virginia slave Gabriel was every bit "as fit for command as Toussaint." Yet the very same acts that won Toussaint gifts from the Adams administration sent Gabriel to the gallows. The upcoming election, added the Democratic-Republican *Aurora*, would be the end of the Federalists and their reckless alliance with the Haitians.[37]

The Federalists threw the blame right back at their rivals. They insisted that it was the Democratic-Republicans and their loose talk of liberty that had inspired the slaves' revolt. "The insurrection of the Negros in Southern states," wrote one, "appears to be organized on the French plan." The Federalist press clinched its argument by pointing to those secret French agents allegedly stirring up trouble.[38]

Some Federalist newspapers went further, denouncing slavery altogether and accusing Democratic-Republicans of championing an immoral institution. The *Connecticut Gazette*, for example, concluded that "Slavery is a monster, the most horrible of all monsters, tyranny excepted. He who affects to be a Democrat, and is, at the same time, an owner of slaves, is a devil incarnate. He tells a damnable and diabolical lie in the face of day."[39]

Most Federalists, however, took the opposite tack and charged the Democratic-Republicans with imperiling the institution. The slaves heard their talk about the rights of man and took it seriously.

As one journalist wrote, "The late revolt . . . will make Jefferson and his party very cautious how they do any act which may stir the sleeping embers of the alarming fire which, were it once rekindled, would probably make all the southern states what Hispaniola [Haiti] now is and fill the chair of Jefferson with a negro successor." The Federalist newspapers claimed to see a silver lining. This conspiracy, reported *Wayne's Gazette*, would surely move "every reflecting man" to vote for President Adams.[40]

The *Aurora*, based in Philadelphia and writing for a northern audience, responded that it was Jefferson—not the tyrannical John Adams—who supported emancipating the slaves. His whole life "has been marked by measures calculated to procure the emancipation of the blacks and to ameliorate the condition of those whom the fatal policy of the British has entailed us." This was a frequent rhetorical strategy of the northern Democratic-Republicans: the blame for slavery rested with the British. Enlightened slaveholders like Jefferson, they argued, would strive to "ameliorate" the unfortunate institution.[41]

As the South grappled with slavery, the political parties each took a different stance. The Federalists may have been unabashed elitists who restricted voting to men with property and fought to exclude the immigrant rabble; however, in many states, they had no objection to letting blacks vote as long as they met the property qualifications. In contrast, when the rising Democrats took power, they struck down the Federalist voting policies—eliminating property qualifications for white men and forbidding African Americans to vote regardless of how rich they might be. The American Revolution had opened a southern conversation about whether slavery belonged in a land of liberty. Gabriel's rebellion and all the agitation surrounding the election of 1800 marked the beginning of the end for those wisps of liberality.

THE CONSTITUTIONAL CONVENTION NEVER SPECIFIED HOW to choose the president. They did dream up the Electoral College but offered no instruction about who would elect the electors and how. Instead, they passed the crucial decisions about the "time, place and manner" to the states. In the charged politics of 1800, the majority parties took advantage of this ambiguity by fiddling the rules to advantage themselves.

In Virginia, electors were chosen by each district. This, Jefferson had long argued, enriched the people's voice. But in the last election, in 1796, Adams had taken a district (and its electoral vote) in Jefferson's home state—and Adams ended up winning the presidency by just three electors. The experience converted Jefferson to a new view. It was folly, he wrote to his ally, Virginia governor James Monroe, to apportion Virginia's votes by districts when ten other states gave their votes entirely to the overall winner. In 1800, a new Democratic-Republican majority in Virginia changed the rules to winner take all, guaranteeing Jefferson all twenty-one of the state's Electoral College votes.[42]

In Massachusetts, the Federalist-controlled legislature changed the rules so that it could choose the electors rather than leave the choice to the voters. That change locked up a unanimous vote for the Federalists. New Hampshire also switched to legislative appointment.

Pennsylvania's divided government fought so long and hard about the voting rules that political observers thought the Keystone State might miss the election altogether—Jefferson tallied his projected totals both with and without the state. A last-minute compromise permitted Pennsylvania to cast votes—eight for Jefferson, seven for Adams.

But for all the fixes and counter fixes, the election came down to New York, where the legislature, which was narrowly controlled by the Federalists, chose the electors, winner take all. The Democratic-Republicans proposed taking the choice away from the legislature and letting the voters chose by district. Naturally, the Federalists swatted down that self-interested proposal.[43]

However, the legislature was closely divided, and an election in April 1800 would decide the majority party—and all twelve of New York's Electoral College votes. The key lay in thirteen assembly seats from New York City. During the last election, in 1796, all thirteen had gone to the Federalists, tipping the legislature, New York's electoral votes, and the presidency to John Adams. Now, those seats were up again. "If the city of N. York is in favor of the [democratic-] republican ticket," wrote Jefferson to Madison, the Democratic-Republicans would win the presidency. If not, Adams would be re-elected. In effect, the election of 1800 came down to the thirteen assembly seats in New York City.[44]

Aaron Burr, an influential New York politician and lawyer, leapt unabashedly into the contest, organized the campaign for the Democratic-Republicans, and almost became president for his trouble. Burr introduced shrewd innovations in the political arts. He began by testing the popularity of different candidates and selecting a slate of household names like American Revolution hero General Horatio Gates. Next, he compiled a roster of voters, meticulously detailing their political views and their wealth. Then he launched what we would call a ground game. He dispatched young men— German speakers for German neighborhoods—who went door to door, soliciting votes and contributions. Burr ticked through the voter lists with his team, advising them whom to ignore ("you will not see him at the polls") and whom to lean on for contributions ("he will pay you the two hundred dollars and thank you for letting him off so easy"). Burr opened the equivalent of a campaign headquarters, with food and drink for the workers. He organized poll watchers to ensure the Federalist authorities did not tamper with Democratic-Republican votes. And on election day, both Burr and Hamilton, who had organized the other side, broke with tradition and crisscrossed the city addressing voters—politely stepping aside for one another when their paths crossed.[45]

On April 5, the Democratic-Republicans swept all thirteen New York City seats and took control of the state legislature. "The result gives a dead majority to the election of Mr. Jefferson to the Presidency," mourned the Federalist *Gazette of the United States*. Crestfallen Federalists in the state legislature tried one last trick. They drafted a letter to Governor John Jay, a member of their own party, asking him to institute the very proposal they had swatted down before they lost control: take the electoral votes away from the legislature and let the voters in each district make the choice. The Democratic-Republican press jeered the transparent turnabout and the governor ignored it. Democratic-Republicans rewarded Burr by nominating him for vice president (he had come in fourth out of eleven men in the previous presidential election in 1796).[46]

The election of 1800 exposed a great irony of American democracy. Because the founders opposed parties and partisanship, they had never established a clear electoral process. Partisans seized the opportunity to bend the procedures to their advantage. Once the process went into motion, it stayed in motion. Despite eight different Constitutional amendments regulating "the time, place and manner" of voting, the partisan scramble would continue through the years—often tangled up with questions about immigration, race, or both. The great silence of the Constitution combined with the rising parties and yielded an enduring battle over the ballot. The restless conflict about who votes and how—so vivid in 1800—would continue year after year, election by election, a feature of US politics that remains unique among established democracies.

ONCE THE STATES HAD FINALLY MADE THEIR CHOICES, THE national parties leapt in and frantically tried to spin the results to their advantage. Jefferson and Burr won the election, seventy-three to sixty-eight. But the results posed a new dilemma. The Constitution clearly specified that the candidate with the most electoral votes would be president and the runner up would be vice president. But now the unexpected parties had sprung up, put the same slate before the entire country, and created a tie between Jefferson and his vice-presidential candidate, Aaron Burr. (The electors were supposed to get around this problem by dropping one vote for the vice-presidential candidate, but the Democratic-Republicans failed to do this).[47]

With Thomas Jefferson and Aaron Burr tied, the election went to the House of Representatives. The Federalists grasped at one last straw. They would vote for Burr over Jefferson. After all, they reasoned, he was an expedient politician who might cast his principles aside and negotiate with the party that thrust him into power. The Federalist newspapers enthusiastically cataloged Burr's supposed virtues and Jefferson's vices.[48]

Would Burr really agree to the Federalist machinations? No one was sure and he refused to say—or to write the letter that acknowledged Jefferson's victory. The tie "has produced dismay and gloom over the republican gentlemen here," reported Jefferson, "and an equal exultation in the federalists." Exultation was an exaggeration, but the Federalists saw a narrow path to power and swung behind Aaron Burr. "It is not to be denied," sighed Madison, "that the Constn. might have been properly full in prescribing the election of P. and V.P." (The chaotic finish to the election of 1800 led to the Twelfth Amendment, which instructed the Electoral College to cast separate ballots for the president and the vice president).[49]

In the House of Representatives, each state delegation cast a single vote—a simple majority (nine votes) would win the presidency. The House voted. And voted. One ballot after another produced exactly the same results: eight states for Jefferson, six for Burr, two abstaining (evenly divided delegations could not agree and abstained). Jefferson was one state short of the majority. To make matters worse, they were all now in the grim little village of Washington, DC—a scattershot of rude boarding houses and taverns. "We want nothing here," said New York's Gouverneur Morris sarcastically, "but houses, cellars, kitchens, well-informed men, amiable women, and other little trifles of this kind, to make our city perfect." After thirty-five ballots, reported Albert Gallatin, the members were feeling "banged badly." Many Democratic-Republicans began to mutter that if the stalemate lasted long enough, the Federalist secretary of state, John Marshall, would become acting president.[50]

The politics grew intense—and bizarre. Hamilton sprayed letters far and wide denouncing Burr—and pushing the members of his own Federalist Party to drop Burr and vote for Jefferson. Burr finally wrote a letter—though we don't know what was in it. On the thirty-sixth ballot, a number of Federalists decided to give up on Burr and simply cast blank votes. That tipped Vermont and Maryland, whose delegations had been tied, into Jefferson's column and gave him the presidency. In the end, ten state delegations voted Jefferson, four states stuck with Burr (the holdouts were all in New England), and two Federalist states abstained (Delaware and South Carolina).

Despite all the drama over the presidency, a powerful Democratic-Republican tide was rising across the country. Besides winning the presidency, Democratic-Republicans took twenty-two new seats in the House (for a sixty-eight to thirty-eight majority) and seven in the Senate (a seventeen to fifteen majority). In context, the Federalist effort to co-opt the Democratic-Republican vice president looks like the desperate measures of a fading majority. The future belonged to Jefferson's party. But the Federalists soon launched a new and bitter attack: Jefferson, they said, had won only because of slavery.

THE FEDERALISTS, ESPECIALLY IN NEW ENGLAND, SEIZED on a simple explanation for their defeat: the Constitution had rigged the rules to inflate the power of the slaveholders by adding three-fifths of each slave to the total white population in allocating representatives in Congress and, therefore, votes in the Electoral College.

The Federalist press loudly insisted that without the inflation for slaves, Adams would have prevailed. "We have proved, by numerical calculation," announced the *Mercury and New England Palladium* (Boston), "*that a majority of the freemen* of the United States have *really* elected Mr. Adams to the Presidency." Jefferson had won, they claimed, only because the Electoral College added votes for men and women "who are no better entitled to representation than cattle and horses." The new president, they said, was "about to ride into the TEMPLE OF LIBERTY upon the *shoulders of slaves*." Similar headlines ran across the New England press: "John Adams has been reelected President of the United States by a MAJORITY OF ALL THE FREE PEOPLE THEREOF," said one. The *Connecticut Courant* added that Adam's real victory "ought to be proclaimed to the world, that the reputation of our country may not sink in the estimation of the wise and good of other countries."[51]

Some contemporary historians add up the numbers exactly the same way. William Freehling, Leonard Richards, and Garry Wills all reckon that the three-fifths rule inflated Jefferson's total by twelve (Richards says thirteen) Electoral College votes. Other historians dismiss the ruckus. There was more to the Federalist decline, they point out, than the constitutional tilt toward slave states. The party was fading because their aristocratic vision was ill-suited to the times, buried by a tumultuous get-ahead age. The artisans in New York and Philadelphia would latch onto the Democratic-Republican vision as heartily as the slaveholders of Richmond, Virginia. After all, it was flipping New York that changed the Democratic-Republicans from losers in 1796 to winners in 1800.[52]

Still, don't overlook the racial dimension. The Constitution may have omitted many details about how elections should be conducted, but one of the few specifications it made stacked the deck in favor of the slaveholders. Then, later, now: the most violent battles about voting rules would cluster around the race line.

———

ON MARCH 4, 1801, THE EDITOR OF THE *AURORA* PUBLISHED three cheers. One for the inauguration of Thomas Jefferson, another for the expiration of the Sedition Act, and one for his own personal victory over the sedition charges that the Federalists had leveled against him.[53]

That same day, the president-elect delivered a radiant inaugural address, the speech of his life. After a call for unity—"We are all republicans, we are all federalists"—Jefferson addressed the rising partisanship. Now that Americans had plunged into unabashed politics, they needed to remember their old values. Jefferson delivered a strong call for tolerance that rings right down through the generations. Of those who would challenge the government, Jefferson said, "let them stand undisturbed as monuments [to] the safety with which error may be tolerated, where reason is left free to combat it." Reason would deal with even the most troublesome speech. There was no need to repress (or, for that matter, to shout down) opposing viewpoints.[54]

Jefferson issued a warning alongside his call for tolerance. The new era had given rise to a serious danger. "Having banished from our land that religious intolerance under which mankind so long bled and suffered," said Jefferson, we will not have gained much if "we countenance a political intolerance, as despotic, as wicked, . . . as bitter and bloody." The new danger arose when party activists turned as fanatical as the Puritans.

Jefferson ended his speech on an especially revealing note. "Every difference of opinion," he said, "is not a difference of principle." What Jefferson meant was that differences could be tolerated without compromising the fundamentals. But there is another way to read the passage. Beneath our policy differences lies something even deeper than principle: the fraught matter of national identity. The election of 1800 injected important ideas into a national debate. But the parties also disagreed on the more primal questions. Who belonged? Who deserved which rights? Who are we?

The Federalists notoriously feared the refugees and the poor and shooed them away from the ballot. Now those barriers would begin to tumble. Jefferson's party controlled American politics for the next twenty-four years. In that period, they won every presidential election (the Federalists only came close once, in 1812); they controlled both chambers of Congress for every single session; and they dominated most state governments outside New England. They used their dominance to build a far more equal society. They threw the vote open to men without property—as long as they were white.

On racial matters, however, it was the Federalists who were the more tolerant party. Looking back on the 1800 election we can see the volcanic issue beginning to rumble. As their party sank, New England Federalists went down cursing slavery and challenging one of the few election rules that the Constitution had not left up for grabs. In contrast, the Democratic-Republican majority would not extend its robust spirit of liberty to slaves or free Africans. On the contrary, as white men without property began to win the vote, black men, even with considerable property, lost it.

President Jefferson eventually rescinded Toussaint's Clause. He banned all trade with the "dangerous brigands" in Haiti who wrought such "horrid scenes," who "destroyed . . . property" and "massacred . . . families." The Democratic-Republicans in Congress cut off all diplomatic and economic relations with the new country. A young John Quincy Adams, the former president's son, denounced the legislation as "among the most disgraceful statues ever enacted in the United States." For a brief time, Adams and the

Federalists had engineered an enlightened policy toward the former slaves in Haiti but the Democratic-Republicans, worried about their own slaves, joined the European empires in cutting off all relations.[55]

THERE WOULD BE STILL ONE MORE RACIAL TWIST AFTER THE election. In 1802, James Callender, a vicious, hard-drinking writer who had been secretly employed by Jefferson, turned on his former patron for refusing him a job and published a blockbuster rumor:

> It is well known that the man, whom it delighteth the people to honor [Thomas Jefferson], keeps and for many years has kept, as his concubine, one of his slaves. Her name is Sally. . . . By this wench . . . our president has had several children.[56]

The Federalist press leapt on the gossip. The papers were alternately pious, gleeful, bawdy, crude, bitter, and deeply racist. Thomas Green Fessenden, a German émigré, published a widely circulated two-volume book of doggerel that channeled Federalist anger into a long, lascivious, race-inflected sneer.

> *Or seek in dark and dirty alley*
> *A Mr. Jefferson's Miss Sally . . .*
> **Great men can never lack supporters**
> **Who manufacture their own voters . . .**
> *And we've no doubt this making brats*
> *Between your blacks and Democrats.*[57]

Nathaniel Hawthorne called Fessenden's doggerel "familiar to every ear" because he expressed "the feelings of the great Federalist Party." But Jefferson's defenders were even more revealing than his critics. "That this servant woman has a child is true," wrote Jefferson's friend, Meriwether Jones. "But . . . is it strange that a servant of Mr. Jefferson's, at a house where so many strangers resort, who is engaged in the ordinary vocations of family, like thousands of others, should have a mulatto child?" Someone else—anyone else—could have done it. Jones casually acknowledges the deeper, more depressing truth. White men insouciantly fathered mixed-race children with slaves. Any guest of the house might have helped themselves to Sally. And every one of them a rape. No one, then or later, mused historian Fawn Brodie, seems to have protested the idea of all those casually fathered mulatto children.[58]

The Federalists, sinking from power, took a kind of glee in muddying Jefferson's reputation. The rumor lingered on the fringe—dismissed as the losers letting off steam—until DNA tests suggested that the story is most probably true. But all the jibes at Jefferson only mirrored the same uneasy race line that kept tangling up the first contested election and that would continue to haunt the United States. The enslaved woman draws no sympathy from rivals mocking President Jefferson. On the contrary, Sally Hemings was transformed into a sexualized cartoon. The scornful takedowns repeatedly returned to blackness and carnality. The songs and jingles that mocked Jefferson all remind us that race runs deeper than elections or power or equality to the bedrock matter of identity. The race line is sexualized out of a primal anxiety about the status of whiteness in a vibrant, biracial society.

The battle over national identity would grow. A new generation of immigrants would land. The slavery debate would slowly come into clearer focus. The parties would evolve. But by the end of the first contested election, there were already hints, to paraphrase W. E. B. Du Bois, that the problem of the nineteenth century would be the problem of the color line.

TWO

"KEEP THE BALL ROLLING"

The First Campaign for the Masses (1840)

The economy crashed in 1837 and Vice President Richard Mentor Johnson, who had been in office for just two months, took off for Kentucky where he opened a tavern on his plantation to help pay off his debts. After some time, President Martin Van Buren dispatched his political fixer, Amos Kendall, to track down the errant VP, and Kendall sent back a disdainful letter. Johnson had thrown himself into "the inglorious pursuit of tavern keeping—even giving his personal superintendence to the—water-melon selling department." Worse, he was devoting "too much of his time to a young Delilah of about the complexion of Shakespears swarthy Othello."[1]

Johnson's personal life was an open secret. He had lived in common-law marriage with one of his slaves, Julia Chen (an octoroon, seven-eighths European). Johnson openly grieved Julia's death, acknowledged their two daughters, educated them, and tried to leave them his estate. Kentucky law rejected all of it—he could not marry a slave, adopt his daughters, or bequeath them anything. Johnson's transgression was not the sex or the children with slaves—that was all familiar enough among white men—but the intimations of equality. Johnson symbolized the times: a financial crash dominated the political headlines. But beneath those headlines lurked the thorny issue of slavery.

American politics had entered into a boisterous new era. It began with Martin Van Buren, who built a political machine in New York and then started to think big. In a letter to southern leaders, written in 1827, Van Buren described the rising tensions over slavery and suggested it could be tempered by a strong political party. The Federalists had vanished, and the Democratic-Republicans had fallen into squabbling factions and minor parties. Resurrecting Jefferson's party, argued Van Buren, would unite the men across the nation around something more solid than squabbles over slavery: the urge to win and the desire for plums (or government jobs).[2]

The rising party, now known as the Democrats, elected a war hero, Andrew Jackson, to the presidency (in 1828 and 1832) and then won again with Vice President Van Buren (in 1836). In the process, a new generation finally buried George Washington's non-partisan dream. Political leaders would no longer pretend to stand apart from the fray; instead, they would unabashedly leap into in partisan conflict. From the start, the party was organized to manage the most dangerous question of the time—what to do about slavery.

During his two terms in office, President Jackson managed to infuriate an opposition party into existence. Rivals accused Jackson of trampling the Constitution and expanding presidential powers. The opposition pointedly named itself the Whigs, after the English party that opposed royal prerogatives.

In the presidential election of 1840, Martin Van Buren and his Democrats ran for reelection against William Henry Harrison and the Whigs. It was the first modern political campaign between two well-organized parties, and it embodied many of the features that we associate with party politics today: nasty, media-driven, full of "mummery" (as the skeptics grumped), a kaleidoscope of torchlight processions, rousing songs, awful doggerel, and histrionic rallies. Every side repeated slogans that were not exactly true. And voter turnout soared to nearly 80 percent, the third highest in US history.

For sheer exuberance, perhaps no campaign has ever topped 1840. But beneath the campaign's hoopla—and there was a lot of hoopla—lurked formidable issues. The Panic of 1837 had triggered a deep downturn just two months into Van Buren's first term, sparking a heated debate about the power of banks—and moving the vice president to sell whisky and watermelons in Kentucky. At the same time, Americans struggled over their identity. The world's first great parties, locked in their first contested campaign for the masses, confronted the overlapping questions of slavery, sexuality, immigrants surging into the country, and just how far that country ought to stretch in the first place.

THE WHIGS GATHERED FOR THEIR FIRST CONVENTION IN December 1839. Senator Henry Clay of Kentucky was the biggest name in the party and a heavy favorite to win the nomination for the presidency. But Clay was a slaveholder, and resistance to slavery was rising in the North. He tried to finesse the issue with a nod to both sides. "I am no friend of slavery," he declared in a famous Senate speech. But, he continued, "I beseech the abolitionists to pause in their mad and fatal course." Their rash solution, he concluded, would inevitably lead either "to the extermination of the blacks or their ascendancy over whites."[3]

Clay's attempt at nuance was agreeable enough to southern Whigs, but it did not come close to satisfying antislavery activists in the North. "Wholly out of the question," scribbled abolitionist William Lloyd Garrison. "There is not, in all this country, an individual more objectionable." At the convention, the northern resistance proved too strong. Clay needed 138 delegates to win the nomination; he won 103 on the first ballot but it soon became clear he was not going to close the gap.[4]

That left two generals in the running: General William Henry Harrison and General Winfield Scott. Harrison had commanded troops against Britain's Native American allies in a celebrated battle on the Tippecanoe River back in 1811 and was fondly known as Old Tip. With the nomination now within reach, his campaign manager, Thaddeus Stevens of Pennsylvania, pulled a famous dirty trick. He had gotten his hands on one of General Scott's letters expressing some sympathy for abolition. To swing delegates to Harrison, Stevens not-so-accidentally dropped the letter in the middle of the Virginia delegation. The Virginians read it and that was the end of General Scott in 1840. General Harrison rolled out of the convention with a huge advantage: no one knew what he stood for. The convention underscored this bonus by declining to write a platform. The most telling feature of the Whig convention was the party's racial vertigo: Clay too pro-slavery, Scott too antislavery, Harrison safely enigmatic.[5]

The convention fatally balanced the ticket with a southern Democrat, John Tyler of Virginia. The candidates went into the campaign with their famous slogan, "Tippecanoe and Tyler too." The downside? Beyond despising Andrew Jackson, Tyler did not share any Whig views. "A democrat, died in the wool," sniffed former President John Quincy Adams, now an irascible antislavery member of Congress representing Boston.[6]

Harrison was sixty-seven years old, the oldest candidate ever to stand for the presidency, and the Democratic press gleefully scorned the "old granny." A writer with the *Baltimore Republican* jeered, "Give him a barrel of hard cider and settle a pension of two thousand a year on him, and take my word for it, he will sit the remainder of his days in his log cabin." And just like that, the Whigs, who had been struggling to overcome the perception that they were elitist, received a populist cudgel, which they gleefully wielded against Democrats, the purported party of the common man.[7]

What was wrong with a poor son of the earth living in an honest log cabin, howled the Whigs. Or with a barrel of good old-fashioned hard cider? The party grasped the homely symbols. Their mass meetings, held in every state, featured log cabins and more log cabins. Whigs drank hard cider out of gourds, carried live eagles, and rolled ten-foot leather balls covered with Harrison slogans from rally to rally. The shouts that greeted the men slid a new phrase into the American political lexicon—"Keep the ball rolling."[8]

The Whig campaign reflected the evangelical style of the era's religious revivals. Barkers stood outside and called the congregations into the frenzy. The sheer size of the gatherings mesmerized Whig partisans. "No eye that witnessed it can convey . . . this grand gathering of the people," recalled one participant of an enormous rally in Dayton, Ohio. "We . . . shall bear [it] to our graves."[9]

The Whigs managed a populist campaign despite being wary of populism and positively alarmed at the prospect of class conflict. The poor would be rich, sniffed the celebrated newspaper editor Horace Greeley, "if they would make the needful sacrifices of ease and mortification of appetite." Their trouble lay in "the groggery, the cigar shop, the gambling den." The Democrats painted their rivals as an anti-immigrant party of big banks, big money, and meddlesome Puritans. This was, of course, a negative spin. But the Whigs *did* fret about morals and about immigrants; they promised an active national government that would sponsor roads, canals, wharves, land grants, tariffs, and—yes—a national bank.[10]

The log cabin and hard cider swelled into nineteenth-century memes that obscured the dull realities. Harrison had grown up on a Virginia plantation and lived in a substantial house on hundreds of acres in Ohio. He drank good wine rather than cider (though lightly, for his son had died an alcoholic). He had been a territorial governor, served in the US Senate, and was notorious for bombarding newly elected presidents with pleas for well-paying government posts (those plums that the parties had begun handing out). But the Whigs were not fact checking. Horace Greeley repeated all the exaggerations in his partisan newspaper, *The Log Cabin*. Even decades later, Greeley was still printing the myth.[11]

Some Whig newspapers casually admitted that, no, Harrison did not *literally* live in a log house. But as Senator Daniel Webster cheerfully reminded listeners, it was the Democratic writers who had invented the image—as a "sneer and reproach" that exposed the contempt they secretly harbored toward the common people they boisterously claimed to champion.[12]

The myths and metaphors signaled something new. The parties had both turned into shrewdly organized people's campaigns. Popular movements had always surged through the United States—pulsating into evangelical revivals, political upheaval, reform movements, workingmen's clubs, self-help groups, and more. Now, the parties channeled all that fervor into their marching, chanting, ranting, singing, torch-lit cadres.[13]

ON THE OTHER SIDE, MARTIN VAN BUREN WAS STANDING for reelection. And, yes, the Democrats are sometimes alleged to have made their own entry into the lexicon of American slang. Van Buren himself was known as Old Kinderhook (he was from Kinderhook, New York) and the party faithful shouted approbation with cries of "OK!"

Historians, following Arthur Schlesinger Jr., once saw Jackson and Van Buren (he stressed Van Buren's role in the rise of Jacksonian Democracy) as tribunes of the common person standing up to the money power—they were something like the FDR of their day. In the 1980s, Jackson morphed into an antebellum Ronald Reagan, bashing big government. And, more recently, historians have focused on Jackson's vicious racial attitudes—especially his genocidal policy toward Native American policy and his pro-slavery policies.

So, what exactly was the Age of Jackson? Egalitarian, antigovernment, or racist? The answer, of course, is all three. The Jackson party has had many heirs—including Franklin Roosevelt, Ronald Reagan, and Donald Trump.[14]

Van Buren had helped to engineer President Andrew Jackson's two landslide victories and, in 1836, Jackson picked Van Buren to succeed him. Van Buren inherited the president's popularity and easily won. But by 1840, the connection to Jackson saddled him with three heavy burdens.

First, there was the simple contrast between the craggy war hero and the plump professional politician. "Van Buren is as opposite to General Jackson," wrote Davey Crockett, a wisecracking Whig representative from Tennessee, "as dung is to a diamond." Harrison's supporters answered the "Granny Harrison" jibes with their own gender benders about Van Buren. "He is laced up in corsets such as women in a town wear. . . . It would be difficult to say, from his appearance whether he was a man or a woman, but for his large red and gray whiskers." The Log Cabin is the famous image of the day. But it sprang to life alongside highly sexualized images of feeble manhood—indeed of unmanly femininity—hurled at each of the candidates.[15]

Secondly, Van Buren inherited Jackson's long roster of enemies. One of the strongest bonds uniting the Whigs was their animosity toward Andrew Jackson, his policies, and his expansion of presidential power. It's one of the few opinions William Henry Harrison shared with his running mate, John Tyler.

Third, and most important, the Panic of 1837 hit the nation five weeks after Van Buren became president, and a deep depression rippled across the country. The Whigs immediately blamed Jackson's policies—especially his fierce battle with the national bank. Jackson had bitterly attacked "the rich and the powerful" who, he thought, were bending the bank to their own interests. He outmaneuvered the bank's supporters and vetoed a bill to renew its charter. At the time, the federal government minted coins but did not print paper money. Instead, individual banks offered their own notes backed by the gold and silver they held (known as specie). The Second National Bank in Philadelphia held the US Government's specie. When Jackson killed the bank, his administration faced a dilemma: Where to deposit all the government gold? The Democrats turned to state banks, sarcastically known as pet banks, and critics soon charged that the pet banks—especially in the west—were issuing more notes than they could cover.[16]

Critics charged Jackson with making a bad policy worse when he issued his Species Circular of 1836, an executive order that required individuals who were buying federal land to pay in gold and silver rather than bank notes. Since western sales were booming, the policy drained gold and silver out of the big eastern banks. In 1837, banks in London called their loans, setting off a run on New York banks, which were now low on specie and began to fail, causing a run on state and local banks, which paid depositors until they, in turn, ran out of gold and silver and shut their doors. Banks across the country collapsed. The blame for the crisis landed squarely on newly elected President Van Buren.[17]

Van Buren's answer to the crisis was to double down on Jackson's war on banks. He removed the federal government's gold and silver from the state banks and placed it in the US Treasury Department— private bankers, he said, would no longer be speculating with federal specie. The administration also tried to cut off future crises by requiring banks to hold more gold and silver to cover their notes. The policies ended up tightening credit in the middle of a depression.[18]

The Whigs attacked this economic policy and pledged to restore the national bank, but they had a funny way of saying so—they bashed the bankers. "I am not a bank man," averred Harrison as he called for a national bank. "Once in my life I was, and they cheated me out of every dollar I placed in their hands." But, he continued, the war on the bank had tightened the money supply, and the only way to loosen it and save the working man was to reverse the Democratic policies. Andrew Jackson had set a defiantly populist tone and the Whigs now played the same game, even mocking the bank they intended to restore.[19]

WHILE THE DEPRESSION AND THE EXUBERANT CAMPAIGNING drew the headlines, slavery also burst into the campaign. Most politicians tried to sidestep the issue, but the national debate had spread too far and grown too hot to permit that. We have already seen how slavery entangled the Whig's nominating convention. During the general election, the Democrats kept finding ways to insinuate that Harrison and the Whigs harbored secret abolitionist thoughts.

For example, early in the campaign, shocking news flashed through the Democratic press—Harrison had voted to sell indebted *white* men into slavery. Congressman Samson Mason, an Ohio Whig, quickly corrected the record. The measure in question was a routine, bipartisan penal bill.[20] Later in the campaign, another Democratic newspaper broke the staggering news—with no evidence or details—that General Harrison was planning to meet with abolitionist Arthur Tappan. That provoked Harrison himself to write a letter to the editor. "A vile fabrication," he wrote, "totally destitute of the least foundation in truth." The flimsy charges revealed a deeper truth. Regardless of their nominee, the Whigs *did* harbor antislavery sentiment in their ranks.[21]

Slavery kept breaking into the campaign because, by 1840, the debate itself had polarized in both North and South. Many white southerners had long soothed themselves with the genteel antislavery of colonization: someday, somehow, the slavers would free their slaves and vanish them out of the country—shipping them to colonies in Africa or Central America. The American Colonization Society had 136 chapters across the South and, in 1837, the erstwhile Whig leader, Henry Clay, became its president. Although a tiny trickle of free African Americans made the journey to Africa, colonization was more fantasy than serious policy. An uncharacteristically sarcastic Alexis de Tocqueville did the math in 1835. While seven hundred thousand people were born into slavery over the past thirteen years, he wrote, a scant three thousand boarded ships with great fanfare and sailed east. The dream of colonization permitted sentimental people to express concern about slavery, imagine a solution in the distant future, and conjure up a completely white society—all without risking their fortunes, which rested on the men and women they held in bondage. As the debate heated up, this easy road to abolition reached a dead end.[22]

Radical abolitionists jolted the debate by demanding an immediate, unconditional, uncompensated end to slavery. In almost jubilant Old Testament language, they called down the wrath of God on the slavers. Immediate abolition was not a new idea—the Quakers had been gently agitating for decades. But during the 1830s, the idea began to spread. Abolitionists exploited new printing technology to produce piles of antislavery tracts, sold for a penny apiece, and mail them to the South.

Moderates were infuriated. This "moral poison," cried the Democratic *Boston Atlas*, was nothing less than a call for "slaves to burn, violate, and murder." In Charleston, South Carolina, the bishop quickly wrote to assure one and all that no Roman Catholic was involved with such mischief. The local post office was uncertain—what should it do with the incendiary material? A mob solved the dilemma by grabbing the abolitionist tracts and making a bonfire out of them—with President Jackson's full-throated blessing.[23]

Riots against the abolitionists erupted across the North. Some were ritualized protests which resulted, as one newspaper put it, "in the loss of a little blood and much reputation." However, the northern mobs turned ugly when they ran into black men and women. "Outrage committed by the mobs form the every-day news of the times," lamented Abraham Lincoln in 1838 and "have pervaded the country, from . . . the eternal snows of . . . New England to . . . the burning suns of . . . Louisiana." Lincoln offered chilling examples, like "the mulatto man seized on the streets [of Saint Louis], dragged to the suburbs of the city, chained to a tree, and actually burned to death; and all within a single hour of the time he had been a freeman, attending to his own business, and at peace with the world."[24]

The abolitionists provoked southerners into rethinking their position—and casting aside their apologies. In 1837, John Calhoun, a Democratic senator from South Carolina who had previously served as vice president, rose in the Senate and, in a famous speech, declared that slavery was a "positive good." The two races could only live "in peace and happiness," he said, if "the inferior race" was enslaved to its own "great benefit." The Africans had arrived on these shores, he continued, "in a low, degraded and savage condition," and thanks to the benevolent masters of the South, "attained a condition so civilized and so improved." Slavery, insisted Calhoun, was nothing less than a providential blessing for the slaves. Southern writers and statesmen would embellish this paternalistic nonsense—slavery as a positive good for the slaves as well as the masters— for the next two decades.[25]

Hardscrabble farmers latched onto a cruder alternative. The African race was "different and inferior," straight and simple. Inferior meant inferior and there was no need to rationalize it with fancy talk about "uplift" and "improvement" for the men and women in chains. These *herrenvolk democrats*, as historian Winthrop Jordan labeled them, ferociously demanded equality for all white men and hard subordination for Africans.

The debate illustrates an important political pattern. Partisans on one side mobilized the partisans on the other. The rising abolitionist societies shouted "Sinner!" The pro-slavery advocates responded by tossing aside their lukewarm colonization plans and celebrating the institution under attack. For the next twenty years, each side upped the emotional temperature of the other.

The changing argument over slavery reflected an economic revolution—the triumph of cotton capitalism. In 1790, the United States had produced 1.5 million pounds of cotton. By the early 1840s, that number had soared more than six hundredfold and surpassed a billion pounds. Cotton became, by far, the most valuable export— and the most valuable single product—in the United States. As historians have recently emphasized, unlimited supplies of land, labor, and capital all protected by a pliant government, made cotton—and the slaves who raised it—the driving force in the rise of American capitalism. It made vast fortunes among New England textile owners and New York merchants as much as southern planters. When we think of industrial capitalism, writes historian Sven Beckert, most people picture factories, railroads, and banks. But they were all driven—all dwarfed—by cotton. Americans framed their arguments about slavery in terms of morality, white men's rights, and what was best for the slaves themselves. But the whole debate rested on a rising cotton empire that powered the economy, the nation, and fortunes around the world.[26]

THE DEBATE OVER SLAVERY CONVULSED CONGRESS. AT THE time, citizens routinely petitioned the legislature. For example, army veterans requested pensions, and growing towns petitioned for funds to dig a harbor. Now, in the 1830s, thousands of petitions engulfed Congress demanding an immediate end to slavery in Washington, DC (which lay under congressional jurisdiction). Some expressed horror at the idea of men, women, and children held in cages within sight of the Capitol dome. John Calhoun led the southern members, who demanded that the antislavery petitions be flatly rejected. But that appeared to violate the First Amendment:

"Congress shall make no law . . . abridging the freedom . . . of the people . . . to petition the government for a redress of grievances."[27]

After a stormy debate, the members agreed to lay all the petitions related to slavery "on the table"—that is, they would be completely ignored. Normally, petitions were presented, printed, and briefly discussed, but the antislavery petitions could not even be mentioned. This offended former president John Quincy Adams, now a member of Congress, who slyly found ways to raise the issue and took wicked delight in provoking shouts of "Order! Order!" from his colleagues. Amid the confusion that greeted one eruption, Adams asked, "Am I gagged or am I not?" And, with his question, the practice of nailing petitions to the table got its infamous title—the "gag rule."[28]

The gag expired at the end of each congressional session and had to be reintroduced at the start of the next one. Days and weeks of heated argument about slavery greeted every new Congress. In 1840, John Calhoun's followers demanded a stronger and more permanent rule. Antislavery petitions should be completely rejected. This stronger gag rule won a narrow victory (114–108). Critics roasted the Slave Power, as they called it, for violating white people's constitutional rights to petition the government.[29]

The conflict over slavery posed the same challenge for each party—how to keep the members from the North and the South united. The Democrats held their ranks together by emphasizing states' rights. The Constitution wisely left the question of slavery to the states, they said, and that was where the matter ought to stay. In 1840, the longest plank in the party's platform declared that the states were "the sole and proper judges of everything appertaining to their own affairs" and warned "that all efforts by "abolitionists . . . to interfere with questions of slavery" would "lead to the most alarming and dangerous consequences," "diminish the happiness of the people," and "endanger the stability and permanency of the union."

The Democrats would continue to draft roughly the same statement right up to the Civil War.[30]

Even radicals went along. Orestes Brownson, for example, was a Democratic political writer from Boston who went so far as to call for abolishing all inheritance. When the wealthy died, he wrote, their property should be distributed to people in the next generation. His essays reverberated with radical defiance of the rich and powerful—President Van Buren denounced him for scaring voters away from the Democrats. But when it came to slavery, Brownson duly recited the states' rights catechism. "Slavery may be a sin, but it is not ours," he wrote in 1838. It may be "a stain, a disgrace, upon the community that tolerates it; but if so, it is not a stain or a disgrace on non-slaveholding communities." Why criticize Boston, he concluded, because there is slavery in Constantinople—or Charleston, South Carolina?[31]

Martin Van Buren had also affirmed the Democrats' creed back during his first inaugural address in 1837. "I must go into the presidential chair inflexible and uncompromising [about] . . . the slightest interference with it [slavery] in the states where it exists." Van Buren was the first president to utter the S-word in his inaugural. And now, here he was, running for reelection, while his own vice president, Richard Mentor Johnson, mocked the race line by trying to treat his children, born into slavery, like legitimate daughters. In a fitting twist for the states' rights party, the Democrats refused to endorse Richard Mentor Johnson for reelection, never agreed on a replacement, and simply left the choice of VP to the states and their electors.[32]

Slavery posed a bigger problem for the Whigs. Their coalition included conservative slaveholders in the South, prosperous bankers in Philadelphia, and radical abolitionists in Boston. Looking across a sample of important votes on the slavery question, one historian discovered that the northern Whigs cast, on average, just one vote with their southern colleagues and forty-nine votes against them.

In contrast, the northern Democrats supported the southern position on slavery by an average margin of fifty-nine to thirty. As the issue rose, Democrats rallied around states' rights while the Whigs cracked into a southern faction that supported slavery and a northern faction that opposed it.[33]

The root of the Whig's problem lay in their districts. Generally speaking, abolition spread in areas swept by evangelical fervor—precisely where the Whigs were strongest. The abolitionists became important swing voters in northern Whig districts. And, beginning in 1840, they had the option of voting for a new third party, the abolitionist Liberty Party, which ran James Birney for president. The Log Cabin campaign generated enough excitement—and ambiguity—to keep most abolitionists with the Whigs. As the election results came in, William Lloyd Garrison wrote in disgust about colleagues who had spurned the abolitionist party. "They violated their solemn pledge and voted for [the Whig] party." But the Whigs were in a difficult position, trapped between aggrieved southern colleagues demanding protections for slavery and northern abolitionists ready to bolt.[34]

The Democrats commitment to states' rights meant keeping a wary eye on the central government as a potential threat to slavery. Power exercised by "any branch of the general government," opined the Democratic *Washington Globe*, threatened the South's struggle to "preserve its *domestic institutions* against the incendiary machinations of its enemies," especially "African Abolitionists." Mind you, Democrats supported the national government's genocidal military campaigns against Native Americans in Georgia, Florida, and Mississippi—after all, it meant more land for white planters and their slaves. But they emphatically ruled out building roads, dredging rivers, and other government programs. On the other side, the Whigs supported a more active government and blamed slavery for blocking national progress. John Quincy Adams wrote a furious report to his constituents decrying how "slavery palsied [the] hand of government" and "stands aghast at the prospective promotion of general welfare."[35]

The Democratic opposition to central government rested on two very different values. There was the familiar Jeffersonian fear that government officials, if given too much power, would nourish an aristocracy—a modest republic required modest national government. But, at the same time, Democrats forcefully expressed their fear that a strong central government imperiled slavery itself. Democrats rallied support for their pro-slavery position in the North by conjuring up the specter of slaves, liberated by the Whigs, competing with whites for jobs, for housing, for prestige, for sexual partners, and for a respectable place in society. This powerful combination—fear of active government, the defense of slavery, and racial anxiety—had already been stirring in 1800. Now it spread, powered by the populist currents sweeping through antebellum America.

WOMEN LEAPT INTO THE CAMPAIGN OF 1840, VIOLATING propriety and outraging Democrats. The rise of evangelical causes, especially abolition, cracked the carefully delineated gender spheres of the era. After all, morality was a central aspect of the woman's role. They joined abolition societies in their capacity as "ministers of Christian love." But moral action drew them irresistibly into the restricted realms of organizing, public speaking, and publishing. They were, for example, especially effective at gathering the antislavery petitions that so enraged Congress. Some of the women's petitions began by invoking their moral status "as wives, as mothers, and as daughters," in the words of one petition.[36]

By the mid-1830s, women had begun to lecture on abolition. At first, they addressed women's sewing circles and parlor groups. However, some of the women were formidable speakers, and before long, they began speaking to mixed crowds. Soon, these "promiscuous assemblies," as they were called, began to break out all over.[37]

In 1840, the gender issue split the largest antislavery organization. Delegates at the annual meeting of the American Anti-Slavery Society narrowly elected Abby Kelley Foster to the executive committee. Lewis Tappan, a wealthy abolitionist and philanthropist, denounced the selection. It is "immoral for a lady to sit behind closed doors with gentlemen," scribbled an angry Tappan. He led the agitated minority out of the convention and formed a rival antislavery group. Through the whole ordeal, "a new and agitating Idea took shape," wrote Lydia Maria Child, a prolific abolitionist. "Why has the women nothing to do with politics?"[38]

The 1840 presidential campaign put Child's "Idea" into action. For starters, all those mass meetings meant that thousands of Whig activists needed to be housed and fed. The wives of local party leaders reported cooking, cleaning, and setting up sleeping quarters. But they also reported something more subversive. They talked politics with the men they hosted. Women's diaries filled with political reflections. And some women broke across another boundary by publishing and distributing pamphlets.[39]

As women transgressed the gender barrier and engaged in the campaign, some Whig leaders cautiously welcomed them. Senator Daniel Webster of New Hampshire, campaigning for Harrison in Virginia, slipped an extra speech into his schedule and addressed the Ladies of Richmond. He began with conventional wisdom. "The rough contests of the political world are not suited to the dignity . . . of your sex." But then he slipped right through the evangelical loophole. "Public morals . . . is a subject on which the moral perceptions of women are both quicker and juster than those of the other sex." John Quincy Adams scribbled the same thought in his diary. "Women so far from being debarred by any rule of delicacy from exercising [political] right . . . are by the Law of their nature fitted above all others for that exercise."[40]

Most Democrats despised the idea of women participating in politics. Vice President Johnson offered a typical grumble. "The rights of women are secure through the courser sex," he wrote to Lewis Tappan in April 1840. "Ladies [are] ordained by nature and by the customs . . . to occupy a higher place in society than . . . the strife of man." Before long, the idea of women in politics became a familiar objection to abolition. Again, and again, the anti-abolition lectures included a recitation about proper gender spheres and segued, inevitably, into expressions of panic about interracial sex. James K. Paulding, a New York Democrat angling for a post in the Van Buren administration, offered a good example of the standard homily: "We take this occasion to remind them that the appropriate sphere of women is their home and their appropriate duties at the cradle or the fireside." Paulding quickly worked his way to the dreaded racial carnality that awaited women if they continued to meddle in politics.

> Surely [the women] cannot be aware of the direct inference which must and will be drawn from their support of the disgusting doctrine of amalgamation, namely that they stand ready and willing to surrender themselves to the embraces of ignorance and barbarity, and to become mothers of a degraded race of wooly headed mulattoes. . . . Gracious heaven! What prostitution![41]

In short, women systematically entered party politics, for the first time, during the 1840 campaign. They provoked a furious backlash because they challenged both the racial and the gendered orders—slavery, white supremacy, and the restricted women's sphere. Some Whigs uneasily accepted the women's role because morality lay in their gender's ambit. Democrats angrily denounced the idea as nothing less than licentious. Few images rallied working-class Democrats like the picture of black men with white women. Every time American identify conflicts heat up, the angry tangle of gender rights, racial fear, and sexual anxiety bubbles to the surface all over again. And beginning with the election of 1840, the anxious politics of gender became still another difference between the parties.

———————

AS SOME WHIGS WARMED TO THE IDEA OF WOMEN IN POLI-tics, the Democrats opened their party to immigrants—and precisely when the topic of immigration became front page news. In the mid-1830s, the number of foreigners entering the country shot up five-fold, reaching sixty thousand a year. Roughly 4 percent of the total US population had arrived in the past decade—about half were Irish and most packed into the cities.[42]

The newcomers leaned heavily toward the Democrats and seized the party's principles—egalitarian populism, laissez faire economics, mind your own business morality, and a full-throated defense of slavery. The northern Whigs stood on the wrong side of all those issues.

To be sure, the immigrants themselves faced plenty of bigotry in their new country. The Irish, in particular, confronted animosity, discrimination, and violence. Even so, the Democratic Party generally welcomed them. Democratic registrars waved the Irish through to the ballot box without asking too many questions. And when challenges did arise, there were always local judges ready to issue the necessary papers.

When the Whigs complained about ineligible foreigners lining up to vote, Democrats mocked them for being hidebound conservatives, out of touch with modern ways. Count on the Whigs, warned Democratic Congressman John Reynolds from Illinois, to "repeal the naturalization laws" and disinter the Alien and Sedition Acts.[43]

The charge got under Harrison's skin during the election campaign. "When those laws were passed," he declared, "I was a soldier in the army of the United States." But the war hero got defensive precisely because his Whigs did support restrictive policies. They were always ready to decry the "perjuries and frauds committed at our elections," as one partisan put it. The Whig newspapers never stinted on the word "shocking." Honest judges were shocked to find their own names forged onto the false naturalization papers. Grand juries were shocked to hear the extent of the foreigners' voting fraud. The American people would be shocked to learn how Van Buren and his minions were cheating their way back to another term. Whig newspapers spread dire warnings about the immigrants and the ways they filled the cities with violence, corruption, shiftlessness, and drunkenness. "Drunken Pat, fresh from the Emerald Isle," joked Frederick Douglass, would cast his vote "leaning on the arms of two of his friends, unable to stand."[44]

Alexis de Tocqueville picked up the alarms and dropped a last-minute footnote into the first volume of *Democracy in America* with a fretful warning about the immigrants. "The crowd of Europeans driven by misfortune and misbehavior to the shores of the new world," he wrote, "formed a rabble more dangerous even than that of European towns." He continued with a dark projection. "I should not hesitate to predict that it is through them that . . . democratic republics of the new world will perish." To address the rising trouble, Tocqueville advised raising a strong national army "capable of suppressing their excesses." Both Tocqueville and Lincoln anxiously described the growing violence in the United States—the Frenchmen called for military force, the American for a renewed commitment to republican virtue.[45]

The clash over the Irish sprang back to the most powerful issue of the day—slavery. Many of the immigrants were virulently anti-abolitionist and harshly anti-black, perhaps in reaction to the prejudice they themselves faced. "The Irish on their own green island," wrote Frederick Douglass mournfully, "are warm-hearted, generous, and sympathizing with oppressed people everywhere." But, here, on American soil, he continued, "they are taught to . . . hate and despise colored people . . . [and] to believe that we eat the bread which of right belongs to them." The Irish parried the nativism they faced by seizing onto the racial prejudices they found in their new land and presenting themselves as members of the dominant, white tribe. The Irish in America, concluded Douglass, are members of "the slavery party." "Don't talk to them of reform," hissed the normally level-headed Lydia Maria Child. "Voting and beating are the [only] moral agencies they have any idea of."[46]

Once again, the parties diffused the angry arguments over identity. In 1800, Jefferson's party had welcomed the refugees while the Federalists made a treaty with former slaves (over loud objections from the other party in both cases). Now, Democrats recruited the Irish, accepted slavery, and abhorred women in politics. The Whigs split on slavery, with many in the North denouncing it; they gave a lukewarm cheer to women in politics; and, for the most part, they fought to curb the influence of the dangerous immigrants. In vivid contrast to our own time, the antebellum parties were divided (sometimes among themselves) about the role of different groups— slaves, free blacks, the Irish, other immigrants, and women. The nineteenth-century experience suggests just how unusual it would be when, in the twenty-first century, the descendants of every one of those groups entered into the same party coalition.

THE STATES HAD ALWAYS JOCKEYED OVER VOTING RULES, each trying to bend them to its advantage. Now, the Democrats (enthusiastically) and the Whigs (reluctantly) built brash electoral machines. The growing parties needed workers, and they recruited them with the promise of government jobs. The system that emerged, known as the spoils system, was crude, corrupt, and democratic.

After each election, the winners served up government posts to loyal party members who filled positions in the post offices, the custom houses, and district attorneys' offices. There was an egalitarian logic to the system. In a raucous, rising, far-flung nation, the people's votes yielded the village postmaster (the rapidly growing postal service accounted for eighty percent of the national bureaucracy). And thanks to the spoils, ordinary men could make a career in politics—they campaigned, seized their plums after the victory, and then keep right on working to keep the party in power (and their appointments safe). Even elite party members got jobs. For example, Orestes Brownson, Nathaniel Hawthorne, and Washington Irving all enjoyed political plums.[47]

During the Log Cabin election, the Whigs, who had never won a presidential election, savaged Van Buren's patronage machine. Harrison thought it augured "the downfall of liberty" and solemnly pledged to staunch "all the patronage of government." A major scandal gave the Whigs a convenient focus. In 1838, Samuel Swartwout, the Collector of Customs for the Port of New York—the biggest plum of them all with six hundred posts at its command—appeared to embezzle $1,225,705.69 and, it was claimed, fled to England (that very precise number comes from a Congressional investigation). President Van Buren devoted four humiliating paragraphs of his Annual Message to Congress, confessing the "gravest defalcation" in American history.[48]

But for all the Whig criticism, the patronage system had grown essential—the crucial grease in the party machinery. The need to galvanize a great political army swept along the unenthusiastic Whig leaders. The party faithful did not share their high-minded ambivalence and clamored for posts as loudly as the Democrats. The Democratic press, in turn, honked at their rival's conversion. "The Whigs," who so "detested the 'spoils' and the 'spoilsmen,'" taunted the *Washington Globe*, "have been changed, by the magic of success, into the fiercest office seekers."[49]

The immense campaigns and the post-election job frenzy became defining features of the mid-nineteenth-century politics. Job seekers gathered after victory, jamming into the White House and accosting newly elected presidents. While Europeans developed public sector bureaucracies that aspired to expertise and statecraft, the United States traded expertise for political muscle. By the election of 1840, parties and patronage had insinuated themselves into almost every cranny of American politics.

The spoils echoed slavery in a subtle way. Each limited the development of a strong, central government. Democrats scrutinized every federal move for potential threats to slavery. Patronage, though it served many useful purposes in its early days, also limited the expertise and the capacity of the government. By 1840, the party system enabled an unprecedented and rowdy electoral democracy, defended a racially bigoted order, and produced a reliably weak central government.

IN THE PARTY SCRAMBLE FOR VICTORY, THE VOTING PROCESS itself went up for grabs. The Whigs were especially anxious about cheating. Foreigners were voting, they said, and strangers tramped into towns on every election day and demanded ballots. Democrats saw no harm in any of that. Why not let men simply vote wherever they find themselves on election day? The real problem, they countered, was the Whig urge to stifle the will of the common people.[50]

The Whigs finally hit upon an effective tactic when they proposed creating a registry of eligible voters and barring anyone who was not listed. An extra hurdle to the ballot box, they reasoned, would ensure that only the eligible voted and limit the flow of Democratic voters. Connecticut imposed a registration system in 1839, just in time for the Log Cabin campaign. Whigs in Pennsylvania introduced registration in 1836 but applied it only to (Democratic) Philadelphia. Whigs in New York clamped the same requirement on New York City, until the Democrats came back into power two years later and repealed it. The new political maneuver—for that's what registration was—spread quickly and voters were soon electing registry boards to oversee the process. Once in office, these boards cracked down on supposedly fraudulent voters—who favored the wrong party.[51]

The constitutional silence about voting continued to haunt American elections. With no guidelines and with elections run by partisans, close votes led to crises. Take the Pennsylvania election of 1838. Democrats insisted that, in one area of Philadelphia, Whig authorities had discarded Democratic ballots, dispatched thugs to intimidate Democratic voters, and stuffed the ballot boxes. One unabashed Whig official allegedly boasted that he himself had cast 120 votes. Eight seats were eventually in dispute and, taken together, they would tip the majority in Pennsylvania's lower chamber to one party or the other. Naturally, the county board split along partisan lines on whether to count or to disqualify the disputed ballots. Since the contested result left no clear majority in the state legislature, that body could not certify the winners either. The Democrats and Whigs each elected a different speaker of the House—pushing and shoving one another on the floor of the chamber. Armed gangs gathered—one mob broke into the statehouse and sent Whigs fleeing through the windows. Whig governor John Ritner called for federal troops, and when the Van Buren administration rejected his request, he turned to the state militia. The commanding officer announced that his troops would protect life and property without taking sides and distributed thirteen rounds of buckshot to each soldier—giving the contretemps its name, the Buckshot War. In the end, the public opinion seems to have swung to the Democrats. In any case, three Whigs defected to the Democrats in the House and eight in the Senate, giving the Democrats control of the Pennsylvania legislature regardless of the disputed votes.[52]

The chaos reflected, once again, the lack of clear voting procedures or authorities. The Constitution offered only weak rules for a new age of formidable parties. On a deeper level, the ballot battles reflected the changing tribalism of the era. The Democrats ended property restrictions and extended the vote to most white men. In the process, however, they restricted black voters. New York, for example, applied property restriction only on black voters, leaving most of them excluded. North Carolina simply added the word "white" to its constitutional requirements for voting. Pennsylvania expanded the franchise to all "white freemen" and, in the process, bowed to intense popular pressure and cut out all black voters (in 1838). Black Pennsylvanians wrote an eloquent appeal against the exclusion, but the majority paid no attention and drove forty thousand African Americans out of the state's elections.[53]

Across the country, a hard color line went up. Back in 1815, black freemen were permitted to vote on the same terms as whites in half the states (nine of eighteen). By 1840, the number of states with racial equality in voting had shrunk to just five of twenty-six. Only New England refused to mark black voters for discrimination or exclusion—and its black population was tiny. American suffrage continued to morph—now it was more white men in, most free black men out, foreigners up for grabs.

WHEN ALL THE MEETINGS AND MARCHES AND SPEECHES were done, the Whigs' decisively won the election of 1840. Harrison took the popular count, 53 percent to 47 percent and routed Van Buren in the Electoral College, 234 to 60. The Whigs also enjoyed a 142 to 98 majority in the House of Representatives and a 27 to 22 majority in the Senate. It was the biggest win in the Whig Party's history and the only time they controlled the White House and both chambers of Congress. Their accession lasted thirty-one days.

Old Tip gave the longest, the most learned, and quite possibly the most boring inaugural address in American history. The usual story is that the sixty-eight-year old Harrison caught a cold delivering his interminable address without a coat or hat. The cold turned into pneumonia and, because he suffered the best medicine available at the time, Harrison was dead within a month. Contemporary epidemiology tells us that it probably did not happen that way. It wasn't the hat (you don't die from no hat). The killer was more likely contaminated water from the open sewer just blocks from the White House—which might well have also killed two of the next three presidents.[54]

What now? No president had ever died in office and the Constitution was ambiguous about whether the vice president simply assumed the powers of the president or stepped into the office itself. But Vice President John Tyler brushed the question aside, declared that the Constitution made him president, and moved into the White House. Any message addressed to Vice President Tyler went right back unopened.

President Tyler—a slave-owning Democrat from Virginia who had been put on the Whig ticket purely for political balance—was just as bold about shutting down his adopted party's policies. When the Whig majority in Congress restored the national bank, Tyler stunned them with a veto. He also knocked down tariffs, killed infrastructure bills, and continued right on vetoing the Whigs' legislation until he broke the record for vetoes in a single session of Congress with ten. His opponents were scornful. John Quincy Adams summed up their judgment: "not above mediocrity . . . with all the interests and passions and vices of slavery rooted in his moral and political constitution." Theodore Roosevelt corrected Adams a half century later: "He has been called a mediocre man, but that is unwarranted flattery." Congress was hostile, the entire cabinet eventually resigned, and the Whigs drummed him out of the party.[55]

Tyler was eager to win his own presidential term in 1844, and the clash with the Whigs posed a problem. He cast about for something that might appeal to his original party, the Democrats. He picked a treacherous issue, the annexation of Texas, which he pursued, as his Secretary of State Daniel Webster put it, with "ardent feelings" unchecked by "prudent judgment."[56]

Texas raised problems that most northern politicians were eager to duck. To understand why, some background is necessary. Mexico had invited American immigrants into its sparsely populated northern territory shortly after its own independence from Spain (in 1821). The American settlers breezily ignored national rules requiring Catholicism, restricting slavery, and regulating commerce. When Mexico began to pay attention—trying to crack down on slavery and limit further settlers—the Americans revolted, won independence in 1836, and immediately applied for statehood in the United States. The Jackson administration, in its final year, turned them down.

There were plenty of reasons to spurn Texas. Annexation might very well lead to war with Mexico, for the Mexicans did not recognize Texan independence and the two sides were still skirmishing. In fact, the two sides set the borders of Texas in very different places so that even when fighting ended, almost half the territory would remain in dispute. And, to complicate matters still further, the Comanche, Cheyenne, and Arapahoe tribes concluded a Great Peace in 1840, and the Comanches began flexing their own muscles in the disputed territories.

If the Democrats were cool to annexation, the Whigs were adamantly opposed. John Quincy Adams charged that the whole thing was engineered to win "bigger pens to cram with slaves." Daniel Webster added some scary math: annexation meant a "slave holding country large enough for . . . a dozen [slave] States"—a terrifying thought to antislavery Whigs. On a more philosophical level, the Whigs opposed a heedless rush to expand the nation. The United States ought to develop the vast lands it already owned rather than grabbing at more.

Both political parties quietly agreed to ignore the whole business and, in 1840, neither candidate had supported annexation. Now, Tyler decided to ride Texas into the next presidential election. In 1843, he secretly sent his second secretary of state, Abel Upshur, to negotiate with the Texans and dispatched newspaper editor Duff Green (another fallen Whig) to England. The capricious Green quickly sent back a sensational but fictitious story. The English, hoping to check American expansion and secure a reliable cotton crop, were also negotiating with the Texans about annexation. Green further claimed that the English planned to abolitionize the country. Never mind official English denials—or the raw implausibility of the Texans agreeing to a deal that outlawed their own slaves. While Washington buzzed over Green's wild rumors, Secretary Upshur secretly hammered out an annexation deal with the Texans, brazenly pledging to dispatch the army and the navy to protect the land from Mexican attacks without congressional approval.

A freak tragedy complicated the situation in 1844. President Tyler and his entourage boarded the new pride of the US Navy, the *Princeton*, for a cruise up the Potomac. The outing included a demonstration of the ship's powerful cannon. As the ship sailed past George Washington's plantation, Mount Vernon, the captain ordered one last cannonade and the great gun exploded. Secretary Upshur was immediately killed. President Tyler, who had been safely below deck, quickly replaced him with the redoubtable John Calhoun.

Secretary Calhoun sent Upshur's secret Texas treaty to the Senate for ratification and included, among other documents, an astonishing exchange with the British foreign office. The English ambassador, Sir Richard Parkenham, had written a letter claiming, in polite diplomatic language, that the reports about England's plan to annex Texas were complete nonsense. Parkenham did acknowledge, in passing, that Britain aspired to see the "abolition of slavery . . . throughout the world," but they had no intention of pursuing it in Texas. The new secretary of state, John Calhoun, would not tolerate even an offhand call for abolition and wrote back, on the president's behalf, instructing the British about the many benefits of slavery. He went on (and on), repeating his familiar argument about slavery as a "positive good" and leavening his memo with snatches of data. For example, the number of "negroes" who were "deaf," "dumb," "blind," "idiots," "insane," "paupers," or "in prison" ran precisely ninety-two times higher where they did not enjoy the benefits of slavery. Protecting slavery in Texas, concluded Calhoun, would be a prime advantage of annexing it to the United States. The diatribe had an important consequence. When Calhoun sent the treaty to Congress, he included this letter and, by doing so, thrust the alleged benefits of slavery right into the debate about annexing Texas. Now, annexation became a point of honor among southern Democrats.[57]

The Tyler administration tried to keep their Texas deal secret, but the story leaked and created an uproar. Democratic Senator Thomas Hart Benton of Missouri summed up the reasons for his colleagues' reluctance. "Mr. Tyler . . . has become infected with the modern notion that gunpowder popularity is the passport to the presidency." But, continued Benton, ratifying the treaty "would be war with Mexico—unjust war, unconstitutionally made . . . upon a weak and groundless pretext." When the roll was called, the senators soundly rejected annexation thirty-five to sixteen. The southern Democrats all voted yes (except for Benton), northern Democrats were narrowly against (seven to five), and Whigs almost unanimously voted nay (twenty-eight to one).[58]

Tyler never got his shot at reelection. The Democrats did not seriously consider nominating someone who had run with the enemy in the last election. But Tyler had fixed his explosive issue on the national agenda. The 1844 presidential frontrunners, Whig Henry Clay and Democrat Martin Van Buren, both repudiated annexation. The issue looked to be blocked in Congress and dead in both the parties. But by turning Texas into a question of slavery's positive good, Calhoun had roused the southern Democrats.

At the Democratic convention, Van Buren won a majority on the first ballot, but southerners rejected him for his unyielding stance on

Texas. The Democrats required their nominees to win two-thirds of the delegates and, with southern opposition, Van Buren could not clear that bar. In a raucous gathering, amid shouts and fistfights, the first dark horse candidate in American history won the nomination on the ninth ballot. James K. Polk, a slaveholder, who had been Speaker of the House and governor of Tennessee, emerged victorious. His signature issue: the annexation of Texas. The Democrats rallied round with a new plank calling for the "reannexation of Texas" and the "reoccupation of Oregon." The odd language—as if the United States were taking back western lands it had never owned—was the first full-throated expression of what the Democratic newspapers began calling "Manifest Destiny."

Manifest Destiny recast national expansion as a providential mission to the west. "Yes, More! More! More!" gushed editor John O'Sullivan, "till our national destiny is fulfilled . . . [and] the whole countless continent is ours." O'Sullivan, who had invented the term *Manifest Destiny*, celebrated "the diffusive instinct in the American character" that could never "be crammed up into a corner of the earth." A glorious tomorrow called down from the future, he declared, and urged today's America to construct a great empire for unborn generations.[59]

The Democrats, the party of states' rights and slavery, had hit upon a soaring cause to match their evangelical rivals. It reverberated, as one historian put it, with energy, plunder, and religious hubris. As the Democrats cheered the new national destiny, the Whigs went wobbly. Henry Clay swept into a united and confident convention and easily won the Whigs' nomination. But the unexpected fire over Texas put him and his party on the defensive. The Whigs' opposition to expanding slavery and their reluctance to jump into a war with Mexico played terribly in the South. By July, Clay was equivocating. The annexation of Texas might actually be OK, he averred, if it could be managed with the common consent of all parties. That hardly appeased the southerners—and it infuriated the abolitionists.[60]

Historians often note that the Whigs' enthusiasm and turnout fell in 1844. A close look at the election returns, however, shows that they still came very close to winning the presidency. The Democrats took New York by just 5,000 votes while abolitionist James Birney, running as a third-party candidate, drew 15,800 votes in that state, mainly in districts that had voted Whig in the last election. If even a fraction of the antislavery voters who bolted for Birney had stuck with the Whigs, the party would have won New York, flipped its thirty-six electoral votes, and Henry Clay would have finally won the office he had so long grasped after. Instead, the Democrats won the presidency, took the Senate (27–24), and kept the majority in the House despite losing six seats (147–79). The "reannexation" of Texas had gone from dead in the water to sure thing. After the election, a lame duck Tyler managed to ram it through the same Congress that had earlier turned it down. Even Senator Benton surrendered.

As predicted, annexation led directly to a bloody war with Mexico. American forces won battle after battle, but volunteers, fighting alongside the regular army, slaughtered civilians and ransacked their villages. An unknown, first-term, Whig congressman named Abraham Lincoln rose and responded to administration's claims that Mexico had invaded American territory by demanding to know "the spot on which the blood of our citizens was shed" and whether the people on that spot "did not flee from the approach of the United States army"—because, after all, they were Mexicans running before invaders.[61]

The war boomeranged right back on American politics. Once the fighting ended and the Americans acquired sprawling lands, an urgent dilemma confronted the nation. Would the new lands be slave or free? That question eventually wrecked the Democratic Party's neat equilibrium. States' rights had given them a reliable answer to the slavery issue, but it offered no obvious solution to the more difficult question they had now forced on the nation: What should be done with the new lands?

Today, Manifest Destiny is often described as a national trait, an insight into the restless American character. But it rose up in the 1840s as something else entirely—part of a fierce partisan debate over fundamental questions about the country. Where should the nation mark its boundaries? How far ought it expand? And, most unsettling of all, as the nation spread, would the new lands be set aside for slavery or for free people?

Because Harrison neglected his hat (or, more likely, because his predecessors, literally, failed to drain the swamp), American history took an unexpected, sideways jump. What might have happened to Manifest Destiny if Harrison and the Whigs had ruled for more than a month? Of course, we'll never know. Once again, an angry foreign policy argument turned the mirror back on the United States and forced the country to grapple with just who was fully American. And who had what right to settle where. That debate would soon blow the nation apart.

PART II

CRACK-UP

The Civil War and America's Identity

THREE

A FIRE BELL IN THE NIGHT
The Path to War (1852–1860)

American politics crashed during the Civil War (1861–1865) and its era. Three treacherous questions charged through the years leading up to the war. First, the United States spread into new lands, and each fresh parcel forced the country to choose: slave lands or free soil? Both sides demanded more.[1]

Second, what role should black Americans play in the republic? Even mainstream politicians who opposed the spread of slavery swore that they stood solidly for white supremacy. At the same time, black Americans themselves would force the nation to face up to the percussive matter of equality.

Finally, what about immigrants? As the debate over slavery heated up, immigration surged and triggered perhaps the greatest nativist backlash in American history. The question of black rights got tangled up with the question of the immigrant's place in politics and society.

The era of mass parties, described in the last chapter, was still going strong. However, these three questions transformed the parties: the Whigs disappeared; nativists briefly surged; a new party, the Republicans, burst onto the national scene; and the Democrats tried to keep themselves together by clinging to states' rights. On a deeper level, all three questions touched the issue of national identity. Each forced Americans to confront the status of millions of people on the margins of power. Each raised the same disruptive question—what kind of country was this going to be? In short, American politics turned intensely tribal.

In the end, the Civil War transformed the nation, crushed the slave economy, and produced nothing less than a second American founding. Three audacious amendments carved the dream of equality into the Constitution. Even the country's name morphed into a singular noun (before the war, they used to say the United States *are*). But after all the blood and sacrifice, actually securing the new rights—actually redeeming the Declaration's proposition that all people are created equal—remained out of reach. Racial equality would remain an elusive aspiration for some future generation.

ANTHONY BURNS WAS WALKING HOME FROM WORK ON A cool Boston evening in May 1854, eager for supper, when a stranger grabbed him and accused him of having robbed a silversmith's shop. In fact, Burns had stolen nothing but himself—he had escaped from slavery the previous year. As he protested his innocence, a gang of men grabbed him, hauled him to the courthouse, and clamped him in chains. A door creaked open and a familiar face peered in and whispered, "How do you do, Mr. Burns?" Before he could stop himself, Burns blurted out, "Master!"[2]

The law gave fugitive slaves almost no chance in court, and Burns knew that his startled comment, "Master," doomed him back to bondage. But this was Boston, hotbed of radical abolitionism, and there were plenty of locals who were itching to confront the slave power. Four years earlier, a fugitive named Shadrach had been snatched by slave catchers and put on trial in Boston, only to be freed when a crowd of African Americans burst into the lightly guarded courtroom and rushed him away. Now, the Democratic Franklin

Pierce administration (1853–1857) was eager to assure the South that the Fugitive Slave Act would be strictly enforced everywhere—even in Boston. The administration turned Anthony Burns into a national example and posted a heavy guard around the courthouse. The abolitionists concocted an elaborate plan to free Burns, but during the chaotic effort, someone in the surging mob of would-be liberators shot a guard dead and the crowd, shocked by the bloodshed, shrank away.[3]

The Pierce administration doubled down by dispatching marines and even cannons into Boston. Nine days after Burns had been snatched off the streets, heavily armed troops escorted him through the city to the harbor, the first leg on a journey back to Virginia. Military guards lined the streets and held back the roiling mob. Antislavery activists had hung the buildings along the route with black crepe. Even moderate New Englanders began to talk about the slave power that had burst into their city with an entire army hell-bent on hounding one man back into bondage. William Grimes, who had been Burn's minister, eventually bought his freedom. Burns went on to attend Oberlin College and remained a free man until he died of tuberculosis in 1862.

Runaways disrupted the slaveholders' dominion in the South and forced people in the North to directly confront slavery. Individuals like Burns generated sympathy, even outrage, in the North. But most white northerners were not ready to face up to the deeper question that every Anthony Burns put before them: What should the nation do with the 3.9 million people in bondage? Free them? Permit them to be politically and socially equal to white people? "My own feelings would not admit of this," said Abraham Lincoln in 1854, "and if mine would, we all know that those of the great mass of whites will not." Most northerners saw no way out.[4]

Even Harriet Beecher Stowe, the single most effective propagandist against slavery, could not face up to black freedom and racial equality. In her monumental 1852 novel, *Uncle Tom's Cabin*, the beautiful slave, Eliza, learns that her seven-year-old son is about to be sold. Desperate, she grabs Harry and flees, chased by slave catchers and their dogs. When the loathsome men trap her on the banks of the Ohio, she leaps onto the perilous blocks of ice floating down the river and makes one of the most famous escapes in American literature. The novel scornfully assails the Fugitive Slave Act of 1850 and mocks those who voted for it just to keep a craven peace. But where does it all end? Eliza, miraculously reunited with her handsome husband George Harris, resolves to emigrate to Africa and help found a truly Christian civilization. *Uncle Tom's Cabin* became the best-selling novel in American history and a formidable critique of slavery, but it can imagine no place in the United States for a brave, talented, black family and arrives at the same conclusion as so many white liberals: former slaves could not stay in America as equals. The happy ending required Stowe to write George and Eliza right out of the country.

Martin Delany, a black leader, drove the hard point home. Free blacks in the North "occupy the very same position politically, religiously, civilly, and socially . . . as the bondman occupies in the slave states." Northerners may have felt sympathy for individual human beings wrenched back into slavery, but the North, in its own way, also subjugated black men and women.[5]

What really bothered most northerners was not the way the slaves were treated but the way the slaveholders were poised to gobble up the west. The *Hartford Courant* bluntly explained the difference in an often quoted 1856 editorial. "We resist the progress of Slavery in this country, not because we feel any burning zeal in the black man's cause," but because we support "the rights of the white man, to labor on his own farm, uncontaminated by the insulting contiguity of black slaves, laboring in the adjoining field." The editors urged Americans to stand up to the slave power and "preserve all of this country that [we] can from the pestilential presence of the black race." The position was simple: no slaves, no black people at all.[6]

Southerners, of course, pushed back against limits to slavery. Barring slavery in the territories trammeled their own rights, threatened their prosperity, weakened their representation in Congress, and violated their sense of honor. The sides could not simply leave one another alone because, again, the nation was spreading and each new territory forced the same debate: Would the new lands be slave or free?

A series of compromises had so far kept a shaky peace. Back in 1820, the nation was in an uproar about admitting Missouri as a slave state. "This momentous question," fretted an aging Thomas Jefferson, "like a fire bell in the night, awakened and filled me with terror." Congressional leaders managed to hush this "knell of the union" by hammering out rules regulating slavery in the vast lands acquired by the Louisiana Purchase. The Compromise of 1820 drew an imaginary line at the 36° 30' parallel. The tracts above the parallel would forbid slavery and come into the union as free states, the land below would permit slavery. Missouri was the exception—it jutted above the line but would be a slave state. By the 1850s, the northern stretches remained undeveloped and unorganized, not even formal territories much less states. But this would soon change.[7]

The war with Mexico (1846–1848) brought still more land into the country, igniting controversy all over again. What should the nation do with its new Southwest? Simply extending the old imaginary line along the 36° 30' parallel would have split California in half. Instead, congressional leaders crafted a rickety compromise. At the heart of the legislation sat a disruptive new idea: popular sovereignty. The people in the Utah and New Mexico territories would decide about slavery for themselves. A tough fugitive slave law went into the books as part of the compromise and, as Anthony Burns illustrated, ensnared northerners in the quandary of the runaways. At first, the legislation failed in the Senate—opponents jeered it as "an omnibus," a term we still use today for legislation larded with all sorts of items. Then, Democratic Senator Stephen Douglas of

Illinois—a hard-drinking, smooth-talking, politically nimble, very short, thirty-seven-year-old force of nature—seized the moment. He broke up the omnibus into separate bills and mustered a majority for each component, though almost everyone despised and voted against at least some features of what became known as the Compromise of 1850.*

TWO FOREIGN POLICY MISADVENTURES, IN CUBA AND NICAragua, illustrated the sprawling conflict about new land for slavery in the 1850s. Many Americans saw Cuba as a potential slave territory just waiting to be seized—but how to manage it? One possibility was to ride in with filibusters—freelance armies that tried to topple foreign governments. Congress was preparing to back an attack on Cuba by a gang of these buccaneers when Democratic President Franklin Pierce (worried about northern backlash) ruled it out. Instead, the Pierce administration turned to diplomacy, aiming to buy or bully the island from Spain. The job went to the flamboyant Pierre Soulé.

---

*The Compromise of 1850 did not replace that of 1820 (which dealt with the land acquired in the Louisiana Purchase) but made rules for new lands, grabbed from Mexico, and included five main points:

1. California entered the union as a free state, tipping the Senate balance against slavery—sixteen free, fifteen slave. However, California agreed to send one pro-slavery and one pro free state member to the Senate.

2. The Utah and New Mexico territories would decide the issue of slavery for themselves. Here was that glittering new idea: popular sovereignty.

3. A tough new fugitive slave law was instituted.

4. Congress banned the slave trade, but not slavery itself, in the District of Columbia.

5. Texas surrendered its claim to what is now New Mexico as well as land north of the 36° 30' parallel. In exchange, the national government took over Texas's debt.

Soulé began his diplomatic mission by wounding the French ambassador in a duel over saucy remarks someone else made about Madame Soulé. The reckless envoy, along with the American ambassadors to England and France, concocted a wild plan known as the Ostend Manifesto, which announced that it was in Spain's interest to sell the island. However, "if Spain, dead to the voice of her own interest and actuated by stubborn pride," refused to sell, then, continued the Manifesto, "by every law human and divine, we shall be justified in wresting it from Spain."[8]

The New York Herald got its hands on the Ostend Manifesto and set off an uproar across the North. Opponents denounced the "shame and "dishonor" of this "highwayman's plea." Spain responded creatively. It emancipated most Cuban slaves and organized the freed Africans into militias. Americans, then as now, liked to think of their nation as the land of the free, but here was an ironic inversion of that idea: an absolutist monarchy liberated its own slaves to block the great republic from grabbing more territory for slavery. Four years later, in 1856, the Democratic Party platform still longed to annex Cuba but specified more respectable terms—"honorable to ourselves and just to Spain."[9]

Down in Central America, a gang of American filibusters barged into Nicaragua in May 1855. Led by William Walker—a lawyer and editor notorious for fighting duels—the Americans managed to conquer the country. Walker seized the nation's presidency, reintroduced slavery (which had been abolished), established English as an official language, and issued new rules designed to push as much real estate as possible "into the hands of the white race." "The wisdom or folly of the American movement in Nicaragua," he later wrote, rested "on the re-establishment of African slavery there." In May 1856, the Democratic Franklin Pierce (1853–1857) administration recognized the Walker government and, later that year, the Democratic Party platform announced that they "sympathize[d]" with his effort to "regenerate . . . Central America." But Walker did not last long. A coalition led by Costa Rica ousted him. When he returned to the United States, he toured the South as a hero. Undaunted by his defeats, Walker kept right on filibustering until he met his end before a Honduran firing squad in 1860.[10]

Critics saw an insatiable slave power, grasping for land far and wide. It snatched men right off the streets of Boston and followed up the recent plunder of Mexico by baldly threatening war with Spain and cheering on the invasion of Nicaragua. Even while the southern representatives searched east and west for new slave lands, they blocked the Homestead Acts designed to help white men and women acquire western land. In 1859, a crude senator from Ohio, Benjamin Wade, jeered the Democrats for being obdurate at home and imperialistic abroad: "When we lacked land, and you had it in your power to give it to us [by voting for the Homestead Act], you went fishing for niggers."* Never "land for the landless" but always "niggers for the niggerless."[11]

Southerners, of course, saw a different reality. Northerners were the ones who wielded too much power. After all, they commanded a solid majority in the House, a small one in the Senate, and a ravenous industrial machine that devoured everything in its path. Worst of all, said the southerners, the reckless agitation against slavery threatened white lives by inciting the slaves to rebellion. Both Soulé and Walker had justified their efforts to seize fresh slave lands by waving the memory of Saint-Domingue and its "horrors to the white race." More than a half century later, Toussaint's rebellion continued to do its work as the white slavers' guilty nightmare sprung to life.[12]

The kinetic Americans kept destabilizing their own intricate compromises over slavery by their own restless motion. Slaves dashed for freedom, filibusters invaded foreign lands, settlers pushed into

---

*This is an awful word and I hesitated about using it. But, in the end, I think a better future means fully facing up to the worst in the past, so I will quote it as it was used at the time.

the west, Congress turned unorganized lands into territories, and territories applied for statehood. But the big blowup came from an unexpected direction. Just three years after he had maneuvered the Compromise of 1850 through Congress, the irrepressible Senator Stephen Douglas demolished it—and eventually crushed both parties in the fallout.

SENATOR DOUGLAS WANTED TO ESTABLISH A RAILROAD LINE between Chicago and San Francisco. The road would open the west to settlers, cut off a rival route from New Orleans, and boost land prices in Chicago where Douglas owned real estate. Douglas led a faction of northern Democrats, known as the Young Americans, who broke with the party's Jeffersonian traditions and supported technology, commerce, and active government. There was just one hitch. Getting Congress to approve the railroad meant formally organizing the lands along the route into territories. And, thanks to the compromise of 1820, the entire area had been set aside for free states. Senator Douglas innocently made his proposal in 1853, and the firestorm began.

Democratic senator David Rice Atchison of Missouri stood in the well of the Senate and announced that he could support the plan only if "the constituents of the slave states . . . could go in . . . carrying that species of property [slaves] with them." The southerners saw an opportunity to extract an enormous concession. Douglas could have his railroad if Congress buried the Compromise of 1820. The lands that had originally been set aside as free soil must be open to slavery.[13]

Douglas tried finesse. The new lands could eventually be admitted as states, he said, "with or without slavery, as their constituents may prescribe." The southerners rejected that idea because the Missouri Compromise would still ban slavery while the lands were territories. Oops, said the incorrigible Douglas, a "clerical error" had omitted a key section of the bill giving the residents control over slavery while the lands were territories. The southern members refused to budge. They insisted that the compromise must be explicitly repealed and backed their demand with an incendiary constitutional claim: Congress did not have the authority to rule out slavery in any territory, as the Missouri Compromise had done. Only the residents of the territory could do that.[14]

Douglas surrendered. His bill, the Kansas Nebraska Act of 1854, flatly repealed the Missouri Compromise of 1820 and declared its ban on slavery north of 36° 30' "inoperative and void." It split the enormous territory into Kansas and Nebraska (the southern part was more likely to choose slavery), and it asserted that the people of the territories should be left "perfectly free to form and regulate their domestic institutions in their own way." President Franklin Pierce underscored the bottom line: "Congress does not possess the power to impose restrictions [on slavery]." In effect, the idea of popular sovereignty (introduced in the Compromise of 1850) would replace the Missouri Compromise and its hard boundary between slave and free territory. The Democrats muscled the legislation through in May 1854 and celebratory cannons roared from the terrace of the Capital building.[15]

Douglas had braced for a detonation, and that's what he got. Even some northern Democrats protested. "A gross violation of a sacred pledge," boomed a group of northern Democrats, "an atrocious plot to exclude immigrants from the Old World and free laborers from our own states and convert [Kansas] into a dreary region of despotism."[16] Abraham Lincoln—an obscure, one-term Whig ex-congressman from the middle of nowhere—leapt onto a platform after Senator Douglas had spoken in Peoria, Illinois, in October 1854 and stated the objection as well as anyone. The two Compromises were two separate bargains dealing with two separate tracts of land. In each case, the North agreed to permit the spread of slavery, "not because they thought it right, but because they were compensated." Now, the slave states, having swallowed their portion of the Missouri Compromise, demanded access to the free territories, "*without any equivalent at all.*" "If you wish the thing again, pay again," summed up Lincoln. "That is the spirit of the compromise." Of the ten free-state legislatures in session, five denounced the bill and four, all in Democratic hands, pointedly refused to endorse it.[17]

The backlash crushed the northern Democrats. Ninety-one went into the 1854 midterm and only twenty-six survived. The destruction of their governors was even worse. The party went from thirteen northern governorships at the start of the year, to five in 1855, and just one (Indiana) by 1857. In the coming years, the northern Democrats would grow increasingly exasperated with their southern brethren who kept devising increasingly forceful pro-slavery positions that played terribly in the North.

Things were a lot worse across the aisle. Most southern Whigs supported the Kansas–Nebraska Act, but not a single northern Whig in either chamber voted aye. The issue of slavery broke the party. A coalition that stretched from abolitionists in New England to slavers in North Carolina could not remain in business when the slavery debate dominated national politics. As the Whigs went down, in 1854, a great question hovered over American politics. Who would replace them as the country's second major party?

TWO NEW FACTIONS, NEITHER OF WHICH HAD QUITE ORGA-
nized into a party, burst onto the scene. Each rallied former Whigs against a different danger. Know Nothings attacked immigrants while Republicans stood against the expansion of slavery. Together, the two new factions reflected something important. Parties are about projecting ideas, winning policies, and serving plums to the faithful. But in a deeper sense, parties also define and defend identities. The raucous marching, singing, torchlight campaigns of the era built communal bonds. As conflict rose through the 1850s, the

identity issues grew more intense. The two factions of orphaned northern Whigs each constructed a forceful answer to the perennial American question, who are we? Or more pointedly, in both cases, who are we not?

Many former Whigs seized on nativism. At this fraught moment, foreigners were landing on American shores in unprecedented numbers. In 1854 alone, four hundred thousand immigrants arrived—1.6 percent of the entire American population and still the all-time high for a single year (as a proportion of the total population). New York City's population had quadrupled in the previous thirty years, and by the 1850s, half of its residents had been born abroad. The newcomers powered the growth of cities, crowded into the Democratic Party, and like every wave of immigration, began to alter the face of the nation.

The immigrants' Catholicism provoked particular angst. American Protestants believed that their faith prepared them to participate in a republic, since it rose out of a rebellion against a corrupted feudal hierarchy, just like the United States itself. Protestants read the Bible for themselves, followed their own conscience, and in many cases elected their ministers. By contrast, Catholics prostrated themselves before a kind of medieval Italian monarch—and to make matters worse, Pope Pious IX had been chased out of Rome in 1848, when he resisted the republicans fighting to unify Italy. Rather than follow their own conscience, said the fearful Protestants, Catholics abided by the dicta of their bishops. They did not even read the Bible (the priests read it during services) and wouldn't dream of voting for their own clergy. Catholic leaders like Cardinal John Hughes of New York stoked the backlash by disparaging Protestantism as a feeble sect that would inevitably fall to the Catholics—exactly what many Protestants feared. And on top of it all, the Catholics unapologetically filled their churches with idolatrous icons and sent their children to Catholic schools where they were indoctrinated by priests and nuns.[18]

In the 1854 midterm election, a nativist backlash against the newcomers blazed onto the political scene. The idea sprang from a secret New York fraternity, formed in 1850, to resist Catholicism and restore Anglo-Saxon culture. Initiates received secret hand-grips, furtive passwords, and instruction to tell nosy outsiders "I know nothing"—and, with that, the new nativism had its name.

The Know Nothings spread and, in the 1854 election, met astonishing success. They elected eight governors across New England, Pennsylvania, Delaware, Kentucky, and California. In Massachusetts, the Know Nothings took the entire congressional delegation, every seat in the state Senate and all but two (out of 378) in the House. In California, they swept every statewide office and won a majority in both legislative chambers. The Know Nothings elected at least fifty-one members to the House of Representatives and combined with other factions to elevate Massachusetts Know-Nothing Nathaniel Banks to Speaker of the House. After the midterms, the rising Know Nothing movement organized itself into a formal political party, the American Party, and gathered an estimated one million members within a year. *The New York Herald* sounded perfectly plausible when it predicted that the next election, in 1856, would put a member of the American Party into the White House.[19]

Men voted Know Nothing for different reasons. Some were disgusted by spoils and corruption. Others were angry at the Democrats for their shenanigans in Kansas. The core of the movement, however, was a rising animosity toward the Irish and German immigrants on the East Coast and the Chinese and Mexicans in California. The Know Nothings' program amounted to an update of the old Alien Acts. They would forbid foreigners from holding office, tighten election procedures, deport foreign paupers and criminals, slow (or even end) naturalization, protect the American common school from the Catholic schools, and legislate temperance to control the heavy drinking of the Irish and German immigrants.[20]

In power, the Know Nothings immediately tripped over the checks and balances of American government. In Massachusetts, the party began, in 1855, by introducing an amendment to the state constitution that would have forbidden all immigrants from ever voting or holding office. As the proposal wound through the process, the prohibition shrank from never, to twenty-one years, to fourteen years, to a two-year delay on voting after naturalization. They did manage to throw up some registration requirements to depress the immigrant turnout. They also took the naturalization procedures out of the hands of Irish-friendly state judges and mandated Bible reading in public schools. Across the country, the Know Nothings won a smattering of temperance laws. California enacted restrictions and taxes on the "Chinese and Mongolians," but the laws were eventually struck down in court.

The nativist surge tested national leaders including three who would be presidential candidates in 1860. The opportunistic Simon Cameron of Pennsylvania damaged his reputation by openly embracing the Know Nothings in an unsuccessful effort to win a seat in the US Senate. New York's William Seward, on the other hand attacked the movement. Standing on the Senate floor, Seward began with a sarcastic play on the movement's name: "It is my purpose to say nothing of the Know Nothings because of the Know Nothings . . . I know nothing at all. [Laughter]." Seward went on to celebrate immigrants for their contributions to building the nation.[21]

Abraham Lincoln, suave and patient, stayed mum, at least in public. Many of his friends had joined the Know Nothings, and he hoped, as he wrote in one letter, "that their organization would die out without the painful necessity of my having to take an open stance against them." Lincoln quietly waited out the Know Nothings in public while eloquently condemning nativism in private. "How could anyone who abhors the oppression of negroes," he wrote in his letters, "be in favor of degrading classes of white people?"

As a nation, we begin by declaring that "all men are created equal." We now practically read it "all men are created equal, except negroes." When the Know-Nothings get control, it will read "all men are created equal, except negroes, and foreigners, and Catholics." When it comes to this, I should prefer emigrating to some country where they make no pretense of loving liberty—to Russia, for instance, where despotism can be taken pure, and without the base alloy of hypocracy.[22]

Lincoln got his wish. The Know Nothings flashed into power in 1854, made a weak show in 1856, and then vanished from the electoral scene. Why did they disappear? Like the Whigs before them, the American Party foundered on slavery. Northern Know Nothings wanted to stand up to the rising slave power, and southerners did not. Like so many other national institutions, the American Party broke into two factions, the North Americans and the South Americans.

The Democratic Party, on the other hand, generally fought the nativists. Every four years, the party platform waved the pro-immigrant flag and denounced their rivals' commitment to the "spirit of the Alien and Sedition acts." The Democrats still reflected the politics of the Jeffersonians back in the first contested election of 1800: they defended slavery while embracing the immigrants; their opponents increasingly objected to slavery and feared the immigrants.

When the American Party disappeared after the election of 1856, much of the nativist sentiment flowed into the Republican Party. As historian David Potter put it, "No event in the history of the Republican Party was more crucial or more fortunate than this sub-rosa union. By it, the Republican Party received a permanent endowment of nativist support which probably elected Abraham Lincoln in 1860 and which strengthened the party in every election for [years] . . . to come."[23]

It is always tempting to dismiss the Know Nothings as a brief, bigoted spasm in an immigrant nation. But rather than a momentary flash, the Know Nothings were part of a deep current running through the American story. Each iteration seems unique. Each generation of nativists insists that the immigrants they despise are different—a far greater threat to the nation—than those who came before (who are now assimilated and respectable). Generation after generation, nativists have scrambled for ways to protect the nation from the inferior masses at the door by barring them from the ballots, limiting their political influence, simplifying the deportation process, or, eventually, shutting the national door to some (or to most) immigrants altogether. At every step, American nativists turned important policy questions—How many people should the nation admit? Whom should we favor and why?—into feverish, even apocalyptic battles about national identity, about looming ruin, about us versus them.

WHILE NATIVISM SWEPT THE NORTHEAST, OPPOSITION TO the Kansas–Nebraska Act dominated the Northwest. "The question of Nebraska is knocking politics all into a cocked hat," reported one Wisconsin newspaper. State conventions across the west pledged, as one Ohio gathering put it, to "work assiduously to render *inoperative and void* . . . the Kansas–Nebraska bill which abolishes . . . the Missouri compromise." One of the protest groups, meeting in Ripon, Wisconsin, called themselves the Republicans and the name stuck.

In 1854, the Republicans, still a loose constellation of groups with different names in different places, elected thirty-seven House members and joined the rising Know Nothings (fifty-one seats) and the fading Whigs (fifty-four) to strip the Democrats (eighty-three, mostly in the south) of their majority. As the controversy over Kansas grew, the Republican Party coalesced and spread across the North, gathering the orphan Whigs, disgruntled Democrats, and former Know Nothings. Whig leaders joined the new party. Senator Seward of New York came over with a large faction and much fanfare in 1855. Abraham Lincoln made a much smaller splash, when he joined the Republicans in time for the 1856 election.

The rising party took a strong stand on slavery: it should not be permitted to spread into any territory. The first party platform, written for the 1856 presidential election, ran twenty-one paragraphs long, and fifteen of them cataloged the different ways that Kansas had been wronged. Another denounced the Ostend Manifesto. Its most famous blast called on Congress to protect all territories from "those twin relics of barbarism, polygamy and slavery"—taunting slaveholders by casting them alongside the despised Mormons. The party also called for an active national government—dredging rivers, improving harbors, and constructing a railroad to the Pacific.[24]

The Republican criticism of slavery reverberated like intimations of Jubilee in the slave quarters. Black men and women learned about the new movement from the anxious white talk declaring that "the streets would run with blood before the [Republicans] should rule." As William Webb, a former slave later put it, this was a thrilling revelation for it "was the first the colored people knew about another Nation wishing for the slaves to be free." The slaves took it upon themselves, as Webb put it, "to study how they should be free." They held meetings where they prayed and called on one another to stand and testify about freedom—always knowing it would be death if the slavers got wind of what they were doing.[25]

But the Republicans themselves did not share the slave's curriculum. The party denounced the expansion of slavery but had no objections to all-white territories in the west. And they remained mum about the fate of the men and women in bondage. Most Republicans loudly distinguished themselves from the radical abolitionists who supported immediate emancipation and equality. For Republicans—for most white northerners—challenging slavery was not at all the same thing as championing African Americans.

Sarcastic Democrats would soon pummel Republicans on this very point: Exactly what did they intend for black America?

THE REPUBLICANS PROSPERED BECAUSE THEIR ISSUE KEPT crowding everything else right out of the headlines. American politics in the mid-1850s became about Kansas, Kansas, and Kansas. Congress called for elections to determine whether Kansas would be a slave state or a free state—without specifying any rules for the territorial election. Political historians focused on the 1850s sometimes comment on what seems like a weird oversight. But, as we've seen, it is the American way of voting—stretching from the Constitution right down to the present. Kansas was only the most extreme example. In six years, the territory faced ten governors, five state capitals, four Constitutions, two competing legislatures, and fourteen elections—many of them stained by violence and every single one wreathed in shouts of "fraud."

In March 1855, Kansas held its first election to select a territorial legislature. Democratic Senator David Atchison, who had pressed Stephen Douglas to repeal the Missouri Compromise of 1820 and open the Kansas and Nebraska territories to slavery, now led thousands of armed Ruffians into Kansas, where they descended on voting districts and imposed their own rules. They shouted that any men who had been in the territory "but five minutes" had every right to vote, and to make their intentions clear, the Ruffians roughed up election officials with yips of "kill the damn nigger thief," "cut his guts out," and "shoot him." They drove off the election monitors, selected new ones on the spot, voted for pro-slavery legislators, and headed home where, according to the antislavery press, they were met with brass bands.[26]

"We have made a clean sweep," exulted one Ruffian leader, "no anti-slavery man will be in the Legislature of Kansas." The final election tally ran 5,427 pro-slavery votes to just 791 for free state candidates—quite an achievement in a territory with just 2,905 resident voters (a census had been taken the previous month). This was all too much for the territory's first governor, Andrew Reeder, who ordered new elections in every district that lodged a complaint. But his order had no impact. The pro-slavery legislature blithely ignored the results from the new elections called by the governor and seated the original winners. It then proceeded to write a slave code that made it a felony to criticize slavery and a capital offense to encourage slave rebellions.[27]

Northern groups scrambled to respond. They organized emigration societies to populate Kansas and tilt the territory against slavery. One pro-slavery newspaper spoke for the ages when it answered charges that its side had violated law, order, and due process: law and order be damned when "hordes of paupers and hirelings are imported into Kansas for the purpose of Abolitionizing the Territory." Neither side accepted the voters on the other side as legitimate. Ruffians cheated on one side, abolitionist émigrés on the other. Without clear rules, every voter could be defended or denounced.[28]

Before long, leaders on both sides were calling for blood. The abolitionists will stop trifling with slave holders, chuckled the *Columbia Missouri Journal*, when they confront our "Arkansas toothpicks [and] six shooters"—Arkansas toothpicks were long-bladed knives. New Yorker, Henry Ward Beecher, one of the best-known preachers of the era, reportedly declared "there is more moral power in one . . . Sharp Rifle . . . than in a hundred bibles." The *New-York Tribune* commended Beecher for "solid sense," and the rifles, which made their way into Kansas, became known as "Beecher Bibles."[29]

By the spring of 1856, the violence had metastasized into guerrilla warfare. Pro-slavery militia with cannons besieged Lawrence, a center of free-state sentiment, and when the town surrendered, marched in and set fire to the hotel and the newspaper offices.[30]

John Brown, a fiery abolitionist, responded by raiding three Kansas homesteads. His small band dragged men out of their houses, hacked them to pieces with swords, or shot them in the head—an eye for an eye, as they saw it. The Pottawatomie massacre, as it became known, fed the cycle of violence. William Halstead, a former Whig congressman from New Jersey, spoke for many Americans when he fretted that "a civil war has commenced." By most estimates, more than fifty people died in this fighting (and some put the number as high as two hundred).[31]

Amid the uproar, Kansas moved to become a state, which required a constitution. The pro-slavery territorial legislature stacked a constitutional convention, held in the town of Lecompton, and in December 1857 the voters were invited to cast their judgment on the proposed Kansas constitution. They could vote for the Lecompton Constitution "with slavery" or "without slavery." But it was a false choice, for all slaves who were already in the state would remain slaves regardless of the outcome—in effect, turning Kansas into a slave state. Free-Staters protested that this was no choice at all and boycotted the vote, which predictably went "with slavery" by more than ten to one. Governor Frederick Stanton (territorial governor number five) called for another vote on the constitution. This time the pro-slavery faction boycotted, and a month after the constitution had been overwhelmingly approved, it was overwhelmingly rejected. The legislature ignored the second vote and sent the Lecompton Constitution to Washington for congressional approval, the final step before entering the union as a slave state. Democratic President James Buchanan (1857–1861) received the pro-slavery constitution, endorsed it, and in February 1858 sent it on to Congress with a long message rejoicing, as he put it, that "a wise spirit" had prevailed among the voters in Kansas. President Buchanan, as we will soon see, never missed an opportunity to stand up for slavery.[32]

Senator Stephen Douglas had championed popular sovereignty, but the rampant cheating offended him, and he charged over to the

White House to protest the Lecompton Constitution. Buchanan threatened Douglas with political destruction if he didn't back off and made voting for the proposed constitution a test of Democratic party fealty. The Senate Democrats got into line, and the chamber narrowly approved the Lecompton Constitution and accepted Kansas as a slave state. The House balked, sent the matter back to Kansas for yet another vote, and on the next round, the voters again decisively rejected the Lecompton Constitution, 11,812 to 1,926. Southern Democrats bitterly denounced Douglas and the northern members in the House who, they charged, supported popular sovereignty only when the voters rejected slavery.

REPUBLICAN SENATOR CHARLES SUMNER OF MASSACHUSETTS fumed over the reports from Kansas. In May 1856, he delivered a sizzling two-day speech to the Senate.

> Are you against sacrilege? I present it for your execration. Are you against robbery—I hold it up for your scorn. Are you for the protection of American citizens? I show you how their dearest rights have been cloven down while a tyrannical usurpation has sought to install itself on their very necks.

Then Senator Sumner got nasty. He singled out Senator Andrew Butler of South Carolina and Senator Douglas, mocking them as Don Quixote and Sancho Panza.

> Senator [Butler] from South Carolina has read many books on chivalry and believes himself a chivalrous knight. . . . Of course, he has chosen a mistress to whom he has made his vows and who, though ugly to others is always lovely to him; though polluted in the sight of the world, is chaste in his sight;—I mean the harlot Slavery.[33]

As Sumner spoke, Douglas paced at the back of the chamber, grumbling "that damn fool will get himself killed by some other damn fool." Two days later, the other damn fool appeared. Congressman Preston Brooks of South Carolina entered the chamber after the Senate had adjourned, primly waited for a woman to leave the gallery, and then approached Sumner, who was writing at his desk. "I have read your speech carefully," said Brooks quietly, "it is a libel on South Carolina and on Mr. Butler who is a [cousin] of mine." And with that, Brooks began to pummel Sumner on the head with his gold tipped walking cane. Sumner, trapped at the desk, which was bolted to the floor, absorbed blow after blow until he finally thrust himself up, ripping the desk from its moorings, and fell to the floor, bleeding and unconscious. Brooks continued to bash him, even after the cane splintered. His colleague, Representative Laurence Keitt (D-SC) stood at his side and blocked anyone else from interfering.[34]

Even northerners who did not especially care about slavery one way or the other, recoiled upon hearing about the assault. The Slave Power, as critics were calling it, had grown insatiable. "If we venture to laugh at them or question their logic or dispute their facts," asked one widely circulated editorial, "are we to be chastised as they chastise their slaves?" Many southerners openly exulted in the long-overdue beating of the vulgar Republican—this was precisely how gentlemen chastised their inferiors. When the House fell short of the two-thirds needed to expel Brooks, he resigned anyway, returned to South Carolina a hero, received dozens of new canes from his grateful countrymen, and was unanimously returned. Sumner took three years to recover from the trauma. He, too, became a hero in his region.[35]

The Sumner caning is only the best-known eruption. Historian Joanne Freeman recently toted up seventy fights with fists or weapons in and near the House and Senate chambers between 1830 and

1860. Henry Hammond, a senator from South Carolina, summed up the mood in Congress: "the only persons who do not have a revolver and a knife are those who have two revolvers."[36]

THE FURY OVER KANSAS IS AN EXTREME EXAMPLE OF THAT old American problem—vague voting rules. The Constitution passed the issue to the states, where the quest to win often swept aside such niceties as clear and consistent procedures. When something fundamental was at stake—and nothing was more fundamental than race and slavery—the rules paled next to the task of saving the country from the other side. Opponents became a dangerous threat to rights, to America, to *us*. That was how the Jeffersonians and the Federalists of the first generation had seen it. And that's how political activists saw it in the 1850s. Civic leaders on both sides endorsed paramilitary groups. Border ruffians faced off against antislavery émigrés. The government lost its monopoly over legitimate violence. To this day, political scientists warn that armed groups, acting outside formal government but with the winking approval of civic leaders, flash a bright warning signal—democracy in peril.[37]

Parties chasing spoils had deflected the slavery conflict for a generation. But, by the 1850s, the question of slavery in the territories dominated national politics. There were few neutral political institutions and no one to impartially oversee the elections in Kansas. Local majorities hammered out the electoral rules—rigging the vote first one way and then the other, prompting boycotts, landslides, and cries of fraud each time.

Bleeding Kansas sends a warning to every generation: it is difficult to contain the conflict when partisans turn normal politics into an existential clash over rights, status, and the meaning of the nation. The fevers rage hottest when they turn on identity, on race or ethnicity or sexuality. And normal politics are always harder to contain without a positive right to vote resting on a foundation of clear, fair, universal rules.

———————

JAMES BUCHANAN WAS BORING, OLD, EXPERIENCED, AND pro-slavery. As the American ambassador to England, he had been about as far from the mess in Kansas as it was possible to get. In 1856, the Democrats nominated Buchanan to run against the first Republican presidential candidate, John Frémont. Buchanan won easily and, at first glance, seemed to restore the Democratic Party after its midterm massacre in 1854. Democrats took the presidency, the Senate, and the House (where they picked up forty-eight seats). But beneath the surface, the roiling slavery issue made the results much closer than they looked at first glance. If the Republicans had flipped just two close states (say, Pennsylvania and Illinois where Buchanan scraped by with 50 percent and 44 percent of the votes in a three-way race), then Frémont would have slipped into the White House without a solitary vote in any of the twelve slave states.

President Buchanan's inaugural address plodded right into the hullabaloo. Buchanan knew that the Supreme Court was about to announce a blockbuster decision about slavery in the territories and he likened the pending judgment to his own presidential election. The campaign may have been passionately contested, but as soon as the results were announced, he said, "instant submission" followed. Likewise, the Supreme Court would announce its ruling and the savage debate over Kansas would end. Like all good citizens, intoned this soul of innocence, "I shall cheerfully submit . . . to their decision . . . whatever it may be." Except that he knew perfectly well what it would be. Buchanan had pushed one northern justice, Robert Cooper Grier of Pennsylvania, to join with the five southern justices in order to improve the optics when the legal bomb detonated.

Two days later, the court released the Dred Scott decision—historically inaccurate, legally implausible, virulently partisan, politically perilous, and the top contender for the worst decision ever rendered by the Court. Yet, for all that, the decision contained cheerless, bigoted grains of truth. It illuminated the Republican's racial agonies. On the other side, Democrats cheered Dred Scott until it broke their party in two.

In 1834, a slave named Dred Scott landed in the free state of Illinois with his owner, an army surgeon named John Emerson. Two years later, the pair moved to Fort Snelling, in the Wisconsin territory (present day Minnesota), where slavery was also banned. While he was in the free territory, Dred Scott got married in a civil ceremony—something that a slave could not have done. The army posted John Emerson back into slave states, and the Scott family (they had two girls) eventually ended up in the slave state of Missouri. In 1846, Dred Scott tried to buy his family's freedom but his bid was rejected. Scott went to court setting off the epic legal saga.[38]

The Scotts lost on a technicality, won their freedom on a second try, and then lost again in the Missouri Supreme Court. Missouri courts had always freed slaves who had lived in free territories—the rule was "once free, always free." Now, the rancor over slavery moved the court to change its practice and it ruled against Scott. "Times are not as they are," explained the court, because "a dark and fell spirit" had ensnared slavery.[39]

Next, Dred Scott turned to the federal courts. As the case snaked through the system, John Emerson, the Scotts' owner, died, and the Scott family was bequeathed first to his widow and then to her brother, John Sanford. By the time the case reached the Supreme Court, an obvious ruling stared the justices in the face: If Scott were a slave, he had no standing in court, and his suit should simply be dismissed. Instead, Chief Justice Roger Taney decided to settle the entire debate over slavery in the territories, once and for all. The result, *Dred Scott v. Sandford*, is a hopeless tangle. Eight justices wrote separate opinions, two of them dissenting. A clerk misspelled the plaintiff's name—it was Sanford—so even the name of this infamous decision memorializes a typo.

At the heart of all the jurisprudence sits Justice Taney's majority opinion, an implacable picture of black people and their status—or more accurately, their complete lack of status—in the American regime. "A negro," wrote Taney, "could not be a citizen in the sense in which that word is used in the Constitution of the United States." Therefore, a black person can "claim none of the rights and privileges which that instrument provides for and secures to citizens of the United States." A state, he conceded, might grant black people rights, but such prerogatives applied only in that state—they were meaningless anywhere else and never entitled black people to US citizenship or constitutional rights. Taney glided serenely past a honking contradiction with the Constitution's Article IV, Section 1: "Full Faith and Credit shall be given in each State to the public Acts, Records and judicial proceedings of every other state."

What about Scott's claim to have lived in free territory? Not valid, ruled Taney for a blockbuster reason: the federal government did not have the authority to prohibit slavery anywhere. Nor could the residents of a territory. What about the Missouri Compromise and its decision to limit slavery below the 36° 30' parallel? "Not warranted by the Constitution and therefore void." The Compromise of 1850, with its provision for popular sovereignty in Utah and New Mexico? Also unconstitutional. The Kansas–Nebraska Act and popular sovereignty in Kansas? Unconstitutional again. All that blood and chaos had been for nothing because no one could interfere with slavery in any territory—not Congress, not the courts, not the residents of the territory. To reach this conclusion, Taney had to torture Article 4, Section 3, which Scott's attorney had emphasized before the court: "The Congress shall have all power to dispose of and make needful Rules and Regulations respecting the Territory or other Property belonging to the United States." Tawney ruled that the provision only applied to territories that already existed in the United States when the Constitution was written.

The decision ultimately rests on a cockeyed view of the founders' ideas about race. When the founders wrote the Declaration of Independence and framed the Constitution, Taney claimed, "the civilized and enlightened portions of the world . . . regarded . . . the unfortunate race . . . as beings of an inferior order, and altogether unfit to associate with the white race." Taney pressed even further, with the most infamous line of the case: the founders considered Negroes "so far inferior, they had no rights which the white man was bound to respect."[40]

Taney had taken the strident pro-slavery argument of his own day and projected it back onto the founders. The early Americans enslaved the Africans for their own good, he wrote, "an axiom in morals as well as politics that no one thought of disputing." To clinch his case, Taney pointed to the most savagely guarded feature of the race line: If there was any doubt about black inferiority, why were marriages between the races regarded as "unnatural and immoral and punished as crimes"? In short, the decision read racial prejudice back into the founders and their Constitution (against all evidence in the document), struck down every chance of restricting slavery in any territory, and snatched all hope of American citizenship away from people of color. Slavery is a right, enshrined in the Constitution, and no one can interfere with it except a state and no further than its own borders.

In dissent, Justice Benjamin Curtis exposed Taney's miserable grasp of history. The founding generation had been far *more* liberal with black rights. Back then, five of the original thirteen states, including North Carolina, permitted free black men to vote under the same rules as white. But now, in 1857, only two states (out of thirty-one) granted free blacks full suffrage on the same terms as white men. In an address at Cooper Union, in early 1860, Lincoln would go on to elaborate upon the dissent, showing in meticulous detail how, again and again, a majority of the Constitution's signers had voted, in one setting or another, to limit slavery in the territories.[41]

Given the many overlapping opinions, Republicans questioned how much of the decision was legally binding. But there was no mistaking the main thrust. The Republican Party had sprung up to stop the spread of slavery into the territories. This decision—the first to strike down a major act of Congress in more than a half century—declared that effort unconstitutional. As historian George Fredrickson put it, the Dred Scott decision was "nothing less than a summons to the Republicans to disband."[42]

The Republicans saw conspiracy. William Seward scornfully described the imperious slave power fouling the republic's institutions and rituals. The president, he said, had whispered the conspiracy into the chief justice's ear and then delivered an inaugural address "as bland as the worst of all the Roman Emperors pronounced when he assumed the purple" (or donned the emperors' colors) while the justices, sitting before him had already decided to fling Dred Scott back into bondage, "without even changing their silken robes for courtier's gowns."[43]

Lincoln developed the plot. The conspiracy stretched across all three branches and the plotters were not finished yet. "Ere long," continued Lincoln, we will find "another Supreme Court decision, declaring that the Constitution of the United States does not permit a State to exclude slavery from its limits." We will wake up one day to find "that the Supreme Court has made Illinois a slave State." He might well have been right. A case was before the courts in which a plaintiff sued for the right to visit New York with his slaves. Once

Taney was through with that case, predicted Lincoln, there would be no legal barriers to slave holding anywhere in the United States.[44]

AN AWKWARD GRAIN OF TRUTH LURKED AT THE HEART OF the Dred Scott decision. Taney had distorted history, jurisprudence, and justice, but by going out of his way to raise the matter of black inferiority—and especially the widespread horror toward marriage between the races—he shrewdly planted his argument firmly in the Republican Party's own prejudice. Many Republicans, even those who opposed slavery, held exactly the same biases, and supported the laws against intermarriage that Taney described.

The Republicans were trapped in their own racial contradiction. They firmly opposed the spread of slavery. They expressed horror at the institution. But they had no idea what to do about the slaves themselves—at least, no idea that an ambitious politician could say out loud in states like Illinois, Iowa, and Oregon. All three had passed laws restricting the entry of free black settlers and stipulated that free black people could be sold into bondage for violating those rules.

A year after the Dred Scott decision, Lincoln and Senator Stephen Douglas held seven famous debates across Illinois. Douglas went straight to the heart of the matter. "Slavery is not the only question," he said at the first debate. "There is a far more important one . . . and that is, what shall be done with the free negro?"[45]

When Democrats started in on this subject of "free negroes," they almost invariably arrived at the topic of interracial sex. In the second debate, held in Freeport, Indiana, Douglas crudely recalled how last time he'd visited the town, he'd seen a magnificent carriage with a beautiful young lady sitting on the box seat, while "Fred Douglass, the negro," reclined inside with her mother. The master of the house meekly drove them around town. By the time he repeated this anecdote at the third debate, Senator Douglas had embellished the details and the beautiful white woman and her mother were now both inside, sitting side by side with "Douglass, the negro." Senator Douglas almost joyfully accused Lincoln of supporting racial and sexual equality.

> If you, black Republicans think, that the negro ought to be on a social equality with your wives and daughters, and ride in a carriage with your wife whilst you drive the team . . . Well, all I can say is, those of you who believe that the negro is your equal and ought to be on an equality with you socially, politically and legally . . . will vote for Mr. Lincoln [cries of "down with the negro"].[46]

Count the tropes: The African American reclining in ease, the beautiful white woman riding right next to him, and the master reduced to driving his own carriage for the black man's comfort. The threat of equality looms. But, even more, the images vibrate with sexuality. The danger lies not just in the realm of work or politics or society. It is more essential. Those 3.9 million Africans chained in the South bid to rise up, leap into the carriage, cross the forbidden line, and menace the white race itself. If you are dupe enough to loosen their chains, warns Douglas, you will lose your own place in the carriage. And worse. You will lose your wives and your daughters and your whiteness itself.

Lincoln squirmed for an answer. He tried multiple rejoinders including a witty insult that effectively conceded his opponent's main point: "I have never had the least apprehension that I or my friends would marry negroes if there was no law to keep them from it. As . . . Douglas and his friends seem to be in great apprehension that they might if there were no law to keep them from it . . . I will to the very last stand by the law . . . which forbids the marrying of white people with negroes." It was one of Lincoln's crispest rejoinders. But beneath the jibe glints the telling concession. He pledges to defend the very laws that Chief Justice Taney drew on to bolster his ruling in Dred Scott.

THE DEBATE ABOUT THE SOCIAL PLACE OF FREE AFRICAN Americans distantly resembled the nativist reaction against the Catholics. The opposition began with the same charge: these people are not ready for political equality in our society. They are inferior. However, the prospect of racial equality provoked the deeper anxiety in the mid-nineteenth century. The constant reference to the rebellion of Saint-Domingue—with its images of blood, fire, black rule, and intermarriage—lent a cataclysmic feel to this deepest of anxieties. As the debate raged into the late 1850s, nothing seemed more unlikely than the abolitionist aspiration for black freedom, much less the utopian aspiration of racial equality.

The recoil from the Dred Scott decision would jar the Court itself. Three years later, Abraham Lincoln and the Republicans would come to power in a dramatic four-way election described in the next chapter. Lincoln and his followers immediately targeted the Court. "The candid citizen must confess that if the policy of the government . . . is to be irrevocably fixed by decisions of the Supreme Court," argued Lincoln in his inaugural address, "the people will have ceased to be their own rulers." The other branches were every bit as capable of judging the Constitution, he continued, and the Court had no business in making those determinations by itself. Republican Senator John Hale of New Hampshire declared "that the Supreme Court . . . has utterly failed," going on to argue that it was time to consider "abolishing the present Supreme Court" and designing a new one. In the following years, the Republican majority added a tenth justice to the court (in 1863), squeezed it down to seven members (in 1866), and finally returned it to nine (in 1869). Plunging into the hottest controversy of the day only turned the political heat up higher—and blew right back on the legitimacy of the Court itself. The failed effort to end a national debate sends a warning to future courts about their own legitimacy in times of soaring partisanship.[47]

But, ironically, the decision did even more damage to the Democratic Party. At first, the Democrats were jubilant, for the Dred Scott decision appeared to take their own claims and etch them into the Constitution: the federal government had no right to limit slavery in any territory. But it turned out to be a hollow victory. The ruling united Republicans and broke the Democrats into angry factions. Northern Democrats could not very well go before their voters—who were eager for western lands—and promote the idea that all territories were opened to slavery regardless of what its population might like. Southern Democrats insisted on nothing less.

In the end, the Dred Scott decision gave the country another hard shove toward disunion. Four years later, North and South would be at war. The Civil War and its aftermath would force Americans to confront its great existential question—Who are we?—in a radically new way.

FOUR

WHO ARE WE?

The Civil War and Its Legacies (1860–1876)

The large side-wheeler backed away from the wharf in the pre-dawn darkness, blew its whistle, and steamed through Charleston harbor flying the Confederate flag. The *Planter* flashed the correct signals, got clearance from the watch, and headed straight at the Federal ships blockading the outer harbor. Alarms soon sounded on the Union vessels and the USS *Onward* came about, lifted big gun number three, and prepared to blast the Confederates speeding toward them. Then someone on deck shouted to hold fire. The *Planter* had run a dirty white sheet up its mast. Soon everyone could see that its jubilant crew were contraband—fleeing slaves. Their leader, Robert Smalls, had meticulously planned the dash for freedom. He became an instant hero and, as the *New York Times* reported, met "wild and prolonged cheering" when he and his family, who had been on board, landed in New York.[1]

Smalls joined the Union Navy and rose to the rank of acting captain for his cool head under fire. After the war, he received a bounty for capturing an enemy ship and used it to buy the McKee house in Beaufort, South Carolina—the very house where he had been kept a slave. Smalls went on to represent South Carolina in the US Congress for five terms. In one of his last political acts, he played a futile role at the 1895 South Carolina constitutional convention

that rewrote the laws to drive African Americans out of politics (after they'd almost defeated Governor "Pitchfork Ben" Tillman), and
clamped a powerful racial apartheid on the state.[2]

Smalls's last frustrated speech at the convention proposed that
any white cohabiting with a black should be banned from public
office and any child from the union should inherit the father's name
and property. After all, he told the delegates, if a black man im-
properly approached a white woman, he would be hanged. But any
convention that was asked to apply justice to a white man who had
debauched a black woman would immediately adjourn for lack of a
quorum. The white delegates, temporarily embarrassed, declined to
adopt Smalls's amendment and pressed white supremacy into law.[3]

Robert Smalls embodied the vertiginous black experience during
the Civil War era. African Americans repeatedly disrupted the
white republic. Slaves ran to freedom before the war, subverting the
rickety compromises that tried to keep the country together by using
harsh fugitive slave laws as a bargaining chip for peace between the
North and the South. They burst out of bondage during the war and
ran (or, in Smalls's case, sailed) toward union lines, transforming the
military facts on the ground. Some two hundred thousand African
Americans served in the Union army and navy—a vital lift in the
grinding war of attrition.

When the Civil War began, abolition remained a radical cause,
barely on the mainstream political agenda. But the terrible war created revolutionary chances. Before it was over, legal slavery was gone,
and by the end of the decade, the nation had ratified the three most
important constitutional amendments outside the Bill of Rights.
Taken together, the Civil War Amendments fashioned nothing less
than a second American founding. The original Constitution had
focused on government powers and individual rights. The second
founding reached for equality.

Meanwhile, the war also made a new country. African Americans
struggled to build communities, unite families, educate children,

enter politics, and get ahead. But, the backlash was ferocious. Black Americans faced a trial by fire—long, violent waves of terror that went on for decades and slowly crushed the civil rights they had won. Smalls went down, at the South Carolina constitutional convention, pointing at the hypocrisy of a society that murdered black men for allegedly crossing the same sexual boundaries that white men insouciantly transgressed.

The struggle to build a new nation can be read, of course, in votes and parties, in arguments and amendments. But it all rested on national identity. Who was a citizen? Who deserved what rights? The former slaves stand at the center of this story. But their journey was complicated by the hopes and fears about the Irish in the Northeast, Asians in the West, Spanish speakers in the Southwest, Germans in the upper Midwest, women in politics, and people who clung to their whiteness everywhere. Democrats and Republicans thrust all these identities into the political maelstrom as each party rallied or repressed different groups.

———

LESS THAN A YEAR BEFORE THE 1860 ELECTION, ABOLITION-ist John Brown tried to incite a slave rebellion. He led twenty-one men, black and white, across the Potomac River into Harper's Ferry, Virginia, and seized a US government arsenal there. The little band had already stockpiled hundreds of guns and almost a thousand pikes, but they needed more weapons for the legions who, if Brown's plan worked, would cast off their bondage, rally to their side, and march down the Alleghenies deep into the South, gathering more and more rebellious slaves as they went.

John Brown had tried to recruit Frederick Douglass into his rebellion, and Douglass warned him "that he was going into a perfect steel-trap. . . . He would never get out alive." Sure enough, the slaves who came running to Harper's Ferry were outnumbered by the enemy—armed townspeople, the local militia, and a company of US Marines led by Colonel Robert E. Lee. The rebels were swiftly killed or captured. John Brown himself was wounded, tried, convicted, and hung within six weeks. At the end of the short trial, Brown famously addressed the court, and even scornful northern newspapers reprinted his "earnest" words.

> I see a book kissed, which I suppose to be the Bible which teaches me that all things whatsoever I would that men should do to me, I should do even so to them. . . . Now, if it is deemed necessary that I should forfeit my life for the furtherance of the ends of justice, and mingle my blood further with the blood of my children [two had died at Harper's Ferry] and with the blood of millions in this slave country whose rights are disregarded by wicked, cruel, and unjust enactments, I say, let it be done.[4]

The South might have shrugged off the rebellion as a crackpot conspiracy except for John Brown's swift apotheosis. Abolitionist preachers extolled him from the pulpits, politicians praised him on the hustings, and newspapers "exalt[ed] old Brown to the rank of demi-god," as the acerbic *New York Daily Herald* put it. Slaveholders had always feared slave rebellions; now they watched northerners celebrating this bloody effort to incite one. Men of property and standing had contributed cash, weapons, and advice. Others, like Frederick Douglass, had known about it in advance and said nothing. The Democratic newspapers sprayed the blame on every politician who had involved themselves in "the mischievous agitation on the slavery question during the last . . . fifteen years."[5]

Mainstream Republicans pushed back. They denounced the violence and denied any connection to it. "Harper's Ferry! John Brown!" said Abraham Lincoln scornfully, "John Brown was no Republican"—and the vast effort to "implicate a single Republican in his Harper's Ferry Enterprise," he continued, "is simply malicious slander."[6]

In the fervid atmosphere, the parties gathered to nominate presidential candidates for the election of 1860. No fewer than six different conventions nominated four men who all ran on platforms dominated by the slavery question. Taken together, the conventions offer a snapshot of mainstream politics on the cusp of the Civil War.

WHEN THE DEMOCRATS GATHERED IN CHARLESTON IN April 1860, Stephen Douglas was the man to beat. The *New York Times* confidently declared him inevitable, but before the convention chose a candidate, it needed to ratify a platform—and that meant taking a stand on the burning issue, the spread of slavery. Northern Democrats wanted to stick with the statement they had used last time, when Buchanan was running in 1856: the white men of each state and territory should decide whether to permit slavery without any interference from Congress. Of course, the Dred Scott decision had sunk that position by ruling that no territory could ban slavery. But, as usual, Douglas had dreamed up a too-clever rejoinder. Despite the Supreme Court decision, the territories were still in control of the decision because slavery "cannot exist for a day or an hour anywhere, unless it is supported by local police regulations." All a territory had to do, chirruped Douglas, was pass "unfriendly legislation" and it could drive slavery right out.[7]

This, of course, infuriated southern Democrats who accused Douglas of casually handing back what the Supreme Court had given them. But Douglas spoke for most northern delegates who had risked their political lives by tearing up the 1820 Compromise and passing the Kansas–Nebraska Act—all to accommodate the southern Democrats. They refused to go further and defend the idea of spreading slavery into all territories, even against the wishes of the voters.

Southerners derided the northern position as yesterday's platform and planted their flag squarely on the logic of the Dred Scott decision—no territory could ever bar slavery. Far from stepping aside and letting the territories vote (their position in 1856), they now insisted that the Democrats should proudly proclaim the new doctrine: Congress had a positive duty to protect slaveholders, "on the high seas, in the territories, and wherever else its constitutional authority extends." The high seas? A sly call to bring back the Atlantic slave trade, which had been outlawed in 1808, but had become a cause among the Fire-Eaters, as slavery's most ardent proponents were dubbed in the North.

As the argument over the Democratic party's platform stretched into the evening, William Lowndes Yancey, a ferocious defender of slavery and an early advocate of breaking from the union, rose to tell it from the southern side. The hall in Charleston, South Carolina, roared for the famous orator. He asked for extra time—an hour was not enough—and the congregation roared again. As Yancey began to speak, darkness fell, the gas lights went up in the hall, and even a cynical journalist marveled at the "extraordinary interest and splendor" of the scene.[8]

The South, said Yancey, had suffered insult after insufferable insult: The nation only grudgingly admitted Missouri as a slave state; a "misnamed compromise" prohibited slavery from vast territories in the middle of the continent; women and children inundated Congress with petitions against the constitutional right to hold slaves; most of the land that bold southern men had won from Mexico was snatched away from them and turned into free states—on and on went Yancey's litany of complaints. His narrative offered a stunning contrast to the Yankee version of the same events. Many northerners listed the very same episodes as evidence of the slavers' insatiability.

American reality had fractured into northern and southern truths, even within the same party.

When Yancey was finished, George Pugh of Ohio rose and met defiance with defiance. "Gentlemen of the South, you mistake us—you mistake us—we will not do it." When the roll was called, the northern delegates narrowly won their version of the platform. Yancey rose and led the Alabama delegates out of the hall. Alabama was followed by the entire delegations of Georgia, Florida, Texas, and Louisiana, and all but one delegate each from South Carolina and Arkansas. The floor managers working for Douglas had calculated that a small eruption of hard-liners would ease the way for their candidate, but this rebellion had spread too far. As the delegates marched out, the galleries roared, and women descended onto the convention floor and placed a single white rose on every vacant chair. The convention then went through fifty-six weary ballots trying to nominate Douglas, who managed an easy majority, but Democrats required two-thirds of total delegates, including those who had walked out, and he never got close. The exhausted delegates agreed to reconvene in Baltimore two months later.[9]

In June, the Democrats tried a second time. Again, there were taunts and jeers. A crude speaker from Georgia provoked the northern representatives by declaring "I glory . . . in slave breeding." The convention voted to reject the delegations from Alabama and Louisiana, who had led the revolt at the last meeting, and replaced them with Douglas Democrats from those states. The southerners walked out all over again. But that act was wearing thin. This time, there was no one to lay white roses on empty chairs. The remaining delegates pushed through a revision of the plank that the Democrats had used in 1856 (with a vague promise to abide by Supreme Court decisions), voted that the nominee only needed two-thirds of those still at the convention, and nominated Stephen Douglas for president.

The southern delegations convened still another Democratic convention. The representatives from more than twenty states met in Richmond, Virginia; acclaimed the Alabama Plank calling on Congress to defend slavery in every territory (though they stopped short of calling for a return of the international slave trade, which was controversial even in the slave states); and swiftly nominated Buchanan's vice president, John Breckenridge of Kentucky, as *their* Democratic candidate for president. President Buchanan promptly endorsed Breckenridge. The last national party had finally broken over slavery.[10]

TWO WEEKS AFTER THE DEMOCRATS' FRACAS IN CHARLES-ton, buoyant Republicans descended on Chicago for their own convention. They gathered, yelled, drank prodigiously, "sang songs not found in hymn books," and threw the more modest members from Ohio into "prayers and perspiration."[11]

Senator William Seward of New York was the biggest name in the party and the easy favorite to win the presidential nomination. He seemed irresistible in the far northern states, but the convention's delegates knew that the election would be decided in a middle tier of states running through Pennsylvania, Ohio, Indiana, and Illinois (which had very narrowly gone for Buchanan and the Democrats last time), and Seward was weaker there. He came with a roster of other liabilities, as well: he was too honest about the Know Nothings (who were thick in Pennsylvania), too radical on slavery, too tangled up with corrupt New York political fixers, and had too many scars from his years in the public limelight. The front runner's supporters brought a three-hundred-piece band and marched behind it to the convention hall, stepping so impressively along the way that they arrived late and found the seats in the gallery taken by rivals—a portent of what was about to happen.

Lincoln's candidacy was based on words rather than deeds. His entire national experience amounted to one term in the House. But his debates and speeches, over the previous three years, offered a formidable explication of the Republican idea. Lincoln clarified, explained, and infused Republicanism with moral commitment. His lecture in February 1860, at New York's Cooper Union, was a kind of tryout before the sophisticated New York audience, and he had slain the Republican leaders. Actor Sam Waterston reenacted the speech in the same hall almost 150 years later and, by the end, the audience was—once again—shouting and applauding the still resonant words.[12]

Lincoln organized a number two strategy. "I suppose I'm not the first choice of very many," he wrote to a former Congressman. "Our policy, then, is to give no offense to others—leave them in a mood to come to us, if they should be compelled to give up their first love." He sent seductive letters far and wide, and then waited patiently while his opponents got ensnared in rivalries, or whispers of corruption, or lost the party's confidence.[13]

There was little disagreement over the party platform, which denounced the spread of slavery, the Kansas–Nebraska Act, the Dred Scott decision, and the Atlantic slave trade as "a crime against humanity." But it also pledged that the party would not interfere with the "right of each state to order and control its own domestic institutions" and "denounced" the "lawless invasion . . . of any state or territory . . . as among the gravest of crimes"—a direct repudiation of John Brown's raid. Overall, the party's position could be summed up simply: We won't touch your slaves, but you can't have so much as another acre for slavery.[14]

Two items provoked questions from the floor and each reflected something essential about the rising party. First, the delegates endorsed a plank that stood up to the Know Nothings by condemning "any changes to our naturalization laws." That led to a challenge and a confused discussion among the delegates—the party, after all, embraced both nativists and people who scorned them—including the frontrunners, Seward and Lincoln. When the vote was called, the plank easily held.[15]

Second, a venerable antislavery Congressman from Ohio rose and proposed an even more controversial addition to the platform, a quotation from the Declaration of Independence: "All men are created equal; that they are endowed by their Creator with certain inalienable rights, that among these are life, liberty and the pursuit of happiness." The chair brushed aside the disruptive proposal and the convention delegates backed his ruling. Then, an impassioned plea from the New York delegation led to a second vote and, this time, the party affirmed the radical sentiment from 1776. Why the fuss? Perhaps because the language gestured toward the perilous question of equality—and what the Creator actually intended for America's black people.[16]

Then the convention turned to its presidential nomination. On the first roll call, Seward led with 173.5 votes—59.5 short of the 233 he needed. Lincoln came in second, with 102. On the next ballot, the strategy of "second love" began to tell as Pennsylvania tumbled into Lincoln's column and he came within three votes of the lead. By the end of the third ballot, the convention turned to him unanimously. Secretaries shouted the results to a man on the roof who announced Lincoln's nomination to the Chicago mob milling around the Hall. The cheering delegates inside could hear celebratory cannons firing outside, and moments later, the smell of gunpowder wafted through the open doors. A joyful celebration eerily foreshadowed the future that awaited the nation as a result of Lincoln's coming victory.

IN MAY, JUST BEFORE THE REPUBLICANS MET, A RUMP GROUP of conservative, mainly former Whigs from the South, gathered in Baltimore for still another convention. Under the banner of a new party they called the Constitutional Union, these delegates aimed to soar above the irksome issue of the day. Each time a speaker said "*Constitution; law; Union; conservative; our fathers; our flag; our country;* or anything of the sort," reported one journalist from the convention, "he had to pause for some time until the general rapture . . . discharged itself." One speaker from Tennessee "thanked God that he had at last found a Convention in which the 'nigger' was not the sole subject of consideration." The delegates airily dispensed with such divisive matters as policies or platforms, and the new party announced that its only principles were "the Constitution," "the Union," and the "Enforcement of the Laws."[17]

The convention nominated John Bell of Tennessee for president and Edward Everett of Massachusetts for vice president. Both men had been born back when George Washington was president—and historians traditionally dismissed the entire ensemble as a meeting of has-beens indulging in grumpy nostalgia. Horace Greeley called it "a great gathering of fossil Know Nothings and South Americans [as the Know Nothings from the South were called]." The proceedings did get a jolt of loud chauvinism from a nativist street gang, the Plug Uglies, who packed noisily into the galleries. Some historians have recently taken a second look. "To dismiss the ticket as too old and too bland," writes A. James Fuller, "is to miss the point that the Constitutional Union Party was an attempt to revive the Whigs and to save the union through compromise." Moreover, they had a plausible strategy. If no candidate won an outright majority in the Electoral College—a real possibility with four in the running—the election would be decided by the House, where the Liberty Union's leaders hoped their vague program might give them a central role in the negotiations. In effect, the party gave voters a way to cast a plea for moderation.[18]

Still, the Constitutional Union was reaching for an old illusion—they would leap right past the national divisions and land on some hazy, ill-defined consensus. That idea sounded seductive to the grey patriarchs in Baltimore as they imagined floating serenely above the democratic charivari. But like the generations that preceded them, they soon confronted the fundamental reality of American politics: There's no resolution lying in some deep agreement about shared principles. The only way to settle differences is to debate and negotiate, to argue and fight. For better and for worse, there is no leaping out of the argument itself. The lesson of the Constitutional Union—and all their nonpartisan look-alikes through the years—is that there is no politics outside of, well, politics. The idylls of nonpartisan unity may stretch back to the founding, but they are no use in the messy, real world of passion and politics.

In sum, it was a four-way race between the Republican Abraham Lincoln; the Liberty Union Party's John Bell; and the Democrats' two candidates, Stephen Douglas and John Breckenridge. Together, the parties covered a great deal of ground—from slavery everywhere to slavery only where it already exists. But no major party called for abolishing slavery. Although Republicans dreamed of freedom someday, they did not argue for freedom now, and only radicals could even imagine pushing beyond freedom and reaching for racial equality. That would all soon change.

IN NOVEMBER, MORE THAN 81 PERCENT OF THE ELIGIBLE voters surged to the polls, still the second highest turnout in a presidential election (after 1876). Lincoln swept the free states. He won big across the northern tier; squeaked by in Ohio, Indiana, and Illinois; and watched California and Oregon fall into his column with barely a third of the tally. Was it a decisive win? Yes and no. In the end, he received 180 Electoral College votes of a total possible 303. At the same time, he received only 39 percent of the popular vote and did not draw a single ballot in eight southern states.

As for the Democrats, their division did not swing the results. The votes for both Democrats—Breckenridge and Douglas—added together would have won seventeen states but fallen fifty-one Electoral College votes short of the presidency. Breckenridge dominated the Deep South, but below the headlines, the slave states were not as defiant as the Breckenridge count suggests. A majority of slave states (eight of fifteen) gave a majority to the moderates in the middle, John Bell and Stephen Douglas added together. Of course, votes are not counted that way. Breckenridge finished first in eleven southern states, Bell won three border states, and Douglas, who had the second highest popular vote, won only Missouri.

The results were no surprise. A month before the presidential vote, three crucial swing states—Indiana, Ohio, and Pennsylvania—held local elections and the returns practically roared Republican. Fire-Eaters in the Deep South prepared their states to break from the union and Douglas, as usual, did the unexpected. "Mr. Lincoln is the next president," he declared, "We must try and save the union. I will go South." And with that, he broke all tradition and became the first presidential candidate to actually campaign for himself, launching a frantic, arduous tour through largely hostile terrain. If he could take the South, he reasoned, he would undermine the more extreme pro-slavery Democrats and keep the union together. His frenetic circuit, combined with his heavy drinking, took their toll on the first modern candidate and Douglas was dead in seven months.[19]

When Lincoln won, two clashing pictures of him filled the media. Opponents saw an unqualified outsider with almost no experience who had lucked into the White House with 39 percent of the vote. Surely, said his critics, he would be gone after four floundering years. Many had shouted "Black Republican" so often that they could only see, in Lincoln, the second coming of John Brown. Hostile cartoons depicted caricatured Africans carrying Lincoln into the White House, where he was poised to dispense benefits to lazy Republicans and enjoy favors from sexualized black women.[20]

Frederick Douglass saw a very different president-elect. "The next four years will see Mr. Lincoln and his administration attacked more bitterly for their pro-slavery truckling than for doing any anti-slavery work." Lincoln immediately seemed to prove Douglass right. His inaugural address pleaded and pledged. "We are not enemies but friends. We must not be enemies." He promised that he harbored no abolitionist fancies. "I have no purpose, directly or indirectly to interfere with the institution of slavery where it exists. I believe I have no lawful right to do so, and I have no inclination to do so." He quoted the Republican Party's states' rights plank and, for good measure, added that the Constitution compelled every American to return fugitive slaves. Lincoln hazily endorsed a proposed Thirteenth Amendment, dreamed up by James Buchanan's administration, that forbade any future amendment designed to "abolish or interfere with" slavery. Congress approved the amendment, but the war cut off ratification, leading, eventually, to a Thirteenth Amendment that did just what this one would have ruled out.[21]

ONE MONTH AFTER THE ELECTION, IN DECEMBER 1860, even before Lincoln had taken office, South Carolina declared its independence from the United States. A secession convention explained why: "An increasing hostility . . . to the institution of slavery" and the election of a president "whose opinions and purposes are hostile to slavery." Seven states followed South Carolina and quickly broke from the union—Mississippi, Florida, Alabama, Georgia, Louisiana, and Texas. Their defiance reflected the voters—all but Georgia had gone strong for Breckenridge. The rest of the slave states teetered on the brink.[22]

The seceding states began to occupy military facilities in their territories and, at the end of January 1861, South Carolina governor Francis Pickens demanded that the United States hand over Fort Sumpter in Charleston Harbor—the unfinished garrison had been under construction, off and on, for years. Five weeks later, the Lincoln administration took office and immediately faced a pivotal decision. Fort Sumpter's supplies were running low. Should the administration resupply the post or surrender it? Lincoln wrote Governor Pickens that he was dispatching relief—but not weapons or troops—to the fort. The newly formed Confederate government responded with the order to attack, and on April 12, 1861, the batteries opened fire. The shells crashing down on Fort Sumpter tipped the wavering states—Virginia, Arkansas, North Carolina, and Tennessee—into the Confederacy. The bloodiest conflict in American history had begun.

The sheer scale of loss and death is still hard to grasp. Somewhere between 600,000 and 750,000 people died, in a nation of thirty-one million, slave and free. Some contemporary estimates put the casualties even higher. The toll was greater than every other war in the nation's history added together.[23]

Two very different countries went to war. Among their many differences were antithetical views about the role of government. Slavery's proponents had always resisted federal programs that might, somehow, insinuate enough national authority to disrupt their institution. We've seen the fear expressed in every historical moment: from Congressman Edward Livingston (who warned in 1798 that the Alien Acts threatened slavery) to John Quincy Adams (who complained in 1841 that slavery "palsied" the hands of government) to Benjamin Wade (who coarsely ripped the Democrats for blocking the Homestead Acts in 1859). Now the clashing governments, the Union and the Confederacy, illustrated the point all over again.

With the slave states gone, the Republican Congress pushed through a long roster of programs that the antigovernment Democrats had blocked. The Homestead Acts, passed between 1862 and 1864, granted men and women 160 acres of public land as long as they resided on and improved it. The Morrill Land Grant Acts sponsored agricultural and engineering colleges. Congress formed the Department of Agriculture, promoted the construction of the transcontinental railroad, established a national currency (until then, the federal government had only minted coin), instituted a progressive income tax, passed protective tariffs, devised new national rules governing corporations, and the list goes on. The national government grew deeply immersed in commerce, industry, agriculture, and the rising power of finance.[24]

Dixie went exactly the opposite way. The Confederate Constitution copied the 1787 original, clause for clause, but meticulously scotched the government's authority to "appropriate money for any internal improvement intended to facilitate commerce"—the constitutional clause that stretched the power of the national government. In a famous speech, newly selected Confederate Vice President Alexander Stephens explained the "cornerstone" of the fledgling country. Above all, the Confederacy was the first government in history founded unapologetically on "a great physical, philosophical and moral truth: that the negro is not equal to the white man; that slavery subordination to the superior race is his natural condition." But Stephens also emphasized a second difference. "Internal improvements," under "the guise of interstate commerce," would be forever "put at rest under our system." There would be no elastic clauses to stretch government authority in Dixie. Bolstering racial hierarchy went hand in hand with diminishing the role of the central government. At least, that was the Confederacy's founding ideal. The imperatives of war would push all kinds of unwelcome changes on the South until, near the very end, they compromised their very first principle and scrambled to recruit slaves into their dwindling armies.[25]

When the war began, both sides focused on union—either restoring it or breaking free. Ironically, a quick victory for either side—North as much as South—would have left slavery intact. As Frederick Douglass ruefully observed, "the South was fighting to take slavery out of the union and the North was fighting to keep it in." Some military historians suggest the North almost managed to have its way and "keep slavery in the union." In mid-1862, General George McClellan cautiously inched his enormous Army of the

Potomac down the Virginia Peninsula toward Richmond, the confederate capital. With a little luck, and lot more dash, he might possibly have broken the Army of Virginia and won the war. Instead, McClellan dithered, General Robert Lee assumed command and pulled together the scattered defenses, and the war went on.[26]

THE SLAVES THEMSELVES FORCED THE NORTH TO DIRECTLY confront slavery by dashing for freedom. As they walked or swam or rowed or ran to the Union lines, Union officers had to decide what to do. At first there was chaos. Some, like General McClellan, returned the fugitives as, he insisted, the Constitution demanded. General Henry Halleck issued an order barring the fugitives from his lines. On the other hand, General John Frémont, commander of the western armies, issued an edict freeing all the slaves in his district. However, he had not consulted anyone up the chain of command, and when President Lincoln learned what he had done, he reversed the edict and soon sacked Frémont.

The breakthrough came just a month into the war. In May 1861, three slaves slipped passed the confederate lines and rowed to Fort Monroe on the end of a peninsula near Newport News, Virginia. They told the Union troops that the Confederates had been constructing defensive batteries across the channel, at Sewell's Point, twenty-six miles away. The Union commander, General Benjamin Butler, was a big, crude, physically unattractive politician, new to the military. He would prove a terrible officer but had a brilliant legal mind (he claimed to have corrected his examiner when he sat for the bar). Now, he declared that offering shelter to the escaped men was a military measure, for they had brought him valuable intelligence. Moreover, keeping the contraband—as the escapees would be called—deprived the enemy of workers. The Lincoln administration liked that logic. Little knots of men and women breaking free turned into hundreds, hundreds turned into thousands, and eventually some half million men and women escaped slavery and fled to the Union lines. They disrupted the southern work force and stunned the slavers—including Confederate President Jefferson Davis—who had come to believe their own fantasies about happy slaves. Slowly but surely, the slaves themselves forced the question that most politicians across the spectrum had so assiduously ducked: What was to be done about the 3.9 million people in bondage?[27]

Even the terrible war did not calm the partisan fury on that question. Angry differences separated the northern parties, which subsequently broke into factions. An internal clash among Republicans quickly rose to the surface as the government debated what to do about the contraband. Radicals in the party pushed for abolition and proposed a series of increasingly stringent Confiscation Acts, instructing the army to take in and shelter the fleeing men and women. To their fury, a smaller group of conservative Republicans opposed them and insisted that stripping the slaveholders of their property violated the Fifth Amendment—taking private property without just compensation. Their constitutional duty, said the conservative Republicans, was clear: return the slaves.

At first, President Lincoln tried to find a middle path. He hated slavery but fretted about the consequences of freeing millions of slaves, all at once. He also kept a worried eye on the border states, which permitted slavery but were not in the Confederacy (they included Missouri, Kentucky, Maryland, Delaware, and Western Virginia, which became a state in 1863). On top of all that, Lincoln was wary of the surging northern Democrats who sprang back to life in the 1862 midterms, doubling their strength in the House (from forty-two to eighty seats) and reducing the Republicans' majority to a plurality.

On the other side of the aisle, the Democrats were also divided, but not about emancipation. Many Democrats supported the war but vehemently opposed freeing slaves. General George McClellan led the faction, known as the War Democrats. He wrote what he described as "a strong, frank letter" ("rude" would be more accurate) hectoring President Lincoln to banish any thoughts about abolishing slavery. "Neither the confiscation of property [nor] the forcible abolition of slavery should be contemplated for a moment," he wrote. He went on to warn Lincoln that the men under his command would never fight to free slaves. "A declaration of radical views, especially upon slavery," he concluded, "will rapidly disintegrate our present armies." Secession was wrong, but so was meddling with slavery.[28]

A second Democratic faction, the Peace Democrats, committed all their energies to stirring up racial furies. Their newspapers shouted out the usual slurs about four million savages poised to overrun the North, steal jobs, demand equality, and rape your daughters. "Nigger at the beginning, nigger in the middle and nigger at the close," griped the *New York Herald*. "It is all nigger. The white man is completely ignored." Bring the troops home, these Democrats insisted, and be done with the pointless bloodletting. Republicans tagged the Peace Democrats "copperheads"—poisonous northeastern snakes— and the Democrats embraced the derogatory, fashioning lapel pins out of copper pennies. The Copperheads gave the South a direct path to success: they did not need to defeat the Union armies but simply fight them until the voters grew sick of the war and voted the Democrats back in. Even Lincoln feared this outcome. In the next presidential election, in 1864, Democrats would balance their two factions, nominating General McClellan for president and Copperhead Representative George Pendleton of Ohio for VP.[29]

The difference between the Democratic factions always blurred at the edges but they vociferously agreed that no one had a right to touch slavery. In 1862, Congress took four roll call votes challenging the institution. Republicans almost all voted aye (99 percent) and Democrats almost all voted nay (96 percent). Perhaps the angry words for and against emancipation amplified the racial animosity, for soon terrible riots—or, more accurately, killing rampages targeting black northerners—erupted in more than a half dozen cities, culminating with the horrific New York City Draft Riot in July 1863. Northern cities vibrated with racial animosity and class antagonism.[30]

In this turbulent context, the Lincoln administration edged toward emancipation, justifying it as a military strategy. In July 1862, fifteen months into a war that was going badly, Lincoln told his cabinet that he intended to issue an Emancipation Proclamation on January 1. William Seward, the secretary of state, warned him to wait for a union victory before announcing the plan or it would look like an act of desperation.

Lincoln groped for a middle way, but his attempted compromises failed at every turn. He tried hard to get the border states to embrace gradual emancipation. The federal government, he said, would reimburse the slaveholders and the process would be gradually implemented, stretching out to the end of the century. These promises were included in a preliminary version of the Emancipation Proclamation but, despite all of Lincoln's arm twisting, the border states wanted nothing to do with his plan.

Lincoln also tried to dampen opposition by advocating colonization. His draft Emancipation Proclamation pledged to continue "the effort to colonize persons of African Descent, with their consent." "Whether it is right or wrong," Lincoln told a committee of African Americans, "I think your race suffer very greatly . . . from living among us, while ours suffers from your presence." Where would the freemen and women go? Lincoln pointed to the Isthmus in Central America. The plan went nowhere. For starters, the nations of Central America responded with a firm "no, thank you." They had, after all, finally rid themselves of William Walker, the erstwhile president of Nicaragua, and his gang of filibusters just two years earlier. The Lincoln administration grasped at another colonizing straw by sponsoring a colony on the Ile a Vache, an island six miles off the southern coast of Haiti. The volunteers went off,

453 strong, and endured fraud by investors, mismanagement by the organizers, a brutal labor system that approximated slavery, and disease and starvation until, a year later, a ship rescued the survivors. But there was a far more fundamental flaw in Lincoln's idea. African Americans were Americans and, for the most part, they intended to stay in their own country, the United States.[31]

Lincoln finally announced his emancipation plan in September 1862, right after the Battle of Antietam—a bloody clash that at least looked vaguely like a Union victory. On New Year's Day, 1863, the Emancipation Proclamation went into effect. The final document dropped all the hemming about gradual implementation or colonization and simply declared that all slaves held by those "still engaged in rebellion against the government of the United States" would be free forever.

There was carping from every direction. "The black blood of the African," warned one newspaper, was cynically being invited to rise up until the white masters' "blood begins to flow and their shrieks come piercing through the darkness." On the other side, abolitionists denounced the moral contradiction: the emancipation only applied to slaves held by rebels. "The principle is not that a human being cannot justly own another," jeered the *Spectator* from London, "but that he cannot own him unless he is loyal to the United States." Worse, as Lincoln himself acknowledged, this was a shaky policy. Slaves might win their freedom one day only to lose it the next as the armies advanced and retreated. And Roger Taney was still chief justice of the Supreme Court (or he would be, until his death in October 1864). It was not at all clear that the Court, under his direction, would let the Emancipation stand. Finally, unless the war took a turn for the better, it seemed entirely possible that the Democrats would sweep back into power and simply revoke the decree. The critics saw a very shaky and partial emancipation.[32]

Even so, the jubilation that greeted the proclamation drowned out all the caveats and criticism. "We shout for joy that we live to record this righteous decree," wrote Frederick Douglass. He quoted the proclamation and repeated what he called the two most important words "to which the President of the United States has ever signed his name." "'*Free forever.*' Oh! Long enslaved millions, whose cries have so vexed the air and sky . . . the hour of your deliverance draws nigh!" Historian Eric Foner estimates that some 3.1 million men and women were covered by the decree. In fact, a joyful (if scholarly) tone seems to filter into his writing too: "Despite the limitations," writes Foner, "this was the largest act of slave emancipation in world history. Never before had so many slaves been declared free on a single day."[33]

The Proclamation changed the war. For one thing, Europeans dropped their talk of intervening. In fact, English leaders were shaken by raw carnage. At the battle of Antietam, twenty-three thousand American lives had been taken in a single day—more than the entire Crimean War had cost the British Empire (though the Russians, French, and Ottomans suffered many times that number). Even more important, the interminable bloodletting had made filling the vast armies increasingly difficult. Now, the North had a huge new pool of eager soldiers. Almost two hundred thousand African Americans joined the army in the next two years—a terrific boost for an army that numbered one million. Those that went into combat fought with courage and, in doing so, exploded long-standing stereotypes. General Benjamin Butler later mused that the African American soldier had "opened new fields of freedom, liberty and equality . . . with his bayonet." The *New York Times* added, "It is no longer possible to doubt the bravery and steadiness of the colored race." Northern magazines, like *Harper's Weekly*, cast aside their odious Sambo images and began to run admiring sketches of the new soldiers. As usual, Lincoln summed it up beautifully in a letter to an Illinois Republican who opposed the Proclamation. When peace comes, he wrote, "there will be some black men who can remember that, with silent tongue and clinched teeth and steady eye and well poised bayonet, they have helped mankind in this great consummation while I fear there will be some white ones, unable to forget that, with malignant heart and deceitful speech, they have strove to hinder it."[34]

It was, however, always about something deeper and more enduring than stout hearts versus malignant ones. The conflict came down to the clash of tribes—before, during, and after the war. Now, with the Emancipation Proclamation in effect, politics turned into a ferocious battle over the nation's fundamental rules—rewriting racial relations, redefining us and them, reaching for rights that would touch all Americans.

ABRAHAM LINCOLN HAD BECOME FAMOUS FOR DESCRIBING the Republican philosophy to the Republican Party. Now he did the same job for the entire nation, defining a new birth of freedom and equality. The original founding, said Lincoln in his incandescent Gettysburg Address, had been "conceived in liberty." But it had also been "dedicated to the *proposition* that all men are created equal." Notice the artful word choice: Propositions have to be argued and won. This proposition of equality rang through the Declaration of Independence and then slipped right out of the Constitution, which focused, instead, on government powers and individual rights.

Back in 1854, Lincoln had waved the Declaration like a flag:

Our republican robe is soiled and trailed in the dust. Let us repurify it. . . . Let us re-adopt the Declaration of Independence, and with it, the practices . . . which harmonize with it. If we do this, we shall not only have saved the Union; but we shall have so saved it, as to make . . . it forever worthy of the saving.

Later, perhaps preparing for his inaugural address, Lincoln scribbled out a fragment: the Declaration of Independence, he wrote, expressed a principle that "entwin[ed] itself around the human heart" and "gave hope to all." The Constitution and the Union was designed "not to conceal" but "to adorn and preserve" the soaring Declaration. Before nominating Lincoln, the Chicago convention had thrown aside caution and quoted the Declaration's most dangerous sentence.[35]

Now, at Gettysburg, Lincoln lifted the Declaration's bold promise of equality right back into equipoise with the Constitution's conception of liberty. The proposition of equality, said Lincoln, was what the whole war was about—it was what all those brave men had given "their last full measure of devotion" to win. By the end of the decade, Lincoln's lapidary words would be carved into the Constitution. Three Civil War amendments gave institutional form to the Declaration's long-lost promise of equality.

IN JANUARY 1865, EVEN BEFORE THE GUNS FELL SILENT Lincoln pushed the Thirteenth Amendment through a balky House of Representatives and achieved exactly what he had entered office swearing not to do—abolish slavery. This amendment introduced something bold. It granted Congress "the power to enforce this article." That phrase could be read narrowly—authorizing the federal government to dismantle slavery. Or, more broadly, a federal mandate to protect and assist the former slaves. Legal historians still argue both sides. This would be the dominant question of the era following the Civil War, known as Reconstruction, when the United States faced the job of rebuilding the South, redefining the former slaves' role in the new regime, and stitching the United States back together.

The Thirteenth Amendment included a fateful loophole. Slavery shall not exist, it read, *except as a punishment for crimes.* The language was simply boilerplate, left over from the abolition of slavery in the Northwest territory back in 1787. But southern states now leapt onto the phrase. Nine states quickly updated their Black Codes, restricting the freedmen's rights to hold jobs, own land, bear arms, or move freely. Some codes forbade African Americans from leaving their jobs before the dates specified in the contract and levied fines on anyone who tried to hire an employed black person. South Carolina introduced stiff taxes on African Americans in any occupation but farming—driving men and women back to the soil. At the heart of the codes lurked vagrancy provisions. African Americans traveling without working papers could be arrested (in some places, by any citizen), whipped, and bound over to private parties for harsh servitude. Slavery was dead. But, thanks to these codes, as one anxious Republican put it, "the blacks at large belong to the whites at large."[36]

In short, the crime loophole enabled new mechanisms for restraining and controlling African Americans. It became part of racial reality—North and South—and lingers on, right down to the present day.

THE WAR EFFECTIVELY ENDED WHEN GENERAL LEE SURRENdered the Army of Virginia on April 9, 1865. Two days later, a jubilant throng gathered outside the White House and heard President Lincoln, speaking from a balcony, sketch out his ideas for reuniting the nation—including his support for what had seemed so impossibly radical before the war— some black male suffrage. But not everyone in the crowd cheered. John Wilkes Booth, a nationally known actor, former Know-Nothing, and Confederate sympathizer, turned to a companion and muttered, "That means nigger citizenship . . . by God, I'll put him through. That is the last speech he will ever make." Two days later, shouting the motto of the state of Virginia—Sic Semper Tyrannis—Booth murdered Lincoln.[37]

The assassination sprang Andrew Johnson, an unabashed white supremacist, into the White House. The Republicans had picked Johnson, the military governor of Tennessee, because he was a Democrat from a border state who had stood with the union—selecting him signaled reconciliation and improved the ticket's chances in the border states. But the party once known as the Whigs had, yet again, chosen a ticket balancer who virulently opposed most of the party's positions—just as John Tyler had after Henry Harrison's death in 1841. The Republicans eventually learned that their unity candidate was a loutish, illiterate, hard-drinking racist.

African American leaders, led by Frederick Douglass, went to see President Johnson to plead for black voting rights. Johnson stunned them with his raw racial animus. "The poor white and the negro have always been enemies," he insisted. "Throw them together at the ballot box and a race war would begin." The federal government, he told them, had no business meddling with the states' rights to determine who votes. Johnson went further. He eagerly pardoned the Confederates, welcomed them back, and sanctioned the Black Codes. The black leaders politely responded to his insults. "Peace between the races is not to be secured by degrading one race and exalting another," wrote Frederick Douglass on behalf of the group. But Johnson did not hear a word that black leaders said and continued to fight every civil rights measure Congress proposed or enacted. Republican Carl Schurz claimed that he was so awful that supporters defended him by attributing his more nasty statements to drunkenness.[38]

Johnson may have been crude, but he did not stand alone. Most Democrats sided with him. They, too, resisted the Thirteenth Amendment and most of the civil rights legislation that followed. They kept repeating his assessment that it invited the federal government to barge into the states' affairs and "revolutionize the whole government." And they, too, repeated racial slurs and insisted on white supremacy.

In February, Congress passed the Civil Rights Act of 1866. The law aimed to put the Thirteenth Amendment's promise of freedom into effect—against the pressure of the Black Codes. Congress aimed to secure the former slaves' right to travel, to work, and to enter into contracts. A Freedmen's Bureau, which had been created for one year in March 1865, was renewed and fortified. The Bureau provided food, clothing, and fuel to the freed men and women. It reconnected black families, taught reading and writing, provided legal services, and pitched into the struggle to find work for the former slaves.

President Johnson jolted Congress by vetoing the bill. Congress, he declared in a blunt veto message, had never provided these services before. And, more pointedly, it had never paid for schools or homes "for the thousands, not to say millions, of the white race who are honestly toiling from day to day for their subsistence." During a political rally, Johnson asked rhetorically, "What does this veto mean?" "It is keeping the nigger down," shouted an enthusiastic supporter. Congress overrode the veto. The lines of conflict were set.[39]

The Thirteenth Amendment was monumental. It formally abolished slavery and freed black Americans to build families, churches, schools, and communities—all things that violated the law in many places just a year earlier. Still, emancipation was not enough. "The uplifting of four million slaves," wrote W. E. B. Du Bois, "would have been a Herculean task," even "in a time of perfect calm . . . and streaming wealth." But now, "gaunt hunger wept beside bereavement." The South was ruined, the people starving, and the lands desolated. The racial order, which ran so deep in the American fabric, had been radically ripped up. Millions of former slaves were, in effect, homeless. And—an even greater disruption—some would soon show signs of success. Some black men and women began rising out of poverty. Their children attended school. And many former slaves brazenly insisted on social equality—a familiar complaint against them was that they refused to submissively step aside when they passed white people on the street. Disgruntled whites began to turn to violence.[40]

TWO CASES EXPLODED INTO NATIONAL NEWS IN EARLY 1866. Like all southern cities, Memphis experienced revolutionary changes. The black population grew as former slaves came into town. Uniformed black soldiers from nearby Camp Pickering were a familiar sight on the city streets. The Freedmen's Bureau built schools and hospitals for the black population. And racial tensions pricked through the city. In May 1866, two horse-drawn carts collided. One was driven by a white man, the other by a black man—and the police promptly arrested the black man. African American soldiers who had been near the scene jumped in and violence erupted. The soldiers eventually returned to their base while an organized mob, led by Irish police and firemen, rampaged through the shanties in the black neighborhoods, which included housing for the wives and families of the black troops at the fort. For three days the white mob killed, burned, and looted. By the end, some forty-six blacks and two whites were dead. Black churches, schools, and roughly ninety homes lay in ashes. The *Chicago Tribune* spoke for the Republicans: even the Copperheads do not bother "to roll the blame on the poor, maltreated, and sorely persecuted blacks of Memphis."[41]

Two months later, in July 1866, Louisiana governor James Madison Wells called a political conclave in New Orleans to consider black voting rights—perhaps among freemen with property and former soldiers. Only a handful of delegates showed up, so it wasn't going to amount to anything but speeches. That didn't stop the police, many of them Confederate army veterans, from leading a vengeful mob against the gathering. They pummeled, shot, and killed black delegates, ignoring men who were frantically waving white cloths of surrender. The mob crushed the skulls of wounded men, lying on the pavement. The killing went on across the city, until the US Army finally marched in and stopped it. Estimates of the death toll ran from forty to more than one hundred. General Philip Sheridan, the military governor for the district, wrote to his superiors, "It was no riot; it was an absolute massacre by the police . . . it was nothing less than pre-meditated murder." Another Civil War veteran wrote the slaughter was worse than anything he had seen in battle.[42]

Congress faced a terrible situation. The former slaves were eagerly participating in communal life. But they were struggling against the organized violence, Black Codes, and powerful efforts to restore a new version of the old plantation economy. The Republican Congress seized Reconstruction away from President Johnson and passed two more constitutional amendments. Neither was conceivable before the war. Together, they redefined American government.

SOUTHERNERS COULD SENSIBLY HAVE EXPECTED THAT THE freedmen in the South would be getting pretty much the same treatment as the free blacks in the North—restrictions and repression on the margin of society. After all, northern states had shown no appetite for racial equality. New Yorkers, for example, had rejected a measure in 1860 that would have given equal voting rights to black Americans, even while they were ticking their ballots for Abraham Lincoln. Between 1865 and 1869, eleven northern states voted on whether to extend the franchise to black men—and nine times they voted no. (The exceptions were Iowa and Minnesota.)

However, Republicans faced a new political calculus. Their allies, struggling to build a new South, were (literally) under fire. Black soldiers had fought bravely for the Union and had a powerful claim on civil rights—they could not be abandoned now, said many Republicans. And there was the politics to consider. Slaves could not vote, of course, but thanks to the infamous constitutional compromise, they each boosted southern representation (in both the House and the Electoral College) by three-fifths of a citizen. Now the former slaves counted as whole people and if they were still kept from voting, the white South—and its preferred party, the Democrats—would get an even larger electoral boost than they had under slavery, one that added up to more than 5 percent of the national population.

The effort to construct new political rules ran a lot deeper than rounding up votes in the South. The debate reached down to the most basic questions in any nation: Who is a citizen? Who has what rights? That opened Pandora's Box of American identity. It would eventually touch the politics of race, immigration, women, and Native Americans. But it began with the political role of the former slaves and the question of citizenship.

In February 1866, Republicans brought the Fourteenth Amendment to the Senate floor in an effort to win equal rights. The amendment would overrule the Dred Scott decision, which held that blacks could never be citizens. Moreover, back in 1833, the Supreme Court had ruled that the Bill of Rights (the first ten amendments to the Constitution, ratified in 1791) protected citizens from the federal government but not from the states. That's because the First Amendment begins "*Congress* shall make no law . . . abridging"—and then goes on to list more than thirty rights across ten amendments. The Fifth Amendment, for example, prohibited the federal government from seizing private property "without just compensation," but, in a famous case, the Supreme Court had ruled that the state of Maryland was perfectly free to do so. And voting, of course, was also in the hands of the state governments. Now, the Fourteenth Amendment aimed to change all that. It would protect the former slaves by requiring the states to respect the people's rights. And, it would give the states a strong incentive to permit black voting.[43]

Democratic Senator Thomas Hendricks of Indiana led his party's small minority (they held just ten of fifty-two seats after the 1864 election) and was blunt about white supremacy. "I am not in favor of giving the colored man a vote because I think we should remain a political community of white people." He dragged out the same old weary sociology that we heard from Andrew Johnson: any effort to force racial equality would only lead to carnage. "The best blood of Europe," said Hendricks, must inevitably, "slaughter the black man." The litany of the trouble that would follow from racial equality worked its inevitable way to sexuality and the end of whiteness. "I am not in favor of attempting to mix these races. I want to see the white race kept a white race . . . without mixture." The Democrats honed their rhetoric of racial fears: Republicans were ready to let loose "a semi-barbarous race of blacks," as Francis P. Blair Jr., the next Democratic vice-presidential candidate put it, with "unbridled lust" for white women. His uncle, Montgomery Blair, had served in Lincoln's cabinet and now advised President Johnson that the radicals seeking to give black men the vote were a despised "miscegenationists party." Again and again, through the years, the Democrats repeated the same fearful mantra against black men voting: it would lead to race war, unleash black sexuality, and imperil whiteness itself.[44]

For all the Democratic bluster, the Republicans had the votes. After much confused debate, they pushed through the Fourteenth Amendment in June 1866. It begins with a radical definition of citizenship: anyone born or naturalized in the United States is a citizen. To this day, few nations offer such a generous notion of inclusion—known as birthright citizenship. The bold definition overturned Justice Taney's categorical denial of black citizenship in Dred Scott. What about Native Americans? After a meandering discussion, the amendment resorted to diktat: "Excluding Indians."[45]

The Fourteenth Amendment introduced a convoluted protection for black voters. If a state abridged the voting rights of "any male inhabitant," that state's "basis of representation" would be reduced in proportion to the male citizens who had been cut out. States would still define who votes—but repressing voters would cost them their voting power. Ironically, the effort to protect black voting injected the word "male" into the Constitution for the first time.

At the time, the debate focused on citizenship and voting rights. But other clauses in the amendment swelled until, today, they are the foundation of more jurisprudence than any constitutional passages outside the Bill of Rights.

Three especially important Fourteenth Amendment clauses stand out.

First, every citizen is entitled to "the equal protection of the laws." No more Black Codes, no more discrimination against any citizen. The phrase firmly lodged Lincoln's proposition—equality before the law—into the Constitution. Eventually, the Supreme Court would use this authority to strike down segregation, discrimination against women, bans on same sex marriage, bussing school children, prohibitions on interracial marriage, and much, much more.

Second, no state could "deprive any person of life, liberty, or property without due process of law." This clause appeared to extend the Bill of Rights to the state governments (since it begins, "no *state* shall . . . "). The courts, however, soon flicked away the extension of rights. Eventually, the courts backtracked and slowly required the states to respect (or "incorporate") the rights listed in the first ten amendments. They did it the long, hard way, incorporating one right at a time over more than a century. The process began in 1897 (states may not seize property without compensation) and stretched all the way to 2020 (they may not impose excessive fines).[46]

Finally, states were also forbidden from abridging "the privileges and immunities of citizens of the United States." This clause appeared to grant citizens a long list of rights that state laws could not violate. It might have been another powerhouse civil rights clause but, as we'll see, the Supreme Court strangled it at birth.[47]

The Fourteenth Amendment went through amid political chaos. Ohio and New Jersey ratified. Then Democrats won in those states and they speedily unratified. Was that legal? Secretary of State

William Seward serenely recorded the positive votes without a word about the reversals.

The Republicans required Confederate states to ratify the Fourteenth Amendment as a condition of reentering the union. That, hoped the Republicans, would protect the former slaves by requiring the states to guarantee "equal protection under the laws" while nudging states to grant voting rights (at the risk of facing reduced representation in Congress).

THE RACIAL VIOLENCE IN THE SOUTH AND THE DEBATE OVER the Fourteenth Amendment dominated the midterm election of 1866, which, in effect, pit two views of Reconstruction against each other. The congressional Republicans (and their recently passed Fourteenth Amendment) versus President Johnson and his tolerant policies toward the old Confederates and their white supremacy. Johnson took the highly unusual step of actively campaigning—he called it a "swing around the circle"—but made a mess of it. He got into verbal brawls, posed pompously as a Black Moses, and whined that he was being treated like Judas. The candidates he supported did badly and the Republicans, now in open opposition to the president, maintained a veto-proof three to one majority in the House and an even larger margin in the Senate. Control of Reconstruction passed to the congressional Republicans.

In February 1869, the large Republican majority passed what, at the time, was the most remarkable amendment of all. The Fifteenth Amendment gave the former slaves a right to vote: no citizen could be denied a ballot "on account of race, color or previous condition of servitude." At long last, the national government had affirmed a national right to vote. Or so it seemed.

However, nativist fears hemmed in the reform. Republican Senator Joseph Fowler of Tennessee had proposed a truly comprehensive right to vote in clear and precise language: "*All* [adult] . . . *citizens of the United States shall be entitled to an equal vote in all elections in the State where they reside.*" Now, *that* would have lodged an affirmative right to vote into the Constitution. But Congress wanted nothing to do with it. The Senate buried Fowler's proposal, which gathered just five votes. Why? Because Congress refused to challenge the barriers that the nativists had thrown up against immigrants voting. The Fifteenth Amendment ignored literacy tests (which were still used by states such as Massachusetts), property qualifications (Rhode Island), poll taxes (Pennsylvania), and California's blunt refusal to let Chinese men vote.[48]

The cramped version of the amendment turned a blind eye to the strategies that would eventually push black voters out of politics. At first, the Republicans plugged the hole with the law that implemented the Fifteenth Amendment. The Enforcement Act of 1870 forbade poll taxes, literacy tests, and other election frauds. But a legislative fix was less enduring than a constitutional amendment, and when Democrats finally gained unified control of government, in 1893, they simply repealed the Enforcement Act—white supremacists would leap right through the loopholes in the amendment and slam the door on black voting.

THERE WAS A TANTALIZING SILENCE IN THE FIFTEEN Amendment. It said nothing about gender. Reformers seized on the chance. The Fourteenth Amendment declared anyone born on American soil a citizen, the Fifteenth forbade denying the right to vote on account of race. Put the two together and perhaps there was a warrant for women voting? Women who tried to cast ballots swiftly learned otherwise. New York police arrested Susan B. Anthony when she tried to vote in 1872, and the Supreme Court rejected the argument two years later. The argument over women's rights soon fractured the old abolitionist coalition (again).

A frustrated Elizabeth Cady Stanton blasted the idea of granting votes to "pauperism, ignorance, and degradation" over the "the wealth, education and refinement of the women of the republic." "Think of Patrick, and Sambo and Hans and Yung Tung," she said later, "who never read . . . Webster's spelling book, making laws for Lydia Maria Child." Stanton and Susan Anthony split with their former abolitionist colleagues and formed the National Woman Suffrage Association. The group pressed for bold reforms that included giving women the right to vote, fair labor laws, and the right to divorce (which conservatives disparaged as "free love" and "free lust").[49]

Many abolitionist comrades turned more conventional when it came to gender. They followed Lucy Stone, who had been a brilliant antislavery orator, and now focused simply on winning the vote for women. The 1872 Republican platform offered half a nod in their direction. "The Republican party is mindful of . . . the loyal woman of America . . . and the honest demand . . . for additional rights should be treated with respectful consideration."[50]

The Civil War Amendments revealed the familiar fissures. Republicans struggled to protect black rights but were hampered by the nativist commitments in their own coalition. They leaned cautiously toward women's rights but not enough to make a federal case out of it. Democrats generally fought back. They stood for white supremacy and their speeches about women's rights were shot through with anxiety about racial mixing.

For all their limits, the Civil War Amendments revolutionized American government. They introduced reforms that shape our understanding of rights right down to the present day. The *proposition of equality*—as Lincoln had put it—was lodged in the Constitution and would eventually rise to match the nation's foundational vision of liberty. But even painstakingly won constitutional rights still have to be won in practice and ratified by courts. The Civil War

Amendments met massive resistance. The rights they promised ran into implacable violence. Many of them slowly vanished.

WHITES IN FIVE SOUTHERN STATES SUDDENLY FACED THE prospect of a black political majority—an early example of majority-minority. The response was what, today, we would call genocide and ethnic cleansing. African Americans in many parts of the South faced murder, rape, and pillaged neighborhoods. The violence grew where the former slaves were politically influential. Or anywhere that a black man or woman might be prospering. The sheer scope of the violence—familiar to historians—has slipped out of collective memory. We recall terrible eruptions, here and there. But the violence went on and on, a sustained campaign designed to do the work that slavery had once done: subordinate an entire race.

In 1868, racial terrorism washed across Louisiana. The state legislature convened an investigative committee which documented 834 killings along with the chilling conclusion that the toll was higher but, in some areas, no one dared testify. "The object," explained one survivor, "is to kill out the leading men [and women]"—often in front of their own children. That would make the rest of the population easier to control.[51]

The guns and knives kept coming out, especially, during election season. During the presidential campaign of 1868, for example, a group of black men in Opelousas tried to join the Louisiana Democratic Party—which indignantly rejected them. The dispute eventually erupted into a massacre followed by attacks on black people across the parish. Although there has never been an accurate count, Republicans claimed that two hundred black people were killed before it was over. That same month, in Camilla, Georgia, a gang of hastily deputized white men opened fire on a black election parade protesting the expulsion of thirty-three African Americans from the Georgia General Assembly. Again, the slaughter was followed by days of rampage.

The violence went on and on. The 1868 election brought Ulysses Grant to the White House (from 1869 to 1877), and his administration scrambled to respond. Contrary to popular legend, they were hamstrung in their efforts to stop the killing. The union army hastily demobilized after the war—their ranks fell from one million soldiers in 1865 to 54,000 in 1866 and just 24,000 by the end of Reconstruction in 1877—with more than half the troops deployed to the west. To be sure, the blue coats responded to riots and protected polling places, but they were stretched thin. And many were black soldiers (roughly 20 percent of the cavalry units), who faced backlash and violence themselves.

State and local governments, in Republican hands during the early days of Reconstruction, also deployed militia and police to quell the violence. Law enforcement officials, black and white, often did their heroic best, but they went home at night. They had families. Like anyone trying to forge a new South, they were always vulnerable to vigilantes who might gather at their doorway waving knives and guns. Sometimes, volunteers ran to the rescue. Congressman Robert Smalls, the naval hero spotlighted at the start of the chapter, was campaigning for reelection to Congress in Gillisonville, South Carolina, when a gang of Red Shirts drove him into a local store and opened fire. Word spread quickly and hundreds of black men and women came running, routed the militia group, and rescued Congressman Smalls.[52]

Across the South, violent paramilitary organizations sprang up—the Ku Klux Klan, the Red Shirts, the Regulators, the Knights of the White Camelia. The terrorists were often led by local police and drew former Confederate soldiers who were struggling with their own hard adjustment to civilian life. Congress strained to meet the threat. It organized a Justice Department in 1870 and passed an effective Enforcement Act against the Ku Klux Klan in 1871. But the paramilitary groups kept rising—and killing. Social scientists sometimes describe governments as having a "monopoly on legitimate use of force." Well, the governments—national, state, and local—lost that monopoly in the South after the Civil War.

In one of the most remarkable partisan turns in American history, the two parties even disagreed about the flowing blood. The Democratic press scoffed at reports of slaughter and often attempted to flip the narrative. The blacks had started it—they were planning to rob or rape or murder whites. "The negroes have organized a regular band of plunderers," reported the *New Orleans Times Picayune* in 1875, "and have murdered and robbed the farming people." When shifting the blame didn't work, the Democratic newspapers charged that the bloodshed had all been exaggerated. "Bogus outrages manufactured for the occasion," scoffed the *Pittsburgh Daily Post* after one bloody episode.[53]

In their effort to shift the blame, Democrats drew on the long legacy of white paranoia about slaves killing masters. The old fears offered a strange purchase for the social revolution before their eyes. Black citizens walked freely through town, read books, cast ballots, bore arms, and proudly wore their old Union Army uniforms. In the Democratic press, this somehow all morphed into a reincarnation of the long-ago revolution in Haiti. "Conservative papers of the state [justify] the massacre," complained President Ulysses Grant about bloodshed in Louisiana. Each federal effort to bring justice, he said, is "denounced as Federal tyranny and despotism." The president continued:

> Fierce denunciations ring through the country while every one of the . . . miscreants goes unwhipped of justice, and no way can be found in this broad land of civilization and Christianity to punish the perpetrators of this bloody and monstrous crime.[54]

Eventually, northern Republicans grew weary of the southern turmoil. The body counts were grisly, but the outrage was difficult to sustain, year after year. Besides, it overlapped with partisan politics and enabled a simple false narrative—the tales of terror were being told for partisan advantage. The inevitable calls to put aside partisan division began to stick. The willingness to fight for black voters began to ebb among many Republicans. Although black men would continue to struggle for the ballot until the end of the century, the debate slipped out of the national news and grew less important to the political parties outside the South. States and communities were left to work things out in their own ways. And that left black men and women to face the violence by themselves.

THE UNITED STATES HAD TRANSFORMED ITS CONSTITUtion—introducing equality in ways that would resonate through history. But who would enforce the changes and protect the former slaves? The Freedmen's Bureau was gone after seven years, the army had swiftly demobilized, and the many national Republicans were losing interest in the southern agonies. The federal courts were soon the only shelter from the storm. And the courts faced a dilemma. They heard a completely different story from the Democrats and the Republicans. Moreover, the Constitution had traditionally rested police powers in the states. Eventually, the courts also declined to protect black Americans. One grisly episode ended up before the Supreme Court and illustrates the legal dynamics of the day.

Elections in Louisiana had become festivals of fraud and violence. In Grant Parish, people of color made up a narrow majority but faced tireless efforts to rig the vote. During the election of 1872, a hole mysteriously appeared in one ballot box that, it turned out, was stuffed with Democratic ballots.

In Colfax, the country seat, both parties claimed victory in the races for sheriff, judge, and mayor. Members of the black community took over the courthouse, camping on the grounds, in an effort to claim the positions they thought they'd won. The newspapers responded by whipping up white outrage. Armed white men galloped into town from the surrounding country to challenge the former slaves for control of the building. Riding into Colfax, one gang came across Jesse McKinney mending a fence on his hardscrabble farm. They shot him dead while his wife and son watched, then rode on— yipping and hollering at their sport.[55]

McKinney's murder frightened black citizens, who, looking for protection, joined those already gathered at the courthouse, turning the grounds into a kind of armed encampment. But it was not much of a redoubt. The building was a converted barn. The freedmen dug a shallow trench, about two feet deep, and brandished old weapons with just enough powder for two rounds each. They pleaded with the governor for help but the only guns that descended on Colfax belonged to the white mob, which kept growing.

On Easter Sunday 1873, the mob attacked. They started firing a tiny four-pound cannon and, after repeated tries, wounded one defender and forced the rest back from the trench into the building. Desultory gunfire kept the attackers at bay until one man snuck around and set fire to the courthouse roof. With the building ablaze, the freedmen surrendered. They came out of the building and piled their weapons on the ground. The jubilant victors lined their captives up, two by two, with one white man behind each pair. Then they marched their prisoners off the courthouse grounds when, suddenly, someone at the head of the parade began to shoot and, in a moment, the white men up and down the line were blasting away.

One of the white leaders, Bill Cruickshank, tried to line up captives to see if he could kill two men with one bullet. The attackers gave increasingly frenzied chase as the wounded captives dashed for their lives. Somewhere between 60 and 150 black people were gunned down that day, perhaps even more; three whites lay dead, though they may have been shot by friendly fire in the havoc. The white supremacists had dehumanized their victims pretending that they were herding cattle—an attitude that often accompanies genocide.

Eventually, the federal government brought charges and managed to convict some of the white leaders, who immediately appealed. Two years later, in the spring of 1875, the case reached the Supreme Court. During oral arguments in *United States v. Cruikshank*, an all-star team of Democratic attorneys argued for reversing the convictions. Police powers belonged to the states. Federal intervention in a local case such as this one, they contended, would be "a fatal departure from the . . . spirit of our institutions." Worse, it would "elevate the black man above the white man," and would "fetter . . . millions of whites who were born free." Perhaps the results from the 1874 midterms, four months earlier, touched the atmosphere in the courthouse—Democrats had swept to power in the House, going from a minority with 88 seats to a majority with 181 (they also won ten seats in the Senate but remained in the minority).[56]

The Supreme Court agreed with the Democrats, threw out the convictions, and issued a far-reaching ruling (by a five to four vote). The Fourteenth Amendment's due process and equal protection clauses, ruled the court, only applied to state governments—not to individuals. "The fourteenth amendment prohibits a State from depriving any person of life, liberty, or property, without due process of law," wrote Chief Justice Morrison Waite, "but this adds nothing to the rights of one citizen as against another." The prosecution had also claimed that the state had not protected the former slaves' First Amendment right to assembly and the Second Amendment right to bear arms. The Supreme Court ruled that while the federal government may not abridge those rights, there was nothing to stop the state governments from doing so. The Court sailed blithely past the Fourteenth Amendment's language, in fact, it's very purpose: "no state shall "deny any person . . . the equal protection of the laws." The

Court would eventually reverse itself in 1937 (the states could not deny the right of assembly) and in 2010 (the right to bear arms).[57]

Other cases shrank the federal protections even further. In what became known as the *Slaughterhouse Cases*, decided the year before *Cruikshank*, the Court conjured a bold distinction out of thin legal air to gut part of the Fourteenth Amendment. The amendment forbade states from abridging "the privileges and immunities of citizens of the United States." In the *Slaughterhouse Cases*, however, the Court decided that the clause protected only the privileges and immunities of *federal* citizenship, not of *state* citizenship. What were those federal rights? The court dreamed up a puny list: access to ports, the right to travel to the seat of government, the ability to run for federal office, and protection on the high seas. Today, very few scholars, on the left or the right, consider this a plausible reading, but the clause remains dead nevertheless. A long series of other federal protections, legislated in the 1860s and 1870s, fell before the courts.

In short, the courts declined to defend black civil rights and struck down Republican efforts to do so. Police power rested with the states and, by the mid-1870s, most southern jurisdictions were not interested in convicting the vigilantes or checking white supremacy. The reign of terror faced no legal check. Future courts would revisit the issues, and the Fourteenth Amendment would grow into a formidable source of rights—but not in time to protect black lives in the nineteenth century.

THE WANING EFFORTS AT RACIAL RECONSTRUCTION FINALLY winked out with the 1876 election. Democrat Samuel Tilden defeated Republican Rutherford B. Hayes in both the popular vote and, so it seemed, in the Electoral College. But Republicans controlled South Carolina, Florida, and Louisiana, and if they could win the disputed vote in all three, Hayes and the Republicans would slip into the White House by a single Electoral College vote. There were plenty of reasons to dispute the vote counts. The campaigns had been marked by fraud and violence—especially in South Carolina, where a Fourth of July celebration marking America's centennial ended with a slaughter of black militia men. Now, claims and counter claims about cheating led Congress to establish a fifteen-person committee that, eventually, handed all three states—and the presidency—to Hayes and the Republicans on an eight to seven party line vote. Democrats—who had not held the White House since Buchanan sixteen years earlier—were outraged. In an effort to calm the storm, representatives of both parties huddled in a Washington hotel and negotiated a truce. We don't really know what kind of deal they made, but the Democrats had been pushing hard for a return to local rule in the South and that's exactly what happened. President Hayes took office and a month later he wrote, "We have got through with the South Carolina and Louisiana [problems] and the troops are ordered away [back to barracks]." The federal government relinquished its oversight over the last southern states. Reconstruction was over. Hayes penned a wan epitaph for the great experiment in Reconstruction. "I now hope for peace and . . . security and prosperity for the colored people." A nice hope, but not one that he or his party would be in a position to advance or defend. Hayes thought it was time to turn to more pressing matters, like an end to patronage and "the evils of office seeking."[58]

THE CIVIL WAR LED TO A NEW AMERICAN FOUNDING—etched by Abraham Lincoln in the Gettysburg Address, enacted by black men and women fighting to make new lives after the Civil War, and lodged in the Constitution where future generations would later find it. The Constitution now included audacious proclamations about citizenship, equality, and male suffrage. But, of course, the new laws had to be won on the desolate ground, in practice as well as in law.

The war's aftermath injected something terrible into the story of partisan conflict in America: a campaign of sustained, organized, vigilante terrorism justified by a major party. It grew especially violent in what we'd now call majority-minority districts. The police and local governments participated alongside private citizens gathered in paramilitary organizations like the KKK or the Red Shirts.

Black Americans eventually found themselves abandoned in hostile territory, but they continued to vote, form alliances, run for office, and occasionally win. Despite the violence, their turnout toward the end of the century still ranged from a remarkable 81 percent in North Carolina, to solid in Georgia (42 percent), Louisiana (44 percent), and Mississippi (45 percent). White supremacists eventually found the loopholes in the Civil War Amendments and, abetted by the Supreme Court, restored white supremacy and crushed the black vote. The next chapter tells that story.[59]

For a long time, the level and scope of the violence was hidden by a quixotic myth. The defeated people dreamed up the romance of the Lost Cause. An honorable region had valiantly fought for liberty against impossible odds. They'd succumbed to the North's overwhelming numbers and returned home to see their devastated communities falling into anarchy because the former slaves were not ready for freedom. Amid the terrible chaos, brave white men, trained in the ways of war, banded together and restored tranquility—disarming black men, taking away their mischievous votes, and protecting white women from rape—now known as the "foul daughter of Reconstruction."[60]

Historians have exploded every aspect of the myth. The South's defeat was not inevitable and the charges against the former slaves were fabrications—black men and women reached for freedom and tried to make new lives in the face of sweltering violence. But the caricatures justified the restoration of white supremacy—and of a new version of the plantation economy.

In its day, The Lost Cause inspired monuments across the region. They hid America's longest spasm of terrorism by reimagining it as a heroic restoration of a traditional order. In Colfax, Louisiana, for example, two monuments memorialized the slaughter of 1873. In the cemetery, a large granite obelisk is inscribed "In Loving Remembrance. Erected to the Memory of the [Three] Heroes Who Fell in the Colfax Riot Fighting for White Supremacy." Not far away, a state historical marker reads: "On this site occurred the Colfax riot in which three white men and 150 negroes were killed. This event . . . marked the end of Carpetbag [or northern] misrule in the South."[61]

The monuments in Colfax point to a history long hidden in plain sight. The memory of the killing fields, the half-forgotten memorials celebrating white supremacy, and the history of the violent twilight that came after slavery and before Jim Crow all remind us of how deep the nation's racial scars go.

But memory grows. People dig. Lost histories get rediscovered. In 1989, a journal called the *Angolite*, published in the Louisiana State Penitentiary at Angola, drew on oral histories to disinter the Colfax killings. The reporters were black inmates, and they delved into the brutal past of a community that, today, has one of the highest incarceration rates in the nation. As the inmates' publication brought the dramatic old story back into the light, it drew the attention of reporters and was repeated in books, blogs, and magazine articles. One reporter, writing in the *Atlantic*, even found the little cannon that had driven the black men from their trench around the courthouse. Today, the story of the Colfax Massacre is famous. The town itself has become a destination for Americans seeking to understand the nation's painful racial history. Many other episodes still wait to be rediscovered and memorialized in new ways.

I've told the story of America's great crack-up as a partisan fight over American identity—about race and ethnicity, and social justice. Even the worst terror campaign in American history was seen differently by Democrats and Republicans. The debate, then and now, has always been about something both deep and familiar. The Civil War, the postwar Amendments, Reconstruction, the Supreme Court's ruling in *Cruikshank*, the *Angolite*'s reporters going back into the past, and the men and women fighting over monuments today all struggle for answers to the most profound question about America: Who are we?

PART III

THE POPULISTS AND THEIR LONG SHADOW

FIVE

POPULISM AND THE RISE OF ACTIVE GOVERNMENT (1890–1900)

"**R**aise less corn and more hell," shouted Mary Lease to the farmers of Kansas. Lease was a Populist orator famous for her "fierce denunciations of the oppressors." "She hurls sentences," wrote one admirer, "as Jove hurled thunderbolts." The Populist movement stormed out of the Great Plains and rallied Americans who felt left behind by the greedy rush for riches during the Gilded Age. This chapter tells the story of the movement that erupted during the 1890s, dreamed up wild ideas, and profoundly shaped the twentieth century.[1]

James "Cyclone" Davis, another Populist orator, was a mountain of a man who lectured at a manic clip, debated like a biblical tempest, clutched Thomas Jefferson's writings in one massive hand, and waved his other arm like a frantic windmill—all while upbraiding the rich and the heartless. Volumes of Populist writing can be summarized in one of Cyclone's famous ditties:

> *The Wall Street bandits / In their Lust*
> *Have trampled the people / Into Dust*
> *They have robbed millions / Of all their feed*
> *In order to gorge / On solid greed . . .* [2]

Thomas Jefferson and Andrew Jackson thought that standing up for the people meant keeping government small—a big national government would only make the speculators and bankers richer. Now, the Populists flipped the script: only a powerful national government could protect the common person from the swaggering power of money. In 1892, the Populists organized themselves into the People's Party, one of the most famous third parties in American history.

The platform that emerged from that 1892 People's Party convention in Omaha, Nebraska (known as the Omaha Platform), reads like a checklist of twentieth-century liberalism. Beyond their planks and policies lay something even more ambitious—a new definition of freedom itself.

"What is freedom worth for a man who is dying of hunger?" asked the Populist leader Ignatius Donnelly. "Can you keep a room warm next winter . . . by reciting the Declaration of Independence?" No. People who are starving or freezing or uneducated cannot be free. And then the big leap: the people—through their government— must guarantee life's basics to everyone. "Government is intended," wrote Donnelly, "to insure every industrious citizen . . . an educated mind, a comfortable home, an abundant supply of food and clothing, and a pleasant, happy life."[3] That view would slowly move to the center of the Democratic Party. By the 1930s, Franklin Roosevelt and his New Deal Democrats took up the Populist's policies, their rhetoric, and their vision of liberty underwritten by the government.

The link between the Populists, the Progressive reformers (1900–1918), and the New Dealers (1933–1948) is controversial among political historians. After all, the tattered, unsophisticated rural Populists—with their shouted speeches and snatches of doggerel— could not be more different than suave gentlemen presidents like Teddy Roosevelt, Woodrow Wilson, or Franklin Roosevelt. But shift the focus from their biographies to their ideas and the populist roots of twentieth-century liberalism shines clear.[4]

POPULISTS ALWAYS ATTACK ELITES IN THE NAME OF THE people. But the same question vexes every uprising—who exactly are the people? Defining us inevitably means differentiating them.

The nineteenth-century Populists built their community in the name of the poor, largely rural populations—and, at least for a time, bravely included both blacks and whites. "You are kept apart," declared Georgia Populist Tom Watson, so "that you may be separately fleeced of your earnings."[5]

The movement arose as inequality remade the nation and hard times pummeled the working class. In 1888, the farming economy turned treacherous. Drought ruined the crops. Homesteaders who had signed up for cheap federal land abandoned their farms and limped back to the East. Others hung on grimly, desperate for help against debt and foreclosure. Cotton prices hit their lowest mark in thirty years. And within five years, the entire economy would collapse.

Strikes swept across the jittery Midwest and flared into violence. Who was to blame? The strikers blamed the owners, the owners accused labor for turning radical, and many on both sides pointed to the new wave of immigrants. The *Chicago Tribune* summed up the new nativism after someone threw a bomb at the police gathered in Haymarket Square in May 1886: The government had been offering "mad dogs" from Germany, Bohemia, Poland and Italy free education, homes, and farms. Now, it was time to "stamp them out . . . without mercy or regret." An ardent new debate rose up again about the nation's open door to immigrants.[6]

Politics was not much help because it had bogged down into a weary stalemate. No presidential candidate broke 50 percent of the popular vote between 1876 and 1896, and two squeaked into the White House after losing the popular vote—something political historians considered remarkable until it happened again in the twenty-first century. In those two decades, partisan control switched party hands six times in the House and seven in the Senate (including the dizzy Forty-Seventh Congress, which saw the Senate spin from tied, to Republican, to Democratic in a single year). Between 1876 and 1896, each party got just one crack at unified control of government and, as we shall see, each smashed things to bits as soon as it took the wheel.

Amid economic and political tumult, the Populists tried to tip the balance. They allied with the weaker party—Democrats in the West, Republicans in the South, and nobody (for they never got anywhere) in the East.

IGNATIUS DONNELLY WAS A SHORT, WILD, CHARISMATIC former congressman named after Ignatius de Loyola (who founded the Jesuits). The press called Donnelly, among many other things, the "Apostle of Protest" and the "Prince of Cranks." He scratched out novels, pamphlets, and platforms expounding the Populist idea.

"The proletariat are desperate," warns one character in his bleak, science fiction novel, *Caesar's Column*. "They are ready, like Blind Samson, to pull down the pillars of the temple, even though they themselves fall, crushed to death in the ruins." Eventually, the people of the novel, goaded beyond endurance by bruising inequality and raw need, slaughter the entire ruling class. Not all Populists were so bleak. In Edward Bellamy's novel *Looking Backward*, the protagonist wakes up in the year 2000 and finds that economic deprivations and class war had evaporated in the inexorable march of industrial progress. In 1892, both Donnelly and Bellamy were active at the People's Party convention—and the former drafted the platform.[7]

The Omaha Platform began by decrying an American society that had split into "two great classes—tramps and millionaires." The rest of the platform can be boiled down to five kinds of demands.[8]

First, the Populists insisted that government was the solution. As the Omaha Platform put it, "the power of government—in other words, of the people—should be expanded." The Post Office, the largest government bureaucracy of the time, offered a model of egalitarian service. Government services should simply replace the avaricious banks and railroads. Cyclone Davis imagined the looming dispensation. When farmers are ready to ship their produce, "instead of chartering a soulless, heartless corporation to . . . rob you, . . . the government will take your goods as it does your letters and distribute them at actual cost."[9]

Over time, more polished movements, the Progressives and the New Deal, would take this idea of government ownership and refine it into business regulation. But the central Populist aspiration—government as a countervailing force to private power—would find its way into the Democratic canon during the twentieth century.

Second, the Omaha Platform called for wresting power from the corrupt parties and restoring it to the people. Government, not the parties, ought to print the ballots and voters should cast them behind a curtain. The people, not the crooked state legislatures, should elect senators. The people should put items on the political agenda through initiatives, vote directly on issues via referenda, and recall politicians who were not properly representing them. The western Populists also pressed for women voting, though southern opposition turned the national platform pleas so vague they were barely detectable.

Third, the populists targeted inequality by calling for an income tax to replace the tariffs on imports and the taxes on liquor, which had funded the government. Congress passed the tax in 1894 but the Supreme Court, in a deeply controversial decision, struck it down the following year. Almost every state (forty-two out of forty-eight) ratified the Sixteenth Amendment, which checked the Court and gave the federal government the power to tax incomes. Eventually, liberals would follow the Populists and come to see the tax as the foundation of fair governance and equality. Conservatives still counter that it infringes personal freedom—and should be cut, and cut, and then cut again.[10]

Fourth, the Populists looked for government assistance, including "fair and liberal pensions" for Civil War veterans and their families. During the depression in 1893, impoverished men and women called on the government to provide payments and create public jobs building streets and railroads. Jacob Coxey led an army of unemployed men to Washington, DC—the first march on Washington for jobs and justice. Coxey was arrested from trespassing on the Capitol lawn, but the essential idea—look to government during hard times—sprang, in part, from the Populist spirit and took root in the nation's reforming imagination.[11]

Finally, Populists championed a looser, more inflationary monetary policy. At the time, the dollar was pegged to gold, which limited the amount of money in circulation. That privileged the banks over the borrowers, charged the People's Party. Its answer was to link the money supply to silver, which was more plentiful, or to a combination of gold and silver. It all sounds archaic today. Gold (the metal of responsibility) clashing with silver (the people's ore), but the fight over money reflected the Populist's primal struggle—voracious financiers versus common people. A later generation would construct the technocratic Federal Reserve system to make money tighter or looser as conditions changed. And FDR would, finally, redeem the metallic dream and take the nation off the gold standard at the start of his administration in 1933.

Beyond the policy details, the Populists championed a view of positive government (and liberty): government itself preserves freedom when it underwrites the basics for everyone—food, shelter, education, health care, and the right to work. As Donnelly had put it, you can't be free if you're cold or hungry. That challenged the traditional view of liberty—keep the government out of my business. The two views, known respectively as positive and negative freedom, still demarcate the left from the right.[12]

Of course, the Populists marched with others. They shared ideas—and members—with organized labor, with the socialists, and with the Farmer's Grange—a cooperative, often radical, farmers' movement with deep roots in rural communities. They all brought the passion of the have-nots to American politics.

———————

WHAT WAS REMARKABLE ABOUT THE 1890 ELECTION CAM-paign in Kansas, reported the dyspeptic editors of one of the state's newspapers, was "the part played by the short-haired sisters." Yes, answered one of those sisters sarcastically, "wimmin was everywhere." Across the West, women played an important—and by nineteenth-century standards, an unusual—role in Populist politics.[13]

Mary Lease rose to address the Omaha convention after being hailed as "our Queen Mary." She was also known as the "Kansas Cyclone"—all those cyclone metaphors hint at the passion blowing through the movement. Lease may have served as an inspiration for Dorothy in the Wizard of Oz, who was also swept out of Kansas on a cyclone.[14]

The most powerful woman of the era, Frances Willard, took over the Woman's Christian Temperance Union (WCTU) in 1879 and built it into the largest women's organization in history. Willard barnstormed around the country, delivering four hundred lectures a year urging her followers to "do everything"—protect their homes from violent husbands, demand the vote, earn equal pay, reach for success in every field, and win social justice for all. A month be-fore the Populist convention, Willard did something remarkable. She summoned the party leaders to Chicago. And the men—they were all men—showed up. In the People's Party, women served as leaders, orators, theorists, and intellectuals, but only up to a point. The Populist leaders tried hard to mollify Willard, but they politely rejected her demands. No, they would not endorse women voting or liquor prohibition. Southern voters would never go for it, they told her.[15]

But Willard and many of her colleagues had something far more revolutionary in mind than suffrage or sobriety—they dreamed of equality between men and women. "Why should the accident of sex surround me with . . . arbitrary limitations?" asks one woman in a Hamlin Garland Populist novel. The story rattles predictably along—boy meets girl, girl inspires boy with her passionate oratory, they fall in love, they get married, he gets elected to Congress—and then an unexpected twist. She insists that she must go back out west and fight the good fight on the speakers' platforms and in the meeting halls. The happy couple parts for the greater good, each doing their bit for the people.[16]

Some pushed into even more perilous sexual territory. The protagonist in George Noyes Miller's novel, *The Strike of a Sex*, awakes one day to find himself in a city where women have gone on strike. The men walk around, unkempt and hungry without their helpmeets. Our narrator is shocked to his marrow when he learns what they want. Not the usual—votes, equal pay, civic equality—but a "guarantee that no woman . . . shall be subjected to the worries of maternity without her free and specific consent." Well, that crossed right over from controversy to crime by violating obscenity laws. A decade later, a fiery socialist named Margaret Sanger would give a name to this disturbing demand, "birth control."[17]

Women were far more politically active in the West. Why? Government policy might have had something to do with it. The Homestead Acts allocated land to any head of household—including widows, single women, and divorcees. By 1913, women owned fully a third of the vast lands that had been distributed by the government. Moreover, the Morrill Land Grant Colleges of the West admitted many more women than the private colleges back east. Finally, farm work blurred gender roles and perhaps the ambiguity spilled over to politics and professions.[18]

The mainstream press remained scornful. One Kansas newspaper called the female activists, "strong minded shrews who abandon their homes and their families to vibrate over the country." They taunted the unmanly men who put up with such stuff. These women are "wearing trowsers" and "lead men who are unable and unfit to successfully cope with their brothers in the fields of politics." The more successful the woman, the harsher the press. "Frances Willard was responsible for [the] pandemonium [that] reigned supreme," ran one widely reprinted dispatch from the Populist convention— filed under the sarcastic headline, "Weeping, Wailing and Gnashing of Teeth."[19] "The speech delivered by Mary E. Lease," sniffed a Kansas newspaper, was "of intolerable length" and "not very well received"—never mind that, as the same paper reported, a whopping ten thousand people had showed up to hear her.[20]

The South was particularly resistant. Women generally did not give speeches and they certainly did not vote. Tom Watson's fictional heroine prettily expresses a rebellious streak in his novel, *Bethany*, but it does not take much to reason her around. "Men are better fitted to fight the rough battle of life," explains a wise minister. "The status women occupy in any system is the best proof of the purity or the depravity of that system." Southern men "throw around their women every possible protection, to guard the home against the slightest impurity." Sustaining white supremacy required the most stringent gender controls—throwing "every possible protection around women" meant constructing every possible taboo against sex across the color line.[21]

While Democrats were more sarcastic about gender rights, neither major party was enthusiastic about them. Frances Willard and the WCTU did manage to win more influence in the corridors of power by emphasizing "home protection" from liquor (which turned men violent) and lust (no more winking at excursions to the red-light districts that flourished in the nineteenth-century city). But building gender rights on a foundation of home protection—on rallying against male violence and marital rape—left the women's movement sadly susceptible to racial hostility. After all, the great lie that justified lynching across the South sounded very similar: white men were protecting women and children from rapacious (black) males. It led Frances Willard to cheer the literacy test in the South. It moved Mary Lease to propose a crackpot idea in her tract, *The Problem of Civilization Solved*: American households would spread south, down the Isthmus and across South America. Each homestead would be allocated inferiors—Chinese, African Americans, chronic paupers—to work their land. The women's movement, in the 1890s, was bold and visionary. But, the logic of home protection bled into the painful racial and ethnic prejudices, even as women fought for their own place in the political economy.[22]

The People's Party, as it crested, engaged women into politics, won women's suffrage in most western states, and imagined bold new forms of equality. But as the Populist wave broke and receded after 1892, reformers lost a powerful source of energy. Women's suffrage would survive and eventually win—first in the western states, then across the nation, but the more ambitious dreams of equality failed. Neither party would endorse that till the 1970s when gender rights would burst back onto the political agenda and help redefine partisan politics.[23]

———

BOTH THE REPUBLICANS AND THE POPULISTS TRIED TO build a coalition across the race line. The Republicans took one last stab at protecting the black vote. "The Negro-Americans . . . died in the trenches and on the battle-fields by hundreds," shouted Representative Henry Cabot Lodge of Massachusetts from the floor of the House in 1890. We owe them, continued Lodge, what we owe every American, rich or poor, black or white: a ballot, counted fairly. The galleries erupted in applause.[24]

In 1888, the Republicans had won control of the federal government for the first time since Reconstruction, and some of their leaders tried to use their majority to win fair congressional elections in the face of racial fraud in the South. The Lodge Bill would empower federal courts to appoint supervisors who could monitor congressional elections. The modest proposal met almost manic opposition. Opponents dubbed it the "Force Bill"—a name that stuck. The *New York Times*'s description was typical: the measure was "foolish," "uncalled for," and "dangerous," marking the return of "bayonet policy." The *Atlanta Journal Constitution* practically chortled over the disastrous political ramifications for Republicans. "The Lodge Force Bill, as an issue, is pie for Democrats."[25]

The southern press occasionally cut through the noise and pointed to the real danger. The bill threatened white supremacy in Congressional elections. "The Lodge force bill was designed to vitalize the 15th amendment," groused the *New York Times*. "The effect would have been to put three states and numerous communities . . . under the political dominion of the negro."[26]

Adroit maneuvering got the controversial bill through the House by six votes—without a single Democrat voting aye. The bill went to the Senate where it encountered the very first filibuster. Opponents figured a Republican majority would prevail if it came to a vote, but party members were not enthusiastic about the measure, so the way to beat it was to keep it off the floor. Senator William Stewart, a Nevada Republican, led the opposition. Week after week, he blocked a direct vote, by pushing more popular measures onto the agenda. Finally, with the end of the congressional session looming, it came down to one last vote. Opponents prevailed again—this time by a single vote. Republican leaders tried to save the bill by playing one final card. Nelson Aldrich of Rhode Island planned to catch the night train to New York and secure the vote of bedridden Senator Leland Stanford (R-CA)—one more aye would create a tie that the vice president could break and finally get the voting bill to the floor.

Senator Stewart overheard two men discussing the plan in the Senate cloakroom. He leapt onto the same train, handsomely tipped the baggage handler to arrange a fast team when they arrived in New York, lavishly tipped the driver to race to the Windsor Hotel on Fifth Avenue and Forty-Seventh Street, dashed into the residence, and talked Senator Stanford's wife into producing the sena-tor's signature—burying the civil rights bill once and for all. As he was walking out, his unsuspecting rival was just entering—too late to save the Force Bill. A more powerful version of the legislation would come back to life, more than seven decades later, as the Voting Rights Act of 1965.[27]

THE SOUTHERN DEMOCRATS FACED AN EVEN GRAVER THREAT from the Populists who—briefly, bravely—tried to connect black and white farmers across the South in an alliance with southern Republicans. "We propose," exulted Ignatius Donnelly during the Populist convention in 1892, "to knock the Mason Dixon line out of geography and the color line out of politics." Congressman Tom Watson, who had founded the Populist Party in Georgia, helped lead the charge. "The millionaires who manage the Democratic party," he declared, have nothing to offer "beyond the cheerful advice to 'work harder and live closer.'" And as to the Republicans, "the millionaires who control that party" respond "with the soothing counsel that the . . . farmer . . . should 'work more and talk less.'"[28]

The People's Party challenged the race line across the South. In Texas, the local organization elected two black members to its governing board. Black and white orators shared the platform in Georgia. And the party's 1890 convention in Ocala, Florida, included black and white Populist groups meeting simultaneously. "The white tenant lives adjoining the colored tenant," wrote Watson in 1892. "Their houses are equally destitute of comforts." Both, he continued, are squeezed by the same taxes, by the same interest rates, by the same landowners, and by the same banks. "You are made to hate one another because upon that hatred rests the keystone of the arch of financial despotism which enslaves you both."[29]

Over and over again, the Populists repeated "self-interest," like a kind of incantation that might finally break the racial spell. If poor white farmers could cast aside their racist attitudes and focus on their economic interests, they would unite with their black compatriots and stand up to the powers that exploited them. The Populists were under no illusions about the limits of their racial alliance. This was an era of unabashed white supremacy and the Populists had to appeal to black voters without offending white ones. "Social equality does not enter into it the calculation at all," tutted Tom Watson.[30]

Newspapers responded to the Populists' biracial efforts with the same jagged charge, said Watson, "negro domination, negro domination, negro domination." "You might prove with mathematical precision that herein lay his way out of poverty into comfort . . . but if the merchant who furnished his farm supplies (at tremendous usury) or the town politician . . . came along and cried 'Negro rule!' the entire fabric of reason . . . would fall and the poor tenant would joyously hug the chains of an actual wretchedness."[31]

Poor whites clung to racial supremacy. We have seen this before, we will see it again. Planter elites rallied hardscrabble white farmers to fight for slavery in 1860 by stressing social status—the poorest whites stood "an infinite remove" above the black people on the ladder of society. Now Democrats mouthed almost the same words to break the Populist threat of an interracial rebellion.[32]

DESPITE ALL THE DIFFICULTIES, A BIRACIAL COALITION swept to victory in North Carolina during the 1890s. A Populist-Republican alliance (or Fusion, as it was called) won both houses of the General Assembly in 1894, and then took every statewide race, including the governorship, in 1896. African Americans entered the governing coalition. Wilmington, the largest city in the state, had a black majority (about 55 percent of the population) and a thriving black middle class. In the mid-1890s, local government included a black justice of the peace, a black deputy clerk of courts, a black coroner, black cops, black men on the board of aldermen, and an all-black health board.

White resentment grew and the newspapers gave it voice. "The superior races have ruled the inferior from the dawn of history" declared the *Wilmington Messenger*. "He that attempts to defy that law must answer the charge of blood guiltiness." The same words run through article after irate article about the city's striving black professionals: "Insolence," "malice," "disrespect," and "corruption."[33]

In the summer of 1897, Rebecca Latimer Felton, one of the few female activists in the South, tossed a verbal firebomb into the charged atmosphere. Felton rose to address the Georgia State Agricultural Society on the anodyne topic of "Women on the Farm" but strayed from her prepared text and ripped "white manhood" for not protecting "innocence and virtue." Then the percussive declaration: "If it needs lynching to protect woman's dearest possession from the ravening human beasts," extemporized Felton, "then I say lynch, a thousand times a week if necessary." That line—"lynch a thousand times"—reverberated across the region. The *Atlanta Constitution* headline summed it up: "Lynch, says Mrs. Felton."[34]

After a Boston newspaper denounced her, Felton tried to clarify her position—and only amplified the detonation. In a long letter to the *Atlanta Journal Constitution*, she began with semi-soothing words, got more agitated as she went along, and ended by raving all over again. "I am in favor of shooting down mad dogs when their mouths are foaming . . . and when a human beast gets ready to . . . destroy my child, the beast should learn to expect a quick bullet or a short rope." Yes, the people of Massachusetts were criticizing lynch mobs, she wrote, but she could explain what they did not seem to comprehend. "The southern people are not of the opinion that . . . young white women [should] be forced into alliances . . . with half-civilized, drunken gorillas."[35]

A year later, Alex Manly, the editor of the *Wilmington Record*, a black daily newspaper, decided to fight fire with fire. "Teach your own men purity," he responded to Felton in a front-page editorial. "It is no worse for a black man to be intimate with a white woman than for the white man to be intimate with a colored woman." Manly brushed right past the primal taboo. "Every Negro lynched is called a 'big, burly, black brute," but it was not so. They are not brutes and not burly but "sufficiently attractive for white girls of culture and refinement to fall in love with them." Manly himself was a handsome man, judging by his photos, and the mixed-race grandson of a former North Carolina governor.[36]

The uproar had leapt from elections to sexuality, from politics to manhood, from virtuous women to inadequate white men. Felton and Manly had both piqued the Ur mythology of racial repression: black leadership, black prosperity, black success—inexorably, inevitably—got transformed into black sexuality, black rapists, and a hushed anxiety about white inadequacy. The sexual worries point to the sharpest fear: the line between us and them won't survive long without strict rules against "their" men having sexual relations with "our" women.

What Manly said might sound like simple common sense—calling out the sexual double standard (exactly as Robert Smalls had done in South Carolina during the convention that drove African Americans out of politics), but it was a dangerous thing to write in a black majority city in the nineteenth-century South. White civic leaders had been plotting to seize control during the next election, in 1898. The Manly editorial—too vile to be described, bawled the *Wilmington Daily Record*—gave them a pretext for restoring order and virtue. Former Congressman Alfred Moore Waddell roused the Wilmington rabble. "You are Anglo Saxons. You are armed and prepared and you will do your duty . . . Go to the polls tomorrow, and if you find the Negro out voting, tell him to leave the polls, and if he refuses, kill him." Intimidation and fraud turned what had been a five thousand vote majority for the Fusion into a Democratic majority of six thousand. The newspapers crowed as if the remarkable swing had not been won by raw intimidation.[37]

The next day, victorious whites held a roaring rally and then followed a Red Shirt militia into the streets. They brandished rifles; pulled a Gatling gun; and, after burning Manly's newspaper office (he had fled the town), they blazed through the black quarter, known as Brooklyn, looting, destroying, and killing. Black men and women lay on the street, dead and dying. Others escaped to the forests where they hid through a cold and terrifying night. The governor called out the state militia, but it joined the Red Shirts hunting down black citizens. The mob's leaders, who had controlled the action throughout, forced the remaining Fusion officials—the mayor, the aldermen, the police chief—to resign at gunpoint. Waddell declared himself mayor and, in the process, accomplished that rare event in American history, a violent coup.

There was nothing rare about the ethnic cleansing that followed. Gangs rounded up the black men and women and, as Waddell himself later put it, "marched them to the railroad station, . . . gave them tickets, and told them to go and to never show up again." Black families streamed out of town by the hundreds, perhaps thousands. "The white people," concluded Reverend Kirk, an African American minister, "intended to remove all the able leaders of the colored race, stating that to do so would leave the better and obedient servants among the Negroes."[38]

WHITE SUPREMACIST LEADERS UNDERSTOOD THAT THEY needed something more reliable than guns and knives to protect their rule. They faced threats from every direction. Republicans pushed their Lodge bill in Washington while Populists aimed to build interracial alliances from Texas to North Carolina. In 1890, Mississippi found a solution—and within two decades, every southern state had followed. The Mississippi legislature, firmly in Democratic hands, organized a constitutional convention with a clear mission: write African Americans out of politics without violating the Fifteenth Amendment. Democrats finally took control of both Congress and the White House, in 1893, and made it easy for white supremacy. They repealed the Reconstruction era laws implementing the Fifteenth Amendment that had prohibited the states from exploiting potential loopholes in the amendment like poll taxes and literacy tests. Now, the legal protection was gone.

Pious pronouncements about good government justified the exercise. A "dense mass of ignorance hovers like a lowering, threatening cloud over the south," offered the *New Mississippian*, "depressing the energies of our people and menacing their safety and civilization." The newspaper did not mince words about who was to blame. "In the presence of an enormous black majority, the cause of good government . . . stand[s] in perpetual jeopardy."

Even Frances Willard, eager to win southern allies for the women's cause, cheered "the wise measures" contemplated by the Mississippi convention. "We have wronged the South," she explained in a newspaper interview. "It is not fair that . . . a plantation Negro, who can neither read nor write, whose ideas are bound by the fence of his own field and the price of his own mule, should be entrusted with the ballot. We ought to have put an education test upon [the] ballot from the first." Frederick Douglass wrote that he felt stung by this twist in Willard's "sweet voice," and anti-lynching crusader Ida B. Wells accused her of abetting the murder of African Americans.[39]

The Mississippi convention—only one delegate (out of 134) was African American—concocted a perfectly legal means of disenfranchisement. Their most important innovation was the literacy test requiring that voters be able to read, write, and properly interpret a public document—often a convoluted passage from the state constitution or a little-known bit of civics (the exact hour that the president's term expires, for example). Political Scientist V. O. Key called the "understanding" clause the crowning achievement of the convention, for it gave registrars plenty of flexibility in administering the test and judging who was literate enough to vote. The Mississippi convention also dreamed up other barriers to voting: poll taxes, residency restrictions, convoluted registration procedures, and the requirement to show fiddly tax receipts and other documents. And the whole thing was legal because, as we saw in the last chapter, the Reconstruction-era Republicans wrote the Fifteenth Amendment with loopholes to permit limits on the Irish in Boston and the Chinese in California. Now, cheered on by good government reformers across the nation and soon facilitated by Democratic control in Washington, the white men of Mississippi used the loopholes to squeeze African Americans out of politics.[40]

The convention also imposed a powerful racial apartheid. In some places across the South, the races were still mingling, even intermarrying. Now, Mississippi led the way—segregating schools, forbidding interracial marriages, limiting African Americans' right to bear arms, and separating the races in public places. The system of segregation would come to be known as Jim Crow—named after a familiar minstrel show character.

The convention's handiwork had startling results. The Mississippi black vote, which had hovered around 44 percent during the previous decade, now plunged to an estimated one percent in a black majority state. The other southern states all followed Mississippi's lead. Louisiana found a creative way to turn the vote over to whites when it added a grandfather clause—men whose fathers or grandfathers could vote before 1867 were entitled to vote. Naturally, that excluded most black men. Every state in Dixie muscled a similar set of rules into place by 1908. The black vote practically vanished from the South.[41]

In 1896 the Supreme Court approved the Jim Crow laws, ruling in *Plessy v. Ferguson* that there was nothing unconstitutional about segregated—"separate but equal"—railway carriages. "If one race be inferior to the other socially," wrote Justice Henry Billings Brown, "the Constitution of the United States cannot put them upon the same plane." Justice John Marshall Harlan wrote a blistering dissent predicting that the judgment would eventually "prove to be quite as pernicious as the decision made . . . in the Dred Scott case." Today, the dissent is often celebrated by civil libertarians, but Harlan built his opinion on a treacherous foundation. The outrageous result of the segregation laws, he wrote, is that "a Chinamen can ride in the same passenger coach with white citizens . . . while citizens of the black race [cannot]." A future court would solve this problem for him, permitting southern districts to clamp segregation on "the yellow races."[42]

The following year, the court turned to the voting restrictions and, in *Williams v. Mississippi*, found, unanimously, that the poll tax and the literacy test "do not on their face discriminate between the races." The court went on to conclude, "it has not been shown that their administration was evil, only that evil was possible under them." Mississippi had successfully threaded the legal needle—they removed black voters without saying a word about race. Even Justice Harlan quietly submitted in *Williams*.[43]

THE NATIONAL REPUBLICANS FINALLY ABANDONED AFRICAN Americans in the South. In December 1898, just one month after the slaughter in North Carolina, President William McKinley (1897–1901) embarked on a southern tour designed to celebrate regional reconciliation. "Reunited! Glorious realization! It . . . is the patriotic refrain of all sections and of all lovers of the republic," he declared to rapturous audiences. Instead of strife and bloodshed, the president saw a country finally and fully at peace across the regions. All it took was for the nation to look away as Dixie mopped up the last, lingering strains of racial justice.[44]

Republican President Theodore Roosevelt (1901–1909) came to office after McKinley was assassinated and waved the entire issue away. Yes, the party still stuck to the rickety campaign platform condemning "discrimination [in] the elective franchise," but it now considered protecting black votes merely an "abstract right" and one that Republicans would be "unable to carry through." Even Henry Cabot Lodge, the original author of the voting rights effort, agreed that "it is something . . . we shall not have the nerve to do." Roosevelt learned his own hard racial lesson when he invited Booker T. Washington to dinner at the White House—and triggered a ferocious outcry. Democratic Senator "Pitchfork Ben" Tillman of South Carolina (the nickname came from his chronic defiance) squawked, "Entertaining that nigger will necessitate our killing a thousand niggers . . . before they will learn their place again." Neither Roosevelt nor his successors would publicly invite another black leader to the White House for almost three decades.[45]

Finally, Roosevelt's successor, Republican President William Howard Taft, intoned a long elegy for civil rights at the beginning of his inaugural address in 1909. "There was a time when northerners who sympathized with the negro . . . sought to give him suffrage," said Taft, but "the movement proved to be a failure." Black Americans "may well have our profound sympathy," he continued, and "personally, I have not the slightest race prejudice," but the sad fact is that "race feeling is so widespread and so acute" that appointing African Americans to office would, in many cases, "do more harm than good." And with that final rhetorical flourish, Republicans gave up on their defense of black men and women.[46]

On one level, it was simple electoral math. Seven Republican-leaning western states came into the union between 1889 and 1896, bringing in fourteen senators and twenty-one Electoral College votes. The Republicans no longer needed those difficult southern votes. They could wash their hands of all that racial trouble and leave the South to the Democrats. But there had always been more to racial justice than maximizing votes. The Republicans (and before them, the Whigs) had been fired by evangelical beliefs, which had led some party members to fight for racial justice—inundating Congress with antislavery petitions, demanding immediate abolition, or pressing for equality after the war. Now, both the practical politicians scratching for votes and the moralists seeking salvation turned to different causes. Neither party would stand alongside black America. Democrats stood for states' rights and white supremacy. Republicans only gave a bit of lip service to the old cause. Both shunned the messy, violent politics of race. It was simpler to cheer American solidarity with William McKinley, leave voting to local government, and ignore the violent, legal apartheid.

Many Populists also cast aside their dreams of an interracial alliance. Tom Watson embodied this shift when, after all his bold talk of the early 1890s, he flipped into a bare-knuckled bigot (or was he simply dropping the mask?). His historical novel, *Bethany*, written in 1905, reverberates with race hatred masquerading as earnest wisdom. "It will take all the coercive . . . power of the white race," intones a judicious colonel, "to keep the blacks of this country from going . . . back, as they have in Hayti, to barbarism." Watson's character falls back on a spiteful variation of the slavery as a positive good argument: "We Southern people took a naked black cannibal and made a human being out of him; but in the contact . . . we ourselves have become morally and mentally lowered. . . . Our children are mentally corrupted by their nigger nursemaids and nigger playmates." The bold pan-racial statesman of 1892 had curdled into a sour white supremacist within a decade.[47]

As the conflict between the parties over race went silent, the fierce partisan politics of the nineteenth century turned calmer. Politics grew less bitter, political institutions became more stable, and polarization declined. Modern social scientists have measured congressional polarization across time and have shown that it would steadily diminish from the turn of the century. It would not begin to rise again until the next time racial justice came back onto the mainstream parties' agenda.[48]

QUIETLY, BLACK AMERICANS RESPONDED TO THE NEW LEGAL apartheid. They organized the National Association for the Advancement of Colored People (NAACP). They began to leave the rural South and head for the northern factories—the start of a Great Migration. And that would change everything.

When they arrived in the North, African Americans audaciously imagined black nationalism. In this new land, the Thirteenth Amendment meant something—black votes counted. Black newspapers weighed the candidates. Local politicians ignored the national parties and began to recruit black voters. Black motion, rising out of the ashes of the 1890s, would once again remake American politics. But all this was barely detectible to the white gaze at the dawn of the twentieth century. National politics ground on without much thought to Black America as it changed and moved and organized.

———

ON A DARK, OVERCAST NIGHT IN OCTOBER 1890, SOMEONE gunned down the police chief in New Orleans—a notoriously violent and corrupt city. As he lay bleeding on the street, he may have whispered, "Dagos." The police swiftly rounded up 150 Italians (most were immigrants) and threw them into jail. White citizens assisted the authorities by roughing up all the unreliable Sicilians they could get their hands on. Eventually, nineteen men were indicted even though no one had seen the murderers' faces and the only person who claimed to have heard the chief's slur never testified. With such flimsy evidence, the first trial returned six innocent verdicts and three mistrials. That enraged the nativists. Angry citizens organized a Committee of Public Safety and called a mass meeting where they whipped up the crowd. A well-organized, well-armed cadre led the mob to the parish jail chanting, "We want the Dagos!" They broke into the jail and murdered eleven men by beating, shooting, and hanging. The backlash was intense. The Italian Consul issued a scorching indictment of the murders. Pope Leo XIII asked for explanation. The president apologized to Italy.[49]

The rising heat reflected powerful demographic trends. In the 1870s, 2.8 million immigrants had arrived in the United States. In the 1880s, the number leapt to 5.2 million. By 1890, the year of the Italian lynching, the percentage of Americans born abroad had reached 14.8 percent of the population—still the all-time high. And people kept coming—8.8 million more arrived in the first decade of the twentieth century. Beyond the sheer numbers were the strange origins. "Greeks, Italians, Poles, Hungarians, Jews," complained one US senator, "Syrians, Portuguese, Magyars . . . ." The unfamiliar people ran into the familiar barrage: They came from inferior countries, they were the wrong race, they practiced dangerous religions, they refused to assimilate, they would drag America down.[50]

The rising numbers fractured the traditional politics of immigration. Both the Democrats, who had long defended most newcomers, and the Republicans, who had largely opposed them, split into competing factions. The Populists, for their part, were ambivalent; they worried about big business importing the contract worker who "crowds out our wage earners," but they also built tentative alliances with Bohemians, Mexicans, and others. All three parties shared one sentiment—animosity toward the Chinese. "No more," promised the Democratic platform in 1892. "An evil of great magnitude," echoed the Republicans. California voters acted on the prejudice when they approved Chinese exclusion, 154,638 to 863.[51]

Immigration opponents fell into two camps: Some feared for the white race, others for the workers. Representative Henry Cabot Lodge, whose voting rights bill had just gone down in the Senate, led the racial skeptics. Immigrants, he said in 1891, posed a danger to American blood. He warned the nation not to miss the "real meaning" of the lynching in New Orleans: good Italians were being replaced by defectives from Sicily and Naples. Lodge latched onto that old standby, literacy tests—not to suppress the black vote in the South but as a way to stop inferior immigrants at American ports.[52]

A new discipline, the social sciences, echoed Lodge with a library of learned alarms. In high academese, deploying reams of dubious data, scholars warned about the dangers of "conferring the privilege of citizenship . . . without any test of . . . fitness." Lodge, who had received the very first PhD in political science issued by Harvard University, flashed his own erudition: "You can take a Hindoo and give him the highest education in the world, but you cannot make him an Englishman." What separates the two groups, he explained, is "the moral and intellectual character which makes the soul of a race, which represent the product of all its past, the inheritances of all its ancestors and motives of all its conduct." And then the warning, repeated countless times over the long debate: "If a lower race mixes with a higher in sufficient numbers, history teaches us that the lower race will prevail."[53]

Furnifold Simmons, who had helped organize the white supremacists in Wilmington, North Carolina, entered the Senate in 1901 and continued his white fight—now against immigrants. The Southern and Eastern Europeans, he declaimed, "belong . . . to a different civilization from that represented by the Anglo-Saxon race . . . .We do not want the ignorant and vicious and undesirable, the scum and riffraff of Europe dumped upon us."[54] These new immigrants, added Richmond Mayo-Smith, an influential economist at Columbia University, introduced anarchism, socialism, crime, pauperism, illiteracy, and high rates of insanity. Furthermore, they fed the corruption of municipal government by keeping the machines in power and brought with them objectionable practices like—recalling the purported villains in New Orleans—"the habit of seeking vengeance for personal wrongs with the stiletto." Edward A. Ross, a sociology professor and advisor to President Teddy Roosevelt, invented the term that summed up all these fears: *race suicide*. Swamped by inferiors mobbing in from the fringes of the Old World, warned Ross, "the higher race quietly and unmurmuringly eliminates itself." Rogers Smith, who took his degree in political science from Harvard a century after William Cabot Lodge, sums it up as "the era of the militant WASP."[55]

A Democratic faction joined the Republican WASPS in the fight. Organized labor bitterly opposed Chinese immigration and grew increasingly agitated about big business deploying foreigners to break strikes and depress wages. By 1897, the labor unions began to press for immigration restriction and threw their support behind Lodge's literacy test. Some unions—the garment workers in New York, for example—stood up for the newcomers. But most organized labor broke with the traditional Democratic position and turned against immigration. Tom Watson crudely summed it up: "The treacherous manufacturing interests [have] . . . dumped . . . the scum of creation on us." Why? Because "they wanted cheap labor and they didn't care a curse . . . [about] the consequence of their heartless policy."[56]

Both high Republicans, fretting over Anglo-Saxon culture, and labor unions, moving toward the Democratic party, opposed immigrants. These strange bedfellows would stick together, across the immigration debates, for almost a century.

On the other side, the coalition supporting immigration was just as unusual. George Washington Plunkitt, a rascally New York City politician, published a day from his diary: "Attended the funeral of an Italian as far as the ferry. Hurried back to make appearance at the funeral of a Hebrew constituent." Plunkitt continued, ticking down his melting-pot checklist. "A man born in Germany can settle down and become a good New Yorker"—the pinnacle of patriotism in Plunkitt's book. Why, "even a Jap or Chinaman can become a New Yorker." The urban machines in the Northeast and Midwest cheerfully mobilized the ethnic voters.

The big city Democratic bosses found unlikely political bedfellows in industry. Business needed workers and pushed for liberal immigration policies. The National Board of Trade opposed the literacy test. California farmers even tried to win a suspension of Chinese exclusion. When the economy was strong, business saw its bottom line reflected in a plentiful labor supply—and never mind the alleged glories of the Anglo-Saxon race.

By 1910, these peculiar coalitions faced off. The WASPs and the workers against the bosses and the business leaders. Over time, slowly but surely, the advantage slipped away from the champions of the open door. But the parties themselves did not whip up passions over the issue because each was divided. For a long time, the Democrats had repressed black voters and the Republicans had repressed immigrants. By the turn of the century, the pattern shifted. Both parties snubbed African Americans and each was internally split over immigrants. By sheer happenstance, the parties continued to restrain the most intense conflicts over identity.

IMMIGRATION LIMITS CAME, SLOWLY BUT STEADILY. IN 1882, the Chinese Exclusion Act banned new workers from China and barred the Chinese from becoming citizens. (Although the few Chinese children born in the United States became citizens—thanks to the Fourteenth Amendment and a Supreme Court ruling in 1898 that upheld birthright citizenship.) The limits came amid violence and discrimination. "Children spit upon us as we passed and called us rats," recalled one immigrant. Congress kept tightening the exclusions until 1906, when it banned all Asian immigrants. That offended Japan, so the Theodore Roosevelt administration negotiated a deal. The United States pledged not to bar Japanese immigrants and the Japanese government promised not to permit any.[57]

A series of small restrictions on immigrants from other countries began to accumulate. Congress imposed bans on prostitutes, paupers, polygamists, lunatics, anarchists, extremists, people likely to become public charges, and individuals suffering from "a loathsome or dangerous communicative disease." Labor got its wish and the United States forbade employers from contracting foreign laborers. Still, all those exclusions did not count for much until government had the capacity to enforce them. The Immigration Act of 1891 created a superintendent of immigration, organized a federal corps of immigration inspectors within the Treasury Department, and declared that the inspectors could not be second-guessed by the meddlesome courts. The new regime opened its famous immigration station on Ellis Island in 1892.

The longest-running immigration conflict turned on Henry Cabot Lodge's literacy test. The 1896 Republican national platform and the labor unions endorsed it. The House and Senate each passed a bill that required immigrants to read at least twenty words of the US Constitution in order to enter the country. The House would eventually approve the literacy test four times, the Senate approved it five times, and four presidents vetoed it until Congress finally rounded up enough votes to overturn Woodrow Wilson's veto of a watered-down version in 1917.[58]

Republican Speaker Joe Cannon finally turfed the debate off to a joint House and Senate commission headed by Republican Senator William P. Dillingham of Vermont. Commissions, then as now, were the savvy politicians' way to bury an issue, but Dillingham returned four years later, in 1911, with an exhaustive, forty-two-volume report that offered immigration opponents thousands of charts and pages of evidence. The abstract, in Volume One, for example, counted up the radical publications in each immigrant language: twenty-seven were in Italian, twenty-three in Hungarian, fifteen in Yiddish, and eleven circulating among the notorious Finns.[59]

The Dillingham Commission, which included Senator Lodge among its ten members, gave a hard shove toward restriction by injecting a new idea into the debate: an annual immigration quota, pegged to the average number of immigrants who had already arrived. The report, and its recommendations, now guided the debate.[60]

Congress finally muscled temporary immigration quotas into place with the Emergency Quota Act of 1921—partially to stop a surge of Jewish immigrants fleeing from persecution in Eastern Europe. In 1924, more permanent limits were put into place and national quotas were tied to the nearly thirty-five-year-old census of 1890—a way to tilt against the more recent immigrant groups. And with that, the United States—the nation of immigrants—cut the flow of new arrivals to a trickle. In 1892, as the Populists gathered in Saint Louis, 579,000 people arrived on American shores; fifteen years later, in 1907, that number had risen to 1.3 million. A quarter century later, as Franklin Roosevelt took the oath of office, the number of newcomers had dwindled to just twenty-three thousand.

The two parties had conspired to bury the great identity issues. Republicans had decided to celebrate national unity and give up on racial justice. Two decades later, the United States closed the door to immigration. Partisanship plummeted. But as we'll see in the next chapter, northern blacks would soon charge back into the parties— and transform American politics once again.

WHAT BECAME OF THE POPULISTS? WE LEFT THEM DEBATing their bold platform at the Omaha convention in 1892. They burst out of that convention and their presidential candidate, James Weaver, took five states and over a million votes (8.5 percent of the total)—the fifth best third-party showing in American history. They ran strong in the West, fell short in most of the South, and never connected at all in the Northeast—1 percent in New York was the most they scraped together.

Meanwhile, Grover Cleveland and the Democrats won it all. They retained the House with a large majority (220–126), took the Senate for the first time in twelve years, and won the presidency with their largest Electoral College margin since James Buchanan thirty-six years earlier. After two decades of divided government and hairsbreadth margins, the Democrats had broken through.

Then the economy collapsed. The 1893 depression was the worst in American history and the economy stayed down for four years. Through the hard times, President Grover Cleveland remained a stiff-necked, small-government conservative. He vetoed 584 bills— more than all his predecessors combined. Cleveland struck down relief bills, dispatched troops to suppress strikes, and broke up protests that sprang up in Washington. As the chaos dragged on, the Democrats divided. Some took up the Populist banner and advocated for loose money pegged to silver. Cleveland's supporters rejected the wild talk and stuck to solid, reliable gold. Four years later, the uproar within the Democratic party generated one of the most colorful elections in American history—and that's really saying something.

THE DEMOCRATIC CONVENTION OF 1896 MET IN CHICAGO and began in chaos. President Cleveland was out, but a half dozen other candidates from across the political spectrum were up and running. Before they got down to nominations, the Democrats debated their contentious platform issue—gold versus silver, tight money versus loose, three speakers to each side.

The first debaters ranged from boring to outrageous. South Carolina Senator "Pitchfork Ben" Tillman (I've already quoted his embarrassing rant about Booker T. Washington's lunch in the White

House) rose to speak for silver and began by announcing that he proudly hailed from "the home of secession." Delegates began to hiss and he hissed right back. He jabbed his finger at the "dictators" from New York, New Jersey, and Connecticut who had "eaten all our substance." They booed him lustily while he banged on, "Why should we write ourselves down as asses and liars?" Sweaty, scruffy, screaming, Tillman was a caricature of pop-eyed extremism.[61]

The final speaker on the question was a thirty-six-year-old former Congressman from Nebraska. Before the age of microphones, William Jennings Bryan's golden voice reached every cranny of the great hall, as he boomed out what may be the most famous oration ever delivered at a national party convention. "From the very first sentence," he later wrote, "the audience was with me. . . . At the close of every sentence it would rise up and shout, and when I began upon another sentence, the room was still as a church." And so it went until he came, at last, to his finale. He knew the majority already believed and that his job was to give them a memorable statement of their own faith.[62]

"Having behind us the producing masses of this nation and the world," blazed Bryan, "we will answer their demand for a gold standard by saying to them, 'You shall not press down upon the brow of labor this crown of thorns.'" Bryan grabbed at his temples and buckled his knees under the agony of the imagined thorns, paused, and from the pained crouch launched his most famous line. "You shall not crucify mankind upon a cross of gold." He raised himself up, stepped forward, pulled his hands off his brow, and threw them out into a crucifixion pose. A deep silence gripped the hall for five ticks at this inspired blasphemy. Then pandemonium. "The floor of the convention seemed to heave up," reported one New York newspaper. Men ran up to Bryan and promised their delegations. Friends wanted to start the roll calls voting right then and there, with the speech still reverberating in the air. Bryan waved them off. "If the desire to nominate me will not last until tomorrow," he reasoned, "would it last through the campaign?" In fact, the other candidates—older, more seasoned—maintained their support and Bryan only managed 15 percent of the votes on the first ballot. He did not take the delegate lead until the fourth round and finally secured the required two-thirds on the fifth.[63]

Opponents remained unmoved. This, they thought, was radical thinking aimed at redistributing the nation's wealth to the unproductive rural districts. "His speech to the Convention was an appeal to one of the worst instincts of the human heart," reported the editors of *The Nation*, "that of getting possession of other people's property without their consent."[64]

The People's Party faced a dilemma when they met to nominate a candidate for the 1896 race. Should they swing behind Bryan, despite his monomania about silver, which they thought, would do nothing to tame the power of the villainous banks and railroads? Or should they nominate one of their own? The Democrats had larded their platform with items to tempt the Populists. They censured Cleveland's action on strikes, condemned the Supreme Court for rejecting the income tax, and called for strong railroad regulation (but not government ownership) to "protect the people from robbery and oppression." However, the Democrats had also nominated a vice presidential candidate, Arthur Sewall, who had three Populist strikes against him—he was a conservative, a banker, and a railroad director.

Some Populists fought bitterly against going over to the Democrats, but many party members had already committed to Bryan. The convention acquiesced and nominated Bryan, but they named Tom Watson as his running mate. Bryan simply ignored Watson. The Democrats came out of their convention torn between the right and left factions. Now, with the same candidate atop two parties' tickets, voters would have a choice of Bryan with right or left running mates. For his part, Watson badgered Arthur Sewall to step down as number two with far more fizz than he devoted to Bryan's cause.

THE REPUBLICAN CONVENTION ENJOYED A LOT LESS DRAMA. The affable William McKinley cruised easily to the nomination on the first ballot. The platform was for sound money, "with every dollar good as gold." McKinley, leaning to the business side of the Republican party, repudiated the nativists and actively courted the growing immigrant vote—on the first day of the convention, the invocation was given by a rabbi, on the second by a black Methodist minister.

The 1896 campaign could be called the first modern election. McKinley's business allies, terrified of Bryan, raised money like no previous campaign ever had. The old era of campaign financing—taking kickbacks from the party faithful who had scored government jobs—now gave way to the seduction of the wealthy. McKinley's handler, Mark Hannah, famously asked business leaders how much Bryan's election would cost them—and then asked for a check.

The traditional nineteenth-century campaigns had organized armies of singing, marching, cheering party workers, Now, all the McKinley money went to something new: distributing information to voters, explaining policy difference, and generating publicity—right down to a new invention, the campaign buttons they handed out. McKinley refused to go out on the hustings, so the party carted voters to his house in Canton, Ohio, where he addressed them, day after day. By the end of the campaign, an astonishing five hundred thousand people had stood before his porch and listened to the candidate. A battalion of orators stumped the country in his name, conjuring up the terrors of a populist wild man in the White House.

William Jennings Bryan countered with a hoarse, merciless, exhausting speaking tour that spanned eighteen thousand miles and addressed millions of people. Pouring over railroad schedules and sleeping in train stations, Bryan was only the third presidential campaign to hit the trail (Stephen Douglas was the first back in 1860). In some places, the mobs roared so loud that no one could hear an introduction and the chair simply motioned Bryan to take the stand. In New Haven, Yale men heckled him—and he hectored them right back. "I am not speaking now to the sons who are sent to college on the proceeds off ill-gotten gains. I will wait until those sons have exhausted what their fathers have left, and I will appeal to their children." Not a bad prediction. One generation later, the economy would crash, many of those Yale men would lose their fortunes, and a new generation of populists would finally break through.[65]

Contemporary campaign strategists, looking back, wonder just what Bryan was doing campaigning in New York or New Haven where he never stood a chance. But Bryan was not just another politician. He was an evangelist, all fired up with dreams of a new, more democratic, more just America—just like the Populists who had embraced him.

HEADLINES SCREAMED THE OUTCOME: "M'KINLEY!" FOR THE first time in a quarter century, the Republicans broke 50 percent of the presidential popular vote (winning 51 percent to 46.7 percent) and took both chambers of Congress. Bryan came within four close states of winning, but the stubborn bottom line remains: the nineteenth-century Populists, on their own or in the Democratic Party, never reached beyond the Bible belt and agrarian heartland. They never won outside the South and West.[66]

Urban workers failed to hear the evangelical cry rising out of the Great Plains. Silver held no magic for laborers who, unlike farmers, were not ensnared by debt. Even Bryan's fabulous oration had reverberated with prairie bias. "You come to us and tell us that the great cities are in favor of the gold standard," Bryan had said.

"We reply . . . burn down your cities and leave our farms, and your cities will spring up again as if by magic; but destroy our farms, and the grass will grow in the streets of every city in the country." No surprise, then, that the cities and the industrial workers didn't hear him.

The 1896 election marked a break in national politics. More than two decades of microscopic differences in the presidential elections and divided government gave way to a comfortable Republican lock of every branch for the next fourteen years. As professionals took over the campaigns and the Republicans dominated, enthusiasm waned, and turnout began to fall. In the five presidential elections before 1896, turnout averaged 78 percent; in the five after, it fell to 65 percent—and kept right on going down.

The Democrats split into populist and conservative factions. The party nominated Bryan three times (in 1896, 1900, and 1908), but he never matched the results of that first crusade. Between Bryan's tries, the Democrats turned the other way and in 1904 nominated Alton Parker—a New York judge, a friend of labor, and a conservative who supported the gold standard. The Democrats learned that there was no market for a second conservative party when it took its worst drubbing of the era in that election. After that, the divided Democrats, saddled with their two-thirds rule, plunged into a series of nightmare conventions that ran to 46 ballots (in 1912) and 103 (in 1924). Gradually, the party moved away from the conservative, states' rights, antifederal government philosophy of Grover Cleveland and toward what skeptics jeered as Bryanism.

CONVENTIONAL WISDOM ENDS THE POPULIST STORY IN 1896. They blundered into the Democratic Party and were never heard from again. But there's another way to see it. The Populists bequeathed to the Democrats a new philosophy and a bold, new attitude about the role of government. "Between 1896 and 1948," sums up political scientist John Gerring, the Democrats turned populist—both in their rhetoric and in their policies.[67]

Listen to Woodrow Wilson, after the Democrats finally broke through for a brief interlude in the era of Republican domination. Always the professor, Wilson used his first inaugural address, in 1913, to tell the people what they had been thinking when they voted for him. Americans, he said, had begun to awaken to something "alien" and "sinister" and "evil" in the land. "We have not stopped to count the [industrial machine's] human cost." Who was to blame? "Those who stood at the levers of control." What should be done? "The government [must] be put at the service of humanity." Woodrow Wilson sounded uncannily like the Populists back in Omaha. One historian summed up that inaugural address as "Bryanism with a Princeton accent."[68]

Franklin Roosevelt took office twenty years later, and his inaugural, too, rang with populist scorn for the greedy rich: "The unscrupulous money changers . . . know only the rules of a generation of self-seekers. They have no vision and where there is no vision, the people perish." Again, FDR reached for strong government that would "put people to work," engage in "redistribution . . . on a national scale," "drive the money changers from the temples of our civilization," and—that essential Populist dream—staunch "the foreclosure of small homes and farms." Eventually, his rhetoric would reimagine freedom itself—along the lines first laid out by the likes of Ignatius Donnelly. Freedom was only possible after life's basic needs were satisfied—and the government would do that job. Former President Herbert Hoover scribbled down his feelings when he first encountered William Jennings Bryan in 1896: "It was my first shock at intellectual dishonesty as the foundation for economics." And FDR? No more than "Bryanism under new words and methods," wrote Hoover in 1933.[69]

For a dangerous and exhilarating moment, the Populists had reached across the race line and tried to build an interracial coalition of poor farmers. They won some victories, but racial fears, intimidation, and violence eventually crushed their project. In the aftermath, a white supremacist backlash twisted southern populism right around—from the shared interests of the poor to savage cries for racial domination.

The Republicans, meanwhile, abandoned their black allies after one last try to pass the Lodge Force Bill. Their campaign platforms made feeble promises that leaders like presidents Theodore Roosevelt and William Howard Taft shrugged off as impractical.

The Democrats remained the party of white supremacy. Woodrow Wilson was the only Democrat to take the presidency between 1896 and 1932. When he first met his cabinet, in 1913, the Postmaster General, Albert Burleson of Texas, immediately raised the issue of race. He wanted to segregate his department (which employed more than half of all federal workers). "It is almost impossible to have different drinking vessels" he explained. And it was entirely improper for black men to supervise white women. The Post Office Building not so quietly closed its dining room to black employees. None of the restaurants in Washington served African Americans, why should the federal government? Over at the second largest department, the Treasury, William McAdoo from Tennessee was also adamant about segregating. Wilson seemed to think it a side issue, acquiesced, and presided over a largely segregated executive branch.[70]

Two years later, D. W. Griffith released his extraordinary movie *The Birth of a Nation*. Before it, cinema had essentially recorded stage plays. Griffith used multiple cameras and different angles to introduce outdoor action. He deployed his technical sorcery to transform the Ku Klux Klan from a terrorist organization into a heroic protector of imperiled innocence. Fantastic scenes, a kind of cinema no one had ever seen before, featured the white knights of the KKK galloping to save the day and protect white innocents from African American brutes in blue (Yankee) uniforms with the usual in mind. Audiences were induced to cheer the KKK riding to the rescue; the KKK ending the reign of (black) terror; the KKK escorting the damsels they had saved; and, in the grand finale, the KKK disarming African Americans and blocking them from the polls. The film was firmly rooted in the mythology of the lost cause that had conquered both history and social science over the past two decades—not least in the historical writing of Woodrow Wilson. Histories, social science monographs, novels, and now movies all embellished the same bigoted mythology: African Americans had not been ready for freedom after the Civil War and they were not ready for it now. The reign of white supremacist violence was rewritten as the restoration of law, order, and good government. The film depicted "the birth of a nation," because with the race question finally tossed aside (and African Americans in their place), North and South could come together in a new and deeper union.[71]

Woodrow Wilson screened *Birth of a Nation* at the White House and is said to have declared, "It is like writing history with lightening. And my only regret is that it is all so terribly true." The comment reflects his own writing about Reconstruction, which made the same points dramatized in the film, but it is probably apocryphal; it did not appear until decades afterward and there is not even any circumstantial evidence to support Wilson having said it. And yet, the quotation stuck to him precisely because it reflected his own attitudes and his administration's policies.[72]

The recently organized NAACP bitterly criticized the Democrats for segregating the federal bureaucracy. A Wilson supporter, William Monroe Trotter, led a black delegation to the White House to protest, and Wilson lost his cool. The president tried to explain that black workers were less efficient—but as an enlightened liberal, he understood that it was only a matter of time before they improved. An unpersuaded Trotter bluntly criticized the segregation of government offices. Wilson barked back, "You are the only American citizen that has ever come into this office [and] talked to me with a tone [like that]. . . . You spoiled the whole cause for which you came." Wilson later lamented that he'd lost his cool but had no second thoughts about his views.[73]

As the Democrats segregated Washington, African Americans were on the move across the country. Beginning in 1916, they left the rural South and headed North, the first wave of a great migration that would run for decades. Once they were up North, black men and women engaged dazzling new ideas—like Marcus Garvey's pan-African nationalism. They would organize, participate, and eventually make their way into the Democratic Party. As they did so, they recreated the same conundrum—and the same perilous opportunity—that had faced the Populists, and before them, the Whigs: How to run a party precariously balanced between southern voters, intent on white supremacy, and reformers committed to racial justice? That is the story of the next chapter—and of the American future.

The other great American identity clash also slipped out of national politics. The parties had clashed over immigration from the very first contested election. For years, the Democrats had puckishly derided their opponents for following in the tradition of the Alien and Sedition Acts, passed by the long-defunct Federalists. Now, the long debate took a new turn. New coalitions rose up and tangled the partisan lines; immigration opponents faced off against supporters within both major parties. Opponents slowly won the argument and steered restrictions through the checks and balances of American politics (including no less than five presidential vetoes for literacy tests alone). As the golden gates closed, a long tribal conflict over the nature of America and Americans slowly faded from view.

By the time the Franklin Roosevelt administration came to power in 1933, the storms that had dominated nineteenth-century

American politics had stilled. Immigration had been reduced to a trickle. Neither party—nor even a major party faction in either party—pressed for racial justice. In the West, bigotry bore down on families from China, Japan, or Mexico. In the South, black communities quietly mobilized against legal repression but failed to engage either party in a major way.

There were, to be sure, terrible political battles. But, for the most part, the parties did not animate them. Instead, the differences between Democrats and Republicans grew fuzzy. Each party split into left and right wings. They debated by day and drank bourbon together by night. By every measure, party conflict and partisanship declined. But quietly, far below the surface of American politics, things were changing.

MEANWHILE, CULTURAL IMAGES AND EXPECTATIONS EVOLVED. Despite all that dire social science data, those dangerous immigrants from dreadful places—Italy or Poland or Finland—raised families that prospered and became American. The kids just chuckled when their grandparents fractured the English language, or reminisced about the old country, or cooked the wonderful foods they had brought with them. Now that there was no danger of taking it seriously, everyone beamed over Emma Lazarus's "give me your huddled masses yearning to breathe free."

My father, the adopted grandson of an uneducated Italian immigrant, attended Columbia University. When he first set foot on campus, in 1940, the Jewish and Italian students didn't feel overt discrimination. But they acknowledged the facts of life. They were limited by quotas and segregated into one fraternity house. They referred to their classmates as "the Americans." Then World War II interrupted their studies. Everyone put on uniforms and went overseas to fight. Those who came back attended a university where every one of them felt 100 percent American.

Except, of course, for the black kids—war heroes who returned to jeers of "boy" or worse. And the Japanese kids who had volunteered to fight from the bleak internment camps where their families had been locked up. And the Mexican kids. All these Americans from all these different backgrounds were heading into a new racial storm. It would remake American politics. It would remake America.

SIX

THE NEW DEAL AND THE ORIGINS OF CONTEMPORARY AMERICA (1933–1948)

Willie Earle was a twenty-four-year old African American who loved his job as a truck driver. But he had epilepsy, and when his boss witnessed a fit, Earle was fired. One evening in February 1947, Willie hired a cab to drive him to his mother's house near Greenville, South Carolina. Later that night someone fatally stabbed the driver and the police immediately nabbed Earle. The taxi-driving fraternity—"tough guys untainted by intelligence," sniffed English critic Rebecca West writing in the *New Yorker*—got together a posse and stormed the jail. They burst in brandishing shotguns, and the jailer helpfully pointed to Willie, who was sharing a cell with a man who had bounced some checks. The cop sternly warned the mob not to cuss while they dragged Earle out of the building. Fifty taxicabs rumbled away, down an isolated road. When the convoy got deep into the countryside, the drivers pulled over, hauled Earle out of his car, dumped him into a slaughtering pen, bashed his head, slashed at him with their knives, and finally shot him dead. The *Greenville News* coolly put the murder in perspective. "The last lynching in Pickens Country, executed in a well-organized manner about 35 years ago, created no flurry of investigations."[1]

This time there *was* a "flurry of investigations." The murderers signed detailed confessions—all had been accessories to murder, all fingered the same triggerman who had actually killed Earle, and thirty-one of them went to trial. On the surface, what followed looked all too familiar. Despite warnings from the bench, the defense played to hard racial attitudes. "Why, you would have thought someone had found a new atomic bomb," purred one attorney, referring to the great crowd that had descended on the trial, and "all it was was a dead nigger boy." "Willie Earle is dead," said another lawyer, "and I wish more like him was dead." Two African American reporters were hustled away from the press table and sent upstairs with the rest of the black folk—though the defense objected, calculating that the presence of black outsiders would help push the all-white South Carolina jury to acquit. They needn't have worried. The defense called no witnesses and the jury took just five hours to find all thirty-one men not guilty.

If the lynching and the trial looked familiar, the national reaction to them was not. Condemnation rang up and down the Democratic Party. The president denounced the lynching. The attorney general dispatched the FBI which made the arrests and recorded the confessions. The South Carolina governor (a Democrat, naturally) called the killing "a disgrace to the state" and assigned a star prosecutor to the case. All reflected a head-spinning political novelty: both parties were after the black vote.[2]

When we left the story in the last chapter, both parties had turned their backs on black voters. Democrats confirmed their status as the party of thumping white supremacy when Woodrow Wilson's administration segregated government offices in 1917. And the Republicans had piously abandoned the fight for black suffrage—it was not, they declared, in the African Americans' best interests. What changed?

Once again, black Americans had gone into motion. Recall how fugitives, racing out of slavery, challenged the fragile political equilibrium before the Civil War. In the first decades of the twentieth century, almost a million black people left the rural South for the north and west, the first stage of a vast internal American migration from the South to the northern and western cities that would number some six million people by its end in 1970. When the newcomers arrived, the city Democrats, often locked in political contests with rural Republicans, began to recruit them away from the party that took their votes for granted. African Americans filtered into a party dominated, on the national level, by white supremacists. Here was a bizarre political alliance—conservative segregationists from the South, African Americans in the North, and organized labor rising on the left.

African Americans came into the Democratic Party in surges over three decades—from the election of 1936, when a majority voted Democratic for the first time, to the election of 1964, when nine out of ten black voters began identifying as Democrats. Their shift helped transform both parties—moving the Democrats left and enabling Republicans to go right.

This breaks with the traditional story in two big ways. First, in popular memory, the fight for civil rights sprang up on a city bus in Montgomery, Alabama, when Rosa Parks courageously refused to move. This chapter shows how the tectonic plates—black activism, southern reaction, and shifting coalitions—began rumbling all the way back in the 1930s. The classic civil rights movement of the 1950s and 1960s was the heroic breakthrough in a battle that had already been raging for decades.[3]

Second, historians have recently stressed the segregationist chokehold on New Deal policy. As Ira Katznelson puts it in his monumental book, *Fear Itself*, the New Deal coalition looked like an alliance between South Africa (apartheid) and Sweden (liberal social policy)—one completely dominated by the white supremacists. All true. But a wider historical gaze shows just how the unhappy alliance was part of a remarkable transformation. African Americans climbed into the party of white supremacy (in 1936), pushed for brash new racial policies, and by the end of the New Deal (in 1948), sent segregationists bolting out of the Democratic convention and running their own Dixiecrat candidate.

This chapter tells the story of how the Democratic Party took on black voters and began its long evolution: from the party of white supremacy to the party of civil rights, from the party of states' rights to the party of big government in the nineteenth-century Populist's mode. The changes in the Democratic Party forced the party of Lincoln to find a new identity of its own.

———

AL CAPONE WAS A FLAMBOYANT THUG WHO DRESSED IN EX-pensive lavender- or lemon-colored suits and dispensed wads of cash to anyone who caught his fancy. He celebrated one birthday by snatching jazz pianist Fats Waller at gunpoint, making him play for three anxious days, then stuffing his pockets with $1,000 bills and sending him home. Capone built an empire unapologetically selling liquor during Prohibition, which outlawed all liquor sales between 1920 and 1933. He raked in up to $105 million a year (the equivalent of over $1.3 billion today) and spent a third of it on bribes—judges, politicians, reporters, and half the cops in Chicago crowded onto his payroll.[4]

The massive payoffs tip us to something new. With Prohibition, the national government had launched an ambitious effort to change the everyday habits of ordinary people. Unscrupulous operators had always bribed important public officials, but now the sheer scope of the government's dry enforcement effort required the vast network of bribes (or bungs, as they were called). Prohibition introduced big government—the New Deal would soon turn it to entirely different purposes.

All the jazz and corruption and booze reflected a vast change. America had turned urban. By 1930, 56 percent of the population lived in cities—up from 39 percent at the turn of the century, and 6 percent a century before that. The big cities and their loose attitudes horrified small-town Americans. Prohibition was, in part, an effort to tame the dangerous metropolis. Instead, it kindled a cultural war. Urban reporters made a sarcastic routine of arriving in an unfamiliar city, setting their watches, and reporting how long it took them to nose out and gulp down an illegal drink. They usually managed in under ten minutes—a sassy measure, they implied, of Prohibition's flat-out failure. But those cynics would have had a much harder time finding their illicit booze in, say, rural Oklahoma or the farm towns of Ohio where people fervently supported the dry regime.[5]

The election of 1928 pitted the two visions of America against one another. The secretary of commerce, Republican Herbert Hoover, nailed the dry flag onto his party's mast and celebrated Prohibition as a "great social and economic experiment, noble in motive and far reaching in purpose" (and never mind that Secretary Hoover himself regularly nipped over to the Belgian Embassy for a beer). The Democrats nominated New York governor Al Smith, who embodied everything the rural conservatives despised: an unapologetic, big city, Roman Catholic, Tammany Hall politician from an immigrant family who wanted to back off national Prohibition and let the states make alcohol policy for themselves.

The election wasn't even close. Al Smith took only eight states (out of forty-eight) and even fell in southern Democratic states like Texas and North Carolina, which had not voted for a Republican president since Reconstruction. But beneath the headlines lay the first signs of the looming political dispensation. The urban vote that had eluded William Jennings Bryan was now trickling to the Democrats. The eight states that Al Smith did carry included a shocker: the rocked-ribbed Republicans in Massachusetts who had not cast a majority vote for a Democrat since James Monroe ran unopposed in 1820. Local Democratic leaders had been busy wooing the new generation of voters that had arrived in the past decades—immigrants from Europe, African Americans from the rural South, and industrial workers from all over.

Herbert Hoover was in the White House for just eight months when the stock market crashed in October 1929, followed by the Great Depression that left almost thirteen million workers—one in four—unemployed. Between the collapse in 1893 (which hit just after Democrats took control of Washington) and the crash in 1929, the Republicans had dominated American politics, electing six presidents to the Democrats' one. Now amid the new economic rubble, the Democrats seized their chance. They would go on to win the next five presidential elections, gather a massive congressional majority for six years, and control both chambers for nine of the next ten congressional sessions. The Democrats won the elbow room to reconstruct American government. By the end of the era, twenty years later, a legion of new programs had redefined government, both parties had reinvented themselves, and Americans had a bold new philosophy of government (and of liberty) to argue about.[6]

THE ELECTION OF 1932 FOLLOWED THREE YEARS OF ECOnomic crisis. The Democrats, meeting in Chicago, made an apparently conventional choice when they picked Governor Franklin D. Roosevelt of New York, but he immediately exploded tradition. Rather than waiting for a delegation to arrive and formally present him with the nomination, Roosevelt flew in to address the delegates—the first presidential candidate to accept the nomination in person. The unexpected speech reverberated with populist verve. We were in an economic fix, said FDR, for a very simple reason. Greed.

> The consumer is forgotten . . . the worker is forgotten. . . . Enormous corporate surpluses piled up—the most stupendous in history. Where, under the spell of delirious speculation, did those surpluses

go? . . . Into the call-money market of Wall Street, either directly by the corporations, or indirectly through the banks. Those are the facts. Why blink at them?[7]

On the campaign trail, Roosevelt put the stamp of modernity to the Populist dream of an active government guaranteeing everyone the basics. "We have to apply the earlier concepts of American Government to the conditions of today," he announced. The mix of old rights and new economic order meant that government "owes to everyone" the chance to possess, "through his own work," enough "plenty sufficient to his need." It was the government's responsibility, he continued, to provide for everyone in "childhood, sickness, [and] old age." The old idea of liberty, proclaimed in the Bill of Rights, begins "Congress shall make no law." Now, Roosevelt and his New Deal submitted a new concept of liberty that called on Congress to do just the opposite—make many laws.[8]

The Democrats defeated incumbent Herbert Hoover in a landslide. They took the popular vote by more than 17 percent and won the Electoral College 472 to 59. Every description of the new administration sounds the same: Pure Frenzy. "The country demands bold, persistent experimentation," said the president. "Take a method and try it. If it fails"—and much of it did—"admit it frankly and try another. But above all, try something." The Democrats tried things with gusto. But below the turbulence, they honored their party's traditions. There was little in the administration's multi-ring circus to agitate the southern oligarchs who still dominated the party. At least, not at first.[9]

At the start of the New Deal, as the administration called its program, every penny the government spent passed through a powerful segregationist filter. The southern Democrats dominated Congress, and with the southern economy devastated by the Great Depression, they enthusiastically approved the ambitious federal programs. However, they crafted each effort around their prime directive:

federal money must never make (southern) black men and women independent—or, needless to say, do anything to disrupt segregation or white supremacy. The New Deal relief programs carefully funneled money through reliable state or local governments, which could be trusted to distribute benefits without disrupting racial relations in the South.

A few programs will illustrate the creative, chaotic, carefully segregated New Deal approach. The administration quickly established a paramilitary Civilian Conservation Corps (or CCC). Army officers supervised young men, dressed in khaki uniforms, who planted trees, erected fire towers, and built bridges. The program eventually employed some three million men in racially segregated units. The Federal Emergency Relief Act (or FERA) made grants to the states to stimulate employment, eventually creating work for twenty million people. The Works Progress Administration (or WPA) put people who had been approved by local welfare agencies to work building highways, bridges, sewers, recreation facilities, and over one hundred airports—including what would eventually become Atlanta-Hartsfield, New York La Guardia, and Los Angeles International.

The United States had never before seen this kind of job creation from the federal government. But at the same time, there was nothing radical or disruptive about the programs' administration—they all operated through reassuringly familiar hierarchies: the military (in the case of the CCC), the states (which oversaw FERA), or the local welfare boards (which oversaw the WPA).

The New Deal constructed something more monumental than airports in 1935 when it designed the Social Security Act, which included seven major programs. Congressional Democrats wrenched one of them, Aid to Families with Dependent Children (AFDC, later known as welfare), out of federal hands and placed it safely within the jurisdiction of state and local authorities. Providing aid to the poor was exactly the sort of thing that might disrupt racial and economic relations. Local officials, reasoned the southern democrats, would know best about touchy matters like the moral character or the race of the beneficiaries.[10]

At the heart of the social security package lay the retirement pensions for people over sixty-five. The administration carefully curated a safe, conservative image for the program (now known simply as Social Security). Workers *earned* their benefits by paying employment taxes during their working years. Although today's taxes flow directly to today's beneficiaries, the program looked more like a mandatory savings plan than like the dole. Congress pushed most African Americans out of the program by excluding the sectors where, at the time, a majority of them worked—agriculture and domestic service. No, no, no, they insisted, when northern liberals asked rude questions, the exclusions had absolutely nothing to do with racial bias or racial anything. It was just "too cumbersome" to ask farmers or domestics to keep the records and pay the taxes that the program required. They had a point. Treasury department officials came before Congress and fretted over the difficulty of overseeing Social Security in exactly these professions. They pushed for the exclusion of farmers and domestic workers—as well as others professions that would be hard to administer, such as sailors. Later, historians would argue about whether it was cautious bureaucrats or anxious segregationists who had excluded most African Americans from Social Security. In fact, it was both. The bureaucrats' concern was perfectly aligned with the southern Democratic obsession—keeping African Americans segregated and subordinated.[11]

The Social Security Act eventually changed American governance. It lodged a large, growing, and enormously popular government benefit firmly in the middle class. The program cracked open divisions within each party. The segregationist Democrats fumed as both parties embraced Social Security and began using their support for the program to bid for voters, black and white. By 1940, the Democratic Party platform would call for an extension of Social Security to those who were not already covered, and by 1944, the

Republican platform would match them and call explicitly for covering agricultural workers. Despite the southerners' efforts, federal money would eventually flow around their carefully contrived filters and into the pockets of black workers.

Social Security sparked an even longer debate among Republicans—one that goes on to the present day. Most Republicans had quietly opposed the program when it came before Congress, and all but one GOP house member voted to bury it in committee before voting aye on the final passage—they voted against it before they voted for it. But once the program had taken root and grown popular, by the end of the New Deal, moderate Republicans acquiesced. "Should any political party attempt to abolish Social Security," wrote Dwight Eisenhower to his skeptical brother, "you should not hear of that party again in our history." Conservatives forcefully disagreed. Social Security posed a formidable barrier to their dreams of a small national government. In their eyes, the program was—and still is—the embodiment of an overweening government buying votes, binding the people to the Democrats, breaking long American traditions of self-reliance, and building an enormous entitlement establishment that would be almost impossible to reverse or even diminish.[12]

IN 1932, HARPER'S MAGAZINE DESCRIBED THE STATE OF THE union movement: "declining," "sick," "dying," "dead," and "no one could revive it." Union membership had dropped from five million in 1920 to under three million in 1930.[13]

What had happened? For starters, employers had always ferociously opposed mass unions that signed up armies of workers as opposed to small groups of skilled craftsmen. The nation's largest union, the American Federation of Labor (or AFL) felt exactly the same way. Skilled workers could wring concessions out of employers;

organizing the masses, on the other hand, would bring retribution from employers, rock the labor organizations (possibly threatening the leaders), and open the door to immigrants. When a group of Italians tried to join the New York Federation of Labor, organizer Bill Collins famously demurred: "My wife can always tell by the smell of my clothes what breed of foreigner I have been hanging out with."[14]

Then the Roosevelt administration barged in. The administration's first recovery effort, the National Industrial Recovery Act (NIRA), encouraged industries to put aside "dog eat dog" competition and negotiate codes of fair competition—agreements that covered prices, production levels, wages, and hours. The government shelved the pesky antitrust laws, which forbade competitors from colluding, and, instead, urged them to work together. Market competition, they reasoned, had created the crisis; perhaps the solution lay in cooperation. Lurking in the NIRA's fine print was a small stick of industrial relations dynamite.[15]

Section 7 (a) of the NIRA included a short line about labor: Employees "shall have the right to organize and bargain collectively through representatives of their own choosing." There were no enforcement mechanisms, but when it came time for the erstwhile competitors in each industry to negotiate codes—wages, hours, and other details—union representatives might be at the table. The clause became important because a handful of union leaders saw its potential and jumped on it. John L. Lewis—the loud, meaty, pompous, shrewd United Mine Workers (UMW) boss—dispatched one hundred organizers into mining areas. "The president wants you to unionize," exaggerated Lewis. "The President Wants You to Unionize," repeated the sound trucks and leaflets and organizers. It wasn't exactly true—but who could argue with the results? Lewis claimed to have brought in 128,000 new members in Pennsylvania, 90 percent of all coal miners in Colorado, and 125 new local union organizations in the oil fields. Across the industrial landscape, workers mobbed into meetings and demanded unions, which still did not want them.[16]

In the summer of 1934, a wave of strikes swept the country, roughly half over the right to unionize. The most dramatic was a longshoreman strike that ran up the West Coast. Workers especially resented the morning "shape-up"—a routine in which longshoremen milled about the docks while imperious company reps picked some and arbitrarily blacklisted others. When the strike began, the owners moved to crush the troublesome workers' movement. The standoff led to gunfire, fistfights, burning cars, and two dead workers. The next day, the National Guard and its tanks rumbled into the city. The clash spread into something rare in American history, a general strike. Workers shut down San Francisco for four days. Eventually, the strike collapsed amid factional fighting between unions. Both sides accepted arbitration and declared victory, but, in the end, the workers won their chief demands: recognition of their union and effective control over hiring.[17]

As the wave of national strikes crested in February 1935, Democratic Senator Robert Wagner of New York proposed more potent labor legislation protecting the right to unionize. Conservative Republicans called it communism; liberals responded that, on the contrary, it would be a bulwark against communism; and the American Communist Party unwittingly boosted the liberals by denouncing the proposal. Despite all the furor, Wagner's National Labor Relations Act floated through the Senate, sixty-three to twelve, won a belated endorsement from the administration, and went on to a resounding victory in the House. As he signed it, President Roosevelt appeared to limit the act, explaining that it only applied when repressing unions would "burden or obstruct interstate commerce."[18]

But there was no repressing what happened next. The new law galvanized the union movement. With his usual bombast, John Lewis and a group of leftist labor leaders formed the Committee (later Congress) of Industrial Organizations (CIO) and signed up industrial workers by the thousands. The hidebound AFL had no choice but to throw off its craft union philosophy and struggle to keep up with the roaring CIO.[19]

Many business leaders continued to resist. The workers developed a new tactic: sit-down strikes in which they would occupy strategically located plants. With workers holding the building, it was more difficult for employers to break the strike by replacing them. A series of dramatic confrontations grabbed national attention. In Flint, Michigan, for example, strikers occupied a GM factory and cut off the production of new cars. Governor Frank Murphy refused to clear the plant by force. John Lewis later imagined that he had convinced the governor not to take sides with a bombastic threat. "I shall walk up to the largest window in the plant . . . bare my bosom . . . [and] when you order your troops to fire, mine will be the first breast that those bullets will strike! And as my body falls . . . to the ground, you listen to the voice of your grandfather [executed for rebellion in Ireland] as he whispers in your ear, 'Frank, are you sure you are doing the right thing?'" The story is fantasy, for Murphy was, as the newspapers put it, "a friend to labor" and was never going to become "Bloody Murphy." But the exchange reflects the drama and intensity of the moment. In the end, GM capitulated and announced that it would negotiate with union representatives as throngs of workers and their families cheered. Powerful union organizations emerged, pulsating with energy, battling recalcitrant industries and fighting amongst themselves. The union ranks swelled from 2.7 million workers in 1929 (under 7 percent of the work force) to 8.8 million by 1939 and 14 million in 1945, comprising more than a third of all nonagricultural workers.[20]

Congress had offered the unions legitimacy—first in the very limited context of the NIRA, then under the more formidable NLRA, which came to be known as the Wagner Act. The wasting labor unions reorganized and rounded up new recruits. The New Dealers reaped the benefits of New Deal labor policy. Organized labor was soon deploying campaign workers, get out the vote drives, policy proposals, and plenty of cash—all to bolster Democrats.

Amid signing up the industrial workers and confronting business, the CIO kicked up all sorts of controversies. But nothing it did was more perilous than its decision to organize across the race line. Leaders, some influenced by the Communists, insisted on class solidarity. Racial exclusion would only divide the workers and offer employers a pool of desperate strikebreakers. Union members and their locals often clung to their racism, but the CIO leadership insisted on organizing both black and white workers. When it came to race politics during the New Deal, black activists sometimes found that they had a vibrant, disruptive ally by their sides.

———————

Two cars crashed on a crowded bridge during a steamy June night in Detroit. The drivers, one black and one white, began to argue, and before long, venomous rumors rippled out from the fender bender. White neighborhoods heard that a black man had raped a white woman. In black districts, a rumor circulated that white thugs had killed a mother and child by hurling them from a bridge. Deep racial resentments that had been building since African Americans had begun moving up from the South now escalated into a riot that shook Detroit for three days. Six thousand federal troops rode in with tanks. By the end, thirty-four people lay dead, over four hundred were wounded, and almost eighteen hundred were arrested—three quarters of each were African Americans. Like the rumors that started the riot, there were two entirely different explanations for the trouble.

Mayor Edward Jeffries blamed "Negro hoodlums" and added, "I am rapidly losing my patience with those negro leaders [who] are more vocal in their caustic criticism of the police department than they are in educating their own people to their responsibilities as citizens."[21]

African Americans (and, later, most historians) saw it differently. Mobs of young men "roam[ed] the streets in search of negro victims," testified the president of the NAACP, Walter White, who had dashed into Detroit during the violence. "The police made no effort to check the assaults." On the contrary, White saw a police captain board a streetcar and tell the black passengers that he would lead them into custody for their own protection. When they came forward, he coldly turned them "over to the mob to be beaten to death." The president of the NAACP's local branch, Dr. James McClendon, directly answered Mayor Jeffries' complaint that black leaders were not "educating their own people" to be proper citizens. "Citizens become educated to their 'responsibilities as citizens' when they are treated as citizens." And if the police department wanted respect, it should stop "killings, vile name calling, wanton, unnecessary arrests of colored citizens, [and addressing] our citizens as 'niggers.'"[22]

Rapid growth exacerbated the simple bigotry. Thirty years earlier, Detroit had been a town of just 459,000 people, 99 percent of them white. Now, the population had more than tripled to 1.6 million. Two hundred thousand African Americans had been lured from the South by the promise of factory jobs. When they arrived, they faced hostility on the streets, discrimination in the workplace, and few neighborhoods where they could live—or even wander through.

The Roosevelt administration tried to ameliorate the problem with a housing project, named after Sojourner Truth, a former slave who had operated an underground railroad in Michigan. But the project was on what whites considered their territory. When the first families tried to move in, a mob attacked the new neighbors and smashed their furniture. When a black crowd gathered and fought back, police broke up the scuffle, arresting two hundred blacks and three whites.[23]

On the surface, the Great Migration seemed to deliver black Americans into another land of prejudice, discrimination, and misery. The explosions in Detroit were just the latest in a long string of riots that greeted the Great Migration. Killing sprees had erupted in Chicago, Baltimore, Tulsa, Omaha, East Saint Louis, Los Angeles, Springfield (Illinois), Springfield (Ohio), and the list runs on.

But the black men and women who had moved up north had a way to fight back. They had the vote. Their ballots would slowly enact deep changes across American politics.

AFRICAN AMERICANS HAD ALWAYS IDENTIFIED WITH THE Party of Lincoln. By 1932, voters had sent twenty-three African Americans to Congress and every one of them a Republican. The first intimations of change came during the presidential campaign that year between Hoover and Roosevelt. Republicans had been out of the civil rights business since the Taft administration. Their 1932 party platform reverberated with indifference, promising "to maintain equal opportunity and rights for Negro citizens." Of course, there was no equal opportunity to maintain. In the sloughs of the depression, 95 percent of black Americans lived in poverty and three out of four in extreme poverty—less than a quarter of a living wage. At least thirty-eight people had been lynched in the past three years. The Republicans seemed more interested in luring southern states away from the Democrats than in helping black voters. But though the national party took them for granted, black voters had become important for Republicans in the northern cities.[24]

Since the alternative was the party of white supremacy, most black voters grimly continued to tick the Republican column. "Four more years [of Hoover]," editorialized a reluctant *Chicago Defender*, the largest black newspaper in the country, "will be better than a possible eight years of any Democrat." The South dominated the Democratic Party. Partially because restrictions on black voters were so effective, Dixie reelected its congressional representatives, year after year, giving them seniority in Congress. They chaired the committees that did the real work in Congress. Democrats in charge meant segregationists in control. Democratic presidents carefully deferred to them.[25]

But cracks had begun to appear in the black vote. In Kansas City, the Democratic political boss, T. J. Prendergast, began to court African American voters in the late 1920s, and now, in 1932, the city's black wards went 1,050 to 388 for Roosevelt and the Democrats. In Pittsburgh, the African American newspaper *Pittsburgh Courier* endorsed FDR and black districts split half and half (the *Courier* would surpass the *Defender* and become the largest black paper in 1937). In the black precincts of South Philadelphia, South Chicago, and Harlem, roughly a quarter of the vote slipped to the Democrats. "Never before . . . have Negros voted Democratic," cheered the *Courier*. In this election, however, "the Negro played a magnificent role and voted a warning to the Republican Party."[26]

The results did not attract much attention in the white press. After all, most African Americans had voted for Hoover. But black observers, including W. E. B. Du Bois, immediately saw that more than two million northern black voters were going into play and might very well swing close elections.[27]

President Roosevelt's political advisors also noticed, and they organized a drive to win the black vote in the next presidential election in 1936. The president and, especially, First Lady Eleanor Roosevelt, gathered an informal group of black political and civic leaders, known as the Black Cabinet. With some fanfare, the Democratic Party organized a national campaign to win the black vote. The president himself went to Howard University, a black school in Washington, DC, with genial words. "There should be no forgotten men and no forgotten races," he said—though, with an eye to his coalition partners from segregated states, he appended the inevitable caveat: "as far as humanly possible."[28]

The returns in 1936 were dramatic and, this time, everyone noticed. After all those years in the Republican Party, black voters overwhelmingly turned to Democrats. At the time, press reports put the figure at 90 percent of black voters. More recent estimates suggest it was closer to 70 percent—still a landslide by any measure. Moderate northern Republicans immediately saw their peril. "If the Republican Party expects to continue as a going concern," ran a typical editorial, "it seems essential to recover lost ground with the Negroes of the North." Northern Republicans would work hard to do just that, and black voters would swing back and forth between the parties for the next two decades. But when asked which party they identified with, the number of African Americans who answered Republican would never again top 40 percent.[29]

Why the great leap to the Democrats? At the time, analysts pointed to the party's programs. New Deal relief touched more than one in four black families. The CCC employed two million black men, even if they were made to work in strictly segregated units. The FERA and the WPA provided more relief than African Americans had ever seen—and all during a time of acute distress. Yes, every program had to pass through a powerful segregationist filter. But despite the limits, federal money flowed into black communities as it never had before. Frank Kent, an influential columnist and a fierce critic of FDR, sarcastically explained why the black vote had gone Democratic. "First, federal patronage. Second federal funds. Third, administration coddling." And then the bottom line: "The job could never have been done without the Works Progress Administration."[30]

Dorothy Thompson, another popular columnist, echoed Kent. The Democrats were winning the black vote, she wrote, because they "pay" for it "with WPA jobs on the same terms as those offered to the whites." That was a wild exaggeration—black workers were not offered much of anything on equal terms as whites—but even the exaggeration would have been unthinkable in the past.

The relief going into black communities stirred anxiety in the white South. One frequently quoted South Carolina farmer put his finger on the danger to white supremacy: "This CWA wage is buzzing in our Niggers' heads." All the strenuous efforts to accommodate segregation were not enough to keep African Americans in their old place.[31]

SOUTHERNERS PERMITTED ONE CHANGE THAT THEY WOULD come to regret. Still basking in his party's approval at the 1936 convention, Roosevelt asked the Democratic convention to end its two-thirds requirement for nominating presidential candidates. The rule had long protected southern interests and had been a defining feature of Democratic conventions for almost a century—it had foiled Stephen Douglas in 1860 and yielded 102 weary ballots in 1924. Amid the good feeling in 1936, the southerners gave up their veto. Roosevelt and the Democrats went on to win their largest victory in modern times, taking over 60 percent of the popular vote and 523 electoral votes. The Republican candidate, Alf Landon of Kansas, carried just two small states worth eight electoral votes and came within 5 percent in only one other state. Congressional returns were just as lopsided: Democrats controlled the House, 334 to 88 and the Senate, 76 to 16.

But, below the surface, all was not easy in the Democratic coalition. Democratic Senator Ellison "Cotton Ed" Smith of South Carolina derided the party convention. "That great hall, bless God, looked like a checkerboard—a spot of white here, and a spot of black there." When an African American minister, Marshall Shepherd, rose to deliver the invocation, Cotton Ed turned foul: "But then, bless God, out on that platform walked a slew-footed, blue-gummed, kinky-headed, Senegambian! And he started praying and I started walking" right out of the convention. The next day, Senator Smith took the whole South Carolina delegation with him when he walked out to protest an address by Representative Arthur Mitchell from Chicago, the first black Democrat ever elected to Congress.[32]

Southern complaints spread and grew louder. "This catering by our National Party to the negro vote," wrote Senator Josiah Bailey, is "extremely distasteful" and "alarming." Cotton Ed Smith was soon contemplating more drastic action. "If we must have a Party in which we are scorned as southern Democrats," he said, "we will find a party which honors us."[33] One columnist immediately put his finger on the problem. The South is saddled with an administration which, through relief funds, federal patronage, and personal cultivation, deliberately has gone after the very vote in the North which the Democrats in the South have barred from the polls."[34]

Facing the menace of civil rights and organized labor, Dixie began to rediscover its fear of the feds. Southern Democrats led by Senator Josiah Bailey of North Carolina began to denounce the New Deal and runaway government. In 1937, he circulated the bipartisan *Conservative Manifesto*, coauthored with Republican Senator Arthur Vandenberg of Michigan, that called for less spending, less taxing, and less federal government—an early intimation of the conservative coalition to come.

At first, conservatives got little traction against the booming New Deal. In 1934, business leaders had organized an association, the American Liberty League, to fight against the taxes and the tyranny. The high-flying New Dealers hooted. Roosevelt scornfully decoded the Liberty League's hymnal: "Love God and forget your neighbor"—and their God, he added, was pronounced "Prop-er-ty." When Josiah Bailey and Arthur Vandenberg circulated their *Conservative Manifesto*, they faced more of the same. The liberal press honked at the *Manifesto*. "If you take every other word of the [*Manifesto*'s] preamble," ran one column in the *Minneapolis Star Tribune*, "it spells out the plutocratic national anthem, 'My heart is in the higher brackets chasing the dough.'"[35]

However, after the election in 1936, the tensions within the Democratic Party began to spread and the conservative opposition gained traction. Southern conservatives stopped supporting New Deal legislation. Many began to join the grumble: they no longer felt respected in their own party. But as one sympathetic columnist wrote, "There isn't any place else [for them] to go." The Republican Party was still despised in the South. And it, too, was split on civil rights. The Republican moderates in the North were still a major force in the party and, now that they were competing with northern Democrats for the black vote, they adamantly opposed any concessions to segregations at the national party conventions. For the time being, most southern conservatives had to content themselves with checking the New Deal liberalism they had once enabled.[36]

By the midterm election of 1938, Roosevelt had become so frustrated with the southern members that he launched a "purge campaign" to dispel the "copperheads" from the party—a reference to the northern Democrats who had opposed the Civil War and fought so hard against emancipation. The campaign was a complete flop. As usual, the conservatives all sailed easily to reelection—and they returned to Washington even more disgruntled. When Cotton Ed Smith was asked whether Roosevelt was his own worst enemy, he answered, "Not while I'm alive."[37]

Far from public view, northern Democrats began to break with their southern colleagues. Political scientist Eric Schickler ran down one straw blowing in the congressional wind. Southern Committee chairs in the House routinely bottled up civil rights bills in their committees. To pry the legislation out of the committee and onto the floor for further action, a majority of the House members had to sign a "discharge petition." Up until 1936, most northern Democrats supported their southern colleagues and refused to sign. But by the 1940s, they openly challenged their fellow party members and lined right up behind the discharges—during some sessions, up to 80 percent signed to bring civil rights measures to the floor.[38]

Liberals were especially frustrated about the party's failure to win legislation against lynching. Southern Democrats in the Senate simply buried each effort with a filibuster. Some did not even bother with the usual high-minded talk about states' rights and went straight to the antediluvian calumny: we need lynching to "protect the fair womanhood of the South from beasts." President Roosevelt ducked. When Walter White of the NAACP came to see the president, FDR bluntly refused to condemn lynching. "The Southerners . . . occupy strategic places on most of the Senate and House Committees," he told White. "If I come out for the anti-lynching bill now, they will block every bill I ask Congress to pass to keep America from collapsing. I just can't take that risk."[39]

As relations between northern and southern Democrats grew rancorous, columnists eagerly tattled about near violence. "North Carolina's lean and icily grim Senator Josiah Bailey," gossiped the *New York Daily News*, "had to be restrained by friends from slapping [FDR advisor Harry] Hopkins' face in the lounge of Washington's Mayflower Hotel." The stories multiplied. During World War II, southern members subverted legislation that would have made it easier for soldiers to vote—worried that the law would enable black soldiers to slip past the literacy tests and poll taxes. That exacerbated tensions within the party still further. "The savageness with which Virginia's [Harry] Bird ripped into [Pennsylvania's Joseph] Guffey" recalled "the days when members of Congress packed their personal shooting irons." Of course, the last time congressmen packed those shooting irons, racial issues were also the question of the day.[40]

IN 1941, CIVIL RIGHTS ACTIVISTS MADE A DARING MOVE. As the United States began gearing up for war, enormous military contracts jolted the American economy back to life and created worker shortages. But that didn't change the blunt facts of segregation. Most firms rejected black workers. "We have not employed Negroes for 25 years," reported Standard Steel "and [we] do not plan to start now." As Interior Secretary Harold Ickes wrote in his secret diary, "Hitler has drawn the color line openly and boldly but I doubt if the Negroes would fair much worse under him than under us."[41]

Black activists, led by A. Philip Randolph, decided to push back. Randolph was the president of the Brotherhood of Sleeping Car Porters, though he was not a porter himself—the union needed an independent leader whom the company could not fire. Randolph hit upon an audacious tactic. Ordinary black Americans would march on Washington to protest discrimination in industry. The idea terrified the white establishment, unnerved mainstream civil rights organizations, made black newspaper editors uneasy, and caught fire in the black communities. Randolph watched the excitement grow and kept boosting his predictions until he was claiming that one hundred thousand marchers would be in Washington, an incredible number in an era when travel was difficult.[42]

The threat agitated President Roosevelt. The Luftwaffe were pulverizing London across the Atlantic—mass protests over racial injustice in the United States would send a terrible message to the entire world. The president called a meeting in the White House. When Randolph and other civil rights leaders arrived, FDR's usual charm fell flat. "What Harvard class were you in, Mr. Randolph?" asked the president. "I never went to Harvard, Mr. President," replied Randolph coldly. Randolph offered to call off the march if Roosevelt issued an executive order forbidding racial discrimination in companies with government contracts.

The president of General Motors, William Knudson, was also present at the meeting, quietly scrutinizing the black men with what one called "ill-concealed hostility." The demand that government force businesses to hire black employees stirred him to life and he loudly objected. Government meddling in private hiring decisions was out of the question, he announced. Randolph fired back saying that GM had one of the worst racial records in the industry.

Roosevelt, growing impatient, curtly demanded an end to the march. Randolph refused. New York Mayor, Fiorella LaGuardia, who was also present, cheerfully waded into the impasse by turning to FDR and telling him that it was time to start drafting that order.

On June 25, 1941, President Roosevelt issued Executive Order 8802 barring racial discrimination in industries holding government contracts for war production and establishing a Fair Employment Practice Committee (FEPC), which would report to the president. Randolph called off the march, though he would be back in the Oval Office in 1963 challenging another reluctant Democratic president with yet another March on Washington. The FEPC had few real powers—it could not even enforce its own decisions. Still, it had a major impact. The first executive order on race since Reconstruction pried open the war industry and gave black workers a shot at its jobs—some 3 percent of the armament jobs went to African Americans by the end of 1942, and the number rose to very roughly 8 percent by 1945.

The order electrified black America. Even black newspapers that had nervously warned against the march now embraced a campaign that the *Pittsburgh Courier* called "Double V for victory." African Americans would defeat the country's adversaries abroad and apartheid at home. The experience taught black leaders that direct action got more results than polite behavior. It also galvanized a new migration of African Americans out of the South—a million moved north (and west) during the war. Some earned wages they had never dreamed of. Of course, they encountered the same old hostility—running into discrimination, hostility, and violence nearly everywhere they went. When a Packard plant in Detroit with twenty-five thousand employees promoted three African American workers, the whites defied their union and struck in protest. "I'd rather see Hitler and Hirohito win the war," screamed one strike organizer, "than work beside a nigger on the assembly line."[43]

For all that, the executive order, wrenched from a reluctant White House and implemented by a recalcitrant industry, became an emblem of pride and political strength. It is perhaps the only executive order in history to have inspired a poem. At Martin Luther King's request, Langston Hughes later wrote "Poem for a Man" to honor Randolph's victory.

> *Poem for a man*
> *Who plays the checkered game*
> *Of king jump king–*
> *And jumps a president:*
> *That order 8802*
> *For me and You.*[44]

The FEPC controversy kept right on growing and eventually split both political parties. Toward the end of the war, labor and civil rights activists tried to make the agency permanent and expand its authority—from government contracts to all hiring. Southern Democrats glimpsed, in that proposal, the apocalypse itself. They did not mince words, labelling the plan "Totalitarian," "Communistic," and "A bill [that] would rape the Magna Carta." They made dire predictions. "White employees will have to work under Negroes." "Every negro in America who is behind movements of this kind . . . dreams of social equality." And, as always, they brandished the primal fear— "intermarriage between whites and blacks" and the end of whiteness itself.[45]

Republicans experienced a more subtle split. The northern moderates were still fighting for black votes, and in 1944 they pushed an expansion of the FEPC explicitly into the party platform. The moderates dominated the party conventions because representation was based on the size of the states—a sore point with Republican conservatives who controlled the congressional delegation and itched to nominate a true conservative for president. In 1946, Republicans took control of Congress for the first time in sixteen years. Joseph Martin of Massachusetts, the new Speaker, curtly explained why the Republican Congress would not be honoring the Republican Party platform pledge. "I'll be frank with you," he told one African American. "We are not going to pass the FEPC bill, but it has nothing to do with the Negro vote. We are supported mainly by New England and Midwestern industrialists who would stop their contributions if we passed a law that would compel them to stop . . . racial discrimination in employment."[46]

Through American history, the Republicans (and before them, the Whigs) had been the party of civil rights and of active government. But, back then, active government had meant supporting business by raising tariffs and building infrastructure—a position first championed by Alexander Hamilton. Now, New Deal Democrats took active government in a new direction. Their version of the FEPC introduced a new threat: deploy government power to thrust civil rights into the private sector. They did not have the strength to push it through, but the effort charts the ascension of the civil rights aspirations within the Democratic coalition—from silence on lynching, to a reluctant FEPC overseeing government contracts, to agitating for an unprecedented intrusion into private hiring practices.

———————

THE NEW DEAL DEMOCRATS DOUBLED DOWN ON THE OLD Populist idea of economic rights. Roosevelt had put it poetically as the nation stood on the cusp of World War II. At the very end of a long speech focused on the war, Roosevelt closed with his famous passage. "Men . . . do not fight by armaments alone." The servicemen and women who defended the nation were also motivated, he said, by an "unshakable belief in the manner of life they are defending." Four great freedoms defined that life. The first two were traditional, plucked from the First Amendment: freedom of speech and freedom of religion. Then came the radical revision: "The third is freedom from want." Roosevelt was actually referring to international trade agreements, but the phrase was capacious enough to embrace the entire New Deal. The freedom from want eventually swelled into a kind of communitarian dream of shared prosperity. The government would boost every American out of need. The fourth freedom was something even more ambitious, the "freedom from fear." Tyrants around the globe threatened free people "with the crash of a bomb," but America would fight back with a bold, modern understanding of what it meant to be free.[47]

Roosevelt's 1944 State of the Union message included his most full-throated statement of the new notion of freedom. Again, a long war speech cheered the recent military triumphs. Then the president shifted to the deepest meaning of the war, to the deepest meaning of America—the economic rights vested in every citizen.

> We have come to a clear realization of the fact that true individual freedom cannot exist without economic security and independence. Necessitous men are not free men. . . . We have accepted, so to speak, a second Bill of Rights. . . .
>
> Among these [rights] are: The right to a useful and remunerative job. . . . The right to earn enough to provide adequate food and clothing and recreation . . . . The right of every family to a decent home. . . . The right to adequate medical care and the opportunity to achieve and enjoy good health; The right to adequate protection from the economic fears of old age, sickness, accident, and unemployment; The right to a good education.[48]

Here, fifty years after the Populists had vanished, was an elegant revision of their wild dream. The people's government takes the negative freedoms of the federal Constitution and adds a positive pledge of personal security: no hungry children, no uneducated youths, no needy families, no old people without a place to live, no suffering Americans turned away from the hospital because they cannot pay.

Liberal Democrats redefined themselves as the party of positive freedom. Even today, progressive candidates like Bernie Sanders enthusiastically read passages from that long-ago State of the Union message while their millennial supporters cheer.

Conservatives recoiled—then, later, and now. Liberty, they insist, meant exactly what the Constitution always said it meant: the right to be left alone. Roosevelt's idea of liberty and rights was, from this perspective, the exact opposite of freedom. It was coercion. The clashing ideas of freedom redefined a central trench running through partisan conflict. Each side imagines a different kind of American community with different kinds of obligations toward one another.

DEMOCRATIC CONGRESSMAN MARTIN DIES WAS A LARGE, truculent, white supremacy publicity hound from a district in Texas where the black population outnumbered the white—though they were, of course, not permitted to vote. In 1938, Dies seized control of the House Committee on Un-American Activities (or HUAC), which had originally investigated fascists, Communists, and other perceived threats, and began to track down the reds he saw skulking in every corner of the country. Dies rode right through the scorn that came down on his committee. It did seem unlikely, after all, that Shirley Temple (age ten) was a communist, even if she did send a greeting to a French newspaper funded by the Communist Party. Or that bookstores should be shut down for carrying books about Marxism. The celebrated striptease artist Gypsy Rose Lee made giggling headlines when she offered "to bare all for the committee."

But the laughter died down as the investigations ground on. "Despite his blustering," reported one columnist, "this red-baiter has actually hung quite a few scalps." Dies helped bring down Michigan governor Frank Murphy, for example, because of his treasonous softness on the sit-down strikers in Flint. After HUAC assailed him, Murphy lost his reelection bid in 1938. The committee's attack on Harry Bridges, who had directed the San Francisco Longshoremen's Strike, led to an effort to deport the labor leader, which would force Bridges in and out of federal courts from 1939 clear out to 1955. Congressman Dies also went after Labor Secretary Frances Perkins (for refusing to deport Bridges), Roosevelt advisor Harry Hopkins, Vice President Henry Wallace, and thirty-five members of the War Economic Board.[49]

Dies and his committee also set their sights on civil rights activists, condemning A. Philip Randolph for his fight "against lynching and all forms of Negro discrimination." The committee also went after mischief makers who sent greetings to the National Negro Conference or made contributions to the Scottsboro Boys Defense Fund (after nine young African Americans were falsely accused of raping two white women). Behind all this racial trouble, explained Dies, lurked the Communists, who "encourage the Negro to demand social equality with the whites." This was the way the reds intended to subvert American freedom, he continued. Pushing African Americans to demand civil rights and even equality would "separate the two races into hostile camps . . . and the resulting clash will be sort of auxiliary to the class struggle and civil war."[50]

An enduring alliance emerged in the House Committee. The Southern Democratic leaders (Dies was from Texas and his major ally, Joe Starnes, from Alabama) worked smoothly with conservative Republicans led by J. Parnell Thomas (from New Jersey) and Noah Mason (from Illinois). Southern Democrats and conservative Republicans were united by their fear of communism, their dislike for labor unions, their antipathy toward racial "agitation," and their animosity toward big government. In the early days of the New Deal, liberals batted aside right-wing criticism with sarcasm about the plutocrats' "snow white whiskers" and "gold-headed canes." But it was harder to scoff at the anticommunists. They were not clinging to their treasure but warning the nation of what they saw as a looming peril. The battle against communism, civil rights, and big government soon began to solidify an alliance of the antigovernment conservatives in both parties.[51]

Republican Senator Karl Mundt of South Dakota eventually launched a campaign to formalize this alliance. "Every major piece of socialistic . . . legislation has been stopped in Congress by a combination of Southern Democrats and Republicans," he wrote. Without this coalition, "our country would be much farther down the road to socialism." Quietly, Mundt asked members of Congress to sign pledges endorsing a cross-party conservative coalition. This alarmed Republican moderates. Congressman Clifford Case, from New Jersey, warned that Mundt's alliance would mean casting aside the civil rights heritage that Abraham Lincoln had bequeathed the party—the Southern Democrats would never accept racial equality. Liberal Republicans began to worry that a conservative coalition would completely lose the black vote in the North and squeeze them right out of the party.[52]

THE CONSERVATIVE ALLIANCE, WHICH COMBINED THE BATtle against communism with resistance to civil rights, fits awkwardly with one bit of conventional nostalgia. Foreign policy, at the start of the Cold War, glows like a lost model of bipartisanship. A month into his fourth term, FDR died, and Harry Truman suddenly found himself in the White House. Truman worked closely with Republican Senator Arthur Vandenberg (who had helped write the *Conservative Manifesto* ten years earlier) in designing a cold war strategy. The administration resolved to stop the Soviet Union from grabbing new lands. To win approval of the tough, and expensive, policy, Vandenberg advised the president to stand before Congress and the nation and "scare the hell out of the American people." This Truman proceeded to do, and, before long, foreign aid flowed to vulnerable allies like Greece and Turkey. Vandenberg himself turned the often-quoted phrase that still sums up this golden moment of consensus: "Politics stops at the water's edge."

Except that the consensus about fighting communism made a formidable post on which to whip radicals, labor agitators, leftists, big-government liberals, and the Democratic Party that housed them. After World War II, the HUAC shifted into overdrive. It rounded up Communists, former Communists, socialists, former socialists, and individuals who had donated to shady causes or signed the wrong petitions or just seemed kind of strange. The Truman administration, queasy of being branded soft on communism, organized a loyalty review board in 1946 and investigated four million government employees over the next five years. The Senate got into the act with its own security committee.

Dies eventually gave way to an even bigger publicity seeker—the canny, crude, tough, disheveled, boozy Senator Joe McCarthy, who barged onto the scene in 1950 waving a file that contained, he said, the names of 205 (later, 57 or perhaps 81, or was it 4?) card-carrying Communists in the State Department.[53]

To this day, Americans remain divided over what exactly hit the country. On the left, this campaign was a witch hunt, tossing aside the rules of justice, ruining lives, and punishing people who leaned to the left. Or had once leaned left. From this angle, the red scare exposed a shocking intolerance running through American thought and culture. When it was over, historians and political scientists pondered how it could have happened here. Conservatives saw it differently. Yes, there were excesses that all regret. But there *were* Communists. They *did* leak secrets back to Moscow. They took instruction from the Soviets. Sometimes they lied about it. Some of them won adulation as martyrs for free speech—until the Soviet files became public and incriminated them.[54]

Which perspective should we believe? Both. Yes, there *were* Communists. But the red scare traumatized the United States and compromised its values because it blurred the line between guarding the homeland and bludgeoning the left. One conservative columnist unwittingly illustrated the danger even as he celebrated national unity. "The people are not divided" except for "the chorus of Communists, left-wingers, soft liberals, [and] cowards [who] sing the Katydid song of 'Peace! Ain't it wonderful.'" Where exactly did the line fall between Communists taking orders from Moscow and the "soft liberals" singing songs of peace and civil rights? Who knew? Who cared? Fearful times are shaky on nuance—from Salem Village (where there really were practicing witches) to the House Committee (where there really were practicing Communists) to the War on Terror (where there were practicing terrorists). In every episode, the deepest danger to the community comes from trampling its established rules of justice. That—not the witches themselves—is what makes a Witch Hunt.[55]

The golden image of bipartisanship in postwar foreign policy obscures an almost creedal enmity between two visions of America. On the right, the anxious war against the powerful Communists could be won only by steely resolve; there was no place for flabby naïveté with everything at stake. The left saw, in contrast, a deep intolerance masquerading as patriotism; it destroyed lives, narrowed the range of permissible opinions, and deployed foreign policy as a powerful wedge between patriots and "soft liberals." Again, and again, international affairs hold a mirror to America's own views of itself, to the tribal conflicts that mark the nation.

THE NEW DEAL SHOOK UP LABOR LAW AND RACE RELATIONS, and at first glance, it looked like it created a revolution in gender roles too. Pa Joad, the patriarch in John Steinbeck's formidable *The Grapes of Wrath*, written in 1939, summed it up: "Time was when a man said what we'd do." Now, "women takin' over." Women seemed to be everywhere.[56]

Eleanor Roosevelt certainly was—her name became synonymous with liberal causes. No presidential spouse had been so influential or sent so many ripples through politics and the media. Activist memoirs from the era often feature Eleanor—fixing up a meeting with Franklin, advising civil rights group on how to approach the White House, pressing for social justice, and even taking heat for stirring up race riots.[57]

Women played important roles up and down the government. Frances Perkins, the first woman to hold a cabinet post, spent twelve years as secretary of labor when labor politics was front page news. Josephine Roche, the assistant secretary of the Treasury, may have done more to nudge national health insurance onto the agenda than any other member of the administration. Mary (Molly) Dawson touted a long list of women candidates for government posts. Over on the federal bench, Florence Allen became the first woman appointed to the Court of Appeals. Women were congregating in the corridors of power like never before.

But Pa Joad's lament touched something else that seemed more essential at the time. The Great Depression had stirred a crisis of masculinity. Men's role had always come from winning the family bread. When the economy collapsed, so did their status. The New Deal aimed to prop it back up.

The federal government constructed benefits not around citizenship but around employment. Social Security, unemployment compensation, the National Recovery Administration, and health care insurance during the war did not specifically flow to men. But the eligibility rules tilted heavily toward male workers. Other programs, like the much loved CCC, recruited only young men. Together, these federal programs designated a special class of citizenship designed to restore male independence and self-respect.[58]

Women worked, of course, but mainly in women's professions—as teachers, nurses, or secretaries, where marriage meant "retirement." In fact, with so many unemployed men, there was strong pressure to limit working women altogether. The federal government made it difficult for the wife of a federal employee to get or keep a government post. Couples clung to jobs by hushing up their marriages. Twenty-six states put explicit limits on hiring married women. A liberal columnist, Norman Cousins, sarcastically summed up the general feeling: "There are approximately 10,000,000 people out of work," he wrote in 1939. "There are also 10,000,000 or more women, married and single, who are job holders. Simply fire the women . . . and hire the men. Presto! No unemployment . . . No depression."[59]

The manly spirit ran strong through the labor movement. Its leaders were withering about Frances Perkins—neither a guy nor a union member. When Perkins went before a congressional committee to testify on behalf of Social Security, she had to shrug aside the condescension of Democratic Senator Thomas Gore from Tennessee—"Isn't this a teensy-weeny bit of socialism?" he asked her.[60]

The art of the period, known as American regionalism, featured brawny muscular men building the great cities in the east, busting sod in the Midwest, taming feral horses in the wild west. The muscular dreams would segue, after the war, into fretting about the "woman problem." When the editors of *Life* published a special issue on "the American Woman," they began with the question of the day. "Has . . . the American woman . . . become too dominant in our society?" FBI Director, J. Edgar Hoover, explained why that would be dangerous: strength, firm and unyielding, was the only thing that could stand up to communism. Masculinity had grown disoriented with the depression; now it was desperately needed for the Cold War.[61]

They all might have taken a second look at the *The Grapes of Wrath* where Ma Joad wisely shepherds the family through one trouble after another—staying the hand of male violence and holding the frayed family bonds together right through the realization that the promised land had been nothing but a mirage. When it came to politics and business during the New Deal, Steinbeck's Ma Joad proved to be the mirage.

———————

THE UNITED STATES ROARED OUT OF WORLD WAR II AS AN economic colossus generating something like 40 percent of the entire world's GDP. Following the war, the great powers of Europe and Asia lay in rubble. The Soviet Union had suffered twenty-five million dead—more than one in ten of its people.

But Americans did not feel colossal. Instead, the nation thrummed with troubles. Millions of soldiers waited to be integrated back into the economy that, in turn, needed to be converted back to peace time. In one month, the Pentagon cancelled $15 billion worth of orders—a full 7 percent of GDP. Shortages popped up everywhere. A tight housing market left the returning soldiers with no place to live—newspapers ran photos of them sitting with their families on the city streets. Inflation leapt 18 percent in 1946 and another 9 percent in 1947. The newly revitalized labor movement launched almost five thousand strikes in 1946 alone.[62]

In 1948, the first presidential election since FDR's death, five very different perspectives spanned the parties. Republicans split into two factions, Democrats into three. Each touched something essential—about politics, about the nation's place in the world, about the government's role in American life, and about national identity itself.

HENRY WALLACE BROKE WITH THE DEMOCRATIC PARTY and ran from the left. Henry Wallace was an oddball. A dreamer, a mystic, a leftist, a civil rights warrior, a once and future Republican, and perhaps the most successful secretary of agriculture in American history. When people were hungry, he pressed farmers to slaughter millions of piglets and plough under thousands of acres. That, he explained to the horrified, was the only way to raise prices and save the farms. President Roosevelt picked him as vice president in 1940 and muscled him through the convention where four out of every ten delegates voted against him. The left was thrilled, the city pols unsettled, the segregationists extremely unhappy.[63]

Once in office, Wallace wrote ditzy letters to a mystic guru and talked FDR into placing the masonic symbol (that strange pyramid-with-an-eye) on the dollar bill. But he lost the president's confidence after a public spat with the secretary of commerce, and the party leaders leapt in and persuaded FDR, now in very ill health, to throw aside Wallace for Senator Harry Truman during the 1944 Democratic convention. The left tried to rebel and force their man back onto the ballot. Claude Pepper of Florida ("Red Pepper," to the right) worked his way to the podium, certain that the party faithful would rise up for Wallace if given the chance. The convention roared. The professional politicians running the convention smoothly adjourned the session before Pepper could do any damage, and, the next day, they slipped Truman in. A month after the inauguration, Roosevelt was dead and Truman was president.

Wallace ferociously opposed the Truman administration's hard line against the Soviet Union. "Hatred breeds hatred," he declared before an exuberant rally at Madison Square Garden. "Getting tough never brought anything real and lasting. . . . The tougher we get, the tougher the Russians will get." Wallace itched to reconstruct the great leftist coalition that had gathered in the early New Deal, when labor was rising and the Communists played an active political role. Back in the mid-1930s, the head of the Communist Party USA had published a syndicated column, looking rather avuncular puffing on his pipe in the accompanying sketch—just one position on the long American spectrum. But now the United States had gone off the rails, said Wallace, with its red baiting, its swollen military, its atomic weaponry. Share the bomb with the Soviets, urged Wallace. Make the Democrats a truly liberal party.[64]

In 1948, Wallace formed the Progressive Party and ran a frenetic campaign. His energetic stumping set off nervous memos at the Democratic National Committee as he toured the South, refusing to speak at any segregated venue, and standing strong against the taunts and the eggs that came flying at him. Leftists gathered around him—he shared the stage with folk singers like the young Pete Seeger. He was insouciant about the Communists who helped organize his campaign and draft his speeches.[65]

Conservatives attacked with gusto. "The important issue . . . isn't whether Henry Wallace and his followers are stooges for Pal Joey [Stalin] in Moscow," wrote one. "The real issue is whether they're nuts." Actually, the real problem was that the Soviet Union refused to live up to Wallace's image of a defensive bear, eager for peace. International crises sprang up, one after another. When the Soviets cut off access to West Berlin, deep in Soviet-occupied East Germany, the United States and Britain responded with a dramatic airlift that fed two million people for eleven tense months running right through the election.[66]

Like most third-party efforts, this one lost altitude as election day drew near. Although he scored over half a million votes (over 8 percent) in New York, throwing the state to the Republicans (who won there by just seven thousand votes), Wallace failed to break 5 percent in any other state and gathered less than 3 percent of the popular vote nationwide.

The often-maligned Wallace effort—conventional wisdom still tags him dangerously naïve—forces us to confront a great counterfactual. Wallace might have been president if Roosevelt had died a year earlier or had refused to replace him as VP. What if, led by President Henry Wallace, the American economic colossus had simply decided not to fight a cold war? What if the nation had refused to drop the atom bomb on Japan and had resisted the rise of its military industrial complex? What sort of world would have emerged? What kind of American nation might that world have witnessed?

THE SEGREGATIONIST DEMOCRATS ALSO BROKE WITH TRU-man and ran their own candidate in 1948. In the process, they dropped the curtain on the solid South—the region's unwavering allegiance to the Democratic Party. A year earlier, an influential book, *Wither Solid South?*, had circulated among southern elites. The Democratic Party, wrote Charles Wallace Collins, had tossed the two-thirds rule, embraced labor, and welcomed black people. The zealots, driven by a blind hatred of southern tradition, were poised to destroy Dixie. "The overweening ambition of the Negro race," wrote Collins, is "to use the sword and the purse of the federal government to force its way into the inner sanctuary of white man's daily life, to work with him, to play with him, to eat with him, to be educated with him, and to worship with him—with the white man and white woman."[67]

These were fears with a long past and a loud future. They had surfaced before the Civil War, roared through Reconstruction, and dominated the debate over the Lodge Force Bill in 1890. Now, historian Richard Hofstadter read Collins as a second coming of John Calhoun and his fierce defense of the South's peculiar institution. The same old fear was back with a vengeance—federal muscle forcing black people into white precincts.[68]

What was to be done? In the long run, wrote Collins, the South should ally with the conservative Republicans. After all, they, too, were outraged at the tyranny of the federal government. But for the time being, he continued, the South would have to unite around a candidate pledged to white supremacy. The southern region, with 170 electoral votes, could block both parties by preventing either from winning a majority of electoral votes in the presidential race. This, of course, would throw the election into the House, where southern leaders could play a decisive role in determining the next president. Unity was the key.[69]

With arguments like Collins' rumbling through the South, the mainstream Democrats gathered in Philadelphia for their political convention. Party leaders, led by Truman himself, tried to calm the racial storm and reunite the party. They failed. First, progressive delegations arrived from South Carolina and Mississippi and demanded that they be seated instead of the party regulars. The official delegates, they charged, represented state parties that repressed black voters and demanded "a thought-control fascistic oath" to uphold segregation. Party leaders politely turned down the protesters and seated the official delegates, but the protest spread to the convention floor. Representatives from the Northeast halted the proceedings and, when they failed to reverse the decision and seat the progressive delegations, they insisted on placing their objection in the record.

Next, southerners tried to restore the party's traditional two-thirds rule—and the convention rebuffed them. One newspaper summed up that debate as "a roaring struggle that often approached the brawl stage."[70]

Then the main event. Party leaders proposed an anodyne race plank that had served them in the last campaign, but northern liberals again bucked the leadership and introduced a civil rights plank to the party platform that touched all the hot buttons: equal voting rights, equal employment, anti-lynching laws, and the desegregation of the military. The fresh-faced Minneapolis mayor, Hubert H. Humphrey, rose out of the uproar. "There are those who say to you—we are rushing this issue of civil rights," shouted Humphrey. "I say we are a hundred and seventy-two years too late. . . . The time has come to get out of the shadow of states' rights and walk forthrightly into the bright sunshine of human rights." George Vaughn, a black delegate from Saint Louis, made his own civil rights plea to cheers, boos, and brutal racist epithets. Southern leaders were appalled, moderates fearful, liberals eager, and many delegates fired by moral conviction. In the end, the ambitious civil rights statement prevailed, passing with 651.5 yay to 582.5 nay.[71]

At that point, as H. L. Mencken reported in the *Baltimore Sun*, "Mississippi and some from the Alabama delegation rose to its legs and began to howl." Mississippi political leaders had instructed the state's delegates to walk out if the convention tried something like this. They hoped to create a spectacle, but this was the wrong time and place. In contrast to the roiling 1860 convention, where the southern delegations blew up the entire meeting, this protest looked small, timid, and rumpled. A little knot of white men announced their displeasure and walked out as boos and catcalls cascaded about them.[72]

The Southern Democrats had prepared for this kind of defeat by planning another convention three days later in Birmingham, Alabama. The Dixiecrats' convention did not attract very many important leaders—only four members of Congress showed up. Instead, the convention swarmed with enthusiastic irregulars. College students waved rebel flags and sang "Dixie." The Mississippi state police, sirens blaring, grandly escorted seventy-five students from the University of Mississippi campus all the way to the Alabama border some ninety miles away.

Governor Frank M. Dixon of Alabama used the keynote address to toss red meat to the throng, warning that if the northerners had their way, black teachers will teach your children and force them to play with black children. Needless to say, "all negroes will be registered to vote, regardless of intelligence." Dixon interspersed his racial animosity with hostility toward the federal government. At the very heart of the American experiment, he argued, was the idea that everyday matters should be handled by state and local government. Placing the federal government in charge of local matters trampled the Constitution. The exegesis led smoothly back to the white supremacists' perennial fear: "This vicious program means . . . to reduce us to the status of a mongrel, inferior race mixed in blood, our Anglo-Saxon heritage a mockery."[73]

The convention unanimously selected Governor Strom Thurmond of South Carolina as their presidential nominee. Thurmond had been in office for just two years and had less to lose than more seasoned politicians. He, too, recited a familiar text: there are not enough troops in the US Army to force "the Southland to admit Negroes into our theaters, into our swimming pools, into our schools, into our homes, into our churches." The convention framed a simple platform. "We stand for segregation of the races" and oppose "totalitarianism at home and abroad."[74]

Even sympathetic observers could see that something was off. The convention kept mixing high-minded talk about liberty with racial hatred. "I was proud and thrilled," wrote one columnist, that someone finally stood up for "all people who believe in freedom from a centralized government and a police state." But the oratory, he continued, "should have been confined to the clear and dignified issue of States Rights" rather than disintegrating into white supremacy and race baiting bristling with "awful nigger jokes," jeering, and laughter.[75]

The Dixiecrats drew on an ancient American tradition as they intermingled two powerful themes: soaring arguments against federal overreach in the name of liberty twined with the malicious caws of racism. In one way or another, we have seen this mixture in every chapter.[76]

The Dixiecrats shambled out of their convention and ran a lackluster, underfunded, and badly organized campaign. Still, they won in four states where they managed to displace the Democrats on the ballot—South Carolina, Louisiana, Mississippi, and Alabama. The Dixiecrats did not get far in 1948, but they left a formidable legacy. The writing and speeches of the 1948 campaign previewed the rhetoric that would greet the civil rights movement for the next two decades. The country would hear the same fears, even the same sentences, that rattled the rafters in Birmingham. More importantly, the Dixiecrats broke the Democrats' grip on the South. Back in the previous election, in 1944, the Democrats had taken the Dixiecrat states with a whopping 83 percent of the vote (across South Carolina, Louisiana, Arkansas, and Mississippi). In the following election, in 1952, Democrats would manage an average of just 54.7 percent across those states while five others (including Texas and Florida) would tumble to the Republicans. To be sure, the Democratic Party would struggle to keep its coalition together. Its next three vice presidential picks included a conservative from Alabama, a liberal from Tennessee, and the enigmatic Lyndon Johnson from Texas. But after 1948, the southern states were in political play. Each would follow its own path out of Dixie, as political scientist Robert Mickey put it, but 1948 marked the start of that journey.

THE REPUBLICANS, WHO HAD BEEN LEFT BARELY BREATHING in 1936, had boomed back between 1938 and 1946, gaining a total of 34 seats in the Senate and 157 in the House across three midterms. In 1946, they took both chambers for the first time in eighteen years, and now, in 1948, they seemed poised to take back the presidency. "The sweet smell of victory is in the Republican nostrils," wrote columnist Drew Pearson from the Republican Party convention. "Nomination is equal to election," ran another dispatch. The Democrats had fractured, the president was unpopular ("to err is Truman," went the familiar jibe), and the Republicans were on a roll. But which Republican Party would win the nomination for president? The presidential race drew the leaders of the party's two factions.[77]

Senator Robert Taft, the majority leader from Ohio, led the conservative wing. Conservatives found much to cheer in "Mr. Republican," for under his leadership (1947–1948), Congress had reduced the power of labor unions with the Taft–Harley Bill (passed over

Truman's veto), exposed Communists in government and society, rolled back New Deal spending, and frustrated Truman at every turn. Taft was brusque, cold, terrible at small talk, and drove liberals crazy. "Shut your mouth," exploded Democratic Senator James Murray of Montana when Taft needled him by calling Truman's health plan "socialistic." "You are so self-opiniated . . . so self-important." The Democrats' discomfort delighted Taft's conservative followers. They were fired up to finally have a real Republican running for the presidency and not just a watered-down Democrat.[78]

Governor Thomas Dewey (NY) represented the establishment, northeastern Republicans. He had signed a strong civil rights act, advocated health care reform, and supported increased funding for education. Dewey was neat, moderate, and methodical. "You have to know Dewey really well to dislike him," quipped one New Yorker. In truth, most Republican conservatives disliked him whether they knew him or not. He stood for everything that they opposed—another politician who offered them nothing more than a less extreme version of the despised New Deal.[79]

Dewey had been nominated back in 1944 and had held FDR to 53 percent of the vote, the closest race in his four runs for the White House. Now, despite plenty of talk about a close contest before the convention met, Dewey easily won another nomination (on the third ballot) and then infuriated conservatives all over again by backing out of a deal to nominate a solid conservative, House Majority Leader Charlie Halleck, for vice president (or so Halleck angrily claimed). Instead, Dewey selected another liberal Republican, Governor Earl Warren of California. After all the high conservative hopes, two liberal Republican governors pushed aside two conservative leaders from Congress and challenged Truman from the moderate center.[80]

Dewey came out of the Republican convention a prohibitive favorite and ran a cautious campaign—why risk the big lead? He shrugged off Truman's incessant attacks on the Republican

Congress. Historians point to a more serious error. Dewey had been one of the most liberal governors in the country on race issues, yet he failed to court black voters. Instead, he unsuccessfully challenged the Dixiecrats and the Democrats for southern support. While Dewey stayed largely quiet on civil rights, his campaign sent Senator Robert Taft on a southern tour where he told audiences that the Republicans were a lot closer to their views than the Truman administration.[81]

FDR had first won the black vote in 1936. Republicans fought hard to wrest some of it back in the subsequent elections. Now, in 1948, the Democrats made a strong play for it. The party had supported a strong civil rights plank and had driven the Dixiecrats right out of their convention and into a separate presidential campaign. Truman had appointed a Committee on Civil Rights that had drafted an ambitious agenda for the administration, including a plan to desegregate the military, which Truman went on to do. The efforts contrasted sharply with Dewey's cool indifference and yielded another great leap toward the Democrats in black precincts. More than three out of four African Americans voted Truman; black party identification now surged strongly Democratic by more than three to one. It never completely fell back. The 1948 election marked an epochal political moment: Republicans lost the majority of the black vote once and for all. Some African Americans would drift back in the next two presidential elections and a cadre of loyal black Republicans clung on for another fifteen years, but the black majority was never seriously in play again.

The losers in both parties would eventually unite. Republican conservatives controlled Congress but were deeply frustrated over their party's presidential nominations. The Southern Democrats also remained powerful on the Hill but had bolted over their party's platform and nominee. The two factions would eventually find one another but, for now, each fought angry battles within its own party. For raw political animosity, 1948 was as hot as any election in our own time—with one very big difference. The hard feelings ran within the political parties much more powerfully than they ran between them. Simply count Democratic and Republican noses during congressional votes and you might call it a bipartisan era—with plenty of cross-party voting. At the same time, gossip columnists were chortling about the poisonous atmosphere—even jibing that members were ready to pack their guns. If they did, not a bullet would have crossed the aisle: Democrats would be firing on Democrats, Republicans on Republicans.

FINALLY, THERE WAS TRUMAN, RUNNING A LONGSHOT CAMpaign for reelection. Truman was an unlikely populist: a straight shooter who had come up through the tough world of party politics—honest, steady, and kind of small. He kept a picture of his old mentor, the Kansas City boss, T. J. Prendergast, even after the old man ended up in jail. His mother offered a homespun variation on the theme: Harry always plowed "the straightest furrow in all Missouri."[82]

When Truman stepped into the White House, everyone expected him to head straight to the middle, where he had spent his Senate career. Three weeks after World War II ended, however, Truman stunned Washington by releasing a blueprint for winning FDR's economic bill of rights—a highly progressive, politically unlikely, twenty-one-point plan for converting the nation's economy from war to peacetime. Liberals were delighted, conservatives dumbfounded. Republican Joe Martin coldly summed up the Republican distaste: "Not even Roosevelt ever asked for so much."[83]

The ambitious domestic agenda went nowhere. Truman faced a hostile conservative coalition in Congress even before the 1946 midterm mowed down liberal Democrats. To make matters worse, Truman had no idea how to move bills through Congress. He was maladroit at both the inside game on Capitol Hill and at going public. But then, in 1948, he found his voice.

First, in his State of the Union Address, he brazenly touted the administration's most controversial proposals—civil rights (infuriating Southern Democrats) and national health insurance (which Republicans despised).[84]

At the tumultuous Democratic convention that year, Truman didn't speak until 2:00 a.m. But when he took the podium, he fired up the weary delegates by declaring that he would call the "do-nothing" Congress back into session (on Turnip Day in rural Missouri) and demand they pass "what they say they're for." The Republican Party platform had promised all kinds of things (expanding Social Security, extending the FEPC, and sponsoring housing programs) that the Republicans in Congress rejected. Truman began the campaign by hammering on the differences between the presidential and congressional wings of the rival party.[85]

Truman then set off on the legendary campaign that, as *Newsweek* put it, "would have killed a less sturdy fighter." He began with an enormous labor rally in Detroit, jumped on a train, and gave his first speeches a little after nine in the morning (in Grand Rapids) and his last just before midnight (in Toledo). Truman kept at it, delivering fifteen speeches in fifteen towns over fifteen hours, day after day. He discovered that he worked best when his staff simply gave him bullet points, banged out on the fly. He would chop the air with his hands and roar out his litany of indictments in short, staccato sentences. Staff members would prime the crowds if they were slow with whoops of "Give 'em hell, Harry!"[86]

Today we call it negative campaigning—and it worked. Truman won by two million votes (or 4.5 percent). The results were both closer and more decisive than the headlines. Truman's margin was less than one percent in five states (worth 138 Electoral College votes) and less than five percent in thirteen more. However, an even bigger surprise lay down the ballot. Democrats netted seventy-five more seats in the House and nine in the Senate. Republicans would win both chambers for just one session in the next forty-six years.

They would not get their 1946 House numbers back until the mid-term elections of 2014.

TRUMAN'S VICTORY IN 1948 HAD ALWAYS STOOD AS THE paragon of lost causes—that is, until Donald Trump managed an even less probable victory in 2016. The media narrative about Hillary Clinton, the loser in that future campaign, uncannily matches the story of Thomas Dewey: too passive, too stiff, too aloof, bad campaign, no substance, no fire, and not very likable. Of course, unlike Dewey, Clinton easily won the popular vote only to trip over the Electoral College.

But the difference between the two Democratic candidates starkly reflects how the Democratic Party itself changed between 1948 and 2016. Harry Truman's mad, angry, staccato, "give 'em hell" speeches read like another coming of the prairie populists. He called the Republicans "gluttons of privilege," "con men with a calculating machine where [their] heart ought to be," and selfish idlers who "want a return of the Wall Street Economic dictatorship." He scoured the greedy rich, contrasting his party as the "haven for ordinary people."[87]

Nor was it simply political posturing. The very same sentiments run throughout Truman's private correspondence while he was in the White House. For example, when Democratic Congressman John Kee of West Virginia forwarded him a constituent letter criticizing the "big strong lazy men" who "lay around and let someone else who is working feed them," Truman blasted back. "Some of our Senators and Representatives . . . are still living in 1890. Perhaps like Rip Van Winkle they will come out of their slumber and find how the world has progressed."[88]

Truman often recalled one of his earliest political projects, back when he was a county official in Kansas City. "There were derelicts who . . . didn't have any ambition. We took good care of them," he said, recalling in particular how he helped build a hospital "to take care of those people . . . who were just [barely] making a living." His attitude was a classic statement of New Deal liberalism. Truman celebrated a government that took care of people who needed help—whether they were hard-working people who had simply fallen on tough times, poor families just getting by, or even losers who "didn't have any ambition." Democrats would soon flee from the idea of helping people who had no ambition and refused to work hard.[89]

The spirit that William Jennings Bryan first thrust into the Democratic Party, the idea that government stood for the people and against the rich, had its last hurrah with Harry Truman. Eventually he retired to the Truman Library where he churned out essays about fighting against the forces of avarice. The Democrats still had big battles and great victories ahead of them. But something fundamental slipped away after the 1948 election: the energetic us-versus-them battle against the rich and powerful. Today, an eternal flame burns behind a glass wall in the courtyard of the Truman Library. As I stared out at it, I couldn't help feeling that it flickered for the distant memory of the populist New Deal vision that Truman took from Roosevelt, unexpectedly embraced, and tried so maladroitly to win.

In that last New Deal election, we get an early glimpse of American politics evolving toward its present form. The Democrats had become the party of active, liberal government and were moving from blunt white supremacy toward active civil rights—though the clash within the party would grind on for almost two decades. On the other side, the northeastern Republican liberals were running out of time and, as they faded, the coalition between conservative Democrats and Republicans finally began to stick. All these changes and more would gather force over the next decade and erupt on the scene in 1964, when the parties as we know them today finally emerged with a bang.

PART IV

AMERICAN POLITICS TURN TRIBAL

SEVEN

THE ELECTION THAT
REMADE AMERICAN POLITICS (1964)

S ix infantrymen leap from a helicopter and dash into the jungle. Their perilous assignment is to locate enemy regiments that the 173rd Airborne will swoop in and destroy. The Americans immediately run into the Vietcong, who swiftly encircle them deep in the bush. The GIs slip away, regroup in a small clearing, lose contact with their unit, dig in, engage in a fierce firefight, reestablish communication, call in a chopper, and get out—mission accomplished without a casualty.

Here's what still counted as news in 1967: the cool, competent lieutenant who led the unit was African American. The *Time* cover story, "Democracy in the Foxhole," was about black men in combat. The dispatch from Southeast Asia ended with a cheer and a warning: "The performance of the Negro G.I. under fire reaffirms the success—and diversity—of the American experiment." But these brave soldiers will be "madder than hell," the article continued, if they return home to segregation and repression.[1]

"Madder than hell" barely covered it. Terrible stories kept rolling through the media. Take just one newsflash that circulated two months before that firefight in the jungle. Wharlest Jackson was the treasurer of the Natchez, Mississippi, chapter of the NAACP and the first black man to win a promotion at the Armstrong Rubber Company plant. After his first day in the new post, he got into his truck and, as he drove home, a bomb detonated, killing him instantly—and leaving five more children without a father. Demonstrators descended on the town. Charles Evers, whose own brother Medgar had been shot and killed in front of his wife and kids, told the press that the Armstrong plant was "infested with Ku Klux Klansmen" and warned that black America's patience "was just about exhausted." That summer, the "long, hot summer" of 1967, saw some 159 race riots—also known as insurrections—culminating in devastating conflagrations in Detroit and Newark.[2]

Race lay at the bottom of the massive changes that transformed American politics in the 1960s. To this day, observers pore over the passion, hope, and violence as they try to make sense of the turbulent decade. The Democratic dominance that began in the New Deal allowed the party to reach for the stars after the 1964 election. They accomplished some remarkable things—we still live in the shadow of the 1965 legislative season. And then it all came crashing down. The Democratic Party lost its coalition, its agenda, its governing majority, and even its sense of purpose. On the other side, conservatives finally captured the Republican Party, transforming it into the party of passion, fresh ideas, small government, moral values, states' rights, and racial backlash. It became more (and less) than a party. It became a movement.

Across every level of government, the passions and intensity of the 1960s would twist and turn and morph into the fierce tribal politics of our time. This final section of the book traces just how we got to our present state—starting with the Big Bang in both parties: the election of 1964.

WHEN GOVERNOR NELSON ROCKEFELLER OF NEW YORK took the stage at the 1964 Republican convention in San Francisco, the crowd erupted into boos and jeers. The chair tried to calm the fury, shouting, "The governor should be allowed to speak. It is only right." A formidable grassroots surge had finally seized the presidential nomination away from the northeastern elites who had for so long dominated the Republican national conventions. The delegates were in no mood to hear from the king of Republican moderates and drowned him out. Rockefeller was proposing an unwelcome plank repudiating right-wing extremists—specifically, the Ku Klux Klan and the John Birch Society. "This is still a free country, ladies and gentlemen," cried Rocky from the podium. But this convention was no place for New York swells. The delegates rejected him and his bleeding-heart proposal.

"From 1936 through 1960," wrote activist Phyllis Schlafly, "a few secret kingmakers based in New York selected every Republican presidential nominee . . . and successfully forced their choice on a free country." Now, at long last, exulted Schlafly, the conservatives had their candidate, Barry Goldwater, and he would give Americans a real Republican alternative, not just an echo of the Big Government Democrats. In a famous essay, historian Richard Hofstadter waved at Schlafly's pamphlet as a prime example of the "paranoid style in American Politics." But, whether or not a cabal of "secret kingmakers" had been picking the nominees, she reflected something very real—the long conservative frustration with party moderates and moderation.[3]

When Barry Goldwater rose to speak, he thrilled the convention with words directed at the despised Rockefeller and his cronies. "I would remind you that extremism in the defense of liberty is no vice. And let me remind you also that moderation in the pursuit of justice is no virtue." He underlined the phrase so the press could not miss it. The modern Republican Party rose up out of that convention and eventually transformed American politics.

Following Goldwater's lead, the convention shrugged off the accusations of extremism within their own ranks and, instead, condemned what they saw as the "real" national problem—crime.

Former President Dwight Eisenhower (1953–1961) took the podium and offered the delegates a tour of the troubles: "Crime in our cities and our parks," "attacks upon law-enforcement officials," "juvenile delinquency," and "disorders arising out of the effort to integrate our institutions of learning." And, without a word about the violence toward black Americans, Ike launched a broadside against a well-worn trope: "Let us not be guilty of maudlin sympathy for the criminal, who roaming the streets with a switchblade knife and an illegal firearm, . . . suddenly becomes, upon apprehension, a poor, underprivileged person who counts upon the compassion of our society." Both Eisenhower and Goldwater promised a "government of law and order," a phrase that Republicans would swing like a cudgel for the next generation. Finally, though it was not in his prepared text, Eisenhower paused for a moment and scornfully attacked the biased, liberal media.[4]

Here was the mix that would power the right through the next two generations: derision toward the smug northeastern establishment, a cry against federal bureaucrats, the call for local independence, a tough stance on law and order, contempt for the urban masses, and attacks on the media—all inflected with something more ominous.

THIRTY-ONE-YEAR-OLD BELVA DAVIS WAS A RADIO JOURnalist reporting from the convention for the Bay Area's soul-gospel-jazz station. "I could feel the hostility rising like steam off a cauldron of vitriol," she later wrote. When Eisenhower spoke, she noted that in the middle of a moderate address, he sent the crowd into a frenzy with his lines about the underprivileged person with a switchblade. "Without uttering the word negro," Davis continued, "the former president spoke in a code that needed no translation for those . . . who regarded black people as an encroaching threat."

The crowd turned menacing when Rockefeller rose to speak. Suddenly, "I heard a voice yell "Hey niggers . . . what the hell are you niggers doing in here?" Davis and her boss swiftly packed up their recording equipment and headed for the exit. "As we began our descent down the ramps . . . a self-appointed posse dangled over the railings, taunting. 'Niggers!' 'Get out of here, boy.' 'You too nigger bitch.' 'Go on get out.' 'I'm going to kill your ass.'" As they walked down the long ramp, the throng began to hurl things at them—"waded up convention programs, mustard-soaked hotdogs, half eaten Snickers bars." A glass soda bottled whizzed within inches of her skull and shattered against the concrete wall. They passed indifferent security guards. In this era, reported Davis, there was no turning to law enforcement for help—"that wasn't a realistic expectation for any African American in 1964."[5]

Jackie Robinson, the star who broke baseball's color barrier, was also at the convention as an alternate delegate for Nelson Rockefeller—part of the dwindling band of black Republicans. "That convention was one of the most unforgettable and frightening experiences of my life," reported Robinson in an editorial. "A new breed of Republican had taken over the GOP. As I watched this steamroller operation in San Francisco, I had a better understanding of how it must have felt to be a Jew in Hitler's Germany." Robinson's description about "the terrible hour for the relatively few black delegates" splashed across the front pages of the black press.[6]

Other black Republicans picked up the theme. "Some Negros are Republicans because of their conservative philosophy," observed the African American vice chair of Georgia's Fulton County Republican committee, Dr. Lee Shelton, "but none are anti-Negro. That's what they are asked to be in the Goldwater campaign." A long roster of black leaders joined the criticism—Martin Luther King, James Farmer, A. Philip Randolph. One journalist summed up the racial fears: "Goldwater's managers will cynically seek to inflame Negro-white tensions in the hope that a civil rights explosion would propel their man into the White House on a tide of segregationist votes."[7]

The 1964 election marked the end of a significant black presence in the Republican Party. The slow African American trek across the party aisle that first stirred in 1932, and swelled in 1948, now came to its conclusion three decades after it began. Almost 95 percent of African Americans would push the Democratic button. By the end of the decade, (white) Republican strategists had seized the great irony of the age: the migration of black voters out of the GOP would foster a new Republican majority.

BACK WHEN THE PHOENIX, ARIZONA, SCHOOLS WERE STILL segregated, the principal of a black school asked Goldwater why his family department store donated gold watches as commencement prizes only to the white schools. Because, replied Goldwater, he did not believe in segregation and did not want to encourage it by awarding prizes to segregated schools. But the white schools are every bit as segregated, responded the principal. Goldwater thought about it and smiled. From then on, the black school got the gold watches too. As Martin Luther King put it, Barry Goldwater was no racist. But—and it was a very large but—he "articulates a philosophy which gives aid and comfort to racists." Goldwater was fair, principled, and unbiased, yet, he managed to finish the job of turning the Republican party white.[8]

Barry Goldwater's message put him on the same perilous crossroad that we have encountered in every chapter of American history: fighting the feds keeps getting linked to projects of racial repression. Goldwater tripped the issue just three weeks before the Republican convention, during the debate over the Civil Rights Act of 1964. The blockbuster legislation, which prohibited employment discrimination and ended legal segregation in public places, was the culmination of the civil rights movement. All eyes were on Congress as it battled over the law. The act passed easily through the House of

Representatives and came before the full Senate on March 30. There it faced the same southern filibuster that had blunted every previous civil rights proposal. Democratic Senator Richard Russell of Georgia enacted the South's familiar routine: "We will resist to the bitter end any measure that will bring about"—what else—the "intermingling and amalgamation of the races in our southern states."[9]

The filibuster ground on and on for sixty working days (including six Saturdays). The bill's manager, Hubert Humphrey, scrambled for the sixty-eight votes necessary to stop the debate and bring the measure to a vote (today, it only takes sixty). Northern Democrats led the charge, Southern Democrats the opposition. The split among Democrats pushed the fate of the Civil Rights Act to the Republicans and, ultimately, their minority leader Everett Dirksen of Illinois. (People used to chuckle about old Ev—in a thousand words or less, Senator Dirksen, are you loquacious?) Dirksen rewrote the act, adding more than seventy amendments that softened the workplace provisions and left more authority for the states. By the end, judged *Time*, it was "Dirksen's bill, bearing his handiwork more than anyone else's." On June 10, after Democratic Senator Robert Byrd of West Virginia completed a fourteen-hour oration, Hubert Humphrey moved for cloture and, for the first time in history, the Senate broke a filibuster over a civil rights bill. On June 19, 1964, the Senate passed its epic Civil Rights Act and on July 2, President Lyndon Johnson signed it into law.

Northern Democrats voted aye (forty-five to one), Southern Democrats nay (one to twenty) and Republicans made the difference (twenty-seven to six). But the victory did not win back black voters because the loudest Republican vote was Barry Goldwater's nay. He had consulted future Supreme Court Chief Justice William Rehnquist and future Supreme Court nominee Robert Bork, and both assured him the act was flatly unconstitutional. Goldwater rose in the Senate and declared that the Civil Rights Act would strip America "of our God-given liberties" and require a "federal police force of mammoth proportions." Here, he said, were "the hallmarks of the police state and landmarks in the destruction of a free society."[10]

It may have been a principled position but consider the context. Even as the Senate debate came to an end, the wires buzzed with news from Philadelphia, Mississippi. A church had been torched and three civil rights activists who'd gone to inspect the damage— James Chaney, Andrew Goodman, and Michael Schwerner—had vanished. Their charred station wagon had been found, and FBI agents descended on Mississippi to look for the killers. Sailors waded through swamps to help with the search, wielding wooden clubs to ward off the water moccasins. Three hundred college students raced in to take up the dangerous cause, while local sheriff Lawrence Rainey scorned the whole fuss. Rainey had shot and killed two black men in the last four years—there were no punishments either time—but he would soon be in the dock for the murder of the three activists. Seventeen other men were also indicted. They came from the police department, the sheriff's office, and the KKK. At the very same time, over in Saint Augustine, Florida, Martin Luther King was leading "wade ins" at a segregated beach while hundreds of angry whites itched for a brawl. "I favor violence to preserve the white race any time, any place, anywhere," screamed one demagogue whipping up the backlash. "Now, I grant you some niggers are gonna get killed in the process, but when war's on, that's what happens."[11]

When Everett Dirksen endorsed Barry Goldwater just ten days after the Civil Rights bill went through the Senate, the Republican's forfeited any credit they might have gotten from black voters for their crucial role in winning the civil rights bill. A different context might have accommodated Goldwater's insistence that racism was a problem of the heart, not of the law. But Mississippi—and America—were burning. And the Goldwater campaign stayed stubbornly mum about the racial hatred screaming all around it.

The media portrayed the Goldwater movement as a white resistance campaign. Walter Lippmann, one of the most respected journalists of the era, put it this way: "When Senator Barry Goldwater went campaigning in the south, his purpose [was] . . . to inaugurate the so-called southern strategy in order to lay the foundations for a radically new Republican party." The Republican's southern strategy meant gathering up the region's white Democrats who resented their party's assault on segregation and white supremacy. The campaign silently accommodated the white supremacists who flocked to their candidate. Goldwater was just one more character tangled in the American crisscross: attacking national government and upholding racial segregation.[12]

The Goldwater campaign was a peculiar mash up of the boring and the incendiary. Goldwater stuck to his principles and bravely challenged popular government programs almost everywhere he went. He attacked Social Security in Florida and pledged to shut down the popular Tennessee Valley Authority when he spoke in Tennessee. Across the South, he stuck earnestly to his attack on government. But he never said a word about the roaring festival of segregation and whiteness that erupted all around him. Strom Thurmond, who had been the Dixiecrat candidate in 1948, now changed parties and enthusiastically campaigned for Goldwater. Ardent segregationists from across Dixie joined Goldwater on his highly publicized southern tour. And through it all, there was never a discouraging word from the campaign or the candidate.[13]

When the campaign arrived in Montgomery, Alabama, it held a rally at a stadium planted with a mass of white lilies. Seven hundred white girls wearing white dresses waved American flags. The candidate rolled into the stadium in a car and gave a meandering speech about how difficult it was to cut government spending. The crowd ignored the talk and roared defiance against the feds as the whiteness pageant—girls, lilies, dresses, and ardent segregationists all buzzing around the candidate—gave the warm autumn night a surreal haze.[14]

The Republicans were finally turning away from their Northeast moderates. Conservative party members had been debating an alliance with the South since the 1940s. Now they finally tied that knot. The Republicans would not nominate another northeasterner for a half century. In Congress, leadership would shift west and south. But the backlash against government and civil rights was not merely a southern phenomenon. Nor was it confined to just Republicans. The biggest surprise of the 1964 campaign was how well it all played up North—among the Democrats.

GEORGE WALLACE WAS ELECTED GOVERNOR OF ALABAMA IN 1962 and barged onto the national scene with a growling inaugural address. "An international colored majority," he warned, was persecuting whites around the world, shedding innocent white blood from the Congo to Cuba to Oxford, Mississippi. Black people were deploying the power of what he called the "federal dictatorship" to sexually transgress the color line and achieve "amalgamation." Over and over, he pitched his fears—foreigners, the feds, interracial sex, and the end of whiteness. His most often quoted defiance summarizes the whole, long speech: "In the name of the greatest people that have ever trod this earth, I draw the line in the dust and toss the gauntlet before the feet of tyranny . . . and I say . . . segregation today . . . segregation tomorrow . . . segregation forever."[15]

Wallace mixed something new into the old bigotry. Danger loomed, not just from the black population in the South but also from blacks on distant shores. Here was a kind of racialized red scare. A multitude of newly independent nations was rising in Africa and Asia. Some had thrown off colonial rule and shed European blood. Now, it was no longer just the implacable Yankees pushing racial equality but a whole world of tribes that the State Department was courting during the Cold War. Six months later, in June 1963, Wallace made the national news when he stood in a doorway at the University of Alabama and theatrically refused admission to two African American students. (Two hours after the show, the students quietly enrolled.)[16]

That fall, Wallace went North to joust with the liberals. During the tour, he skipped the racist epithets, brushed up his act, posed as a mischievous rapscallion from the South, and debated the students who packed into a Harvard University theater to resist him. "Oh, I know you," he said to one, "you're Bob Zellner and you're a renowned Alabamian. In fact, you've been in a number of jails in Alabama." At least, that's how it was reported in the Alabama press—a low-key, rather charming quip to a well-known civil rights activist. None of the Boston papers made any mention of the exchange. As Wallace slickly worked the enemy territory, a wild idea took shape. He could run for president.[17]

Wallace challenged President Lyndon Johnson and entered the Wisconsin primary in 1964. At the time, only fourteen states held Democratic primaries and they were low key affairs—in fact, Wisconsin governor John Reynolds was on the ballot as a surrogate for President Johnson and he laughingly dismissed Wallace as a "kook." But, on the campaign trail, Wallace returned to his hot, race-baiting mode and ominously warned the whites in Wisconsin that the Civil Rights Act would drive them from their jobs, their homes, their farms, and their schools. On primary day, the returns stunned everyone. Wallace captured 266,000 votes—more than 33 percent of the Democratic votes cast. He didn't win but, as the *New York Times* put it, Wallace had managed "to win without winning." One anonymous Democrat spoke the party's fear: "When a nationally disliked racist from deep Dixie can get 25 percent of the vote [across both parties] in a state like Wisconsin, I'd say we're all in for a hot summer. And who can dare predict anything?"[18]

Next, it was on to Indiana where, a month later, Wallace managed just under 30 percent. And then Maryland, where his blunt segregationist appeal carried fifteen out of twenty-three counties and a total of 43 percent of the Democratic vote, smashing all turnout records. Only a large black vote in Baltimore salvaged President Johnson's surrogate. Wallace was not actually winning the primaries, but he was gathering hundreds of thousands of votes. Liberal politicians were flummoxed. Wallace spun civil rights as a terrible threat to whites—and, in many communities, the people responded. "If the civil rights bill was what governor Wallace said it was," complained Attorney General Robert Kennedy, "I'd be against it too." Black leaders kept reminding the swarming journalists that "Negroes were not trying to take jobs away from whites" but simply "fighting centuries of discrimination." On the other side, southern politicians cheered the "tremendous protest vote against the so-called Civil Rights Bill."[19]

Primaries had not yet spread beyond a handful of states, and the president remained in firm control of the party and its convention, so Wallace had no chance to build on his strong showing. But the Wallace tallies sent a loud, clear message. The civil rights struggle was more than a regional conflict in which a bipartisan coalition of Democrats and Republicans from the North imposed human rights on the stubborn segregationists in the South. There were, it turned out, plenty of fretful white northerners who thought their tribe would lose out in the liberation of black America. To them, civil rights were not a matter of simple justice, but raised deep-seated fears. They tuned right into Wallace's message—a different people were getting a boost at the expense of people like you.

We have seen the same feeling in every chapter—igniting the Detroit race riots, for example, or cheering Senator Stephen Douglas's contempt for "Frederick Douglass, the negro" riding in the carriage with the wife and daughter back in 1858. And in Abraham Lincoln's agonized rejection of racial equality before the Civil War: "My own feelings would not admit of this and if mine would, we all know that those of the great mass of whites will not." Now, the roaring reaction to Wallace in the ethnic enclaves of Wisconsin and the rural districts of Maryland hinted at what was coming—the end of the old Roosevelt–New Deal coalition. These were districts that celebrated FDR's Social Security Act but were uneasy about LBJ's civil rights legislation. Wallace explained how civil rights was unfair to their people—and, in some quarters, white ethnic loyalty to the Democratic Party began to crack.[20]

Wallace himself would not cash in on the ruckus he created in 1964. Once the Republicans had safely selected Goldwater, the Southern Democrats pushed Wallace aside. Former Georgia governor Marvin Griffin, a strong Wallace supporter, now announced that he should "get out of the race to avoid hurting Mr. Goldwater's chances." "We ought not divide our forces," he explained. Over the years, the cerebral Arizonan would come to be celebrated as the godfather of the conservative revival while the pugnacious Wallace is largely forgotten—a fringe, atavistic cry against racial progress. Back in 1964, however, they both provoked the same tribal fervor against the coming racial revolution—in the North and the South, among Republicans and Democrats. Conservative Republicans and Southern Democrats were perfectly frank about the need to avoid "dividing their forces."[21]

Together, each in a different way, Goldwater and Wallace point to the stresses that run right across American history. Goldwater blithely ignored the fervid racial passion of his supporters. Wallace went out of his way to provoke the tribal feelings. They expressed attitudes that would sweep the country before long. But neither got very far in 1964. Instead, LBJ and the Democrats swept the election and, in the next two years, changed American government and what it does.

———

PRESIDENT LYNDON JOHNSON AND THE DEMOCRATS WON their biggest landslide in modern history. LBJ grabbed over 61 percent of the popular vote—more than Franklin Roosevelt at the height of his popularity. The Democrats racked up their second highest electoral vote total (after 1936) and stormed to super majorities in Congress (68–32 in the Senate, 295–140 in the House). The Republicans, temporarily cast into the political darkness, would have been consoled to know that Goldwater presaged the future. True, he only managed five states outside his own, but they all lay in the Deep South. The faithful Dixie Democrats were finally turning to the Republicans. Before long, the south would anchor a new Republican majority. The Democrats would manage no more than a single southern state in eight of the next eleven presidential contests. On the Democratic side of the historical ledger, the massive liberal majority, led by LBJ's legislative wizardry, redefined American governance. To this day, Americans live and fight in the shadow of the mighty Eighty-Ninth Congress. Our own political debates spring directly from the laws that followed the landslide of 1964. Consider four of them.

In most history books, northern and southern Democrats are always on the verge of blows. Almost every description—including mine—emphasizes their passionate differences. The strange rise of federal health policy, however, illustrates a very different side to the story. One of the Eighty-Ninth Congress's most far-reaching achievements was winning two massive health care programs, Medicare and Medicaid. But they would never have passed if, as today, the conservatives and liberals were in different parties.

In his powerful role as chairman of the House Ways and Means Committee, Arkansas Congressman Wilbur Mills, a Democrat, had quashed Medicare proposals, year after year. In late 1964, he almost managed to "kill Medicare forever," as one flummoxed liberal put it, by proposing an enormous increase in Social Security benefits and the payroll taxes that paid for them. Since Medicare would also be paid for by payroll taxes, a very large increase would make additional tax hikes (and therefore Medicare itself) extremely difficult to legislate for a long time to come. At the last minute, the president managed to outmaneuver Mills and kill the increase.[22]

Six weeks later, the Democratic landslide made Medicare seem inevitable. By one count, forty-four pro-Medicare liberals swept into the House. Now Wilbur Mills somersaulted. He led the House Ways and Means Committee through its paces on the Medicare proposal, and suddenly, at the very end of the markups and in secret collaboration with President Johnson (revealed in recently released White House tapes), he pulled a legendary coup. There were three different bills before the committee. The administration's Medicare proposal covered hospital care for people over sixty-five (now Medicare Part A). Wisconsin Republican John Byrnes proposed an alternative, which he thought would be smaller—covering physician services for elderly Americans who voluntarily signed up (now Medicare Part B). And a conservative plan proposed health insurance for low income Americans through a nationally organized but state-administered program (now known as Medicaid). Mills shocked everyone in the room when he took the three competing proposals, folded them all into a single big bill, and sent them to the House floor for an immediate vote. President Johnson, feigning surprise at a bill that was almost three times the size of the administration proposal, approved the package and—as he had secretly promised he would in multiple phone calls—passed all the credit back to Congressman Mills, who had suddenly gone from the program's enemy to "a hero for the old folks," as LBJ put it.[23]

What explains Mills's switch? Most scholars speculate that once the reform seemed inevitable, he wanted to maintain his own influence. Or that he was aiming to limit future program expansions by covering the neediest—the old and the poor. At the time, it all looked like politics as usual. But from the perspective of our own era—where conservatives have gathered into the rival party and oppose all big government proposals with an iron consistency—the Mills flip shows us just how unusual and how fluid the New Deal Democratic coalition could be.

Beyond race and labor issues, the regional sides negotiated and logrolled, adjusting to the political alignment of the moment—as Wilbur Mills and the Southern Democrats did on Medicare and Medicaid. Southerners, in particular, were committed to Congress as an institution. Yes, they routinely frustrated liberal reformers. And the horror they expressed over the most basic civil rights—like African Americans voting, or prospering, or marrying whom they liked—indicts them for all time. But there is more to the story of this strange coalition. Left, right, or center, Democrats were members of the same party and shared overlapping goals. Being part of a majority coalition kept the liberal agenda in play and offered the left occasional opportunities. Conservative Democrats fought hard against Medicare when they were in control, but they led the way to a robust and popular program when their liberal colleagues had the votes. The two sides accommodated one another—for better and for worse—in ways that would no longer be possible when liberals and conservatives had sorted themselves into rival parties. Two of the most significant consequences, Medicare and Medicaid, would soon redefine American medical care, and today, the two together pay for more than one out of every three health care dollars spent in the United States. Every major health reform proposal since that time—from both Democrats and Republicans—would build on the foundations of Wilbur Mill's unexpected coup.

THE BIGGEST HISTORICAL BANG MADE THE SMALLEST SOUND as it passed into law. In 1965, Congress quietly, almost casually, threw the United States open to immigration again. Congress had shut off most immigration in 1921, and it had stayed shut—strict national quotas squeezed the number of newcomers to a thin trickle.

In 1960, for example, only thirty-five thousand foreigners landed on American shores—almost all of them (84 percent) from Europe and Canada. The almost-closed door clashed with the image of the United States as the leader of the free world. President Truman called it an "absurdity" from the dead age of isolationism. His successors Eisenhower and Kennedy both echoed him. Now, the Johnson administration reframed the idea for the times. Small national quotas were just another form of racial discrimination. Why not accept people on the basis of the skills they brought to America rather than the countries they happened to be from? Why not open the United States to the world? Johnson sent a special message to Congress two months after his landslide, and supporters lined up to denounce still another form of senseless racial discrimination.[24]

Framing immigration as a civil rights issue inevitably agitated some opposition. Democratic Senator Sam Ervin of North Carolina charged that the proposal discriminated "against the people who have made the greatest contribution to building up our country." Why, asked Erwin, would we put northern Europeans on "the same basis as Ethiopia?" "I don't know what contribution Ethiopia has made," he cracked. But in the middle of the fiery civil rights protests, the immigration debate fell to page two—a side issue with the same sides but a lot less heat.[25]

Once again, the 1964 landslide changed the political calculus. And once again an unlikely conservative rewrote the reform. The chair of the House Judiciary Committee, Congressman Michael Feighan, was a veteran Democrat from Cleveland. He was not enthusiastic about immigration reform but soon succumbed to the famous Johnson treatment—dinner in the White House, chats in the Oval Office, and flights on Air Force One. He finally agreed not to bury the reform in his committee, but he insisted on rewriting the proposal. (When LBJ conquered a legislator, he backed off and let them define the details.) In his rewrite, Feighan changed the entry rules. Rather than recruit immigrants on the basis of their skills, as the administration proposed, the Feighan revision emphasized family reunification. That, he reasoned, would bring lots of Irish and Germans (who already had family on these shores) while cutting off the Ethiopians (who did not). As a result, the Hart–Celler Immigration Act of 1965 repealed the national quotas and reestablished immigration based primarily on uniting families.

Everybody was wrong. Standing in the shadow of the Statue of Liberty in October 1965, President Johnson signed the law and predicted it was "not . . . revolutionary." Senator Ted Kennedy, who helped guide the bill through the Senate, pledged that "the ethnic mix of this country will not be upset." But in trying to ensure just that, Congressman Feighan rewrote the legislation in a way that ended up achieving the opposite. The prosperous Europeans were not itching to move to the United States, but people from poorer nations were. And as they arrived, the new system tilted immigration toward their relatives.

A long-delayed law, passed in the shadow of the civil rights movement, created a slow-motion revolution in the nation's ethnic composition. A formidable culture war—and perhaps the most explosive issue of the 2010s—flowed out of this quiet effort to restore "the faith that brought thousands to these shores," as LBJ had put it. The legislation would bring not "thousands" but millions. And, despite all the predictions to the contrary, it once again remade the face of the nation. It would also change the face of the political parties. Immigration reform was, from the start, linked to civil rights—the issue that was already transforming the parties. What lay just ahead—as a direct result of this casual legislation—was something new in American history. For the first time, the same political faction would support both liberal civil rights policies and liberal immigration policies. The other side came to oppose both. The political parties would, for the first time, join the fierce passion (and the fury) of America's two most powerful identity issues—race and immigration.

CIVIL RIGHTS ACTIVISTS WERE GROWING IMPATIENT. CONgress had passed the Civil Rights Act, but African Americans still couldn't vote in much of the South. President Johnson juggled his blockbuster bills. He wanted to win Medicare and follow that with an ambitious education bill before taking on voting rights. Civil rights activists, however, led by the Students Nonviolent Coordinating Committee (or SNCC) took to the streets to speed up LBJ's timetable.

They targeted Selma, Alabama. The city had 29,500 people with a slight black majority, but the voting rolls remained almost entirely white. Selma's Sheriff James Clark, an implacable segregationist, led the resistance, sporting his famous lapel pin inscribed "*Never*." *Time* called him "a bully-boy segregationist who leads a club-swinging, mounted posse of deputy volunteers, many of them Ku Klux Klansmen." Across all of Alabama, black registration had reached just 19 percent, and the situation in Mississippi was even worse with just 6 percent registered.[26]

On one February night in 1965, protesters marched through Marion, twenty-five miles northwest of Selma. Suddenly, the streetlights went dark and troopers, along with white "volunteers," charged the protesters, beating them with clubs and blinding them with flashlights. One protester, Jimmie Lee Jackson, fled with his mother and grandfather into Mack's Café where police chased after them, threw him against a cigarette machine, and fatally shot him in the stomach. Another American bled to death for the right to vote. Jimmie Lee's murder riveted national attention on the Selma campaign.

On March 7, just five days after Wilbur Mills had pulled his Medicare coup, some six hundred civil rights activists began a march from Selma to Montgomery, the state capital fifty miles away. The marchers walked out of a Methodist church carrying bed rolls and lunch sacks, and went six blocks to the Edmund Pettus Bridge. On

the other side, at the edge of the business district, they encountered helmeted state troopers, local cops, mounted possemen, and
hostile white spectators. As the marchers approached, State Police
Major John Cloud commanded them to go back. The troops donned
gas masks. The marchers stopped and quietly stood their ground.
Suddenly, the troopers rushed forward in a wedge, wielding their
clubs. The civil rights marchers began to stumble, fall, and scream.
Horsemen rode in, some cracking bullwhips. The white bystanders
"whooped and cheered" while the marchers scrambled to get out of
harm's way. Then tear gas canisters burst on the melee and a thick
grey cloud obscured the newsmen's view.[27]

As Sheriff Clark and his men tried to force the marchers all the
way back into the church, the marchers began to fight back. They
threw bricks and bottles at the cops and forced them to retreat.
Many activists had been marching and bleeding and suffering arrests
for years—and they were running out of patience. As the marchers limped back into the church, SNCC chair John Lewis made a
roaring speech. "I don't see how President Johnson can send troops
to Vietnam—I don't see how he can send troops to the Congo—I
don't see how he can send troops to Africa—and can't send troops
to Selma, Alabama." Then he went to the hospital to be treated for
his broken skull.[28]

ABC news interrupted its programming to broadcast live footage
of the clash—something new in television technology. The brutal
images stunned most Americans. As one administration official put
it, this "was the deepest sense of outrage [the public] has ever felt on
a civil rights question." Protests sprang up across the nation. Demonstrators clogged the hallway of the justice department demanding federal intervention. Clerics from around the country dropped
everything they were doing and raced to Selma to stand with the
marchers. Within a week, one of them, Unitarian Minister James
Reeb of Roxbury, Massachusetts, had been beaten to death by four
white men outside the Silver Moon Cafe.[29]

Johnson had been secretly negotiating a voting rights bill with Republican minority leader Everett Dirksen while he finagled his health and education bills through Congress. Now the mayhem in Selma forced his hand. The speaker of the House invited the president to address a joint session of Congress, the first (other than State of the Union addresses) since Harry Truman had declared the Cold War in 1946. On March 15, 1965, Johnson delivered the most powerful and moving speech of his presidency, a soaring sermon about the American mission in the twentieth century:

> Rarely in any time does an issue lay bare the secret heart of America itself. Rarely are we met with a challenge, not to our growth or abundance, our welfare or our security but rather to the values and the purposes and the meaning of our beloved nation.
>
> The issue of equal rights for American Negroes is such an issue. And should we defeat every enemy, should we double our wealth and conquer the stars, and still be unequal to this issue, then we will have failed as a people and a nation.
>
> For with a whole country, as with a person, "What is a man profited, if he shall gain the whole world, and lose his own soul?"[30]

As he delivered the address, Congress sat in deep silence and then five minutes into the address, at the end of the passage quoted here, exploded into applause. After that, almost every sentence provoked cheering. Senate Majority Leader Mike Mansfield visibly choked back tears. Supreme Court justices put aside their "judicial stillness" and cheered. The next day, in a glowing report, the *New York Times* commented that "no other president had so completely identified himself with the cause of the American Negro. No other president had made the issue of equality for negroes so clearly a moral cause . . . for all Americans."[31]

Not everyone cheered. Senator George Smathers of Florida clapped "tentatively." Senator Allan Ellender of Louisiana slumped "gloomily" in his seat." But the inevitable southern filibuster was no longer what it had once been, and after twenty-four days of drama for the folks back home, the Senate voted to cut off debate and easily passed the bill.[32]

The Voting Rights Act of 1965 banned literacy tests and injected federal oversight into areas where less than 50 percent of the non-white population had registered. The bill authorized federal surveillance in seven states: Alabama, Georgia, Louisiana, Mississippi, South Carolina, Virginia, and Alaska, and in 26 counties in North Carolina and one in Arizona. Johnson signed the voting rights act on August 6, 1965—exactly a week after signing Medicare.

Most legislation takes years to have an impact, but not this one. Within the week, federal marshals were in the South overseeing registration. The attorney general had every reason to feel "elated" as people rushed to register. "They came," enthused *Time*, "in battered autos and chartered buses and on foot. They stood in the shimmering heat of midsummer and they waited," in many cases doubling and tripling the number of registered African Americans in a town or county. Within months, 250,000 black Americans registered to vote. Almost fifty years later, in 2012, when Barack Obama was running for reelection, the national percentage of black people voting inched past the percentage of whites for the first time in American history. Journalist David Remnick penned a beautiful image: on the other side of Edmund Pettus bridge, finally, stood an African American president.

The Voting Rights Act of 1965 offered a rare challenge to state control over voting. States and localities with a history of discrimination—mostly in the South—would now be required to receive approval from the Department of Justice for their election procedures and any changes they made to them. Those national rules would remain in place until June 2013 when the Supreme Court ruled (five to four) that, in Chief Justice John Roberts's phrase, "the United States has changed." Within two hours, Texas had pushed through restrictive legislation that the Department of Justice had previously forbidden. Twenty-three other states swiftly followed with new voting rules.[33]

The Voting Rights Act was a blockbuster—one of the great civil rights achievements in American history. But it was also part of a long, bitter, and often forgotten history. Americans have wrestled over who votes and how since the very first contested election. And that conflict always grew hottest—and most violent—around the race line. We saw the "appeal of 40,000 citizens" back in 1838 when the Democrats in Philadelphia extended the franchise to poor white men and stripped it from black men with property. We saw it again during Reconstruction, when the effort to empower black voters got tangled up in nativist fears about the Irish or the Chinese coming to power. And, again, when Senator Henry Cabot Lodge proposed a Voting Rights bill in 1890—derided as a "force" bill and buried in the very first filibuster. Or when Frances Willard, the inspiring women's leader, cheered on the Mississippi convention organized to strip the vote from black men. In a larger historical context, the Voting Rights Act was not a metaphorical bridge to power but one victory for voting rights in a very long and bloody history that has seen each advance followed, eventually, by backlash. Still, the civil rights legislation seemed—and was—monumental when it passed.

Time itself seemed to compress. Selma's Bloody Sunday erupted on March 7. The next day, marines splashed onto the beaches of Danang, Vietnam, marking the start of a massive war effort that would peak with more than a half million American servicemen and women in Southeast Asia. President Johnson signed the Medicare and Medicaid bills on July 30 and the Voting Rights Act on August 6. Five days after that, Los Angeles burst into flames.

IN AUGUST 1965, POLICE MADE A ROUTINE TRAFFIC STOP IN Watts, a poor, black neighborhood in Los Angeles. The cops charged twenty-one-year-old Marquette Frye with driving while intoxicated, and a crowd began to gather. Frye's mother came to the scene to keep the car from being towed away and loudly scolded her son. Marquette began to shout that he was not going to jail, and suddenly, one cop drew a revolver and another brandished a shotgun at the restless crowd. "This officer had this man handcuffed in the car," reported a nearby grocery store owner. "The officer took his club and kept jamming it into his stomach. All the people standing around got mad." The crowd exploded into riot that went on for six days. By the time it ended, thirty-four people lay dead, over one thousand were injured, and whole blocks had been torched. Some fourteen thousand National Guard troops deployed to Watts and arrested thousands.

Time had planned a cover celebrating the voting rights breakthrough. Instead, it ran pictures from the war zone in Watts and commented that the two stories were "intricately intertwined." The violence grew and spread over the next four summers, as riots burst out in black districts across the nation.[34]

African American leaders like Dr. King had focused on the South, and through their long, difficult, patient strategy of peaceful protest, demanded basic human rights in the face of terrible violence. Despite the agonizing pace, the strategy seemed to work. All those stories of murder, arson, beating, whipping, fire hoses, police dogs, castrations, and derision drew many Americans to the moral cause. But there was an audience that the civil rights leaders had not reckoned with. Young black Americans in other parts of the country watched the implacable violence over simple things—a walk in the park, a seat at the lunch counter, a place in the pew. Yet, scarcely a word about the troubles they faced every day. In Los Angeles, the black population had leapt from 63,000 in 1950 to 350,000 by 1965. Good jobs and good neighborhoods were closed to them. Black Angelinos lived in dilapidated areas and were attacked when they ventured into nicer ones. Republicans in the state legislature had passed the Rumford Fair Housing Act in 1963, which would have limited racial discrimination by rental agencies and property owners, but the following year, opponents put it to the public in a referendum and the act was buried in a landslide, two to one.

The largely white and often violent LAPD added to the friction. While the press flooded into Selma and Birmingham, there was no national audience denouncing the everyday brutality in Los Angeles. Along with everyone else, young African Americans watched white folks cheer as white cops in Selma beat and whipped and cursed black people on live television. And all for what? The right to vote, which the young people in LA already had.

Martin Luther King tried desperately to juggle all sides of the movement. White liberal allies could no longer dash in and stand alongside black activists when prayers and songs and marches morphed into "burn baby burn." This, they warned, would lose the sympathy of the nation. As Watts blazed, King deplored the violence. "It is absolutely wrong, socially detestable and self-defeating," he said. But King also scrambled to keep up with the angry youngsters: "I equally deplore," he added, "the continuation of ghetto life that millions of Negroes have to live. They are in hopeless despair and they feel that they have no stake in the society."[35]

Many African Americans had lost patience with the practice of turning the other cheek. How many times could they march peacefully into horrific violence without fighting back? Many began to give up on implacable white America. James Baldwin put it bluntly: "To be a negro in this country . . . is to be in a rage all the time." And black journalist Louis Lomax: "The negro masses are angry and restless, tired of prolonged legal battles that end in paper decrees." Black nationalists—the Panthers, the LA street gangs, the Nation of Islam—called on black Americans to stop being submissive, to stand up and fight back. African Americans refused to remain the "submissive," "dominated," "timid," "female" race, as historian Gerald Horne put it. They would stand their ground.

The real shock in Watts, barely comprehensible to the media covering the riot, lay in the self-conscious black insurrection. Men grabbed guns and fired on the police and state troopers. "One man," ran a shocked dispatch from the scene, "had incredibly taken up a post on a rooftop overlooking the Watts Seventy-Fourth Street precinct station" and directed fire at the police and National Guard. He blazed away until the National Guard sharpshooters shot and killed him.[36]

By the end of the Watts riots, jarring news accounts depicted a tribal war. White backlash surged across the North. Young white men formed vigilante gangs, "organized to fight marauding Negroes," as one of the men put it. The *New York Times* quoted a minister in Pasadena: "The racial hatred among white people will take years to erase." The run on gun stores was "fantastic," concluded a television writer, and "there is a . . . terrifying . . . smell of violence in both the white and negro communities."[37]

King went to Chicago the following January to begin a campaign against racial discrimination in housing and neighborhoods, and was stunned by the reaction. He testified that he had "never seen— even in Mississippi and Alabama—mobs as hostile and hate filled as I've seen in Chicago." Now his brand of nonviolence faced hostility on the (white) right and derision on the (black) left. His former allies were out of patience. Nonviolence was yesterday's plan. King just did not seem to understand, they said, what had to be done to win a revolution. "I had preached to them about my dream," wrote a mournful King, "I had urged them to have faith in America and in white society." But in Chicago, his own people booed him "because they felt we were unable to deliver on our promises."[38]

In April 1968, a paid assassin and ardent racist shot and killed Martin Luther King—as murderers had gunned down so many civil rights activists before him. The cities across the nation exploded into riots. Now, who would call upon protesters to love thy enemy? "The next black man who comes into a black neighborhood preaching nonviolence," responded militant Julius Hobson, "should get a taste of violence." Nonviolence," said one long-suffering black leader, is "as foreign to this violent country as speaking Russian." "White America understands no other language," added another.[39]

WHEN LBJ STOOD IN THE WELL OF THE HOUSE AND DELIVered his soaring address calling for passage of the Voting Rights Act, the economy was booming—GDP growth hovered around 6 percent per year. Medicare and Medicaid stood poised to pass through Congress. The launch pads for the Apollo space mission were almost ready. The United States—and the Johnson administration—was flying high. But the president boldly waved all that aside and insisted on a far more demanding metric of national worth. None of it mattered if the United States failed to win civil rights. Racial equality was the true test of American ideals, of American democracy, of America itself.[40]

Johnson had directly challenged the country. "If we are unequal to this issue," he had said, "we will have failed as a people and a nation." For a whole generation, at least on the left, the results spoke for themselves. The shots that struck down Martin Luther King three years later seemed to sound a terrible verdict on Johnson's soaring challenge to the nation.

I was in high school at the time and it is impossible to describe the horror we felt when we heard the news. Our classes came to a standstill. What kind of country *was* this? One thing was for sure. This nation did not feel like a city on a hill. We didn't remember LBJ's speech, but if you'd asked my schoolmates, we'd all have said the same thing: Yes, we had "failed as a people and a nation."

Liberals and conservatives would divide on this perilous ground. Conventional wisdom suggests that the Vietnam War and Watergate turned Americans cynical. But the real disenchantment sprang from something more fundamental. It rose up from the vanishing dream of racial justice, from the gauntlet that the president himself had thrown down to the nation, from a long crusade for justice that, after decades, seemed to crash in failure.

Fifteen years later, Ronald Reagan made it his mission to reverse the judgment. His deepest conviction, the thought he most often repeated, was a soaring pride in his county. There was nothing to apologize for, he said again and again. And with that high-flying patriotism, an inchoate fissure between liberals and conservatives came into view. Pride and shame, patriots versus skeptics, the shining city on a hill versus the nation that was not quite up to the great challenge of civil rights and, at the very least, ought to keep struggling for elusive social justice.

The landslide of 1964 had permitted the Democrats to win policies they had been reaching for since the Truman administration. The programs remade American politics. But, at the time, it did not feel like enough, especially to the winners. And the backlash against those policies ended the Democratic era. In its place, a brash new Republican Party would rise up and dominate American politics.

EIGHT

WE WIN, THEY LOSE

Tribal Politics at High Tide (1968–2020)

G eorge Wallace rocked New York's Madison Square Garden in October 1968. Twenty thousand supporters stood on their seats, waved Confederate flags, and roared at his provocations. "We don't have riots in Alabama," he shouted. "They start a riot down there, first one of 'em to pick up a brick gets a bullet in the brain."[1]

Protesters dangled a noose from the balcony, and the intoxicated crowd began to scream "kill 'em, kill 'em, kill 'em." A small group of African Americans from a Baptist church in Harlem sat quietly near the back, but the mob turned on them too. "Hey niggers, get out of here, niggers," they shouted. Police dashed from eruption to eruption, breaking up fights and ejecting troublemakers. Outside the Garden, protesters brawled with Wallace supporters. Through the uproar, Wallace ticked through his list of aggravations: "the punks, the queers, the demonstrators and the hippies. . . . Their day is *over*."[2]

Wallace supporters in New York explained their passion to roving reporters. One young man spat it right out. "Whites don't want to live with them [Negroes]. I don't believe in forced integration." Others delighted in this bull smashing the china shop. "He says what he thinks," "He tells it like it is." An off-duty cop at the rally put his finger directly on the issue that loomed over the whole election: "He is the only guy who stands for law and order." Many supporters were ready for a walk on the dark side. He might break the rules, but he'd restore the nation.[3]

This time, Wallace was running as a third-party candidate and his campaign seemed to catch fire across the North. He drew fifteen thousand in Pittsburgh, sixteen thousand in Baltimore, and seventy thousand to the Boston Common. Wallace joined the long and varied list of American populists. The original Populists had tried to reach across the race line only to stoke a bigoted backlash that would become known as "southern populism." Franklin Roosevelt had also stood in a roaring Madison Square Garden during his first reelection campaign and channeled popular resentment against the financial classes. The "malefactors of great wealth," he had said, "are unanimous in their hate for me—and I welcome their hatred." Now, Wallace rode that resentment hard to the right.[4]

The Wallace numbers dwindled as the election neared. After polling at 20 percent in mid-summer, he ended up taking just 13 percent of the popular vote and five Deep South states. Still, his forty-five electoral votes represent the second largest total of any third-party candidate in American history. The Wallace eruption seemed, for many years, like a historical footnote—anger bubbling on the political fringes during a tumultuous time. But we always read the past from where we stand in the present, and today the Wallace rallies and resentments sound eerily like President Donald Trump's rallies and resentments. Wallace deployed a tribal fury, an identification with whiteness, a fear of the racial other, and a sexual resentment about new mores (which others called liberation). His supporters thrilled at the smashed taboos. He touched a dark streak running through American culture—one that broke to the surface once again in the late 2010s.

The Democrats had dominated American politics from 1933 to 1966. Now, they lost their way—their peculiar coalition, spanning segregationists and civil rights activists, finally flew apart. The party ran out of ideas, lost control of the political agenda, and found itself with no regional base at all. Now, it was the Republicans' turn. Between 1968 and 1988, they built a formidable coalition rooted in the dynamic South and the West. Led by presidents Richard Nixon (1969–1974) and, especially, Ronald Reagan (1983–1989), the Republicans turned from a traditional party coalition into a kind of movement. They attacked government, squashed the unions, presided over a new Gilded Age, and yearned to restore traditional moral values as they understood them. Like the majority in every era, they came up short of their high-flying hopes. But in the process, they changed the norms and assumptions of American politics.[5]

The Republican ascendancy was followed by something unprecedented. Control over the branches of government changed hands more frequently between 2000 and 2020 than in any other two-decade period in American history—in ten national elections, control of the White House or a chamber of Congress shifted ten times.

By the 2000s, the two parties had organized themselves around ideological poles: conservatives Republicans versus liberals Democrats—and each at roughly equal strength. More important, the parties now sorted themselves by race, nativism, and sexuality—tribal differences, intensified by a new media, that all reflected the most passionate divisions running through American history. The themes we have been following through American history clicked into the new and passionate alignment that marks the screaming politics in the United States today.

IN 1968, A FAR SHREWDER POLITICIAN SEIZED WALLACE'S truculent message, smoothed out the rough edges, and dropped it into the mainstream. Richard Nixon's campaign rang with the promise to restore order. Our central cities, wrote Nixon in *Reader's*

Digest, "have been abandoned to snipers, looters, and arsonists." The entire nation, he continued, "was blazing in an inferno of urban anarchy." And the answer, he promised, was simple. More cops. Tougher cops. Better equipped cops. Fewer liberal judges. And less concern about rights that set criminals free on technicalities. The Nixon program could be summarized in the same phrase that echoed through the Goldwater convention four years earlier: "Law and Order." The tough talk brought Strom Thurmond, now a senator, round to Nixon's side. When some conservative Republicans moved to draft Governor Ronald Reagan of California to run for president in 1968, Thurmond shot them down. The party had finally vanquished the old moderate establishment and it could not afford a split in the conservative ranks. "We just can't take that chance and let Rockefeller slip in," said Thurmond."[6]

Nixon set a template that candidates would use for years to come. He ran a racially charged campaign without using overtly racist language—at least, not in public. His private conversations were quite another thing. That "hits it right in the nose," exulted Nixon when his team rolled out a tough-on-crime advertisement, "It's all about law and order and the damn Negro–Puerto-Rican groups out there." As *Time* put it, the law and order issue that had originally elevated George Wallace's candidacy now had "lured Richard Nixon . . . to the edge of demagogy." The only campaign issue conservative politicians seemed to be talking about, groused the magazine, is "Negro Crime."[7]

But racial backlash was not the whole story. Crime *was* rising fast—the murder rate had jumped almost 60 percent in the past decade. The chaotic war in Vietnam increasingly bewildered Americans, and universities were in an uproar over it. But the most important thing about the election had nothing to do with Richard Nixon or George Wallace or the Republicans. The Democratic Party was at war with itself.

EVERYONE ASSUMED LYNDON JOHNSON WOULD RUN FOR RE-election, and 1968 should have been an incumbent's dream. The economy was humming—GDP rose 4.9 percent that year, unemployment stood at a low 3.7 percent (in July), hourly wages were up a snappy 2.6 percent from the previous year, and, in today's dollars, the minimum wage stood at $11 an hour. But, in late March 1968, President Johnson gave a televised address and at the end, out of the blue, bowed out of the election.[8]

We might trace LBJ's decision back to the reverberations from an episode in Saigon, the South Vietnamese capital, five years earlier. Word had filtered through the media that something worth seeing was about to happen at a busy intersection. As the reporters arrived, a Buddhist monk sat in a lotus position while two colleagues doused him with gasoline and then stood back as he lit himself on fire. Journalist David Halberstam remembered the horror that swept the crowd, the smell of burning flesh, and the eerie composure of the flaming man. "I was too shocked to cry," he later wrote, "too confused to take notes or ask questions, too bewildered to even think." A photograph of the event flashed around the world. Four more monks immolated themselves in the following weeks. They were protesting South Vietnamese President Ngo Dinh Diem's anti-Buddhist policies such as outlawing prayer flags. Diem came from Vietnam's Catholic minority.[9]

The burnings symbolized a war that had lost its purpose. At the start, during the height of the Cold War, it seemed like a simple matter of democracy standing up to communist tyranny. But, through the 1960s, that bright moral cause faded into gray amid corruption, coups, counter coups, terror, counterterror, monks immolating themselves, and an insurgency by South Vietnamese people known as the Vietcong. Worse, the whole idea of a monolithic communist threat had fractured into squabbling nations that were as likely to battle one another as to fight the United States. Americans intellectuals, college students, and (eventually) congressional leaders began questioning the entire enterprise.

The civil rights movement had spilled out of the black churches, the antiwar movement rose out of the university campuses. But the two were powerfully linked. Many antiwar protesters had started out as civil rights activists. And by the mid-1960s, they began to see the same foe in both fights. The long, hard battle for racial justice seemed to expose a deep reactionary streak running through America. So did the implacable war machine. Liberals began to think that the cops bashing peaceful marchers in Selma echoed the boots treading in Saigon—American power shedding the blood of nonwhite people. Segregationists made the connection more plausible with their strident support for the war (though there were some notable exceptions). And civil rights leaders, starting with Martin Luther King, further reinforced the link by ardently criticizing the conflict. Heavyweight boxing champion Muhammad Ali probably reached more people than anyone when, at the height of his prowess, he spurned his draft board and refused induction into the military. "I ain't got no quarrel with no Vietcong," he famously said.[10]

When young black men turned to black power, they mesmerized young white radicals. Norman Mailer, reporting on the antiwar demonstrations in 1967, described it beautifully.

> The new left was impressed . . . by the criminally suggestive cool of Black Power, by the snipers, the Molotov cocktails thrown from the rooftops. . . . Young, college-bred middle class . . . felt the militancy of the blacks as a reproof to their own secure, relatively unthreatened mass demonstrations.[11]

Here was an unexpected variation of an old theme—black freedom struggles always seem to stir up insecurities among white men. The antiwar demonstrations grew larger, angrier, and more contemptuous. The kids waved North Vietnamese flags and burned the stars and stripes. They clashed with police. The establishment Democrats were baffled. What were they to make of the sarcastic anarchist, Abbie Hoffman, who led a few hundred radicals past police cordons and onto the grounds of the Pentagon where they tried to levitate the building—with chants, incantations, and prayer bells—in order to shake out the evil spirits lurking within? The Democratic Party had been brawling over civil rights. Now it divided again over the war in Vietnam. The two conflicts overlapped, heating up old party enmities between North and South, black and white, union organizers and college professors.

Then, disaster struck the Johnson administration's war policy right as the reelection campaign was about to begin. In late January 1968, the Vietcong attacked five of the six largest cities and most of the provincial capitals across South Vietnam. In Saigon, the enemy brazenly charged the presidential palace, assaulted the airport, and blasted their way into the American embassy where they held out against the US Marines all night. The Vietcong hung on for three weeks in the provincial capital of Hue. In simple military terms, the offensive was suicidal. The rebels carried out their bold attack expecting that it would trigger a massive uprising. When that didn't happen, their ranks were decimated. But the Tet Offensive, as it was called, shook up the debate back home.

The Johnson administration had countered the rising criticism of the war with a dogged stream of optimistic reports—regions pacified, enemy killed, infrastructure destroyed. Now it all looked like flimflam. The war's opponents had insisted the United States could not win the brutal and confusing conflict. At the time, the Tet Offensive seemed to vindicate the pessimists. And the confusing images, streaming live on television, gave the moral criticisms of the war a terrible immediacy. Twenty million Americans sat in their living rooms and watched the Saigon police chief, Nguyen Ngoc Loan, stride into the camera's frame, pull out his pistol, put it to the head of a bound man in street clothes (Vietcong Captain Nguyen

Tat Dat), and pull the trigger. To this day, the video is agonizing to watch. At the time, it insinuated the uncomfortable thought: perhaps the protesters and civil rights leaders had a point. Perhaps American policy was not just confused but immoral.[12]

Senator Eugene McCarthy of Wisconsin had launched a quixotic, antiwar challenge to President Johnson for the Democratic nomination. After Tet, he suddenly found traction. "A few months ago," said McCarthy, "we were told sixty-five percent of the population was secure. Now we know that even the American embassy is not secure." The following month, McCarthy almost upset Johnson in the New Hampshire primary, 42 percent to 49 percent. Four days later, Senator Robert Kennedy of New York jumped into the race, also promising to campaign against the war. And at the end of the month, a weary President Johnson dropped out and Vice President Hubert Humphrey became the Democratic Establishment's candidate.[13]

At the time, only fourteen states held primaries, and Humphrey did not bother entering them. He would rely on the party leaders to secure the nomination while McCarthy and Kennedy used the primaries to joust for the party's left wing. They went head-to-head in four states and Kennedy took three of them. Then, both turned to California, where McCarthy was lionized on the college campuses, Kennedy in the barrios. On June 4, Kennedy narrowly won the state. The fight for the soul of the Democratic Party looked to be on: it would be Bobby Kennedy and the left versus Hubert Humphrey and the establishment. On the night of his California victory, Bobby addressed jubilant supporters at the Ambassador Hotel in Los Angeles, then made his way through the hotel kitchen to a press conference. A young man sprang up and shot him three times at point blank range. Twenty-four hours later, Bobby Kennedy was dead.

Two months after an assassin had murdered Martin Luther King, another killed Bobby Kennedy. Young people—stunned, numb—watched Kennedy's coffin loaded off the train in Washington, DC, as his forlorn supporters sang the "Battle Hymn of the Republic." In the last chapter, I emphasized the challenge in Lyndon Johnson's sermon: "Should we . . . be unequal to this issue [of civil rights], then we will have failed as a people and a nation." What was there to say now? What was there, for those on the left, besides cynicism or despair?

Most political historians think Kennedy was too far behind in the delegate count to catch up to Humphrey. Of course, we'll never know if his charisma might have united a fractured party. The Democratic convention, in August, showcased all the party's agonized divisions. Peace delegates fought the establishment, northern party members clashed with southern, and police battered young antiwar protesters in the streets.

Humphrey staggered to the nomination and started the general election far behind. But he was an exuberant campaigner and almost made up the difference, closing the gap from approximately 12 percent in September to less than 1 percent on election day. He lost five states by less than three percent that, together, would have won him the election. But this was the end of the exhausted Democratic coalition. The party had won seven of the last nine presidential elections and taken every state at one point or another during its long dispensation. Now, the Republicans would take the White House five of the next six times, and across that run, they, too, would win in every state. They would have the space to build a new coalition, introduce a new philosophy, and remake the assumptions of American politics.[14]

RICHARD NIXON WON THE 1968 ELECTION, GATHERED BOTH liberals and conservatives around him, and flashed bold policy proposals before the country, one after another. In an era of big government programs, Nixon aimed to build a legacy by rethinking popular social reforms in more Republican terms. His administration's welfare reform, for example, would have guaranteed all Americans an annual income—that way, reasoned his advisors, everyone could participate in the economy while the welfare agencies providing food assistance, housing, or other services could be reduced and someday eliminated. He quietly negotiated a national health insurance proposal with Democratic Congressman Wilbur Mills of Arkansas that relied on private insurers and remains, to this day, the most ambitious program ever to make it through the House Ways and Means Committee (in the spring of 1974). He transmuted the Cold War in February 1972 with a surprise visit to China, which had been completely closed to the United States, and leveraged that into a détente with the Soviet Union, culminating with a summit in Moscow several months later.

Conservative leaders were furious about all that liberalism, especially in foreign policy. Some, like the conservative activist Phyllis Schlafly, denounced the administration and supported a primary challenge from Congressman John Ashbrook of Ohio when Nixon was up for reelection in 1972. But Ashbrook did not win a single delegate. Nixon's conservative opponents ran smack into a hard reality—they may not have liked many of the programs that the administration proposed, but the president's support ran deeper than policy. He understood the tribal currents running through American politics and built a powerful new coalition around them.

Those currents were no secret. During Nixon's first year in office, a blockbuster book hit Washington and was immediately acclaimed (and deplored) as prophetic. In *The Emerging Republican Majority*, a numbers geek and Nixon campaign strategist named Kevin Phillips added up the votes that went Nixon and Wallace in 1968 and summed them to a lopsided conservative majority of 57 percent. The apparently squeaker election in which Nixon beat Humphrey by just 0.7 percent, wrote Phillips, actually showed a public moving decisively to the right. And they would stay to the right, he prophesied, thanks to two big changes.

First, population and voting power were shifting from the old Northeast toward what Phillips called "the sun belt." Republicans could forget all about the crumbling northern cities and their troublesome (African American) populations. Instead, all they had to do was cater to white voters basking in their warm, tidy, sunlit suburbs far from the all the turmoil.

Second, and more important, Phillips gave Republicans some ironic advice. The winning move for them, he wrote, was to stop resisting black suffrage and, quite the reverse, protect black voting rights across the South. Why? Phillips was brutally direct. Because blacks had become Democrats and, as a direct result, most southern whites would flee the party. "Negro voting rights in Dixie, far from being contrary to GOP interests," he summed up, are "essential if Southern conservatives are to be pressured into switching to the Republican Party." Phillips spelled it all right out. "Ethnic polarization is a long-standing hallmark of American politics." Today, black enfranchisement—and, crucially, the reaction against it—"almost inevitably had to result in political realignment." The "negro's social economic revolution" and black influence in the Democratic Party "virtually dictates the coming alignment of the Deep South."[15]

The Democrats, continued Phillips, had been a populist party defending "farm, highway, health education, and pension expenditures" from unpopular "conservative budget cuts." But when they "turned to social engineering, [they] lost the support of poor whites." Nixon read the book in December 1969 and circulated it to his staff, for it described exactly what he already knew. The Jews, the blacks, and the Puerto Ricans, as he put it privately, would deliver conservative whites to his party. Phillips warned Republicans of the one peril in their path to majority. They would send white voters right back to the Democrats if they messed with the entitlement programs—Social Security, Medicare, and aid to education. They could rail against government. They could blast unworthy beneficiaries. They could run against welfare. But they must not lay a finger on the fat programs that benefited the middle class.

The book immediately became the "talk of political Washington," as the *New York Times* put it. "It is a little depressing," wrote the *Times* reviewer, to hear that elections turn on "deep divisive conflicts between black and white" and that "Americans vote only on their bloodline, church, neighborhood or caste." Politics was not just about policies. Instead, it had become—in fact, had always been—about us versus them. Nixon felt it in his political bones—the quest for racial equality was tilting tribal politics toward him and his party.[16]

The South had been drifting, slowly, toward the Republicans ever since the Dixiecrats bolted in 1948. Phillips helped politicians see how and why. As the white southern majority switched from solid blue (or Democratic) to red (Republican), the Republicans began to dominate presidential politics. Putting aside the anomalous Watergate election of 1976, Democratic candidates averaged a meagre seventy-six Electoral College votes (out of 538) between 1968 and 1992. The Republican landslides came one after another and mark the most lopsided run in the Electoral College since mass parties rose up in the 1820s. Democrats scraped together scanty Electoral College totals of seventeen (against Nixon running for reelection in 1972), forty-nine (for incumbent president Jimmy Carter, running for reelection in 1980), and thirteen (for Walter Mondale running against President Ronald Reagan in 1984). A Democrat would not win with a majority of the popular vote (again, putting 1976 aside) until Barack Obama broke through in 2008, forty years after Hubert Humphrey led the party into the wilderness.

The collapse was more than just a fall of coalitions. The party lost its message. The one Democratic administration that squeaked into office during this period—with 50.1 percent of the vote during the backlash against Watergate—dramatically illustrated the problem.

President-elect Jimmy Carter's pollster, Hamilton Jordan, circulated a remarkable memo one month before the inauguration. "Governor Carter's political situation is precarious for . . . the Democratic Party is in serious trouble—with a shrinking and ill-defined coalition." What should the incoming team do? Jordan offered a most unusual piece of advice. The president's advisors must aggressively "educate" the incoming cabinet members about Jimmy Carter's "goals and philosophy." Imagine. Carter had run a national campaign for two years and, still, his own appointees would have to be "educated" about what he stood for. Most presidents lead a movement or a party or at least a faction into power. This one offered only a cool promise of efficiency and clean government—a good process in the name of only the vaguest substance. With no party message or cause, the Democrats could find no foothold on the presidential map. Carter himself managed just six states and the District of Columbia when he ran for reelection.[17]

The Republican wave took longer to roll over Congress. The powerful Democrats from the South kept their seats until they retired—and when they did, they were generally replaced by Republicans. The GOP finally took control of the Senate in 1980 and the House in 1994, dominating each chamber until 2006 when every elected branch of government began careening wildly from party to party with each election.

IN THE 1970S, TWO CLASHING WOMEN'S MOVEMENTS GAVE each party a cause that would help define it for the next half century. Reformers from both left and right drew on a long legacy of gender politics.

In the past, women had often entered politics to pursue moral causes—for religion and morality fell safely in the feminine sphere. But, as we have seen, politically engaged women ran straight into gender barriers—the campaign for moral causes led directly to the fight for equal rights. For example, women joined the antislavery movement, grew frustrated by the limits they faced, and began to demand the right to vote, to hold a job, and to be treated equally by the laws. Decades later, Frances Willard led the Woman's Christian Temperance Union in its crusade against alcohol—and quickly moved on to press for the women's right to vote, earn equal pay, and other reforms.

Now, in the 1970s, the two sides of women's politics split. A powerful campaign for gender and sexual rights went quickly from the fringes of national politics into the heart of the Democratic coalition. Conservative women, who were often active in their churches, reacted against the "women's libbers," articulated strong moral positions, and eventually, made them a defining feature of modern Republican politics.

The split had a curious origin. It emerged from a segregationist effort to kill the Civil Rights Act of 1964. Congressman Howard Smith of Virginia half seriously proposed dropping the word "sex" into the Act. His amendment would prohibit discrimination on the basis of race, color, religion, *sex*, or national origin. Smith announced his proposal sarcastically, with guffaws ringing through the chamber. "Now, I am very serious about this," he chortled, as he regaled his colleagues with a letter from a woman who could not find a husband. "In this election year, it is pretty nearly half the voters that are affected, so you had better sit up and take notice." Smith generally supported women's rights, but he and the southern Democrats were desperately fighting to protect segregation, and they imagined that adding the word *sex* might turn the Civil Rights Act into a farce and give northern representatives a cover for voting nay.

The Johnson administration and most (male) liberals nervously opposed Smith's upgrade to the law. With a long filibuster looming in the Senate, the last thing they needed was a debate about women's rights, of all things. At the time, there were twelve female representatives, and most of them seized the opportunity that Smith's cynical ploy offered them. "Women and Negroes occupy the same positions in American society," argued Democratic Congresswoman Martha Griffiths of Michigan. If anyone doubted that "women were second class citizens," said Griffiths pointedly, the laughter that greeted this proposal "would have proved it." In the end, eleven of the twelve women in Congress joined with the segregationists and pressed for the change. With their support, the gender provision stuck and passed into law with the Civil Rights Act.[18]

At first, even liberals dismissed the change. "A mischievous joke perpetrated on the floor of the House of Representatives," scoffed the *New Republic*. The agency charged with implementing the employment provision, the Equal Employment Opportunity Commission, declined to enforce the gender provision. That galvanized a group of activists to organize the National Organization of Women (or NOW) in 1966 to prod a reluctant Johnson administration to move ahead on forbidding discrimination on the basis of sex.

NOW lobbied, demonstrated, and sued. Before long, the government began to respond, first by enforcing the gender provisions in the Civil Rights Act and then by going further. After NOW disrupted committee hearings in 1972, Congress approved the Equal Rights Amendment to the Constitution. The ERA, as it was called, put it directly: "Equality of rights . . . shall not be denied or abridged by the United States or by any State on account of sex." At first, it seemed uncontroversial—it had strong, well-organized supporters and few opponents. It went through Congress by lopsided majorities in both the House (354–24) and Senate (84–8) and then began to sail through the ratification process. Thirty-five states quickly approved (twenty-eight within the first year)—just three states short of victory.

AS THE AMENDMENT RACED TOWARD RATIFICATION, A WOMen's group asked conservative activist Phyllis Schlafly to participate in a debate about it. She wasn't particularly interested—her specialty was defense policy—but Schlafly agreed, studied the issue, and discovered the cause of a lifetime.

At the very last minute, Schlafly organized a campaign called STOP ERA, arguing that the amendment would strip women of treasured privileges—like the right to be supported and the privilege of staying home and watching her children grow up (the "STOP" in STOP ERA was an acronym for Stop Taking Our Privileges). The Christian tradition of chivalry had always protected women, warned Schlafly. Now, the government would barge into the sacred family and push women out of their traditional marriages and into the military, into single sex bathrooms, and into a world without protection or alimony. Her campaign took off among conservative women's groups.[19]

The cry from the right froze the ERA. States stopped ratifying. Four that had already done so voted to rescind their approval (though it was not clear if they could legally do so). The battle against the ERA spread to other moral issues. In 1973, the Supreme Court had struck down a Texas law banning abortion (in *Roe v. Wade*). At first, reaction was muted, but by the mid-1970s, the coalition fighting for traditional morality was in the field and they rapidly gathered allies for the battle against abortion. And homosexuality. The widening division across gender issues was illuminated by a massive conference on women's rights held in Houston in 1977, the only one of its kind. Three presidential spouses served as honorary co-chairs.

Delegates from fifty states endorsed the Equal Rights Amendment and public funding for abortions. Then some delegates introduced a more controversial item that had not been on the agenda—lesbian rights. All eyes turned to Betty Friedan, NOW's co-founder, who had long argued that getting entangled with homosexuality would harm the woman's movement. She made her way to the dais and surprised the delegates. "As someone who has grown up in middle America and has loved men—perhaps too well—I've had trouble with this issue," she said. But, now, she averred, she could hear her sisters' call. "We must help women who are lesbians to their own civil rights." The galleries roared and pink and yellow balloons cascaded onto the delegates.

Not everyone cheered. The Mississippi delegation rose, turned their backs on the podium and bowed their heads in prayer. Across town, eleven thousand women, men, and children gathered in a counter rally. They condemned abortion and homosexuality. "I have enough civil rights to choke a hungry goat," proclaimed one Texas state representative. "I want a right to segregate my family from these misfits and perverts." A man rose up and confessed that he had been gay for twenty-six years but now his faith had delivered him from his sin.[20]

The lines were drawn for the culture war to come. One side championed gender equality, gay rights, and reproductive choice—all explicitly built on the template of civil rights. The other side defended traditional families, traditional marriages, and traditional gender roles—and vehemently opposed abortion and homosexuality.[21]

The clash led conservatives to swipe moral politics away from the left. The civil rights movement had long invoked Christian images. Martin Luther King had used the Bible as his text and mixed gentle images of Jesus with jeremiads from the Old Testament. Now, the righteous fervor passed from the left to the right. It invested conservative politics with fervor and hellfire. As morality surged into the Republican coalition, it infused a wide range of issues and causes, including the debates over race and immigration.

White supremacy had always been tangled with sexual anxiety— the Ku Klux Klan and other terrorist organizations defined themselves as protectors of white women and carried out their campaigns of violence in the name of chivalry. Again, and again, we've seen conservative white men warn women about the racial consequences of political activism—often with blunt references to a "degraded race of wooly headed mulattoes." Now, this long, tangled skein of race and sexuality clicked into its contemporary place within the political parties. The party of civil rights would also be the party of gender rights. On the other side, the campaign to reinforce traditional gender roles fused with a backlash against civil rights, active government, and what party members saw as reverse discrimination against white people. The long linkage between racial and gendered anxieties continued to play its powerful role.[22]

AT THIS SAME TIME IN THE LATE 1970S AS THE CRUSADE for family values helped define the Republican coalition, two other groups rethought their politics and joined the rising alliance.

Kevin Phillips had correctly predicted the first development. White sunbelt voters fled the Democratic Party as it became identified with African Americans. White conservatives were repelled by what they saw as the Democrats' pandering to civil rights, its lenient approach to urban disorder, its defense of high taxes, and its turning soft on patriotism. In some places, the late 1970s brought still another racial grievance. Many communities had ducked integration by creating private schools—known by friends and foes, respectively, as Freedom of Choice schools or Segregation Academies. Most were Christian schools, and when the courts stripped them of their tax-exempt status, conservative church leaders in the South had an economic reason to damn the Democrats.

Second, business conservatives had grown anxious about the fate of capitalism. The kids kept quoting Henry David Thoreau and mocking the drive to buckle down and get ahead. In a now famous memo to the US Chamber of Commerce, written in 1971, corporate lawyer and future Supreme Court Justice Lewis Powell warned that "members of the intellectual community were waging ideological warfare against the enterprise system." Capitalism needed protection. Powell urged business to build a powerful network—think tanks, magazines, scholarly journals, a speaker's bureau, business schools—all to promote capitalism. Powell's most important recommendation seemed controversial at the time: "As unwelcome as it may be," he wrote, business must play "a broader and more vigorous role in the political arena." In the decades ahead, the chamber and its allies enacted many of Powell's recommendations. Business leaders became even more influential in the Republican Party, which grew passionate about lowering taxes, cutting government regulation, and celebrating capitalism. The network of unabashed free market defenders spread far and wide—though it never quite managed to conquer the universities—except in economics and law.[23]

The three interests—moral, racial, economic—all converged on a familiar demand. This nation—in fact, any nation—should shrink the state, liberate markets, and restore traditional values. The rising conservative Republicans of the late 1970s lucked into a charismatic leader in the next presidential election.

———

RONALD REAGAN TOOK THE THEMES RISING ON THE RIGHT and brightly pitched them to the country. He offered himself—his history, his tall tales, his body itself—as an embodiment of the conservative revolution. In the process, he and his allies changed American politics. The progressive logic of the Democratic era now gave way to the market thinking of the Reagan epoch.

Dutch Reagan—he was born crying like a Dutchman, said his father—often recalled his idyllic, small-town, "Huck Finn childhood." He painted a picture of swimming, fishing, and occasional fistfights with young bigots who mocked his dad's Catholicism. The Reagans did not have much money, but "I never thought of our family as disadvantaged. Only later did the government decide it had to tell people they were poor." Always the Reagan antimony: his family lives happily in the golden past, the government butts in to define poverty and stir up discontent.[24]

Reagan's charming autobiographies have the same tone and narrative line as Horatio Alger's nineteenth-century books for boys. A virtuous, hardworking fellow, full of pluck and good cheer, works his way up to success. At every turn, he catches the eye of a benign patron who magically open doors—don't worry about money, say the business leaders who appear from nowhere and recruit him to run for governor of California. A superficial reading might suggest a simple moral: hard work and virtue leads to success. But, like the Alger novels, the deeper lesson is about the country itself. America is a nation of generous communities, full of people who are ready to offer an honest fellow a hand. In this land, good cheer and hard work earn their just rewards. The personal history lays an engaging foundation for a new philosophy. Put aside government and New Deals and return to the old idylls of individualism.[25]

The sunny tales always raised the same nagging question—did that really happen? Is it true? Take Reagan's favorite story—he apologizes to the reader for telling it, yet again, in his second autobiography. After college, Dutch became a sports announcer for a small radio station in Des Moines, Iowa. He recreated baseball games in the studio while a telegraph operator sat by his side and handed him summaries of each play. In the nineth inning of a scoreless game between the Chicago Cubs and the Saint Louis Cardinals, the wire went dead. If he leveled with his audience, he'd lose them to a station broadcasting directly from the park. So, he kept right on talking. "I knew there was only one thing that wouldn't get into the score column and betray me—a foul ball." In Reagan's ballgame, the batter, Billy Jurges, fouled off pitch after pitch after pitch. For seven minutes the audience heard nothing but fouls. When the telegraph started working again, Reagan learns that "Billy popped out on the first ball pitched." Well, "not in my game he didn't," quipped Reagan. For days people asked him about all those foul balls—Was it some kind of record?—while Reagan shook his head and agreed that it had been amazing, and never let on.[26]

Most Reagan biographers focus on his easy blurring of fact and fiction—he is a raconteur, a fabulist, a man who stretches the truth, a damn good liar. In fact, the stories go to the heart of Reagan's success—and his limitations. He focused on parables rather than on policies. His airy indifference to the analytical world of evidence and arguments freed him to repeat his handful of verities and impress them on American discourse. He reimagined the United States while the tougher characters who rallied to his administration reconstructed the nation's political institutions.[27]

The Reagan story always casts racial shadows. For example, did he really start the 1980 presidential campaign with a dog whistle to white supremacy? Well, sort of. His first campaign appearance, following the Republican convention, was at the Neshoba County Fair, just outside of Philadelphia, Mississippi, where three civil rights workers had been murdered sixteen years earlier. At the fair, Reagan told a white audience, "I believe in states' rights; I believe in people doing as much as they can at the private level." That echo of Barry Goldwater made the headlines. A subtle wink to white supremacy? When he appeared before a black audience in New York two days later, he got a "tepid" reaction, perhaps, speculated the *New York Times*, because of his "appearance [on] Sunday . . . in Philadelphia, Miss." In the heat of the campaign, journalists called in a blunder. Later, political historians added Reagan's appearance to the long roster of racial semaphores Republican candidates flashed at white voters.[28]

Wait a minute, say Reagan's supporters. The Neshoba fair was a popular Mississippi event that went back to 1899. It was an obvious place to hunt for southern votes. After all, two days later candidate Reagan was addressing the Urban League in New York and campaigning in African American neighborhoods in the Bronx. That racial dog whistle sprang straight out of the hostile, liberal mind.[29]

Which is it? Dog whistle or perfectly innocent speech? Well, both. The Philadelphia criticism stuck because, exactly like Reagan's own parables, it captured something essential. After a long debate stretching back to the late 1930s, the conservatives in the Republican Party finally tossed aside their black alliances and—free from civil rights—went after the white vote in Dixie. This required accepting the support of avowed segregationists without demurring. Regardless of the campaign's motives, the critics are right to remember the long and tangled lines between states' rights and white supremacy— and the dirty hands in a party that did what it had to do to gather backlash votes in the decades after Birmingham and Selma. White supremacy by no means defined the party—in fact, it was less prominent among Republicans than it had been among Democrats three generations earlier. But, like it or not, it was now part of the Republican coalition. Ronald Reagan, like Richard Nixon before him, did what he had to do to maintain his coalition.

RONALD REAGAN EASILY WON THE 1980 PRESIDENTIAL election—he took almost 51 percent in a three-way race but gathered 489 electoral votes (out of 538). His Republicans picked up a stunning twelve seats in the Senate and took the majority in that chamber for the first time in a quarter century. And then, five weeks after his inauguration, Reagan walked out of the Washington Hilton, paused for a question, and heard a series of pops, like firecrackers. "What the hell is that?" he shouted. His security guards knew all too well. Agent Tim McCarthy stepped in front of the gunman, spread his arms wide, and took a bullet to the chest. Other agents pushed the president into the car and raced to George Washington University Hospital where Reagan, always mindful of his appearance, buttoned his jacket and tried to walk toward the doors. He struggled to get a breath and collapsed.[30]

One month after the assassination attempt, President Reagan stood before a joint session of Congress and a national television audience. After an ecstatic ovation, the president turned all the personal good will into political momentum for his plan to cut government spending. The administration proceeded to squeeze what seemed like astonishing figures out of the Democratic House: a $750 billion cut in taxes (chopping the top tax rate from 70 percent to 28 percent) and a $35 billion cut to domestic programs (more than 5 percent of total expenditures). The administration also removed four hundred thousand people from the food stamp program, closed the public service hospitals (which dated back to the John Adams administration), and pinched the federal flow of money to the states by taking twenty-one federal programs and converting them into block grants to the states—the state government got fewer dollars but far more discretion in how they would be spent.[31]

That was supposed to be just the start. The budget promised $44 billion in additional cuts—and possibly even more. Where would they cut? The administration did not say, but the budget director, David Stockman, knew the cuts would come from where the money was—the Social Security program. That, after all, was the mother of all entitlements and the foundation of Big Government, as Stockman explained in his memoirs.[32]

Reagan didn't pay much attention to the policy details and, in one meeting, two advisors talked him into reducing Social Security benefits for people who retired at age sixty-two. The normally adroit administration proposed the plan, not in some distant future, but the very following year—threatening to upend people's immediate retirement plans. When the plan went public, Reagan's approval ratings plunged—by sixteen points in one poll. The administration withdrew the plan, but not fast enough to stop the Democratic House (405–13) and the Republican-controlled Senate (96–0) from stomping on the dead proposal.

The warriors on the right complained that it did not all add up to anything like the revolution they had been promised. By the time Reagan left office, government spending was up 18 percent (in real terms), the federal deficit was 186 percent higher, and the government's share of the economy had only inched down from 19.6 percent to 18.3 percent—more a result of a strong economy than program cuts. The administration introduced a major benefit for low income workers (the Earned Income Tax Credit), negotiated an immigration reform that offered amnesty to undocumented people, and—over the objection of every member of the cabinet but one—the president approved the largest expansion of Medicare in that program's history, a catastrophic care package (though it was quickly repealed in the next session of Congress—after Reagan had left office).[33]

When the Medicare expansion first passed, Budget Director Stockman wrote what seemed, at the time, the eulogy for the Reagan revolution. Ending Big Government required "draconian reductions" that would "hurt millions of people in the short run," he wrote. Only an "iron chancellor" could make those changes stick. "Reagan had no business trying to make a revolution," groused Stockman, because he was "gentle" and "sentimental"—it "wasn't in his bones." On the face of it, Stockman had the measure of his boss. Reagan's staff took the stacks of mail he loved to read and carefully culled letters with hard-luck stories to stop him from writing small checks to his fans. Stockman summed up his frustration in the subtitle of his memoirs, *How the Reagan Revolution Failed.*[34]

With a bit of historical distance, we can see that Stockman was both right (Big Government is still going strong) and wrong. Reagan's most enduring legacy lay in the three fixed verities he returned to, again and again. Each would have a long partisan legacy, each helped shape politics as we know it today.

First, a boundless patriotism. Anything that moved Ronald Reagan—a choir, a space launch, an encouraging letter, an old movie—inspired the same thought. "You have to feel good about our country." This thought, more than any other, dominates his personal diaries. "I am more and more convinced," he wrote after watching astronauts return from space, "that Americans are hungering to feel proud and patriotic again."[35] Reagan cemented his vision with an imaginary quote from Alexis de Tocqueville. "America is good. And if America ever ceases to be good, America will cease to be great." Good, great, best—Reagan's first verity: cheer the homeland. Reagan's supporters welcomed the end of national self-criticism and started waving the flag.[36]

Fifteen years earlier, President Johnson had offered Americans his racial jeremiad about the nation's mission. That soaring appeal to civil rights was followed by bleak demonstrations, urban insurrections, terrible assassinations, protests, and backlash. Did Reagan's resurgent patriotism mean casting aside the search for social justice? What about the unmet challenge that the civil rights revolution had put before the nation? Surely, said many on the left, the murder of so many civil rights leaders—Martin Luther King had been killed just twelve years earlier—should humble the nation and redouble its quest for social justice.

Reagan pushed all that aside. Patriotism developed a partisan edge. Republicans began to scorn their rivals for being soft on national pride. During the 1988 election to succeed Reagan, Republican George H. W. Bush pummeled a startled Michael Dukakis for not standing up for the Pledge of Allegiance (as governor, scruples about the freedom of speech had led Dukakis to veto a bill that required the pledge in all schools). In 2004, Democrats nominated John Kerry, a decorated combat vet and war hero who came home and, in Democratic eyes, thoughtfully questioned the war in Vietnam. They were stunned when Republicans blasted Kerry as a traitor whose antiwar protests had run down America even while his comrades were still fighting in the field. The politics of patriotism grew nastier with each election cycle. "There is a determined group of radicals," wrote Newt Gingrich in 2011, with President Barack Obama very much on his mind, "who outright oppose American Exceptionalism [and are] convinced America is a brutal, racist, malevolent country." Reagan's deep-felt, gauzy patriotism hardened in the next generations, and turned into a partisan weapon.[37]

Second, communism is evil, and we fight for our lives against it. Reagan saw the Red Scare as an epic struggle for the soul of the nation. He believed that "America faced no more insidious or evil threat than communism." "My theory about the cold war," he told his future national security advisor Richard Allen, "is simple: we win, they lose."[38]

Reagan's anticommunism ran into a larger Manichean reflex. A simple conflict lurked within every debate—the good *us* fights a malevolent *them*. Patriots face up to cynics "who believe ours is a sick society." Honest students stand up to spoiled protesters. Hard working Americans resent welfare queens. Forty brave Democrats loudly applaud the president's tax cuts surrounded by glowering liberals sitting on their hands. By raising Republicans to parity with the Democrats in Congress and wielding his *us versus them*, Reagan helped frame a new era of bare-knuckle party politics. All this was hard to see while Reagan was in office. His tough talk was always tempered by optimism and geniality. He relished swapping tall tales with Democratic Speaker Tip O'Neill. "It was a nice evening," he wrote in his diary after one night, "but maybe Tip and I told too many Irish stories." The political generation that followed seized onto "we win, they lose" without the guilty pleasure of swapping tall tales with the other side.[39]

Finally, and most important, Reagan came to Washington pitching a big idea: "Government is not the solution to our problem; government is the problem." Roosevelt, Truman, Kennedy, and Johnson had all passionately believed in the power of collective action to lift individuals and communities. Even Nixon had announced "I am a government man." Not Reagan. Government was no instrument for the common good. On the contrary, it was elitist, stifling, even tyrannical—a dead weight on the shoulders of the common man and woman.[40]

There was a story about this deep truth at every turn. Was it really true, as he reported in his memoirs, that the army bureaucrats back at headquarters had granted Reagan's unit permission to destroy a warehouse full of useless files provided they kept copies of every piece of paper? Who knows? Who cares? The parable is irresistible: government bureaucracies will choke the life out of any enterprise. Whatever he did or did not accomplish, the Reagan idea was clear: cut spending, roll back regulations, and shrink the federal government. Let the free market work its wonders.

That idea was the conservatives' greatest legacy. It came to dominate American politics. It profoundly shifted the lines of conflict in American partisan politics. It changed the argument between Democrats and Republicans. The Republicans would become the party that despised the government. And the Democrats would go along—adding anxious caveats.

BACK IN THE 1890S, THE POPULISTS HAD ROARED OUT OF the prairies with a radical idea that government should reflect the collective will of the little people and stand up to the rich and mighty. That spirit flowed, eventually, into the Democratic Party and flourished between 1933 and the early 1950s. Now, the Reagan revolution pushed the other way. As they saw it, government was a force defined by incompetence and malevolence, a view Reagan himself expressed in one of his most famous quips: "The most terrifying words in the English language are 'I'm from the government and I'm here to help.'"[41]

Reagan and the Republicans rejected the Populist's premise: Rather than attack the rich and the powerful, they admired and encouraged them. The Reagans flashed the new spirit right from the start when Nancy Reagan appeared at the inaugural ball in a beaded haute couture gown designed by James Galanos—the first of many designer dresses. It was as opposite to Eleanor Roosevelt as one could get. The image foretold the policies. The administration began to dismantle the many limits on wealth that the Democrats had constructed: they cut taxes, squeezed labor unions, reduced regulation, and swapped out the nanny state for the market's *caveat emptor*.

For example, the Reagan administration took a tough new stance toward labor unions. The federally employed airport flight controllers—part of the Federal Aviation Authority—went on strike in August 1981. As part of the Teamsters Union, they had bucked the rest of organized labor and endorsed Reagan's presidential run the previous year. Now, the president gave them forty-eight hours to return to work, and when most of them (some eleven thousand) defied the order, Reagan fired them and imposed a lifetime ban on every striker. To the union's chagrin, military personnel and supervisors broke the strike and kept the planes flying. By October, the union itself had been decertified. Was there a whiff of racial animus in the union busting? Recently, political historian Desmond King has discovered that the union had rapidly gone from two to ten percent African American. In any case, the larger change remade labor relations. The New Deal had placed the government firmly on the side of the unions, protecting the right to organize and roughly balancing the interests of labor and capital. Now, Ronald Reagan sent a loud, clear message: The government's thumb would be firmly on the other side of the scale. Federal officials—and their labor policies—gave employers the green light to resist the inconvenient unions.[42]

Meanwhile, Reagan's tax cuts left a lot more money in the bespoke pockets of the wealthy. Margaret Thatcher's banking deregulation in London (known as the Big Bang) unleashed a new era of global finance, and international markets soon put terrific riches in the hands of anyone with the right pitch. A new era of inequality—a new Gilded Age—began to rise.

Our numbers geek, Kevin Phillips, who'd predicted the emerging Republican majority back in 1968, now fingered another powerful development in American political life. "The liberal style that had prevailed from 1932 to 1968," he wrote, "left a legacy of angry conservatives indignant over two generations of downward income distribution." Now, that era was over. Wealth shot back up. Inequality grew. It was the "best of times for the wealthy," wrote Phillips. Incredible riches ran to what he called "the top 1%." But Phillips delivered a warning to the rising rich: the nation had swung too far, he said, and would now see a political backlash against the Republicans' aggressive efforts to protect the wealthy. This time, Phillips was just plain wrong.[43]

Popular culture illustrated the strange nonreaction. Director Oliver Stone, for example, set out to mock the brazen, big money cheats in his 1987 film *Wall Street*. He created a slick, amoral villain who broke every rule and double-crossed every partner on his way to fabulous wealth. Yes, he ends up in jail, but the satire fell flat because the director seemed to fall under the spell of his Wall Street rogue. Gordon Gekko sounded a little bit like Ronald Reagan when, in the movie's climactic scene, he rose at a shareholder's meeting and growled that the company, like the nation, was being "royally screwed over by . . . bureaucrats." The remedy was Greed. "Greed . . . is good," he said. "Greed is right. Greed works."

In 1960, John F. Kennedy had called the young to public service—elite universities watched their graduates rush into the Peace Corps or head to Mississippi to fight for civil rights. Now, the Reagan administration pushed in the opposite direction. Self-interest was just fine, the race for riches was the American way. "Greed is good" became the mantra of a new generation who hustled after the fabulous riches of investment banking. From high-brow books (*Bonfire of the Vanities*, *Bright Lights, Big City*) to low-brow television (*Dynasty*, *Dallas*, *Lifestyles of the Rich and Famous*), the culture served up irony, grudging admiration, or cheap voyeuristic thrills about the rising money culture. Talented young people worked sixty-hour weeks, reaped the rewards they felt they deserved, and left their fellow citizens far behind without a backward glance.

At first, critics like Phillips thought the rising inequality would leave Republicans vulnerable. But, like the cultural critics, the

Democrats did not touch the theme in a serious way. On the contrary, the Democrats adjusted. When Bill Clinton broke the Republican lock on the White House in 1992 (winning 43 percent of the vote in a three-way race), his administration offered vivid testimony to Reagan's view of government as the problem. The new Democratic regime constructed their policies on Ronald Reagan's foundation, harnessing the markets to solve policy problems. The administration championed NAFTA, a trade agreement negotiated by the Republican George H. W. Bush administration—turning it a little bit Democratic by adding some feeble protections for workers and the environment. Clinton also devised an intricate health care plan that largely ignored the old big government programs (Medicaid and Medicare) and relied, instead, on the magic of the market—competition between private insurers overseen by federal and state regulators.

By 1990s, the difference between the parties had changed with the times. Back in the last generation, conservative Republicans like Robert Taft or Barry Goldwater fiercely opposed big government Democrats like Harry Truman or Lyndon Johnson who believed that federal programs—idealistic, ambitious, and far-reaching—should offer a boost to Americans who needed help.

Now, Republicans promised to shut down the big government programs and let unfettered markets rip. The new Democrats countered that governments ought to regulate those markets in order to protect consumers, limit inequality, and buff off the hard edges. Republicans cheerfully denounced the Democrats as socialists, but they had all become marketeers.

To be sure, there were still real differences between the parties. President Clinton expounded on the Democrat's market dispensation in his 1996 State of the Union Address. "The era of big government is over," he declared. And just to be sure the country heard him right, he repeated the idea three times during the address.

Careful listeners would have also heard, however, that each cheer for the markets came with the Democratic Caveat. "We cannot go back to the time when our citizens were left to fend for themselves." A smaller government would still have to help citizens make their way by raising the minimum wage, making private health insurance easier to buy, and guaranteeing that private pension plans were more secure. In the Reagan era, big government remained suspect. The parties wrangled over how to organize markets—with less oversight or with more.[44]

All these forces—lower taxes, weaker unions, fewer government programs—led inequality to rise faster and further in the United States than in other wealthy countries (except for Great Britain). The United States went from inequality levels roughly equivalent to France and Japan in 1970 to levels closer to Mexico and Brazil by 2010. The rapid growth of inequality unsettled American society and added a new intensity to political debates. But neither party pitched a sustained program to reverse inequality.[45]

Instead, the political winds began to blow in a different direction. The parties began to focus on clashing visions of American identity. And as they did, a formidable new media ecology emerged to amplify the partisan storm.

IN 1986, THE REAGAN ADMINISTRATION REPEALED AN FCC regulation from 1949 that had required broadcasters to give equal time to both sides of a political issue. The Fairness Doctrine, as it was known, compelled every station to balance Democrats and Republicans, conservatives and liberals. The rule had helped maintain the Cold War ideal—a centrist, unified nation could trust the sober, nonpartisan information that was delivered every evening on the nightly news. Democrats tried to restore the rule, but Reagan and the rising Republican majority blocked them and pressed a simple new philosophy on the media: let the people decide what they wanted to watch and hear without any government meddling.

And just in time for a technological revolution. Cable television arrived. An upstart station named CNN demonstrated its potential when it broadcast live from Baghdad during the first gulf war in 1991; unlike the traditional networks, which had fled when the war began, CNN didn't wait till 6:00 p.m. but ran the news all day long. Changes also revolutionized radio. Music moved to the FM band when the military relinquished control of the wavelengths and the AM channels went hunting for new content. Loquacious conservatives made the leap from sports to politics and filled the airwaves. By the early 1990s, the raucous, free-form world of cable news and talk shows had erupted.

The right had bitterly attacked the media as far back as the Goldwater convention in 1964. Now they created their own information ecosystem. Conservative views spread across the AM dial. Fox News, launched in 1996, quickly became a conservative powerhouse. In one survey, 53 percent of Republicans called it their primary source for news. Democrats never developed a comparable allegiance to any one provider—they were as likely to get their information from Comedy Central (which broadcast the Daily Show) as from CNN. With the rise of the internet, the news became even more fragmented, and every political niche and passion could curate its own information.[46]

On the surface, the new media era looked like its no-holds-barred nineteenth-century counterparts. But there was one big difference. Back then, the partisan newspapers agreed on the central facts. The Republican *Aurora* printed columns from Federalist *Gazette of the United States* and then responded. *The Gazette* shot back. Each side put its own spin on the issues and derided its adversary's version, but their clash turned on how they interpreted the facts of the day. Likewise, in the 1850s, southern fire-eaters and northern abolitionists saw different realities in the same events. But, as the free-form media took hold in the 1990s, each side featured not just different interpretations but entirely different facts. The right dished out reports that the left rejected as, well, loony.

One example illustrates just how far reality fractured. Glenn Beck, a voluble (and once highly popular) Fox News personality, took a dull, voluntary United Nations agreement on sustainability called *Agenda 21*, which was gathering dust on the shelves, and spun it into a dark plan to impose "centralized control over all of human life on planet earth." Big global government would impose "a sustainable environment," "social justice," and "economic justice" at the expense of all our liberties. The internationalists would drive Americans people out of the countryside and pack them into the dense and sustainable cities. They would take away their cars and force them onto public transit. Crazy? Yes and no.[47]

Yes, it *was* a crackpot conspiracy. Beck had alighted on a random bureaucratic tome and imagined it into a blueprint for world domination. But beneath the craziness lay a deeper truth. Globalization was leaping across national differences. Elites comfortably jetted from country to country. "European" attitudes—secular, feminist, cosmopolitan, sexually liberated, "sophisticated"—were spreading across America. Coddled third-world people seemed, at least to people tuning into the Glenn Beck show, to be getting rich and fat while Americans like them struggled. And, yes, environmentalists warned of a looming catastrophe that could be avoided only with significant lifestyle changes. Many (older, white, rural) Americans felt, in their gut, that Glenn Beck was making sense. The crackpot conspiracy reflected a deep discomfort with the state of the world and its smug elites preaching about the changes that had to be made. And that discomfort filtered right back into party politics with a new intensity fostered by the partisan media that spoke hidden truths to just one side.[48]

The fractured reality spread far and wide. I saw it flash all the way down to my town meeting in Lempster, New Hampshire (population 950). The selectman proposed adding our town-owned forests to a greenway that conservationists were creating across the center of the state. As soon as the issue was raised, one woman—well known in town because she and her husband operate a snowplow business that has been around for two generations—leapt up and asked, anxiously, "Is this Agenda 21?" Several young men muttered that of course it was. Neither the town moderator nor the elected officials knew what she was talking about. Their obvious puzzlement seemed to refute the charge and the proposal slipped through. But even in a small, local town meeting, the national news media had splintered the people's ideas about reality.

A REVOLUTION IN CONGRESS FED THE PARTISAN FIRE BLAZing from the new media. Congress had developed norms of civility and careful process—these norms usually held, more or less, as long as the members were not debating civil rights. Then, in the late 1980s, a new generation of Republican rebels burst onto the scene. Congressman Newt Gingrich of Georgia stepped into a leadership role (the Minority Whip, responsible for corralling Republican votes) in 1989 and he excoriated his party colleagues for growing fat and lazy as they languished in the minority. The Republicans had dominated the White House since Richard Nixon's ascension in 1968 and the Senate had turned competitive in 1980, but the House Republicans still lingered in the minority where they had sat for most of the last sixty years.

The only path to victory, preached Gingrich, lay in all-out, take-no-prisoners, political war. Get "nasty," he hectored his polite older colleagues. The Democrats are the enemy, he said again and again. Gingrich seized Reagan's "we win, they lose" philosophy, raised it to a new level, and spread it through Congress.[49]

For example, when the cable TV channel C-SPAN put cameras in the House, any member could go speak to the empty chamber after hours. The cameras were fixed on the dais, so viewers did not see that there was no one else in the room. Gingrich stuck. He rose and denounced fifty-one Democrats for believing that America was "stupid" and its allies "rotten and corrupt." As he delivered his after-hours speeches, Gingrich pretended that the absent Democrats were sitting there in front of him, too cowed or too callow to object to his rant. An outraged Democratic Speaker, Tip O'Neill, confronted him for "the lowest thing I've seen in my 32 years in Congress." The Republicans snapped right back and got the House to rebuke O'Neill for being derogatory to another member—the first speaker to be censured in almost two centuries. The young rebels who had gathered around Gingrich gave him a standing ovation at the end of the episode.[50]

The Gingrich wars were personal. He tried to get Democratic representative Charlie Diggs from Detroit, a founder of the Black Congressional Caucus, expelled from Congress after Diggs was convicted of fraud. That move fell short, but Gingrich did manage to knock off Democratic Speaker Jim Wright for slipping around limits in speaking fees by peddling a self-published book. Wright went down deploring the "mindless cannibalism" of the other side. After a grisly murder in Illinois, Newt offered this: "Let's talk about the moral decay . . . the left is defending." When a woman in South Carolina drowned her two sons in 1995, Newt leapt up again to point the finger at "liberalism" and offered just one path to social safety—"vote Republican." "The new zeitgeist of ascendant conservatism continues to vent its anger," demurred the *Washington Post* after the South Carolina incident.[51]

The roaring on the right stunned old Washington hands in both parties. They remembered a past era of spirited debates between people who respected the institutions—and one another. The memories of comity were exaggerated—the Red Scares and the debates over civil rights had been vicious and personal. Even so, by the 1990s, Congress was enacting a bare-knuckle politics of personal destruction that had few precedents since the Civil War. *We win, they lose* became the axiom of the day. And, sure enough, as Gingrich had predicted, congressional Republicans began to win majorities after their sixty years out in the cold.

From the Democrats' perspective, the Republicans became a ferocious, inflexible party that turned on any leader who dared to compromise with "the enemy." One leader after another fell to a new and more conservative wave of activists. Gingrich became Speaker after Republicans stormed to the majority in 1995—and then fell just four years later. "In a fractured Republican caucus," concluded the *New York Times*, "he could never satisfy every ideological instinct and faction." Three Republican speakers followed, each toppled or swept away by the next more conservative wave. The Gingrich Republicans had pushed aside the Reaganites, the Tea Party threw off the Gingrich Republicans, and the Trumpists routed them all. Political scientists called it asymmetrical polarization—Republicans moving right further and faster than the Democrats went to the left.[52]

But something odd emerged from the furor. Each side felt the polity slipping away from them. Republicans did not feel they had redefined the debate or moved too far to the right. On the contrary, they saw ruin in every direction. Government was no smaller than it had been when the Reagan revolution began. Entitlement programs kept growing. The culture had turned crass, hypersexualized, and antireligious. Back at the dawn of the current cultural war, Phyllis Schlafly had warned about the damage lurking in the Equal Rights Amendment: women in combat, same sex bathrooms, single mothers, the demise of traditional families, and the decline of Christian chivalry. By the late 1990s, every one of Schlafly's fears had sprung to life. Conservatives believed they had no choice—like partisans right back to 1800, they feared that their rivals would destroy the nation that they loved.

The Democrats, meanwhile, complained bitterly about the bare-knuckle politics by which a minority Republican Party—as they saw it—clung to power and refused to cooperate in the smooth running of government and the programs that Democrats valued. As the battles wore on, each political perspective, left and right, told pollsters the same thing: on issues that matter, their own side was losing. Only one in four felt like a winner.[53]

———

WE HAVE FOLLOWED THE LONG, SLOW SORTING OF TRIBAL identities into the two parties. The Republicans had once been the party of civil rights, and though their commitment had been waning, it was still no great surprise, in the mid-1960s, when they salvaged the Civil Rights Act and the Voting Rights Act from the southern Democrats—making the laws a bit more business friendly along the way. But that was the last hurrah for the party of Lincoln. As black voters settled into the Democratic Party, Richard Nixon and his Republican strategists drew their cynical conclusion: the racial backlash—South and North—would send many whites fleeing their way.

Frustrated liberals began calling out racial dog whistles—Why was Reagan opening his campaign just down the road from Philadelphia, Mississippi?—but racial attitudes were locking in and, like the solid South's Democratic voters in the past, required relatively little maintenance.

One of the biggest surprises, as I researched this book, was the length and the strength of the connection between white supremacy and the resistance to national government. Democrats vastly over-simplify when they tag Republicans as a band of racists. Many conservatives are baffled to hear their party denounced that way. But every coalition is a mash up of different attitudes. Whites who feel resentful on racial issues—those who score high on tests of racial intolerance—vote overwhelmingly Republican. On the other side of the party divide, nine out of ten African Americans punch the Democratic ticket. Those lopsided numbers reflect the ardent debates across both parties that first began to stir in 1932 and grew right through the 1964 election.

What's more, the racial divisions now link up to the immigration debates in a new way. The Great Society Democrats casually reopened immigration as a civil rights measure—to the distinct discomfort of the segregationists. The strangers in the land remained a minor issue until the trickle of thirty-five thousand newcomers in 1960 turned into a vast wave—fifty-nine million immigrants landed in the next half century. The political divide over immigration began to clarify in 1994 when California Republicans introduced a ballot measure barring undocumented immigrants from most social services. Proposition 187, also known as SOS for "Save Our State," roared through by almost twenty points. Congressional Republicans got the message and, two years later, rewrote national welfare laws to bar legal immigrants from food stamps, Medicaid, and other programs for five years after their arrival. President Clinton vetoed the bill twice and denounced the limits but finally capitulated and signed it into law—wanly pledging to overturn the bans someday. Some benefits have been restored and a handful of states have used their own funds to extend some programs to some immigrants. But in most places, most of the restrictions remain in place.[54]

The war on terror launched by the George Bush administration after the World Trade Center attack in 2001 further cemented the tribal loyalties. Despite the president's earnest efforts to avoid stereotypes, immigrants found themselves thrust into the glare of militarized security. One of my friends, an Indian American, made the point sardonically when I turned to him in the San Francisco airport and said, "Let's dash or we'll miss the flight." "You dash, Jim," he responded, "Brown people don't dash through airports anymore."[55]

The Republicans had dominated the Asian American vote right through the 1990s. But by 2010, it had slipped away to the Democrats. Some 70 percent of both Asian and Latino Americans regularly vote blue. The difference between the parties' views hardened as the Census Bureau jacked up the heat with their prediction that the United States would become majority-minority in just one generation. Surveys reported that four out of five Republicans worried that people of color "weaken our values and customs." Most reported feeling "uncomfortable" when they heard foreign languages spoken in the streets. As an often-quoted sign in Gino's cheesesteak stand in Philadelphia put it, "This Is America. When Ordering 'Speak English.'"

Two out three Democrats felt exactly the opposite way. They told pollsters that immigrants "strengthen our values and customs." For the first time in American history, the same party stood for both black rights and immigrants' rights. By 2020, the members of Congress reflected the division. There were 117 black, Hispanic, or Asian members in the House of Representatives and 107 were Democrats.[56]

The party differences have grown still hotter because the parties are evenly matched. The identity issues—whites on one side, people of color on the other—give the tight political competition a special intensity. Not only are they "the enemy" but they come from a visibly different tribe—and they could win it all in the next election. Donald Trump vividly demonstrated the worries running through the Republican Party base as he trampled his Republican rivals on his march to power in 2016. With his election, the new Republican ethos fully emerged: a fierce movement, dominated by white voters, often anxious about race and immigration.[57]

The tribal divisions were intensified yet again by the two women's movements that sprang up in the 1970s and grew more passionate—and influential—across the years. On the left—and in the Democratic Party—gender activists embrace reproductive free-dom, gender equality, and LBGTQ rights. (When Gino's gay son took over the cheesesteak shop, he quietly took down the famous sign and cheerfully took orders in Spanish.) Conservatives continue to fight for what they see as traditional families, gender roles, and sexual behavior. By 2020, the House of Representatives illustrated this difference too: ninety-one Democratic women including a Speaker versus fifteen Republicans.[58]

In short, political differences were intensified by the unprece-dented alignment. White people, especially those without a college education, increasingly came to feel that their very identity was under threat. People vaguely like them and their families had always been in charge. Now African Americans, Asians, Latinas, and powerful women like Democratic House Speaker Nancy Pelosi were pushing them aside. If they complained, or even used the wrong words, they were cast right into the Democrats' basket of deplorables.

Have we ever seen anything like this before? We sure have. This was the feeling that raced across white communities in the black majority districts in the South after the Civil War. That time, the fears of majority-minority triggered a long reign of terror that won back white supremacy at a very high price—the slow extinction of popular rule in Dixie.

Of course, every era is different. In contrast to the Reconstruc-tion period, the clashing tribes are now evenly matched across the entire nation, though they may not be for long. Every year another million new Americans come online. And they are moving toward the Democrats. The screaming divisions over race, immigration, and sexuality are far less marked among young people. Perhaps that's no surprise: they are the most diverse generation in American history. And they blithely cross the most savagely guarded line in American history. Every move toward racial equality brought howls about amalgamation—now more than one in seven millennials (and almost one in five black millennials) marry people from other races and ethnicities.[59]

Even so, the partisan past sends up its warning. In one generation after another, tribal conflicts eroded popular rule. As we have seen, democracy in America is surprisingly fragile. Especially when the screaming question of the day becomes "Who are we?"

What do we do now? What lessons should we take away from 200 years of ardent political conflict? And the roiling identity conflict the parties fire up today? The next chapter turns to where America might go next.

CONCLUSION

What Next?

B ack in the late 1940s, anxious rumors percolated through the white South. A white woman in South Carolina (or perhaps it was Louisiana or Georgia) had offered a job to a black woman as a cook (or a maid or a laundress) only to be told, "Well, I was looking for someone to work for me." Black women, so the stories went, were meeting in Eleanor Clubs (inspired by you know who) and plotting their move to the big houses where they would trade places with their former mistresses and feast on asparagus. The rumors grew edgier when they turned to black men, who were said to be ordering pistols in Memphis, buying knives in Mississippi, and pushing white folk off street cars on Thursdays in Washington, DC. It was the old fear of slave rebellions, sprung back to life and reimagined for a new era.[1]

The fantasies reflected something real. By the late 1940s, African Americans were beginning to rise. Their demands for jobs and justice were beginning to find traction inside the majority party, which narrowly voted a bold civil rights statement into the party platform at its raucous 1948 convention. African Americans did not really go around pushing white people off the street cars on Thursdays, but they were, slowly but surely, doing something much bolder. They were pushing white supremacists out of the Democratic Party.

We have followed the long, hard rise of civil rights to its break-through in the mid-1960s. Just two months after winning the Voting Rights Act of 1965—and fired up by their campaign for social justice—liberals opened the country to immigration for the first time in forty years. No one imagined the epic consequences. Fifty-nine million newcomers would land in the United States over the next half century. In the past, the shifting demographics would not have translated directly into power for one party since, as we have seen, the parties diffused identity politics. In an earlier era, Republicans offered most African Americans a political home while Irish immigrants headed straight to the Democrats.

Slowly, across the twentieth century, our contemporary coalitions developed. Democrats gathered African Americans (between 1932 and 1965), immigrants (from 1965 to the 2000s – each national group turned toward the Democrats at a different pace), and women fighting for equal rights (beginning in 1964). The politics of all three were built on a civil rights model. The Republicans harvested the backlash—whites uneasy about civil rights, natives worried about strangers in the land, conservative women eager to restore old-fashioned morals. One recent survey found more than one in five Republicans at the extreme end of a 100-point scale measuring racial resentment; a majority registered at least some resentment. A spate of studies followed, all showing the same anxieties on the right. Democratic respondents to the same surveys clustered at the opposite end of the scale.[2]

I recently overheard two men at the town dump in Lempster, New Hampshire, parsing the tribal politics. "If we don't find a way to stop those people," said one, "we'll never elect another Republican president. It'll be all over." They shared a worry that ran back through the years—recall those unruly George Wallace rallies in 1968. A different tribe is using the federal government to disrespect our people and push us aside. Identity passions have torn the nation apart more than once, but now the parties are built around the passionate American us versus them. Each side goes into every election with the same grim thought—if we lose, "it'll all be over."

In our own time, two successive presidents reflected the clashing visions of America. Barack Obama brilliantly embodied the multiracial, immigrant, urban, cosmopolitan nation. He became a star at the 2004 Democratic National Convention by offering himself up as an avatar of the rising new country. "My father was a foreign student, born and raised in a small village in Kenya. He grew up herding goats, went to school in a tin-roof shack. . . . I stand here today, grateful for the diversity of my heritage . . . knowing . . . that in no other country on earth, is my story even possible." For anyone who lived through the 1960s, it was extraordinary to see a man like Obama elected president—and by a larger margin than any Democrat since Lyndon Johnson forty-four years earlier. The nation seemed to be changing before our eyes. Perhaps, in the long run, the United States had lived up to Lyndon Johnson's rousing call after the bloodshed in Selma. Perhaps it had finally proved itself equal to the issue of civil rights.

On the other side of the great division stand the two men at the Lempster dump—and their local, white, native-born, traditional, heartland nation. In 2016, presidential candidate Donald Trump offered them a crackpot theory that reflected something serious. He peddled the calumny that President Obama was not American—despite all the evidence to the contrary. And, somehow, it rang true to people who felt that Barack Hussein Obama—they put a heavy emphasis on his middle name—did not reflect the country they grew up in. Trump offered his followers precisely the opposite message from Obama's. From interracial, international parents reaching for the stars to terrible people overrunning the homeland. He launched his unlikely presidential campaign with a bigoted blast: "They're bringing drugs," he said, referring to immigrants. "They're bringing crime. They're rapists. . . . It's coming from all over South and Latin America, and its coming—probably, from the Mideast."

For most Democrats, still thrilled by the racial breakthrough of the Obama elections, it seemed impossible that a man this intolerant and abrasive could be elected president—and by a larger Electoral College margin than any Republican in twenty-eight years.

Trump managed it, in part, by taking the country's inchoate tribal anxieties and bringing them to consciousness with a message carefully catered to low information voters. As political scientists say, he mobilized whiteness among racially anxious voters and added that surge to the traditional Republican electorate. He also tapped a deep dissatisfaction with the traditional political leadership in the United States, stoked at least in part by the new Gilded Age and its five decades of growing inequality. George Wallace touched the same resentments when he went north and uncorked an almost fanatic fervor from crowds who cheered his "telling it like it is."[3]

The United States has faced darker times in the past. We have seen worse violence and more blood. But today's divisions ought to worry us, for they go deep. They are not simply about policy preferences but about essential identity—about who we are and what Americans look like. For the first time, the parties gather all the forceful feelings of us versus them and channel them straight into politics.

What should we do? Let's begin with what *not* to do. Two familiar exhortations are plausible, appealing, and wrong.

AMERICANS OFTEN INVOKE THE DEEP BEDROCK VALUES THAT lie beneath all the screaming differences. Pundits, politicians, and philosophers routinely tick through the reassuring roster of principles: equality, liberty, markets, religious faith, the American Dream, and (or) the rule of the law. Together they sum to the idea of America—the foundations of our national exceptionalism, the consensus beneath the disharmony.

But, pace Jefferson, there are no self-evident truths or inalienable rights lodged at the heart of the nation. What we've seen is something more challenging—passionate disagreement. Americans have long quarreled about the meaning of liberty—does it require more government or less? We disagree about the promises and perils of equality, the role of religion in the public square, or whether Manifest Destiny was our country's providential mission or its terrible crime.

Partisans in every era invoke the revered traditions (as you can see, there is a long list to choose from) as they try to win elections or rally the people to their policies. But each of those often-invoked verities turn out to be a hotly contested debate. They are, most of them, rousing ideas. They have inspired reformers throughout the country's history. But Americans have never agreed on what any of them actually mean and to whom they apply.

Reading American politics with an eye to the people on the margins of power forcefully brings this point home. The fight to win civil rights, for example, has come and gone (and come and gone) with the vicissitudes of each era. For every Obama election, a Trump backlash. If the arc of American history bends toward social justice (or equality, or democracy, or the rule of law), it is only because idealists fight to achieve the soaring values lodged in the Declaration of Independence and manage to prevail, often against long odds.

ANOTHER PERENNIAL HOPE LIES IN BIPARTISAN CONSENSUS. Sensible people ought to be able to cast aside their differences and address the nation's needs. The dream of rising above the fray goes right back to George Washington. It didn't work for the founders and it doesn't work today. That's because politics is about choosing between deeply felt values. Do we want a stronger central government or one that leaves most power with the states? Do people have a right to health care or is it simply another service to purchase? Do we need more immigrants to enrich a diverse nation or fewer (or none) to protect our traditional culture? These questions do not have correct answers that high-minded bipartisans might simply discern. They are clashing values that have to be debated and decided.[4]

How about times of national peril? The coronavirus and an economic meltdown hit the United States just after I finished this book. At the time, some basic cooperation seemed essential. But that is not what we have seen during the crises in the past. Northern Democrats and Republicans fought bitterly during the Civil War—and even more bitterly during Reconstruction. Franklin Roosevelt spurned calls to cooperate with the lame duck Hoover administration during the Great Depression. And Republicans clobbered Obama during the Great Recession of 2009.

Americans often look back nostalgically to an imagined consensus that never actually was—a time when partisans came together for the greater good or when politics "stopped at the water's edge." They forget that Senator Arthur Vandenberg minted the famous aphorism as conservatives were pummeling liberals for being soft on Communists. In fact, that fight against communists, liberals, socialists, and civil rights activists is what first forged an alliance between conservatives in the two parties—and introduced the Republican Party we know today.[5]

Of course, civil discourse is always something to reach for, even to celebrate. Screaming partisans make many people uneasy and drive young people right out of politics. But civility is not the same as insisting that we agree. The founders' dilemma remains our own: partisanship is the oxygen to democracy. It is how people who disagree decide what to do. They join parties, persuade others, and hold a vote. Partisanship—arguments between intensely held views—is how vibrant republics work. Our job is not to tamp the differences down but to build a political system that can hash out the disagreements and let the majority govern.

The real problem lies not in the disagreement but in a political system that is not well suited for two parties pressing for advantage with no quarter given. We have no firm election rules, no bedrock right to vote, and the opportunity for shenanigans at many points in the electoral process. The contest over who gets a ballot (and how easily) always runs hot when the old majority is confronted by a new tribe—when the Sicilians and the Poles arrive from across the sea or African Americans move up from Dixie. Today's tribal fears will require clear, strong, democratic rules to keep contemporary politics within republican bounds. How do we build such a system?

Reformers can start by remembering two basic historical truths. First, politics is always changing. Today's rock-solid certainties will sound positively quaint tomorrow. You can mark the rate of change simply by checking an election map from a generation ago. In 1988, for instance, when Michael Dukakis was running against George H. W. Bush, Democrats knew that they would win West Virginia (now the single reddest state with more than two out of three voters picking Trump in 2016) and that they had almost no chance in California (now bright blue but, back then, it had gone Democratic just once in the previous nine presidential elections). We usually process politics in two years stanzas, extrapolating the future from the last midterm election. But a longer view reminds us how small, steady changes add up. Power shifts, the economy changes, groups drift out of old coalitions, new alignments emerge, new crises shake the established verities, and blue regions run to red—or vice versa.

Second, change takes time. Big shifts often appear to come on suddenly—a bolt from the blue. But, in reality, the storms gather slowly, over many years. The first black newspaper editorials urging

African Americans to abandon the Republicans appeared in 1932, but the migration of black voters into the Democratic Party took more than three decades. Or to take an even slower change, it took the South sixty years to go from solid Democratic to rock-ribbed Republican. Nor did the evolution stop then—after all, American politics is always in flux. After a couple of decades locked into red America, large swaths of the southland are moving back into play all over again.

Thinking about the future means imagining where Texas or Georgia or Alaska or New York will be, not two years from now during the next election but two decades from now for the next generation. More important, how will Dominican Americans or Chinese Americans or Indian Americans or African Americans or postmillennials evolve as voters? Will the parties court them, shun them, or make the mistake of taking them for granted? Neither geography nor demography is destiny. Parties, presidents, economic crashes, pandemics, and sheer chance will all play their part in shaping the next political era.

Looking backward gives us a very rough way to think about what may lie ahead—and why. The following five proposals all emerge from our exploration of the American past.

Secure the Vote

My dad voted for a Democratic presidential candidate just once in his long life. He was fighting in the European theater during the 1944 election, and after he'd voted, his commanding officer called him in, waving his ballot with disdain. "Morone," he growled, "you're the only man in this unit who voted against the commander in chief. Now get the hell back in that tent and do it right." And so, my father went back into the designated tent and voted to reelect President Franklin D. Roosevelt.

My dad was experiencing an all-American tradition when that officer casually tossed aside his right to vote—it's an apt metaphor for 220 years of American elections. The single most important reform to leap out of our long history is this: secure the right to vote. For everyone. Automatically. Register every American when they turn eighteen. No caveats. No paperwork. No convoluted residency tests. Today, technology makes it possible to identify voters without ID cards—much less the rigamarole of taking two different days to register and cast a ballot.

There's more we can do. Elections—national, state, and local—ought to be held on the same day. Why, for example, does Chicago vote for mayor in the frozen middle of February during the off-years between midterm and presidential elections? So only the most faithful party members will bother, of course. Voting should be easy to do. We should debate an even stronger position: *require* voting, as countries like Belgium and Australia already do.

Turning more people out to vote might very well lower the political temperature. With plenty of barriers to voting, only the most intense partisans turn out. A larger electorate would require the true believers to rally their neighbors now lingering on the sidelines. Less committed partisans may very well be open to, well, less partisan arguments. As John Dewey famously put it, "the cure for the ailments of democracy is more democracy."[6]

There is one problem with this suggestion. The whole idea of turnout has itself grown partisan. Democrats piously press for voting rights, expand access to the ballot in blue states, and coast to office amid high turnout. Of course, they do. Low turnout voters—young people, Latinx, Asian Americans, people with low incomes—all lean blue. Republicans, by contrast, do exactly what the Democrats did for so many generations, especially in the South. They win, in many places, by squeezing down the vote. President Trump has been refreshingly straight about how big turnouts would kill Republicans.

The vote suppressors make the same arguments in every era. Voting should be reserved for the better informed, for those with more at stake (like the wealthy), and for those who are willing to take the trouble. People who recite these old arguments don't know that they are echoing a long, violent tradition of racial repression. It was the argument of white supremacy in the South, the cry against Spanish speakers in California, the charge against Irish voters in New England. And it continues to do the same work today.

But thoughtful Republicans ought to reconsider for a more important reason. In the long term, it will be impossible to suppress the growing numbers of multiracial and young voters. A million new voters come online each year—either young people turning eighteen or immigrants naturalizing. Both groups trend heavily Democratic. In the long run, the Republicans (and the republic itself) will prosper only if the party finds a way, once again, to appeal to these populations. Remember, politics is always in flux. Every one of these Democratic groups once tilted Republican. In the long run, conversion will be more successful than suppression. And suppression strong enough to maintain control would require the end of popular government.

Unrig the Electoral Machinery

It's the same idea in every sport. The rules have to be clear and impartially applied. Then, go ahead and compete as hard as you can. Our problem is that in the United States, the contestants fix the rules as they go along. Political scientists Jacob Hacker and Paul Pierson call it "Calvinball," named after the six-year-old terror in the comic strip *Calvin and Hobbes*. Calvin dreams up one crazy rule after another in the middle of play—anything goes as long as it boosts his chances of winning.[7]

Our political Calvinball goes right back to the first contested election. But the tradition of changing the rules took deep root when the political parties rose up and built the electoral machinery to accommodate the (white male) masses in the 1820s and 1830s. The parties carved up the districts, printed their own ballots, organized the voters, marched them to the polls, watched them cast their votes, occasionally paid them for their trouble, and then counted the votes themselves.

Reformers eventually ended the most egregious practices. Parties don't print the ballots, voters slip behind a curtain, and paying them could land you in prison. But the reformers left the job half finished. In many places, partisans continue to carve up the election districts, run the elections, count the ballots, and certify the winners. The nation got a crash course in how that works when the presidential election of 2000, between George Bush and Al Gore, came down to a few thousand disputed ballots in Florida—the voting machines failed to cleanly punch through the ballots and they had to be inspected by hand. I watched the recount with people who were shocked to see the panel of three Broward County registrars accepting or rejecting ballots seemingly on a pure party-line vote, two to one in favor of the Republicans almost every time. It may have looked unsavory, but it was business as usual in American politics.

It's time to finish the job the reformers began more than a century ago. The basic principle is simple: take the entire electoral process out of partisan hands. No system can do so entirely, but today's contests reflect far too much of the swashbuckling (ruthless and corrupt) nineteenth-century parties. Nonpartisan referees ought to oversee elections. Partisanship is for candidates, campaigns, and issues, but we should minimize the role it plays in refereeing the game.

Here are a few illustrative steps toward less brazenly partisan election procedures:

First, the United States ought to have clear, simple standards for how people cast their ballots, with a paper (or computerized) record to make recounts easy.

Second, the process should be overseen, the votes counted, and the results certified by nonpartisans. This is a job for a civil service agency dedicated to the job.

Third, a more controversial idea: nonpartisan commissions ought to design the districts. Yes, the gerrymander goes back to the earliest elections—the name itself mocks Elbridge Gerry of Massachusetts for dreaming up an election district that looked like a salamander in 1812. But high partisanship and data technology have made politicians surgically precise at carving up populations for their own advantage. Today, over twenty states, both blue and red, have reined in gerrymanders and turned the districting process over to nonpartisan commissions. But in many others, it remains politics all the way down. Democrats often exaggerate the consequences (the party's real electoral problem is that they pack into urban areas where they "waste votes" when huge majorities go Democratic). Still, extreme gerrymandering diminishes democratic competition.

Finally, we ought to push further and challenge the many practices that permit minorities to rule majorities. The Electoral College is the most dramatic example. We should go back to Jefferson's original principle and allocate electors to each candidate according to their percentage of the popular vote. Donald Trump won 37 percent of the vote in New York and that ought to net him ten New York electors rather than none. Changing the rules in this way would push candidates to campaign across the country rather than waging billion-dollar elections in a handful of competitive states. Jefferson abandoned his own democratic principle to eke out an extra electoral vote in Virginia. Today, the rules make it too easy to overrule popular majorities. It's time to switch back to Jefferson's original position.

Beneath all these examples rests a simple principle: make strong, universal voting rules that maximize the public's voice. Then, once a robust electoral process is set . . .

Embrace Partisanship

Let the arguments roar. The bluster may not look pretty, but it's how we chose between different values. It's the whole point of democracy.

Great presidents have always broken partisan deadlocks, not by reaching out to the other party but by overwhelming it with a new vision. Franklin Roosevelt did not offer a hand to the defeated Hooverites. Nor did the Republicans rally round the president during the Great Depression—they almost unanimously tried to bury Social Security back in committee. Roosevelt's success lay not in cooperation but in the force of the collective, social-gospel vision he articulated during tough times. Likewise, Ronald Reagan fervently enacted his vision of patriotism, anticommunism, and limited government. Yes, he compromised when he had to. But there was never any doubt what he was for and why. Roosevelt and Reagan reveal the dirty little secret of bipartisanship. It generally happens when one side is cowed or beaten or out of fresh ideas.

Even so, Democrats just can't seem to put aside the bipartisan idyll. That's no surprise. They are the party of government trying to operate an institutional machinery that evolved to require cooperation across the aisle. But that prospect has evaporated—at least for now. President Barack Obama faced an opposition that voted almost unanimously against his every move and became increasingly reluctant to accept him as a citizen—only one in four Republicans were ready to call him an American. And still he dreamed that his reelection would "break the partisan fever." Of course, reelection did no such thing.[8]

Nor should it have. Republicans believe in different principles than Democrats. It's not a fever. It is what democracies do—argue over basic principles and take them to the voters.

The problems that subvert a vibrant democracy are not the partisan fevers but barriers to voting. And parties that fail to articulate clear, strong principles. Which brings us to the Democrats' dilemma.

The Task for Democrats: Confront Inequality

Throughout American history, there has always been a party or a faction that defended the common person against the money power—usually, the Democrats. In the 1890s, the Populists bequeathed the Democrats a bold version for modern times. Forty years later, President Franklin Roosevelt refined it into four freedoms and an ambitious economic bill of rights. We the people—through our government—owed each person the basics: food, shelter, health care, security, and a good shot at the American dream.

On the campaign trail, during the worst economy since the Great Depression, candidate Barack Obama resurrected the Democrats' old dream. At one campaign stop, a large, muscular man with a shaved head and antigovernment principles (soon famous as "Joe the Plumber") challenged Obama about taxes. Obama responded with a powerful restatement of the familiar creed:

> My attitude is that if the economy's good for folks from the bottom up, it's gonna be good for everybody. If you've got a plumbing business, you're gonna be better off if you've got a whole bunch of customers who can afford to hire you, and right now everybody's so pinched that business is bad for everybody and I think when you spread the wealth around, it's good for everybody.[9]

Republicans pounced on the line "spread the wealth around" and branded Obama a socialist. Obama stuck to the trusty populist canon. The parties each laid a clear principle face up before the electorate: positive freedom and the power of collective action to lift everyone versus the primacy of the markets, low taxes, and limited government.

But when Obama's "spread the wealth" entered the halls of power, the message turned murky and the populist call to champion the little guy morphed into a search for managerial efficiency. The signature move of the new Democrat (connecting the Democratic presidents of the last half century—Jimmy Carter, Bill Clinton, and Barak Obama) sets aside the Populist idea ("spread the wealth") and reaches for expertise and good government to lift us beyond partisanship and politics. The shift in perspectives rattled through President Obama's first inaugural address:

> The question we ask today is not whether our government is too big or too small, but whether it works. . . . Where the answer is yes, we intend to move forward. Where the answer is no, programs will end. And those of us who manage the public's dollars will be held to account, to spend wisely, reform bad habits, and do our business in the light of day, because only then can we restore the vital trust between a people and their government.[10]

The clarion calls to share, to spread the wealth, and to lift the poor all vanished—displaced by pledges of efficiency. The president promised to manage wisely. He called for reforming—not the rampant inequality of a roaring Gilded Age but government's "bad business habits."

Back in the twilight of the Reagan administration, political analysts like Kevin Phillips expected Democrats to make an issue of the emerging inequality. The gap between the very rich and everyone else had grown politically dangerous—or so it seemed. Of course, we now know that that was just the start of the era. The gap between rich and poor has expanded far beyond the inequality of any other wealthy country. During the Great Depression of the 1930s, the

Democrats built their half-century majority by squarely addressing this issue. Then, during the Johnson years, a smash up: the politic of lifting up the common person ran into racial furies.

The white majority came to see "spreading the wealth around" as spending "our" money on "those" people. As the majority of whites abandoned the Democrats amid the tumult of the 1960s and '70s, there were no longer enough votes to keep the New Deal vision intact. Now, as the United States grows more and more diverse, the votes just might be there.[11]

The problem grows. Both inequality and poverty have created havoc across all kinds of communities: rural as much as urban; white as well as Latino, Asian, and black. The fading American dream destabilizes our politics and depresses entire areas. The benefits of a long economic boom went straight to the very top. The pain of contagions and contractions goes straight to the middle and bottom. We have become a country of private jets and hungry children.

Of course, every generation updates its populism for the times. Democrats ought to find a new way to champion the old dream. As FDR put it in his first inaugural address, "These dark days will be worth all they cost us if they teach us that our true destiny is . . . to minister . . . to our fellow man." The fallout from coronavirus, the economic crash, and the shocking discovery that life expectancy has been falling among middle-aged white men ought to give this old aspiration a new urgency.

How should contemporary populists face up to the problem of inequality? Democrats across the party spectrum ought to make that long-neglected question their urgent business and begin a debate within the party about what such a program will look like. It is always tempting for the party of government to fix on what can be accomplished now, today. But every chapter in this book offers examples of reformers dreaming big and—slowly, slowly—changing everything.

The Task for Republicans

Bashing the federal government has always been entangled with protecting white supremacy. We saw the connection stirring in the election of 1800 and in full cry by 1840. More recently, segregationists swarmed around Barry Goldwater's earnest antigovernment message—recall the soda bottle whizzing past the heads of the black broadcasters as they tried to flee the Republican convention of 1964 unharmed.

In 1968, after four tumultuous years, Richard Nixon cashed in as disaffected white voters tumbled into his column. Following Nixon, the party's links to white supremacy could be confined to winks and dog whistles—that is, until Donald Trump. His victory stands as the greatest underdog win in modern presidential history. And he managed it, in part, by emulating George Wallace—rousing the people who were sick and tired of hearing know-it-all elites preaching politeness toward the different tribes who were transforming the USA right out from under them. In President Trump's hands, the old dog whistles became full-throated invectives against Mexicans, Muslims, and people of color. Now, the winks went out to the white nationalists—imagining their status might, somehow, be lifted up if only they pummel African Americans or Muslims or Jews. Or disinter the nineteenth-century bunkum about the mighty Anglo-Saxon race.

Understandably, many Republicans despise all that. They have their gaze fixed on entirely more honorable matters: less government, lower taxes, fewer regulations, religion, patriotism, the military, protection for the traditional family. And above all, a philosophy of leaving people alone. What do any of those priorities have to do with past segregation or the president's offensive language? The answer lies in the coalition. All those honorable positions get their political juice—generation after generation, North and South—from a persistent strain of white anxiety. Racial demons have always crawled into the antigovernment coalition. They always gave it energy and power.

Democrats are sometimes criticized for overemphasizing identity. Ironically, it's the Republican version of identity politics—the long, hard tradition of grasping for whiteness—that most feeds our roaring differences.

The job facing contemporary Republicans is to untangle the strands. Cull conservatism from white hostility and nativist fears. How? By taking the Republican message directly to people of color. It means winning back Asians, Hispanics, and African Americans. There are plenty of connections between the conservative message and each of these groups—black and Latino populations, for example, are far more churched (and in socially conservative churches, for that matter) than are whites.[12]

Young conservatives may be especially eager to start the operation. It's one way they can rescue the party from the grandparents and connect it to the young. What's more, as Republicans make inroads among African Americans, Latinos, or Asians, the tribal passions will begin to ebb—differences of principle and policy will stop firing up differences of tribal identity.

Impossible? Not for those who take a longer historical view. Ethnic and racial politics are always changing—alliances shift, attitudes develop, opinions turn. Recall what lured black voters into a party run by segregationists. Local party leaders recruited them, labor allies organized with them, New Deal policies appealed to them, and their own party took them for granted.

———

WALK DOWN TO THE VERY LOWEST LEVEL OF THE MUSEUM of African American History in Washington, DC, past the wreck of a slave ship and the declaration that all men are created equal, and you'll find something that President Obama fixed on when he dedicated the museum. "A block of stone. On top of this stone sits a historical marker, weathered by the ages," said Obama, "and that marker reads 'Gen. Andrew Jackson and Henry Clay spoke from this slave block during the year 1830.'" The important thing, continued Obama, is what we remember and what we forget—and for many years that stone was remembered "not for a child, shackled and bound, and bought and sold, and bid like cattle on a stone worn down by the tragedy of a thousand bare feet" but for "the unmemorable speeches of two powerful men." Understanding history, he concluded, is the way we build a better present. It's why we construct museums, confront the past, and topple monuments to white supremacy. It's why students at my university insist on a full reckoning with Brown's long connection to the slave trade. Or why the editors of a prison newspaper at a maximum-security jail in Louisiana rediscovered the story of the Colfax massacre, described in chapter 4. And, to take a much smaller example, it is why I wrote this book.[13]

The history of black America was, for a long time, ignored or simply misrepresented to justify terrible repression. Then, as the civil rights movement rolled across the country, it became about black people and the challenges they faced and overcame—celebrated, heroic, and still fenced off from the national narrative. Now a new generation understands, finally, that black history is American history. It is an essential part of the nation's founding and its laws, its culture and its mythologies, its past and its present. The year 1619, when the first twenty African slaves came ashore, was as decisive as 1776 and the declaration that all were equal.

The American story has many passionate narratives spiraling through it and none more dynamic than the stories of the people on the margins of power, pressing in—African Americans, recent immigrants, poor people, and women reaching for morality and justice. They add up to the story, not of different people, but of us, of America. Obama reminded us, in that memorable dedication speech, that the connections run both ways—"the African American experience has been shaped just as much by Europeans and Asians and Native Americans and Latinos. We have informed each other. We are polyglot, a stew."

Divided societies always struggle over memory. Over how to face up to the painful past—and its echoes in the present. The effort can be loud and angry and difficult, as it often is today. Or it can be mindful and careful and kind. Facing up to the past, and the many kinds of people who made it, is as important as anything else that Americans can do, as important as any other item on this list. It is how we can find ourselves. It is a vital first step toward restoring the better angels of our nature.

ACKNOWLEDGMENTS

I originally signed up to do a short book on ideas in American politics. I sat down to discuss it with my friend and editor, Lara Heimert, who shook her head and asked me, "Look, what's really important, right now?" By the end of our lunch, the idea for this book was on the table. Lara meticulously read through multiple drafts, made exactly the right comments each time, and then turned it over to the wonderful Connor Guy, who did outstanding line edits. I am grateful to my fabulous agent, Rafe Sagalyn, and his trusty mantra: "Show us, don't tell us." And I lucked into a wonderful, free-form seminar about writing with Theresa Winchell, who did a superb job with the copy edits.

Unfortunately, this book became entangled with another one I had also promised to deliver—a fat textbook on American politics. I sensibly thought I should choose between the two. I met my pal and collaborator, Rogan Kersh, in a café in Paris, and he talked me right out of giving up a book. "Just do them both," said the always-exuberant Rogan—terrible advice for which I will always be grateful.

And, as long as I'm on the subject of coauthors, a big thanks to all my collaborators on other projects: Elizabeth Fauquert, Larry Jacobs, David Blumenthal, Dan Ehlke, Ryan Emanaker, and my honorary coauthor, Jeremy Johnson. Shep Melnick and Bruce Miroff read the entire manuscript and made very valuable comments.

Margaret Weir served as discussant on multiple presentations and gave me something valuable to ponder every time.

As I wrote the book, I traveled to colleges and universities to try out my thoughts. The book is so much better for all the hands that shot up with questions, quibbles, and subversive ideas. Extra thanks to Christine Zumello, who set up a lecture in the amphitheater at the Sorbonne—the world's most fabulous venue. I'm also grateful to my friends at Oxford University, especially Des King, Karthik Ramada, and Ngaire Woods, who shared fabulous suggestions, nourishing conversations, and pints of stout.

Other stops along my way included the University of Chicago, Fondation des États-Unis in Paris, University of Virginia, Woodrow Wilson School of Government at Princeton, Yale Law School, West Point Military Academy, Holy Cross, Aurora Historical Society, George Washington University Law School, University of Toronto, NYU, John Jay University, and Skidmore College—where I'm especially grateful to the faculty of the political science, history, and American studies departments for a wonderful interdisciplinary discussion. Extra special thanks to the cheerful students and faculty at Oklahoma City Community College and El Paso Community College.

A wonderful network of people pitched in with comments on the book and a change of subject when I needed it. I'm especially grateful to Peter Andreas, Tim Bartlett, Mark Blyth, Corey (and Ali and Sophie) Brettschneider, Francoise de Chantal, John Cell, Bill Galston, Lindsay Evans, Marie Gottschalk, Alex Gourevitch, Jacob Hacker, Bonnie Honig, Ira Katznelson, Jerry Karabel, Jen Lawless, Ricky Locke, Glenn Loury, Colella Mackenzie, Ted Marmor, Suzanne Mettler, Vincent Michelot, James Evans Morone (a rising political scientist who just got his degree from Penn), Joe Evans Morone, CC Morone, Jon Oberlander, Paul Freedman, Rich Snyder, Eric Patashnik, Mark Peterson, Melvin Rogers, Wendy Schiller, Tom Sugrue, Steve Skowronek, Natalie Taylor, Caroline Touhy, Robert

Vipond, Nick Ziegler, Linda and Endres, and the remarkable Ashu Varshney. My brothers, Joe and Pete Morone, have been talking politics and history with me for a half century, and this book was one more chapter in our life-long conversation. Special thanks to Anthony Sparacino, who generously shared what he had found in an archive in Boise, Idaho.

When I first figured out where this book was going, I tried the argument out on David Robertson—his enthusiasm was the essential first test for me. And I struck more gold when Sid Milkis, a marvelous scholar, listened to my thoughts about race, immigration, and the parties, and said, "David Hackett Fisher and I once discussed exactly this pattern and thought there'd be a great book in it, someday." On the shoulders of giants . . .

My wonderful son, Harry, taught me to walk across scary mountain passes without looking down. He had something interesting to say—in the same calm, soothing, guide's voice—every time I pitched the evolving storyline to him. My current and former graduate students have also been superb and patient teachers. Special thanks to Rachel Meade, Tony Dell'Aera, Aaron Weinstein, Kevin McGravey, Dan Carrigg, KR White, Kaitlin Sidorsky, and Megean Bourgeois. My undergraduate seminar in American political development read the manuscript, turned the tables on their professor, and offered me terrific comments, corrections, and exhortations. And special thanks to the fabulous team at Basic Books: Katie Lambright, Michelle Welsh-Horst, and Melissa Raymond.

On a more somber note, writing a book is a journey, and during this one, I lost two lifelong guides. My mother, Stasia, died just around the time I was hitting send on the final manuscript. At ninety-two, she kept asking to hear the story of the book and always said the same wonderful thing: "Oh, how interesting." My mom, born in Krakow, spent World War II in a Soviet work camp before escaping to a golden life in Rio de Janeiro, where I spent my childhood. Perhaps it was her remarkable adventures, but she relentlessly sought out the other side of every story. Each time I'd come home from school with some tale the nuns had told me, she gently suggested what the Protestants might say about it. Her urge to see more and see it differently is one of the things that got me here.

Another was the high school teacher who most inspired me to do what I do—a remarkable former Augustinian priest named Richard O'Donnell. He introduced me to Shakespeare, Plato, the romantic poets, Dante, James Joyce, and more. To this day, I marvel at the mesmerizing lectures he seemed to deliver effortlessly, one after another. He also taught us to drink espresso, to appreciate good red wine, and how to get to Lincoln Center. Richard—ROD, as we knew him—slipped away suddenly, just as I was finishing the edits.

Finally, I've dedicated this book to Rebecca Henderson, my wonderful partner. There's much to say about Rebecca but, for now, I'll just remember our routine during a joint sabbatical in Paris. The morning began with a run to our boulangerie for baguette and croissant; then, we worked feverishly on our books until a late lunch time (I was drafting chapters 3 and 4); and then, writing done, we haunted the markets, museums, concert halls, and bistros. This book was delivered a bit later because of all the things we saw and did. But the cheer you might occasionally see flashing through its pages reflects the joyous times Rebecca and I have had as we each scribbled away.

NOTES

Introduction: How American Politics Turned Tribal

1. Social scientists have done a terrific job writing accessible books about contemporary partisanship and the danger of government breakdown. See, for just a few outstanding examples, Steven Levitsky and Daniel Ziblatt, *How Democracies Die* (New York: Crown, 2018); John Sides, Michael Tesler, and Lynn Vavreck, *Identity Crisis: The 2016 Presidential Campaign and the Battle for the Meaning of American* (Princeton, NJ: Princeton University Press, 2018)—which opens with a good description of the Trump rallies; Doug McAdam and Karina Kloos, *Deeply Divided: Racial Politics and Social Movements in Postwar America* (New York: Oxford University Press, 2014); Matt Grossmann and David Hopkins, *Asymmetric Politics: Ideological Republicans and Group Interest Democrats* (New York: Oxford University Press, 2016); and Kathy Cramer, *The Politics of Resentment: Rural Politics in Wisconsin and the Rise of Scott Walker* (Chicago: University of Chicago Press, 2016). On the public opinion data, see Pew Research Center, "Partisanship and Political Animosity in 2016," June 22, 2016, survey conducted March 2–28 and April 5–May 2, 2016. On intermarriage, Lynn Vavreck, "A Measure of Identity: Are You Married to Your Party?" *New York Times*, January 30, 2017.

2. The US Census Bureau prediction is controversial, and many demographers criticize it for taking a simplistic view of who counts as minority. See Richard Alba, "The Likely Persistence of a White Majority: How the Census Bureau Statistics Have Mislead Thinking About the American Future," *American Prospect*, January 11, 2016, www.prospect.org/civil-rights/likely-persistence-white-majority/.

3. Conservative Democrats have latched on to the idea that the party is too focused on identity politics, but this is an essential feature of both parties. See Mark Lilla, *The Once and Future Liberal: After Identity Politics* (New York: HarperCollins, 2017).

4. Bush v. Gore, 531 U.S. 98 (2000). See Alan Lichtman, *The Embattled Right to Vote in America: From the Founding to the Present* (Cambridge, MA: Harvard University Press, 2018). For the classic account, Alexander Keyssar, *The Right to Vote* (New York: Basic Books, 2000).

5. "Trump Is Racist, Half of U.S. Voters Say," *Quinnipiac University Poll*, July 30, 2019, https://poll.qu.edu/national/release-detail?ReleaseID =3636. The response was 51 percent "yes," 45 percent "no."

6. George Washington scrawled a series of letters describing the event: General Order, Head Quarters, Newburgh, March 11, 1783 [changing the meeting date]; Letter to Alexander Hamilton, Newburgh, March 12, 1783 [on the affair being managed from Philadelphia]; Letter to Joseph Jones, Newburgh, March 12, 1783; Letter to Elias Boudinot [president of the Continental Congress], Head Quarters, March 12, 1783 [a kind of official report to Congress]; and Speech to the Officers of the Army, Head Quarters, Newburgh, March 15, 1783. The anonymous letter calling for officers to assume a bolder tone is generally attributed to John Armstrong. The letter can be found in George Washington, *Writings* (New York: Library of America, 1997), 1107–1109. For a description of this famous story, see Richard H. Cohn, "The Inside History of the Newburgh Conspiracy: America and the Coup d'Etat," *William and Mary Quarterly* 27, no. 2 (April 1970): 187–220, https://doi.org/10.2307/1918650.

7. George Washington, *Circular to State Governments*, Head Quarters, Newburgh, June 8, 1783.

8. George Washington, Farewell Address, United States, September 19, 1796. The address—really a letter published in newspapers—is often thought to be a statement of isolationism in foreign policy. It is not. The real theme and passion in this forceful letter is a warning against the spirit of division between parties and regions—in fact, "the passionate attachment of one nation for another" is simply presented as one issue (a major one in the 1790s) dividing Americans against each other.

9. James Madison, *Notes of Debates in the Federal Convention of 1787*, June 2, 1787 [quoting Franklin]. James Madison, "Federalist No. 10." Unlike the others quoted here, the nimble Madison thought the answer to the problem of faction was more faction—lots of small interests all feverishly buzzing with deals and compromises. His elegant scheme would be compromised if all those interests froze into both a majority and a minority party that spanned the nation. John Quincy Adams, Inaugural Address, Washington, DC, March 4, 1825. By Adams's day, this sentiment was being overrun by the political parties of the 1820s. *A Compilation of the Messages and Papers of the Presidents*, ed. James D. Richardson (Washington, DC: Bureau of National Literature, 1911), 2:861–862. Thomas Jefferson to

Frances Hopkinson, Paris, March 13, 1789. Thomas Jefferson, *Writings* (New York, Library of America, 1984) 941.

10. The term *parties* does appear some seventy times in the Federalist papers, but generally in reference to factions or interests. The most notable exception is a brief discussion by Madison in "Federalist No. 50."

11. Drew Desilver, "US Trails Most Developed Countries in Voter Turnout," Pew Research Center, Fact Tank: News in the Numbers, May 21, 2018, www.pewresearch.org/fact-tank/2018/05/21/u-s-voter-turnout-trails -most-developed-countries/.

12. For example, a half century later, the 1852 Democratic Party platform put it this way: "ours [is] the land of liberty and the asylum of the oppressed of every nation . . . and every attempt to abridge the privilege of becoming citizens and the owners of the soil among us ought to be resisted with the same spirit that swept the alien and sedition laws from our statute-books." "1852 Democratic Party Platform," American Presidency Project, www .presidency.ucsb.edu/node/273166.

13. Martin Van Buren to Thomas Ritchie, January 13, 1827, Washington, DC, *Papers of Martin Van Buren*, Series 5, January 1, 1925–March 3, 1829 (Washington, DC: Library of Congress).

14. See Orestes A. Brownson, "Abolition Proceedings," October 1838, 331, and "The Laboring Classes," July 1940, in *Works in Political Philosophy, Vol. 2: 1828–1841*, ed. Gregory S. Butler (Wilmington, DE: Intercollegiate Studies Institute, 2007).

15. The turnout data is from the 1938 midterm and is computed from Ira Kastznelson, *Fear Itself: The New Deal and the Origins of Our Time* (New York: Liveright, 2013), 143.

16. Political scientists have found many different ways to measure partisanship. They generally agree on a sharp decline on partisanship at the start of the twentieth century, bottoming out in the 1940s, and then rising sharply beginning in the 1970s. See figs. 1.2 and 1.3 in Nolan McCarthy, Keith Poole, and Howard Rosenthal, *Polarized America: The Dance of Ideology and Unequal Riches*, 2nd ed. (Cambridge, MA: MIT Press, 2016), 10.

17. Frank Kent, "The Parties and the Poll Tax," *News Journal*, May 15, 1940.

18. Original Inaugural Address of George C. Wallace, January 14, 1963, Montgomery, Alabama. http://digital.archives.alabama.gov/cdm/ref /collection/voices/id/2952.

19. Greg MacGregor, "Reaction Divided on Wallace Vote: Showing Is Discounted in North and Hailed in South"; and Ben A. Franklin, "Brewster Victor, Wallace Has 43% in Maryland Vote: Alabaman Does Better Than

in Wisconsin and Indiana: Elated at Showing," *New York Times*, May 20, 1964.

20. Phyllis Schlafly, *A Choice Not an Echo* (Alton, IL: Pere Marquette Press, 1964).

21. Jackie Robinson, "New Breed's Weapons Are Hate, Murder," *Pittsburgh Currier*, July 25, 1964.

22. Letter from George Romney to Barry Goldwater, December 21, 1964, MS 280, Box 7, Papers of Robert E. Smylie, Republican Governors Association, Idaho Historical Society. Special thanks to Anthony Sparacino of the University of Virginia, who generously shared this material.

23. John Avril, "Rusk Hit on Immigration Law Change: Revision of Quota Setup Challenged by Ervin," *Los Angeles Times*, February 25, 1965.

24. Ron Machtley, personal conversation, February 1994. Gingrich was one of the Republican whips.

25. Former Senate majority leader Tom Daschle, conversation with me, May 2014. Lauren Holter, "Some Members of Congress Sleep in Their Office and There's a Couple of Problems with That," *Bustle*, March 6, 2018, www.bustle.com/p/some-members-of-congress-sleep-in-their-office-theres-a-couple-problems-with-that-8420692.

26. "Is There a Clinton Mandate? Dole Implies 43% Vote Justifies GOP Opposition to Legislative Programs," *Los Angeles Times*, November 8, 1992, http://articles.latimes.com/1992-11-08/opinion/op-186_1_popular-vote. On the Senate vote, only five Republicans found Clinton "not guilty" of either of the two charges against him.

27. Josh Clinton and Carrie Roush, "Poll: Persistent Partisan Divide over 'Birther' Question," *NBC News*, August 10, 2016, www.nbcnews.com/politics/2016-election/poll-persistent-partisan-divide-over-birther-question-n627446. Gregory Krieg, "14 of Trump's Most Outrageous 'Birther' Claims," *CNN Politics*, September 16, 2016, www.cnn.com/2016/09/09/politics/donald-trump-birther/index.html.

28. James A. Morone, "Diminishing Democracy in Health Policy," *Journal of Health Politics, Policy and Law* 45, no. 5 (Stamford, CT: Centage, 2014).

29. CNN, "Roberts: "My Job Is to Call Balls and Strikes and Not to Pitch or Bat," September 12, 2005, www.cnn.com/2005/POLITICS/09/12/roberts.statement/. Kevin Buckler and Elizabeth L. Gilmore, "Originalism, Pragmatic Conservatism, and Living Document Judicial Philosophies: Explaining Variation in US Supreme Court Votes in Criminal Procedure Cases for the 1994–2004 Terms of Court," *American Journal of Criminal Justice* 42, no. 1 (July, 2016): 28–54, https://doi.org/10.1007/s12103-016-9354-6. Jeffrey Segal, Lee Epstein, Charles Cameron, and Harold Spaeth,

"Ideological Values and the Votes of US Supreme Court Justices Revisited," *Journal of Politics* 57, no. 3 (August 1995): 812–823.

30. From Justice Brandeis's dissenting opinion in New State Ice Co. v. Liebmann, 285 U.S. 262, 311 (1932).

31. New State Ice Co., 285 U.S. 262, 311 (1932). Steven Levitsky and Daniel Ziblatt, *How Democracies Die* (New York: Crown, 2018), 2.

Chapter 1: Into the Temple of Liberty on the Shoulders of Slaves

1. This is the plan as it was originally reported in the newspapers. The version described here is from the *Connecticut Gazette*, September 10, 1800. For a fine description of the rebellion, see Douglas R. Egerton, *Gabriel's Rebellion: The Virginia Slave Conspiracies of 1800 and 1802* (Chapel Hill: University of North Carolina Press, 1993). Patrick Henry was a native of nearby Hanover County and a friend of the Prossers, Gabriel's owners.

2. The only source for the famous dinner is Thomas Jefferson, who wrote two quite similar descriptions of the event. See *The Complete Anas of Thomas Jefferson*, ed. Franklin B. Sawvel (New York: Round Table Press, 1903), 33–37. All quotes in the following two paragraphs are from Jefferson. Ron Chernow, *Alexander Hamilton* (New York, Penguin, 2005), 330, judged this "the most celebrated dinner."

3. There is much historical debate about the famous deal. Stanley Elkins and Eric McKitrick, in their superb study of the Federalists, suggest that the Virginia and Pennsylvania congressional delegations had already agreed about siting the capital. But even so, they argue, Jefferson was probably right: getting Jefferson, Madison, and Hamilton to sign on clinched the agreement and kept it from unraveling over the tumultuous months and years. Stanley Elkins and Eric McKitrick, "Adams and Hamilton," in *The Age of Federalism: The Early American Republic. 1788–1800* (New York: Oxford University Press, 1993).

4. For a vivid view of New York, which was still rude thirty years later, see Sean Wilentz, *Chants Democratic* (New York: Oxford University Press, 1984).

5. "Contradiction," *Boston Gazette*, October 9, 1800. Washington, Farewell Address. For a similar warning, delivered at length from the floor of Congress, see Representative Fisher Ames, *Annals of Congress*, House of Representatives, 3rd Congress, Session 2 (November 26, 1794), 920–932, www.memory.loc.gov/cgi-bin/ampage?collId=llac&fileName=004/llac004 .db&recNum=457.

6. Thomas Jefferson, "Query XIX," in *Notes on the State of Virginia*; "First Inaugural Address," March 4, 1801. On the rising democracy, see Sean Wilentz, *Chants Democratic*.

7. "A Favorite Beer-House Song," *Gazette of the United States*, September 15, 1800. "A Federal Republican," *Philadelphia Gazette*, March 2, 1800.

8. See for example, the affidavit by Tench Coxe, *Aurora*, October 9, 1800. Coxe had been a member of the Washington administration who was removed by John Adams and became a Republican. Jefferson repeats a variation of the loose talk taking place at President Washington's table in *Anas*, 667, 671 [glare].

9. George Washington to Thomas Pickering, Secretary of State, July 11, 1798. As we'll see, Washington was especially concerned about the French fomenting rebellion among the slaves.

10. John Adams, Special Message to the House and Senate, May 16, 1797, in *A Compilation of the Messages and Papers of the Presidents*, ed. James D. Richardson (Washington, DC: Bureau of National Literature, 1897), 2:223–229. For a fine description of the conflict with France, see Elkins and McKitrick, *The Age of Federalism*, chap. 14, negotiations in Paris described at 549–579.

11. John Adams to James McHenry, October 22, 1798.

12. *Gazette of the United States*, April 12, 1789. For a lengthy and eye-opening excerpt from the dispatch see, *Aurora*, April 10, 1798.

13. Julian Ursyn Niemcewicz, *Under the Vine and Fig Tree: Travels Through America in 1797–1799, 1805*, trans. and ed. Metchie J. E. Budka (Elizabeth, NJ: Grassmann, 1965), 125.

14. William Cobbett (an Englishman), *Porcupine's Gazette*, December 24, 1798 (emphasis original). George Washington, Letter to Alexander Spotswood, Philadelphia, November 22, 1798. For an oration on the subject that offers a good summary of the fears, see "Is the Alien Law Consistent with the Principles of the Constitution or of Sound Policy?" *Commercial Advertiser*, February 21, 1798, 1.

15. John Adams to Tenche Coxe, May 1792. Reprinted in *Porcupine's Works: Containing Various Writings and Selections Exhibiting a Faithful Picture of the United States of America* (London: Cobbett and Morgan, 1801), 11:142–143. Coxe created considerable trouble by releasing the private letter to the press. He would go on to certify in the *Aurora* that both Hamilton and Adams were *monarchists*.

16. *Gazette of the United States*, February 14, 1798.

17. For my own take on this vast theme, see James A. Morone, *Hellfire Nation: The Politics of Sin in American History* (New Haven: Yale, 1993). See also, Aristide Zolberg, *A Nation by Design* (Cambridge: Harvard University Press, 2006).

18. Representative Edward Livingston, "Speech of Edward Livingston, in the House of Representatives of the United States, on the Third Reading of the Alien Bill," *The Debates and Proceedings in the Congress of the United*

States (Washington, DC: Gales and Seaton, 1834–1856), June 21, 1798, 2008–2010 [deporting slaves], 2013–2014 [dark]. The literature on the American fear of government is voluminous. For a nice summation, see Robert H. Wiebe, *Self-Rule: A Cultural History of American Democracy*, rev. ed. (Chicago: University of Chicago Press, 1996). And for my own effort, James A. Morone, *The Democratic Wish* (New Haven, CT: Yale University Press, 1998).

19. George Washington to Thomas Pickering, Secretary of State, July 11, 1798. Washington thought that the slaves might join the invaders—as some had done during the revolution when Britain promised them freedom. Back then, Washington had demanded the return of the slaves but Britain flatly refused.

20. James Callender, *The Prospect Before Us*, vol. 2, pt. 2 (Richmond, VA: Printed for the author and sold by M. Jones, S. Pleasants Jr., and J. Lyon, 1800–1801), 7.

21. For a good description of the Federalist worldview (and their anxieties), see Joanne B. Freeman, *Affairs of Honor: National Politics in the New Republic* (New Haven, CT: Yale University Press, 2002).

22. *Aurora*, July 31, 1799.

23. *Aurora*, October 4, 1799. For a scholarly description of the cases, see Philip Blumberg, *Repressive Jurisprudence in the Early American Republic* (New York: Cambridge University Press, 2010), 112ff.

24. "Sedition Is Slavery," *Aurora*, July 19, 1798.

25. See Donna Demac, *Liberty Denied* (New Brunswick: Rutgers University Press, 1990).

26. For a description of the rebellion, see Philippe Girard, *Toussaint Louverture: A Revolutionary Life* (New York: Basic Books, 2016). See also Laurent Dubois, *Avengers of the New World: The Story of the Haitian Revolution* (Cambridge, MA: Harvard University Press, 2004).

27. For details of the negotiation, see Gordon Brown, *Toussaint's Clause: The Founding Fathers and the Haitian Revolution* (Jackson: University Press of Mississippi, 2005).

28. Congress would soon reverberate with racial charges—against Louverture, against Esteve, against the people of Haiti. But there is only silence about Bunel's race—an unlikely oversight if he was, indeed, a man of color. For a fine analysis, see Phillipe R. Girard's essay, "Trading Races: Joseph and Marie Bunel," *Journal of the Early Republic* 30 (Fall 2012): 351–376. Most histories repeat the first person of color line—see for one example, David McCullough, *John Adams* (New York: Simon and Schuster, 2001), 519.

29. Albert Gallatin, January 21, 1799, in Thomas Hart Benton, *Abridgement of the Debates of Congress from 1789 to 1856*, vol. 2 (New York: D. Appleton, 1861).

30. From Thomas Jefferson to James Madison, February 12, 1799, *The Papers of Thomas Jefferson*, vol. 31, ed. Barbara B. Oberg (Princeton, NJ: Princeton University Press, 2004).

31. The political science textbooks illustrate an interesting amnesia about the 1800 election. When I wrote my own textbook, reviewers (textbooks get endless reviews) immediately reminded my coauthor and me to include a description of the Alien and Sedition Acts. But never across hundreds of reviews did the election of 1800 elicit a word about Toussaint or Gabriel from any reviewer. As far as I can see, all the other major texts emphasize the Alien and Sedition Acts and are silent on the racial upheaval. See the other best-selling texts for illustration: Ginsberg et al., *We the People* (New York, Norton, 2017) and Samuel Kernell et al., *The Logic of American Politics* (Thousand Oaks, CA: Sage, 2018).

32. See Brown, *Toussaint's Clause*, 161–227, Jefferson quoted at 195. For a version that is more critical of Jefferson, see Douglas R. Egerton *Gabriel's Rebellion* (Chapel Hill: University of North Carolina Press, 1993), Jefferson quoted at 170.

33. On women fighting for liberty in Haiti, see Stephanie McCurry, *Confederate Reckoning: Power and Politics in the Civil War South* (Cambridge: Harvard University Press, 2010), 246–247. On the French invasion, see David Brion Davis, *The Problem of Slavery in the Age of Emancipation* (New York: Knopf, 2014), Leclerc quoted at 76.

34. David Walker, *Appeal to the Coloured Citizens of the World* (Boston: David Walker, 1829), article 2.

35. Douglas R. Egerton, *Death or Liberty: African Americans and Revolutionary America* (New York: Oxford University Press, 2009), 259–260.

36. Egerton, *Death or Liberty*, 280.

37. *Herald of Liberty*, October 27, 1800, 1. *Aurora*, September 23, 1800.

38. *Herald of Liberty*, October 27, 1800 [denying French involvement]. For the argument that there were indeed elusive Frenchmen, see Egerton, *Gabrielle's Rebellion*, 40, 102, Appendix 2. *Wayne's Gazette of the United States*, September 23, 1800 [French plan].

39. *Connecticut Gazette*, October 8, 1800, 1. *Boston Gazette*, October 9, 1800.

40. Cobbett, *Porcupine's Works*, 141. *Wayne's Gazette of the United States*, September 23, 1800.

41. *Aurora*, September 24, 1800.

42. For a summation of the voting machinations, see Edward J. Larson's superb *A Magnificent Catastrophe: The Tumultuous Election of 1800, America's First Presidential Campaign* (New York: Free Press, 2007), chap. 2. I recommend Larson as the ideal introduction to this election.

43. On the New York election, see Thomas Jefferson to James Madison, March 4/8, 1800. The letter is dated March 4 and then continued on March 8. In *The Writings of Thomas Jefferson*, vol. 7, ed. Thomas Ford (New York: Putnam, 1896), 429–434. A copy of the original can be found at www.loc.gov/resource/mjm.06_0749_0751/?sp=1. For a summation of the voting machinations, see Larson, *A Magnificent Catastrophe*, chap. 2.

44. *Writings of Thomas Jefferson*, 434.

45. Matthew L. Davis, *Memoirs of Aaron Burr* (New York: Harper, 1837), 2:6–7. This is the best original source for the New York campaign. For a more recent account, with juicy detail, see Aaron Lomask, *Aaron Burr: The Years from Princeton to Vice President* (New York: Farrar, Straus and Giroux, 1979), 239–240.

46. *Aurora*, May 5, 1800. *Gazette of the United States*, May 5, 1800.

47. Hamilton had concocted a byzantine scheme to put Federalist vice-president candidate, Charles C. Pinckney from South Carolina, into the presidency by pushing South Carolina to give all eight of its Electoral College votes for their native son (and none for Adams). But Hamilton pushed too hard and turned even Pinckney against the scheme.

48. "Chronicle Impudence," *Columbia Centinel*, January 3, 1801.

49. Thomas Jefferson letter to James Madison, December 19, 1800, *Writings of Thomas Jefferson*, 342–343 [exultation]. James Madison, Letter to Thomas Jefferson, March 15, 1800, *The Writings of James Madison*, ed. Gaillard Hunt (New York: Putnam, 1906), 6:407.

50. "The Early American Presidents," *Harper's New Monthly Magazine*, March 1984, 555.

51. "A Plain Fact," *Mercury and New England Palladium*, January 21, 1801 [shoulder of slaves]. "A Plain Case Stated," *Boston Columbian Centinel*, December 24, 1800 [horses, hogs, and oxen]. "Great National Election," *Connecticut Courant*, December 27, 1800 [proclaim to world].

52. Leonard Richards, *The Slave Power: The Free North and Southern Domination, 1780–1860* (Baton Rouge: Louisiana University Press, 2000); Garry Wills, *The First Negro President: Jefferson and the Slave Power* (New York: Houghton Mifflin, 2005); and William Freehling, *The Road to Disunion: Secessionists at Bay, 1776–1854*, vol. 1 (New York: Oxford University Press, 1990). For an ardent counter to the argument, see Sean Wilentz, *The Politicians and the Egalitarians* (New York: Norton, 2016), chap. 4.

53. *Aurora*, March 6, 1801.

54. Thomas Jefferson, First Inaugural Address, March 4, 1801, *Messages and Papers*, 1:309–312, quoted at 310.

55. For a fine description of the debate in Congress, see Brown, *Toussaint's Clause*, 269–278. John Quincy Adams, *Diaries: 1779–1848*, ed. David Waldstreicher (New York: Library of America, 2017), 1:110.

56. James Callender, "The President Again," *Recorder*, September 1, 1802.

57. Christopher Caustic [Thomas Green Fessenden], *Democracy Unveiled or Tyranny Stripped of the Garb of Patriotism*, 3rd ed. (New York: Riley, 1806). Couplets from vol. 2, pp. 7, 19, 21 (emphasis original).

58. Hawthorne included Fessenden in a collection of biographical sketches. "Thomas Green Fessenden," *The Works of Nathaniel Hawthorne* (Boston: Houghton Mifflin, 1850), 12:246–263, quoted at 254. The Federalist uproar included a poem by future president John Quincy Adams written as an anonymous lark in the *Monthly Anthology*, a newsletter for a Boston literary club. See the full poem in the *Proceedings of the Massachusetts Historical Society*, 1910, 41:243.

Fawn M. Brodie, *Thomas Jefferson: An Intimate History* (New York: Norton, 2010), 465. The Jones argument appeared in the *Richmond Examiner*, February 9, 1803. Brodie's book, originally published in 1974, exploded Jefferson historiography by disinterring the Sally Hemings story and placing it front and center. Considerable evidence, including DNA tests, very strongly support the thesis (but, there is no definitive prove and many conservatives cling to the story that other family members might have been responsible for the children). For a recent sorting of the evidence, see Annette Gordon-Reed, *The Hemingses of Monticello: An American Family* (New York: Norton, 2008).

Chapter 2. "Keep the Ball Rolling"

1. On Kendall, see John Quincy Adams, *Diaries, Vol. 1: 1779-1821*, ed. David Waldstreicher (New York: Library of America, 2017), 486. On Johnson, see Christina Snyder, *Great Crossings: Indians, Settlers and Slaves in the Age of Jackson* (New York: Oxford University Press, 2017), chap. 8.

2. Martin Van Buren to Thomas Ritchie, January 13, 1827, Washington, DC, *Papers of Martin Van Buren*, Series 5, January 1, 1925–March 3, 1829 (Washington, DC: Library of Congress).

3. "Speech of the Honorable Henry Clay, in the Senate of the United States: On the subject of abolition petitions." February 7, 1839. (Boston: J. Munroe, 1839), 40, 33, 41.

4. William Lloyd Garrison to Oliver Johnson, *The Letters of William Lloyd Garrison 1836–1840* (Cambridge: Cambridge University Press, 1971), 2:525. Nominating conventions were new and some southern states failed to send delegates, which hurt Clay.

5. Although Clay and Scott would each be nominated in the future. On the Whigs in general and this campaign in context, see the works of Daniel Walker Howe, especially *What Hath God Wrought: The Transformation of America, 1815–1848* (New York: Oxford, 2007) and *The Political Culture of*

American Whigs (Chicago: University of Chicago Press, 1979). The most thorough analysis of the party is Michael F. Holt's extraordinarily researched *The Rise and Fall of the American Whig Party* (New York: Oxford University Press, 1999). Holt delves into the patronage patterns on the national, state, and local levels. Two popular books give lively accounts of the campaign: Ronald Schafer's delightful *The Carnival Campaign* (Chicago: Chicago Review Press, 2017) and the classic Robert Gray Gunderson, *The Log Cabin Campaign* (Lexington: University of Kentucky Press, 1957).

6. John Quincy Adams, *Address of John Quincy Adams to His Constituents, of the Twelfth Congressional District at Braintree, September, 17, 1842* (Boston: J. H. Eastburn), 30; for another biting description, see *Diaries, Vol. 2: 1821–1848*, ed. David Waldstreicher (New York: Library of America, 2017), 505.

7. For a lively account of the campaign, see Schafer, *Carnival Campaign*, 12 [granny and cider].

8. "The Rolling of the Ball," *National Intelligencer*, June 8, 1840, 3; see also Lucy Kenney, *The Strongest of All Government Is That Which Is Most Free: An Address to the People of the United States* (no publisher listed, 1840), 5–6.

9. Thomas Hart Benton, *Thirty Years View; or A History of the Working of the American Government for Thirty Years from 1820 to 1850* (New York: Appleton, 1856), 2:205–206.

10. Horace Greeley, *Hints Towards Reform* (New York: Harper, 1850), 16–17.

11. Horace Greeley and Robert Dale Owen, *Reflections of a Busy Life* (New York: J. B. Ford, 1869), chap. 17, quoted at 132.

12. Greeley and Owen, *Reflections*, quoted at 132. For an example of a more accurate piece, see the reprinted puff piece, which is perfectly direct: "The general's home is far from being a log cabin," in "General Harrison at Home," *Fayetteville Observer*, May 22, 1840. Daniel Webster, "The Log Cabin Candidate," August 12, 1840, in *The Speeches and Orations of Daniel Webster* (Boston: Little, Brown, 1879), 476.

13. On the people rising, see James A. Morone, *The Democratic Wish: Popular Participation and the Limits of American Democracy* (New Haven, CT: Yale University Press, 1998). On the religious uprisings, more generally, and moral politics in the nineteenth century, see James A. Morone, *Hellfire Nation: The Politics of Sin in American History* (New Haven, CT, Yale University Press, 2003), 100–221.

14. Arthur M. Schlesinger, *The Age of Jackson* (Boston: Little, Brown, 1945), 505, and *The Idea of a Party System* (Berkeley: University of California Press, 1969), chap. 6. Rogers Smith, *Civic Ideals* (New Haven, CT: Yale University Press, 1997), chap. 8, pointedly titled "High Noon of the White Republic: The Age of Jackson."

15. David Crockett, *The Life of Martin Van Buren: Heir Apparent to the "Government" and the Appointed Successor of General Andrew Jackson* (Philadelphia: Robert Wright, 1935), 13, 81.

16. Andrew Jackson's Veto Message Against Rechartering the Bank of the United States, 1832, in *A Compilation of the Messages and Papers of the Presidents*, ed. James D. Richardson (Washington, DC: US Government Printing Office, 1908), 2:576–591. Some economic historians now suggest that the pet banks were not as flimsy as contemporaries charged.

17. For an overview of the economic arguments, See Mike Connor, *A Commercial Republic: America's Enduring Debate over Democratic Capitalism* (Lawrence: University of Kansas, 2014), chap 2.

18. For a summary of the Whig's list of harms produced by Van Buren's bank policies, see "A Retrospect," *National Intelligencer*, November 4, 1840.

19. William Henry Harrison, *General Harrison's Speech at the Dayton Convention, September 10, 1840* (Whig Republican Association, 1840), 5. On Jackson as transformative, see Stephen Skowronek, *The Politics Presidents Make* (Cambridge, MA: Harvard University Press, 1993), chap. 5.

20. "Charge Against Gen. Harrison for Voting to Sell White Men for Debt: Speech of Mr. Mason of Ohio," *National Intelligencer*, June 4, 1840, and "A Concise Statement of Facts Relating to the Charge Against General Harrison of Voting to Sell White Men for Debt," *National Intelligencer*, May 6, 1840.

21. William H. Harrison, letter to the editor, *The Republican*, October 27, 1840, "And Yet Another Forgery," *National Intelligencer*, November 2, 1840.

22. Alexis de Tocqueville, *De la Democratie en Amerique* (Paris: G. F. Flammarion, 1981), 1:476. For more detail on the material in this section, see Morone, *Hellfire Nation*, 117–215.

23. "Detestable Villainy," *Niles' Register*, August 8, 1835, 402–403. The paper includes outraged accounts from a dozen newspapers around the country, including the *Charleston Southern Patriot* [detestable] and the *Boston Atlas*.

24. *Niles' Register*, November 6, 1824, 160. Abraham Lincoln, Address Before the Young Men's Lyceum of Springfield, Illinois, January 27, 1838, in *The Collected Works of Abraham Lincoln*, ed. Roy Basler (New Brunswick, NJ: Rutgers University Press, 1953), 1:109, 110.

25. John Calhoun, Speech on the Reception of Abolition Petitions, February 6, 1837, *The Works of John C. Calhoun* (Farmington, MI: Gale, Sabin Americana, 2012) *Collected Works*, 2:630.

26. Sven Beckert, *An Empire of Cotton: A Global History* (New York: Knopf, 2014). Sven Beckert and Seth Rockman, eds. *Slavery's Capitalism* (Philadelphia: University of Pennsylvania Press, 2016).

27. See, for example, the list of petitions—including pensions and harbors—in *Niles' National Register*, April 11, 1840, 13.

28. John Quincy Adams, *Diaries, Vol. 2*, 427–428. See other descriptions on 425, 407–408 (September 1837), 511 (June 1841), and passim. Senator John Henderson (D-MI), "Congressional—The Right of Petition—Remarks of Mr. Henderson," *Washington Globe*, February 21, 1840.

29. "Congressional—Abolition Petitions—In Senate," *Washington Globe*, February 17, 1840. For a political analysis, see Jeffrey A. Jenkins and Charles Stewart III, "The Gag Rule, Congressional Politics, and the Growth of Anti-Slavery Popular Politics" (unpublished manuscript, April 16, 2005), http://web.mit.edu/cstewart/www/gag_rule_v12.pdf.

30. "1840 Democratic Party Platform," Article 7, adopted at the Democratic Party Convention, Baltimore, Maryland, May 5, 1840.

31. Orestes A. Brownson, "The Laboring Classes," Orestes Brownson, *Works in Political Philosophy, Vol. 2: 1828–1841*, ed. Gregory S. Butler (Wilmington, DE: Intercollegiate Studies Institute, 2007), 411–439, quoted at 418, 419, 439. Brownson, "Abolition Proceedings," *Works*, 321–343, quoted at 331 [Charleston]. For context, see Alex Gourevitch, *From Slavery to Comparative Commonwealth: Labor and Republican Liberty in the Nineteenth Century* (New York: Cambridge University Press, 2015). For the classic, see Arthur Schlesinger, *Orestes A. Brownson: A Pilgrim's Progress* (Boston: Little, Brown, 1939), quoted at 101.

32. Martin Van Buren, Inaugural Address, March 4, 1837.

33. Computed from Leonard Richards, *The Slave Power: The Free North and Southern Domination* (Baton Rouge: Louisiana State University Press, 2000), 111. For a feel for the debate among the Whigs, see "Congressional," *Washington Globe*, February 18, 1840. The debate is continued four days later, "Congressional," *Washington Globe*, February 21, 1840.

34. William Lloyd Garrison to John Collins, December 1, 1840, *The Letters of William Lloyd Garrison, Volume 2: A House Dividing Against Itself*, ed. Louis Ruchames (Cambridge, MA: Harvard University Press, 1971), 725.

35. John Quincy Adams, *Address of John Quincy Adams to His Constituents, of the Twelfth Congressional District at Braintree, September, 17, 1842* (Boston: J. H. Eastburn), 23. Adams made the same point his diary. John Quincy Adams, *Diaries, Vol. 2*, 427.

36. Daniel Carpenter and Colin Moore, "When Canvassers Became Activists: Antislavery Petitioning and the Mobilization of American Women," *American Political Science Review* 108, no. 3 (August 2014): 479–498.

37. See Garrison's marvelous description of Sarah Grimké's speech at Pennsylvania Hall—just before it was torched. William Lloyd Garrison to Mrs. Sarah Benson, *Letters of William Lloyd Garrison*, 2:362–364.

38. Lewis Tappan to Theodore Dwight Weld, May 26, 1840, *Letters of Theodore Dwight Weld, Angelina Grimké Weld, and Sarah Grimké*, ed. Gilbert Barnes and Dwight Dumond (New York: Appleton-Century, 1934), 2:836. Recall that the Democratic press accused Harrison of plotting to meet with Lewis's brother, Arthur. Lydia Maria Child, "To Abolitionists," *Lydia Maria Child Reader*, ed. Carolyn Karcher (Durham, NC: Duke University Press, 1997), 194–195.

39. The pamphlet that got most attention, a mélange of campaign songs, blasts at Democratic corruption, and celebrations of General Harrison, was penned by Lucy Kenney, *The Strongest of All Government Is That Which Is Most Free: An Address to the People of the United States* (no publisher listed, 1840). On diaries, see Ronald J. Zboray and Mary Saracino Zboray, "Whig Women, Politics and Culture in the Campaign of 1840," *Journal of the Early Republic* 17, no. 2 (Summer 1997): 277–315.

40. Daniel Webster, Address to the Ladies of Richmond, Richmond, Virginia, October 5, 1840, *The Speeches and Orations of Daniel Webster* (Boston: Little, Brown, 1879), 478. John Quincy Adams, *Diaries, Vol. 2*, 431.

41. Letter from the Vice President to Lewis Tappan. *Niles' National Register*, April 18, 1840, 4–5. James Kirke Paulding, *Slavery in the United States* (New York: Harper and Brothers, 1836), 310.

42. Computed from United States Bureau of the Census, *The Statistical History of the United States, From Colonial Times to the Present: Historical Statistics of the United States, Colonial Times to 1970* (New York: Basic Books, 1976).

43. "To the people of Illinois," *National Intelligencer*, July 7, 1840.

44. William Henry Harrison, Speech at Dayton Convention, September 10, 1800. "Van Buren Frauds," *Daily National Intelligencer*, October 31, 1840, 3 [grand jury]. "The Philadelphia Locofoco Frauds," *Daily National Intelligencer*, November 2, 1840, 3 [respected judges]. David Blight, *Frederick Douglass: Prophet of Freedom* (New York: Simon and Schuster, 2018), 414 [drunken Pat].

45. Alexis de Tocqueville, *De la Democratie en Amerique* (Paris: G. F. Flammarion, 1981), 1:381. On immigrant vices and virtues, see Morone, *Hellfire Nation*, chap. 7.

46. Frederick Douglass, "The Slavery Party: Extracts from a Speech Delivered Before the A.A. Society," New York, May 1831. Appendix to *My Bondage and My Freedom*, in *Frederick Douglass: Autobiographies* (New York: Library of America, 1994), 440–444. Lydia Maria Child, *Selected Letters*, eds. Milton Meltzer and Patricia Holland (Amherst: University of Massachusetts Press, 1982), 383. For an extended discussion on the Irish and the abolitionists, see Morone, *Hellfire Nation*, pt. 2.

47. When the election of 1848 cost Hawthorne his post, he wrote an acid satire of his days in the Boston Custom House and appended it as a preface to *The Scarlet Letter*.

48. William Henry Harrison, Dayton Convention Speech, September 10, 1840 [downfall], and Inaugural Address, March 4, 1841, in Richardson, *Messages and Papers*, 3:1868 [staunch patronage]. Martin Van Buren, Second Annual Message, December 3, 1838, in Richardson, *Messages and Papers*, 3:1709–1710 [defalcation]. On the Whigs and Patronage, the seminal work is Holt, *American Whig Party*.

49. William Henry Harrison, Dayton Convention Speech, September 10, 1840, City of Washington, *Washington Globe*, November 21, 1840, 3 [spoils and spoilsmen].

50. "The Philadelphia Locofoco Frauds," *National Intelligencer*, November 2, 1840. For more detailed descriptions of the registration movement, see Alexander Keyssar, *The Right to Vote* (New York: Basic Books, 2000), chap. 3, and Tracy Campbell, *Deliver the Vote* (New York: Carrol and Graf, 2005), chap. 1, quoted at 14–15 [safe].

51. Capen v. Foster, in *The American Decisions: Cases of General Value and Authority Decided by the Courts of the Several States*, ed. A. C. Freeman (Rochester, NY: Bancroft–Whitney, The Lawyers' Cooperative, 1910), 23:632–635.

52. On the Buckshot War, and more generally, the conflicts over voting, see Edward B. Foley, *Ballot Battles: The History of Disputed Elections in the United States* (New York: Oxford University Press, 2016), 79–84.

53. *Appeal of Forty Thousand Citizens Threatened with Disenfranchisement to the People of Pennsylvania* (Philadelphia: Merrihew and Gunn, 1838), 1.

54. Polk (1845–1849) would die soon after leaving office and his successor, Zachary Taylor (1849–1850), would die in office—too much ice cream on a hot summer day, said his contemporaries. See Jane McHugh and Philip Mackowiak, "What Really Killed William Henry Harrison," *New York Times*, April 1, 2014.

55. John Quincy Adams, *Diaries, Vol. 2*, April 1841, 505. Theodore Roosevelt, *Life of Thomas Hart Benton* (1897; London: Forgotten Books, 2012), 237.

56. John Quincy Adams, *Diaries, Vol. 2*, April 1841, 508. Daniel Webster, "Objects of the Mexican War," March 23, 1848, in *The Great Speeches and Orations of Daniel Webster* (Boston: Little, Brown & Co., 1879), 560.

57. *The Works of John Calhoun*, ed. Richard Crallé (New York: D. Appleton, 1883), 5:331–339, quoted at 331–332, 338–339.

58. Benton, *Thirty Years View*, 2:613, 612. He is frequently quoted as saying "a cry of wolf where there was no wolf," but that was a different speech on a different issue.

59. "More! More! More!" *New York Morning News*, February 7, 1845.

60. Sean Wilentz, *The Rise of American Democracy* (New York: Norton, 2005), 562. The seminal work on Manifest Destiny remains Frederick Merc, *Manifest Destiny and Mission in American History* (New York: Vintage, 1963).

61. Abraham Lincoln, "Spot Resolution in the United States House of Representatives," December 22, 1847, in Lincoln, *Collected Works*, 1:420–422.

Chapter 3. A Fire Bell in the Night

1. "The Law and Order Party," *Kansas Weekly Herald*, June 22, 1855. Lincoln, Speech at Peoria, in *The Collected Works of Abraham Lincoln*, ed. Roy Basler (New Brunswick, NJ: Rutgers University Press, 1953), 2:271.

2. Burns himself described the episode in a lecture, widely reprinted in northern newspapers. "Anthony Burns in New York," *Liberator*, March 9, 1855.

3. For a vivid description of the rescue attempt from one of the white ringleaders, see Thomas Wentworth Higginson, *The Writings of Thomas Wentworth Higginson* (1898; New York: De Capo Press, 2000), 65–73. On the administration's response to the earlier case, see Gary Collison, "'This Flagitious Offense': Daniel Webster and the Shadrach Rescue Cases," *New England Quarterly* 68 (December 1, 1995): 609–625, quoted at 610.

4. Lincoln, *Collected Works*, 2:255–256.

5. Martin Robison Delany, *The Condition, Elevation, Emigration, and Destiny of the Colored People of the United States* (no publisher listed, 1852), 3.

6. "Sam and Sambo," *Hartford Courant*, March 6, 1856.

7. Thomas Jefferson letter to John Holmes, April 22, 1820, in *Jefferson: Public and Private Papers* (New York: Library of America, 1984), 1433–1435.

8. James Buchanan, J. Y. Mason, and Pierre Soulé, Aix-las Cappelle, *The Ostend Manifesto*, October 15, 1854, www.historyofcuba.com/history /havana/Ostend2.htm.

9. "Republican Party Platform of 1856," June 18, 1856, www.presidency .ucsb.edu/documents/republican-party-platform-1856, and "1860 Democratic Party Platform," June 18, 1860, American Presidency Project, www .presidency.ucsb.edu/documents/1860-democratic-party-platform.

10. William Walker, *The War in Nicaragua* (New York: S. H. Goetzel, 1860), quoted at 253–254 [white race], 256 [wisdom].

11. *Congressional Globe*, 35th Congress, Session 2 (February 25, 1859), 1354.

12. Buchanan, Mason, and Soulé, *Ostend Manifesto* [horrors].

13. *Congressional Globe*, Senate, 32nd Congress, Session 2 (March 3, 1853), 1113.

14. The back and forth is detailed, with considerable sarcasm, in "Appeal of the Independent Democrats in Congress, to the People of the United States: Shall Slavery be Permitted in Nebraska?" Washington, January 19, 1854, 8–9. For a description of the episode, see David M. Potter, *The Impending Crisis: America Before the Civil War: 1848–1861* (New York: Harper, 1976), chap. 7.

15. An Act to Organize the Territories of Nebraska and Kansas, 1854 (10 stat. 277), Section 14, and Franklin Pierce, 4th Annual Message, December 2, 1856, in *A Compilation of the Messages and Papers of the Presidents*, ed. James D. Richardson (Washington, DC: US Government Printing Office, 1908), 4:2, 934.

16. *An Appeal of the Independent Democrats in Congress to the People of the United States: Shall Slavery Be Permitted in Nebraska?* Washington, January 19, 1854, 1, Oberlin College Anti-Slavery Collection.

17. Lincoln, *Collected Works*, vol. 2, quoted at 259.

18. For a good example of the charges, Samuel F. B. Morse, *Foreign Conspiracy Against the Liberties of the United States*, 7th ed. (New York: American and Foreign Christian Union, 1855), 16. The Most Reverend John Hughes, *The Decline of Protestantism and Its Causes* (New York: Edward Dunigan and Brother, 1851).

19. For a fine overview of the eastern Know Nothings, See Tyler Anbinder, *Nativism and Slavery: The Northern Know Nothings and the Politics of the 1850s* (New York: Oxford University Press, 1992).

20. Senator William Seward, speaking against an effort to limit or exclude the foreign born from a proposed Homestead Act, read the articles of the society on the floor of the Senate. Although his language is mocking, the principles are quite close to the published planks of the Massachusetts Party. *Congressional Globe*, Senate, 33rd Congress, Session 1 (July 12, 1853), 1708.

21. *Congressional Globe*, 1708.

22. Abraham Lincoln, Letter to Owen Lovejoy, August 11, 1855, *Collected Works*, 2:316 [painful necessity]; Letter to Joshua Speed, August 24, 1855, *Collected Works*, 2:323 [degeneracy]; and for a variation of the same line, see Letter to Theodore Canisius, May 17, 1859, *Collected Works*, 3:380.

23. Potter, *Impending Crisis*, 259.

24. "Republican Party Platform of 1856," American Presidency Project.

25. William Webb, *The History of William Webb, Composed by Himself* (Detroit: Egbert Hoekstra, 1873), 9.

26. Report of the Special Committee Appointed to Investigate the Troubles in Kansas, 34th Congress, Session 1, Report no. 200 (Washington, DC: Cornelius Wendell, 1856), quoted at 15, 16, voting data on table 1,

p. 30. The report runs to more than one thousand pages bristling with Bowie knives and cocked pistols. There was a minority report that disputed all this, but it offered few details. President Pierce sided with the minority report and refused to accept the findings—though historians generally find the report plausible.

27. "Kansas Election Fraud," *National Era*, Washington, DC, April 9, 1855.

28. "Law and Order Party," *Kansas Weekly Herald*, June 22, 1855.

29. "Kansas Election Fraud," *National Era*, April 9, 1855. A more benign account appeared in "Kansas," *St. Joseph (Missouri) Cycle*, May 25, 1855.

30. "Civil War," *New York Herald*, June 15, 1856.

31. "Kansas Affairs: Mr. Oliver's Minority Report," *Daily Union*, July 19, 1856. This is a reprinting of the minority report to the House investigation in Kansas and offers a detailed account of the evidence delivered regarding the John Brown murders. "Civil War," *New York Herald*, June 15, 1856.

32. James Buchanan, "To the Senate and House of Representatives of the United States," February 2, 1858, in *Messages and Papers*, 4:3002–3012.

33. *The Crime Against Kansas: Speech of the Hon Charles Sumner in the Senate of the United States*, May 19 and 20, 1856 (Boston: Jewett, 1856), quoted at 5 [sacrilege], 9 [harlot].

34. Testimony of Governor A. G. Brown, Select Committee on the Assault of Charles Sumner, 34th Congress, *Records of the Early Select Committees, Compiled 1793–1909*, United States House of Representatives, https://history.house.gov/Records-and-Research/Listing/hi_003/. Brown met both Brooks and Keitt shortly after the incident and reported their conversation to the committee.

35. New York Evening Post editorial was widely reprinted in the Northern papers. See "From the New York Evening Post," *Buffalo Daily Republic*, May 26, 1856.

36. Joanne Freeman, *The Field of Blood: Violence in Congress and the Road to Civil War* (New York: Farrar, Straus and Giroux, 2018).

37. See Timothy Snyder, *On Democracy: Twenty Lessons from the Twentieth Century* (New York: Penguin Random House, 2017).

38. For a good description of the convoluted details, see Don E. Fehrenbacher, *The Dred Scott Case: Its Significance in American Law and Politics* (New York: Oxford University Press, 1978).

39. Scott v. Emerson, 15 Mo. 576, 586 (Mo. 1852).

40. Dred Scott v. Sandford, 60 US (19 How) 393 (1857).

41. Lincoln, Address at Cooper Institute, February 27, 1860, *Collected Works*, 3:523.

42. Fehrenbacher, *The Dred Scott Case*, 3 [partisan], 70 [attorney general]. George Fredrickson, *The Black Image in the White Mind: The Debate on*

Afro-American Character and Destiny, 1817–1914 (New York: Wesleyan University Press, 1971), xi.

43. *Congressional Globe*, Senate, 35th Congress, Session 1 (March 3, 1858), 941.

44. Lincoln, "House Divided," June 16, 1858, Springfield, Illinois. *Collected Works*, 2:465–467.

45. Stephen Douglas, First Debate, Ottawa, Illinois, August 21, 1858, Lincoln, *Collected Works*, 3:11. For a text that contrasts Democratic and Republican newspaper accounts of the debates, see Harold Holzer, ed., *The Lincoln Douglas Debates: The First Complete, Unexpurgated Text* (New York: Harper Collins, 1993).

46. Stephen Douglas, Second Debate at Freeport, August 27, Third Debate at Jonesboro, September 15, 1858, Lincoln, *Collected Works*, 3:56, 105.

47. Lincoln, First Inaugural Address: Final Text, March 4, 1861, Washington, DC, in *Collected Works*, 4:268. Senator John P. Hale, *Congressional Globe*, 37th Congress, Session 2 (1861), 26. For discussion, documents, and analysis, see Howard Gillman, Mark Graber, and Keith Wittington, *American Constitutionalism: Structures of Government.* (New York: Oxford University Press, 2013), 1:253–254.

Chapter 4. Who Are We?

1. "The Hero of the Planter," *New York Times*, October 3, 1862.

2. "Tillman's Big Speech: In the Constitutional Convention on the Suffrage Plan: The Hideousness of Negro Rule in All its Deformity," *Manning [South Carolina] Times*, November 13, 1895.

3. "Afro-American Notes," *New York Sun*, September 10, 1895. For a description of Small's role at the Convention, see Okon Edet Uya, *From Slavery to Public Service: Robert Smalls* (New York: Oxford University Press, 1971), chap. 6.

4. Frederick Douglass, *The Life and Times of Frederick Douglass*, in *Frederick Douglass: Autobiographies* (1893; New York: Library of America, 1994), chap. 18, 754–773. "Speech of Old Brown," *New York Herald*, November 3, 1859. For a fascinating account by an African American participant who survived, see Osborne Anderson, *A Voice from Harper's Ferry* (Boston: Printed for the author, 1861).

5. "Alarming Condition of the Country—Probable Triumph of Black Republican Revolution," *New York Herald*, November 3, 1859.

6. Abraham Lincoln, Address at Cooper Institute, February 27, 1860, *The Collected Works of Abraham Lincoln*, vol. 3, ed. Roy Basler (New Brunswick: Rutgers University Press, 1953). For a broader collection of reactions to the raid, see John Stauffer and Zoe Trodd, *The Tribunal: Responses to John*

Brown and the Harper's Ferry Raid (Cambridge: Harvard University Press, 2012).

7. Stephen Douglas, "Second Debate at Freeport," August 27, in Lincoln, *Collected Works*, 3:56. The Douglas position became known as the Freeport Doctrine.

8. William L. Yancey of Alabama, "Speech Delivered to the National Democratic Convention with the Protest of the Alabama Delegation," Charleston, SC, April 28, 1860. For a similar address, put less flamboyantly, see Yancey's "Speech at Cooper Union," reprinted in the *New York Times*, October 11, 1860. On the election of 1860, the indispensable source is a downright heroic journalist who covered every convention—dashing back and forth between opposing groups when they divided. His colorful reports have been compiled in Mural Halstead, *Three Against Lincoln* (1860; Baton Rouge: Louisiana State University Press, 1960), Yancey speech described at 52–54.

9. Halstead, 54–55.

10. Halstead, 276.

11. Halstead, 142, 164.

12. Sam Waterston's reenactment of Lincoln's Cooper Union Address can be found at www.youtube.com/watch?v=aQ2De8VcSLw. The event marked publication of Harold Holzer, *Lincoln at Cooper Union: The Speech That Made Abraham Lincoln President* (New York: Simon and Schuster, 2004).

13. Abraham Lincoln letter to Samuel Galloway, March 24, 1860, *Collected Works*, 4:33–34.

14. Quotations from the "Republican Party Platform of 1860," Chicago, May 17, 1860, American Presidency Project, www.presidency.ucsb.edu /node/273296.

15. "Gov. Seward Will be Nominated," *New-York Tribune*, May 18, 1860. Halstead, 167.

16. Carl Schurz, *The Reminiscences of Carl Schurz*, vol. 2 (New York: McClure, 1908), chap. 5, 175–186. Schurz, a German immigrant, drafted the plank.

17. Halstead, 127; and "Constitutional Union Party Platform of 1860," May 9, 1860, American Presidency Project, www.presidency.ucsb.edu /documents/constitutional-union-party-platform-1860.

18. A. James Fuller, "The Last True Whig: John Bell and the Politics of Compromise in 1860," in *The Election of 1860 Reconsidered*, ed. A. James Fuller (Kent, Ohio: Kent State University Press, 2013), 118.

19. Robert W. Johannsen, "Stephen Douglas and the South," *Journal of Southern History* 33, no 1 (February 1967): 46.

20. See, for example, "The Republican Party Going to the Right House," published by Currier and Ives, 1860.

21. Frederick Douglass, "The Late Election," *Douglass' Monthly*, vol. 3, no. 7 (December 1860): 370; and Abraham Lincoln, First Inaugural Address, March 4, 1861, Lincoln, *Collected Works*, 4:263–264. Lincoln claimed, implausibly, not to have read the amendment.

22. *Declaration of the Immediate Causes Which Induce and Justify the Secession of South Carolina from the Federal Union*, December 24, 1860, https://avalon.law.yale.edu/19th_century/csa_scarsec.asp.

23. The classic nineteenth-century estimate put the number at 618,222. A more recent calculation, using newly digitized census data, recalculates the total to 750,000 with an estimate range of between 650,000 and 850,000. Guy Gugliotta, "New Estimate Raises Civil War Death Toll," *New York Times*, April 3, 2012.

24. For a fine description, see Stephen Skowronek, *The Politics Presidents Make* (Cambridge: Harvard University Press, 1993), 217ff. See also James McPherson, *Abraham Lincoln and the Second American Revolution* (New York: Oxford University Press, 1990), 40.

25. *Constitution of the Confederate States of America*, March 11, 1861, art. 1, sec. 8, para. 3; and Alexander H. Stephens, Corner Stone Speech, Savannah, Georgia, March 21, 1861.

26. Douglass quoted in W. E. B. Du Bois, *Black Reconstruction in America* (1935; New York, Athenaeum, 1992), 61.

27. For a description of the battle for the plantation, see Stephanie McCurry, *Confederate Reckoning: Power and Politics in the Civil War South* (Cambridge, MA: Harvard University Press, 2010); for the rebellion on the Davis Plantation, 252–259.

28. George McClellan, *McClellan's Own Story: The War for the Union* (New York: Charles L. Webster, 1887), 491 [frank], 537–538 [disintegration].

29. "Important Points Demonstrated by the Recent Attack at Charleston," *New York Herald*, April 17, 1863. The editor, James Gordon Bennett (who, two decades earlier, had coined the term *Manifest Destiny*) kept spinning from side to side. Soon he would bash the administration for moving toward emancipation too slowly.

30. The roll call votes from James McPherson, *Battle Cry of Freedom: The Civil War Era, 1848–1865* (New York: Oxford University Press, 2003), 506.

31. Abraham Lincoln, "Address on Colonization to a Deputation of Negroes," August 4, 1862; *Preliminary Emancipation Proclamation*, September 22, 1862, Lincoln, *Collected Works*, 5:371, 433–436.

32. See Amanda Foreman's fine *A World on Fire: Britain's Crucial Role in the American Civil War* (New York: Random House, 2010), 317–319.

33. "Emancipation Proclaimed," *Douglass' Monthly*, October 1862, quoted at 517. Eric Foner, *The Second Founding: How the Civil War and Reconstruction Remade the Constitution* (New York: Norton, 2019), 26.

34. *New York Times*, June 11, 1863. Lincoln, "Letter to James C. Conkling," August 26, 1863, Lincoln, *Works*, 6:406–410, quoted at 410. The term *Sambo* went into popular American culture with *Uncle Tom's Cabin*. For Butler quotations and discussion of the changing iconography of black America, see James A. Morone, *Hellfire Nation: The Politics of Sin in American History* (New Haven, CT, Yale University Press, 2003), 209–213.

35. Lincoln fragment, John Hay Library, Brown University.

36. See "Northwest Ordinance: An Ordinance for the Government of the Territory of the United States Northwest of the Ohio River," July 13, 1787, https://avalon.law.yale.edu/18th_century/nworder.asp. The article also excluded fugitive slaves who were to be "conveyed" back to person claiming them. The crestfallen Republican quoted by Jeffrey Tulis and Nicole Mellow, *Legacies of Losing in American Politics* (Chicago: University of Chicago Press, 2018), 78.

37. Abraham Lincoln, "Last Public Address," April 11, 1865, Lincoln, *Collected Works* 8:399–405. Booth himself received regular notices in New York and London. See, for example, *The (London) Era*, "Foreign Dramatic Intelligence," December 25, 1864, or *Brooklyn Union*, January 9, 1864.

38. The meeting is famously described in "Reply of the Colored Delegation to the President," February 7, 1866, in Frederick Douglass, *Selected Speeches and Writings* (Chicago: Lawrence Hill Books, 1999), 586–589. Carl Schurz, *Reminiscences*, 3:225–228.

39. Eric Foner, *Reconstruction: America's Unfinished Revolution: 1863–1877* (New York: Harper and Row, 1988), 251.

40. Du Bois, *Black Reconstruction*, 166. For a fine description of the Thirteenth Amendment and the legal arguments that surrounded it, see Rogers Smith, *Civic Ideals* (New Haven, CT: Yale University Press, 1997), 282–284.

41. "Reconstruction in Memphis," *Chicago Tribune*, May 5, 1866.

42. Du Bois, *Black Reconstruction*, 464–466 [murder]. Foner, *Reconstruction*, 263 [slaughter].

43. In Barron v. Baltimore, 32 U.S. 243, 1833, the Court ruled that Congress could not "take private property . . . for public use, without just compensation" (as the Fifth Amendment stipulates), but Maryland or Baltimore could. The Bill of Rights did not apply to state governments.

44. *Congressional Globe*, Senate, 39th Congress, Session 1, February 16, 1866, 880 [Hendricks]. Blair quoted in Foner, *Reconstruction*, 340 [Frances], 218 [Montgomery]. Blair was bitterly criticized for his language after the Democratic ticket was crushed in 1868, but it was hardly unusual.

45. Many of the nations in South America and the Caribbean adopted the same definition of citizenship, but it remains extremely rare outside of the Americas.

46. See James A. Morone and Rogan Kersh, *By the People: Debating American Government* (New York: Oxford University Press, 2018), chap. 5.

47. See Corey Brettschneider, *Constitutional Law and American Democracy: Cases and Readings* (New York: Wolters Kluwer, 2012), 1132.

48. *Congressional Globe*, 40th Congress, 3rd Session 3, February 9, 1869, 1029. For discussion, see Rachel Nusbaum, "What Right Has Any State to Abridge the Franchise: The Strange and Disappointing History of the 15th Amendment's Not Quite Right to Vote" (paper presented at the Annual Meetings of the *New England Political Science Association*, April 26, 2019), emphasis mine.

49. Ann Gordon, ed., *The Selected Papers of Elizabeth Cady Stanton and Susan B. Anthony* (New Brunswick, NJ: Rutgers University Press, 1997), 1:594, 2:127.

50. "Republican Party Platform of 1872," June 5, 1872, American Presidency Project, www.presidency.ucsb.edu/documents/republican-party -platform-1872.

51. *Supplemental Report of the Joint Committee of the General Assembly of Louisiana on the Conduct of the Late Elections and the Condition of Peace and Order in the State* (New Orleans: A. L. Lee, State Printer, 1869), 111–115.

52. The episode is described in Luis Alejandro Dinnella-Borrego, *The Risen Phoenix* (Charlottesville: University of Virginia Press, 2016), 1.

53. "South Carolina Banditti of the Other Sort," *New Orleans Times Picayune*, April 26, 1875. "Bogus Outrages," *Pittsburgh Daily Post*, October 10, 1872.

54. President U. S. Grant, Message to the Senate, January 13, 1875, *Messages and Papers of the Presidents*, ed. James D. Richardson (Washington, DC: Bureau of National Literature, 1911), 6:4262.

55. For the Colfax story, see Charles Lane, *The Day Freedom Died: The Colfax Massacre and the Betrayal of Reconstruction* (New York: Holt, 2008).

56. For a fine description of the trial, see Lane, *The Day Freedom Died*, chap. 11, attorneys quoted at 237 [elevate], 235 [shackles].

57. United States v. Cruikshank, 92 U.S. 542 (1876).

58. Letter to W. D. Howells, April 22, 1877, in *Diary and Letters of Rutherford Birchard Hayes*, ed. Charles Richard Williams (Columbus: Ohio State Archeological and Historical Society, 1924), 3:430.

59. Results reported in Richard Valelly, *The Two Reconstructions: The Struggle for Black Enfranchisement* (Chicago: University of Chicago Press, 2004), 128.

60. See Gary Gallagher and Alan Nolan, eds., *The Myth of the Lost Cause and Civil War History* (Bloomington: Indiana University Press, 2000).

61. See Richard Rubin, "The Colfax Riot: Stumbling on a Forgotten Reconstruction Tragedy," *Atlantic*, July/August 2003.

Chapter 5. Populism and the Rise of Active Government

1. Mary E. Lease, *The Problem of Civilization Solved* (Chicago: Laird and Lee, 1895), 365–367; and Annie L. Diggs, "Women in the Alliance Movement," *Arena* 6 (1892): 166. Lease later claimed that the quote about raising hell was invented by the newspapers, but it sounded so good she adopted it.

2. James H. "Cyclone" Davis, *Memoir by Cyclone Davis* (Sherman, TX: Courier Press, 1935), 98.

3. Ignatius Donnelly [writing as Edmund Boisgilbert, MD], *Caesar's Column: A Story of the 20th Century* (Chicago: F. J. Shulte, 1890), 236, and for the entire utopian scheme, see chapter 40 ("The Garden in the Mountains"). Gerald Magliocca, *The Tragedy of William Jennings Bryan: Constitutional Law and the Politics of Backlash* (New Haven, CT: Yale University Press, 2011), 378 [what is freedom].

4. The connection is ably made by Elizabeth Sanders, *Roots of Reform: Farmers, Workers, and the American State* (Chicago: University of Chicago Press, 1999) and John Gerring, *Party Ideologies in America: 1828–1996* (New York: Cambridge University Press, 1998). Among historians, the connection is drawn by Michael Kazin, *The Populist Persuasion: An American History*, rev. ed. (Ithaca, NY: Cornell University Press, 2017), esp. preface and chap. 1; and Charles Postel, *The Populist Vision* (New York: Oxford University Press, 2007). On the other side, the classic is Richard Hofstadter, *The Age of Reform* (New York: Random House, 1955) and, in a classic analysis that emphasizes how FDR broke with the past, Sidney Milkis, *The President and the Parties: The Transformation of the American Party System since the New Deal* (New York: Oxford University Press, 1993), pt. 1.

5. Tom E. Watson, "The Negro Question in the South," *Arena* 6 (1892): 540–550, quoted at 545.

6. "Stamp out the Anarchists," and "the Mayor and the Communists," *Chicago Tribune*, Friday May 7, 1886.

7. Donnelly, *Caesar's Column*, 54–55. For more on Donnelly's nicknames, see Nicholas Rudick, "Introduction," in *Caesar's Column* (1890; repr., Middletown, CT: Wesleyan University Press, 2003), xvi.

8. The Populists published two major platforms. The most important was the *Omaha Platform* (written by Ignatius Donnelly and adopted by the 1892 convention meeting in Omaha). Two years earlier, the Farmer's

Alliance met in Ocala, Florida, and published thirteen reforms known as the *Ocala Demands*. Almost all the demands overlap in the two platforms, and I've drawn on both to summarize the populist philosophy in the next seven paragraphs.

9. James H. ["Cyclone"] Davis, *A Political Revelation* (Dallas, TX: Advance Publishing, 1894), xx.

10. In Pollock v. Farmer's Loan and Trust Co. 157 U.S. 429 (1895), a five to four majority took constitutional language designed to bar the taxation of slaves and awkwardly applied it to the income tax. For discussion, see Magliocca, *Tragedy of William Jennings Bryan*.

11. See Theda Skocpol, *Protecting Soldiers and Mothers: The Political Origins of Social Policy in the United States* (Cambridge, MA: Harvard University Press, 1995).

12. See Isaiah Berlin's classic, "Two Concepts of Liberty," in *The Proper Study of Mankind: An Anthology of Essays* (New York: Farrar, Straus and Giroux, 1997), 191–242.

13. "The Sisters in Politics," *Western Spirit* (Paolo, KS), November 14, 1890. Annie L. Diggs, "Women in the Alliance Movement," *Arena* 6 (July, 1892): 161–179, quoted at 161 [winmin]. On other groups, see Elisabeth Clemens, "Organizational Repertoires and Institutional Change: Women's Groups and the Transformation of US Politics, 1890–1920," *American Journal of Sociology* 98, no. 4 (January 1993): 755–798.

14. Diggs, "Women in the Alliance Movement," 161, 165. Sarah E. V. Emery, *Seven Financial Conspiracies That Have Enslaved the American People* (Lansing, MI: Robert Smith, 1894).

15. Frances Elizabeth Willard, *Glimpses of Fifty Years: The Autobiography of an American Woman* (Chicago: H. J. Smith, 1889), 380 [do everything]. Frances Willard, *How to Win: A Book for Girls* (New York: Funk and Wagnalls, 1887), 26.

16. Hamlin Garland, *A Spoil of Office: A Story of the Modern West* (New York: Appleton, 1897), preface, 144, 145. Originally serialized in *Arena*, 1892.

17. George Noyes Miller, *The Strike of a Sex* (London: William Reeves, 1891), 19, 51. Margaret Sanger, "What Every Girl Should Know," *New York Call*, a twelve-part series beginning on November 17, 1912. The Comstock censorship laws were whittled down over thirty years, but the final blows were Griswold v. Connecticut, 381 U.S. 479 (1965) and Miller v. California, 413 U.S. 15 (1973).

18. Holly McCammon and Karen Campbell, "Winning the Vote in the West: The Political Successes of the Women's Suffrage Movements, 1866–1919," *Gender and Society* 15, no. 1 (February 2001), 55–82, table 2.

19. "A Wild Mob. Exciting Scenes in the Labor Conference. Without a Parallel in Convention History. Weeping, Wailing and Gnashing of Teeth . . . ," *Akron Beacon Journal*, February 25, 1892.

20. "Farmers and Laborers," *Globe-Republican*, August 20, 1890. "Sisters in Politics," *Western Spirit*, November 4, 1890. Diggs, "Women in the Alliance Movement," 161–179, describes the sarcasm and responds.

21. Thomas E. Watson, *Bethany: A Story of the Old South* (New York: Appleton, 1905), 236–239.

22. Lease, *Problem of Civilization Solved*.

23. Eileen McDonagh, "Race, Class and Gender in the Progressive Era," in *Progressivism and the New Democracy*, ed. Sidney Milkis and Jerome Mileur (Amherst: University of Massachusetts Press, 1999), 145–191. Suzanne Mettler, *Dividing Citizens: Gender and Federalism in New Deal Policy* (Ithaca, NY: Cornell University Press, 1997).

24. *Congressional Record*, 51st Congress, Session 1, vol. 21, pt. 7 (June 23, 1890), 6538–6547, quoted at 6543. See also the restatement in Henry Cabot Lodge and T. V. Powderly, "The Federal Election Bill," *North American Review* 151, no. 406 (September 1890): 257–273.

25. "The Unwise Force Bill" and "Republicans Do Protest," *New York Times*, July 24, 1890. Van Woodward, *Origins of the New South, 1877–1913* (Baton Rouge: Louisiana State University Press, 1951), 255. The original Force Bill was a measure pushed by President Andrew Jackson fifty years earlier.

26. "Republicans Do Protest," *New York Times*. Savoyard, "Henry Cabot Lodge," *Washington Post*, February 9, 1908.

27. Senator William M. Stewart, *Reminiscences of Senator William M. Stewart* (New York: Neal, 1908), 301–306.

28. Tom E. Watson, "The Negro Question in the South," *Arena* 6 (1892): 540–550, quoted at 545.

29. Watson, "Negro Question," 548–549.

30. See Charles Postel, *The Populist Vision* (New York: Oxford University Press, 2007); Kazin, *Populist Persuasion*; and Watson, "Negro Question," 550.

31. Watson, "Negro Question," 541.

32. James Dunwoody Brownson De Bow, *The Interest in Slavery of the Southern Non-Slaveholder* (Charleston, SC: Evans and Cogswell, 1860), quoted at 9–10 [infinite remove].

33. "Let Us Heed the Lesson," *Wilmington Semi-Weekly Messenger*, August 26, 1898 [taxed], November 15, 1898 [blood guiltiness]. For the classic overview of the event, see H. Leon Prather Sr., "We Have Taken a City: A Centennial Essay," *Democracy Betrayed: The Wilmington Race Riot of 1898*

and Its Legacy, ed. David Cecelski and Timothy Tyson (Chapel Hill: University of North Carolina Press, 1998), 16–41.

34. "Mrs. Felton's Letter," *Atlanta Journal Constitution*, Friday, August 20, 1897. For a fine description, see LeeAnn Whites, "Love, Hate, Rape, Lynching: Rebecca Latimer Felton and the Gender Politics of Racial Violence," *Democracy Betrayed*, Cecelski and Tyson, 143–161, quoted at 149.

35. Mrs. W. H. Felton, "Mrs. Felton Not for Lynching: Her "Ifs" Were Overlooked—Answers the Boston Transcript," letter to the editor, *Atlanta Journal Constitution*, Friday, August 20, 1897.

36. *Daily Record (Wilmington, NC)*, Thursday Evening, August, 18, 1898.

37. Reverend J. Allen Kirk, *A Statement of the Facts Concerning the Bloody Riot in Wilmington, N.C.: Bloody Riot Perpetrated upon the Helpless and Inoffensive Negro*, Wilmington, NC, November 10, 1898. "Election Aftermath," *The Semi-Weekly Messenger (Wilmington, NC)*, November 15, 1898.

38. Kirk, *Statement of the Facts*, 16.

39. "Intelligent Suffrage" [cloud] and "Food for Reflection" [enormous black majority], *New Mississippian*, April 23, 1890. Frances Willard, *Voice*, October 28, 1890, http://gildedage.lib.niu.edu/lessonplan1group1. The interview is a painful pander throughout. Willard had imagined that, with a literacy test, the Convention would also accept women's suffrage. Of course, it did no such thing.

40. For details, two classics analyze the politics of disenfranchisement. V. O. Key, *Southern Politics in State and Nation* (New York: Knopf, 1949), chap. 25, quoted at 537; and Rick Valelly, *Two Reconstructions: The Struggle for Black Enfranchisement* (Chicago: University of Chicago, 2004), chap. 6.

41. The voting data is reported in Valelly, *Two Reconstructions*, 128, table 6.3.

42. Plessy v. Ferguson, 163 U.S. 537 (1896). On Harlan's flawed vision, see Jackson Chin, "The Plessy Myth: Justice Harlan and the Chinese Cases," *Iowa Law Review* 82 (1996): 151–183. Lum v. Rice, 275 U.S. 78 (1927) [yellow races].

43. Williams v. Mississippi, 170 U.S. 213 (1898).

44. President William McKinley, "Speech at the Banquet at Atlanta, Georgia," December 15, 1898, *Speeches and Addresses of William McKinley: From March 1, 1897 to May 30, 1900* (New York: Doubleday and McClure, 1900), 160–165, quoted at 165.

45. Roosevelt quoted in Valelly, *Two Reconstructions*, 132–134; Tillman quoted in Stephen Kantrowitz, *Ben Tillman and the Reconstruction of White Supremacy* (Chapel Hill: University of North Carolina, 2000), 259. Desmond King, *Separate but Unequal: African Americans and the US Federal Government* (New York: Oxford University Press, 2007). Herbert Hoover broke the bigotry in 1929.

46. William Howard Taft, Inaugural Address, Washington, DC, March 4, 1909.

47. Thomas E. Watson, *Bethany: A Story of the Old South* (New York: Appleton, 1905), ix, 235, 292. The charge that Watson only tried racial conciliation as a political expedient is developed in Eugen Fingerhut, "Tom Watson, Blacks, and Southern Reform," *Georgia Historical Quarterly* 60, no. 4 (Winter 1976): 324–343.

48. On partisanship in Congress from 1880 to the present, see esp. Nolan McCarthy, Keith Poole, and Howard Rosenthal, *Polarized America: The Dance of Ideology and Unequal Riches* (Cambridge, MA: MIT Press, 2016), 2:10, fig. 1.3.

49. "Signor Corte's Farewell: His Story of the Lynching of the Italians." *New York Times*, May 24, 1891.

50. Immigration data from *Historical Statistics of the United States* (New York: Basic Books, 1976), 117–118. Senator Furnifold M. Simmons, *Congressional Record*, 59th Congress, Session 1, vol 40, pt. 8 (May 23, 1906), 7295 [list of foreign nations].

51. Speech of Mr. Miller of California, *Congressional Record*, 47th Congress, Session 1, vol. 13, pt. 2 (February 28, 1882), 1481–1488, quoted at 1482.

52. Henry Cabot Lodge, "Lynch Law and Unrestricted Immigration," *North American Review* 152 (1891): 602–612, quoted at 603, 608.

53. Henry Cabot Lodge, "The Restriction of Immigration," Speech in Senate, March 6, 1896. *Henry Cabot Lodge, Speeches and Addresses: 1884–1909* (Boston: Houghton Mifflin, 1909), 261, 264–265.

54. Simmons, *Congressional Record*, 59th Congress.

55. Richard Mayo-Smith, *Emigration and Immigration: A Study in the Social Sciences* (New York: Scribner's, 1890), quoted at 84, 87–88, 157, 166. Edward A. Ross, "The Causes of Race Superiority," *Annals of the American Academy of Political and Social Science* 18: 67–89, and *America's Race Problems: Address at the Fifth Annual Meeting of the American Academy of Political and Social Science, April 12–13, 1901* (July 1901), 67–89. Ross wrote a lively, biased, and influential popular book, *The Old World in the New* (New York: Century, 1913). Rogers Smith, *Civic Ideals: Conflicting Visions of Citizenship in U.S. History* (New Haven, CT: Yale University Press, 1997). For fine descriptions and analyses of this literature, see Daniel Tichenor, *Dividing Lines: The Politics of Immigration Control in America* (Princeton, NJ: Princeton University Press, 2002); Desmond King, *Making Americans: Immigration, Race and the Origins of the Diverse Democracy* (Cambridge, MA: Harvard University Press, 2000); and Aristide Zolberg, *A Nation by Design* (Cambridge: Harvard University Press, 2006).

56. Magliocca, *Tragedy of William Jennings Bryan*, 38–39.

57. United States v. Wong Kim Ark, 169 U.S. 649 (1898). There were not many children because most of the Chinese who came to the United States were male workers. On the violence and the exclusion movement, see Beth Lew-Williams, *The Chinese Must Go: Violence, Exclusion, and the Making of the Alien in America* (Cambridge, MA: Harvard University Press, 2015), 24 [spit].

58. Grover Cleveland, Veto Message, March 2, 1897, *Messages and Papers of the Presidents*, ed. James D. Richardson (Washington, DC: Bureau of National Literature, 1911), 8:6189–6193.

59. *Abstracts of Reports of the Immigration Commission: Presented by Mr. Dillingham*, December 5, 1910 (Washington, DC: US Government Printing Office, 1911), 1:55.

60. For a good account of the commission, see King, *Making Americans*, chap. 3.

61. "Ben Tillman's Address to the 1896 Democratic Convention, Chicago Il.," *Public Opinion* 21, no. 16 (July 1896): 69–71. Michael Kazin, *A Godly Hero: The Life of William Jennings Bryan* (New York: Knopf, 2006), quoted at 56-57.

62. William Jennings Bryan and Mary Baird Bryan, *The Memoirs of William Jennings Bryan* (Chicago: John Winston, 1925), 113–116. Among the many accounts of the convention, see esp. Richard Bensil, *Passion and Preferences: William Jennings Bryan and the 1896 Democratic Convention* (New York: Cambridge University Press, 2008).

63. Bryan and Bryan, *Memoirs*, 11.

64. "The Chicago Nominee," *The Nation*, July 16, 1896, 42.

65. For a fascinating look at the campaign through the eyes of a modern campaign professional, see Karl Rove, *the Triumph of William McKinley: Why the Election of 1896 Still Matters* (New York: Simon and Shuster, 2015), quoted at 330.

66. "M'Kinley! An Overwhelming Vote for National Honor," *New York Sun*, November 4, 1896.

67. Gerring, *Party Ideologies*, 188 (emphasis original).

68. Woodrow Wilson, "Inaugural Address. Delivered at Washington. March 4, 1913," *Messages and Papers*, 7868. David Sarasohn, *The Party of Reform: Democrats in the Progressive Era* (Jackson: University Press of Mississippi, 1989), 123 [Bryanism]. Jeffrey Tulis, *The Rhetorical Presidency* (Princeton, NJ: Princeton University Press, 1987), suggests that Wilson broke with the older constitutional forms and made the presidency an office that, through rhetoric, directly engaged the public.

69. Franklin D. Roosevelt, Inaugural Address, Delivered in Washington. March 4, 1933, *The Public Papers and Addresses of Franklin D. Roosevelt: The Year of Crisis, 1933* (New York: Random House, 1938), 2:12. Herbert

Hoover, *The Memoirs of Herbert Hoover* (New York: Macmillan, 1951), 1:28 [dishonesty]. Joan Huff Wilson, *Herbert Hoover: Forgotten Progressive* (Boston: Little, Brown, 1975), 212. See also the fine discussion of Bryanism in Wilson and FDR in John Gerring, *Party Ideologies,* 226–231, 230 [Bryanism in words]; and Sarasohn, *Party of Reform,* 123 [accent, Times].

70. Computed from *Historical Statistics of the United States* (New York: Basic Books, 1976), 1102. A. Scott Berg, *Wilson* (New York: Putnam, 2013), 306–331 [post office].

71. The vast literature, much of it from the South, includes history, social science, and novels—all borrowing the same phrases to construct variations on the theme: African Americans are moral inferiors and not ready for freedom. William Dunning, *Reconstruction: Political and Economic* (New York: Harper, 1907). Frederick Hoffman, *Race Traits of the American Negro* (New York: Macmillan, 1896), esp. 328–329. Benjamin Andrews, *The History of the Last Quarter Century in the United States, 1879–1895* (New York: Scribner's, 1896), 2:373. Woodrow Wilson, *History of the American People* (New York: Harper, 1902).

72. Mark E. Benbow, "Birth of a Quotation: Woodrow Wilson and 'Like Writing History with Lightning,'" *Journal of the Gilded Age and Progressive Era* 9, no. 4 (October 2010): 509–533.

73. Kerri Greenidge, *Black Radical: The Life and Times of William Monroe Trotter* (New York: Liverwright, 2020), 198–199. See also, Berg, *Wilson,* 345–347.

Chapter 6. The New Deal and the Origins of Contemporary America

1. Manuel J. Rogers, "Pickens Lynch Case Recalled. Negro Was Lynched About 35 Years Ago in Pickens," *Greenville News,* February 18, 1947. Rebecca West, "Opera in Greenville," June 14, 1947. The national news covered the story extensively. For a fine summary, see Kari Frederickson, *The Dixiecrat Revolt and the End of the Solid South, 1932–1968* (Chapel Hill: University of North Carolina Press, 2001), chap 2.

2. "Justice Prevails," *Index-Journal (Greenville, SC),* February 28, 1947.

3. This scholarly literature resetting the clock is now voluminous. In political science, I especially admire and was influenced by Eric Schickler, *Racial Realignment: The Transformation of American Liberalism, 1932–1965* (Princeton, NJ: Princeton University Press, 2016); David Karol, *Party Position Change in American Politics: Coalition Management* (New York: Cambridge University Press, 2009); Alan Ware, *The Democratic Party Heads North, 1877–1962* (New York: Cambridge University Press, 2006); and Robert Mickey, *Paths Out of Dixie: The Democratization of Authoritarian Enclaves in America's Deep South* (Princeton, NJ: Princeton University Press,

2015). The historical literature is even larger. See, for starters, two outstanding books: Kevin Kruse, *White Flight: Atlanta and the Making of Modern Conservatism* (Princeton, NJ: Princeton University Press, 2005), and Frederickson, *Dixiecrat Revolt*.

4. On Capone, see James A. Morone, "Scarface," *New York Times Sunday Book Review*, December 4, 2016.

5. For details, see James A. Morone, *Hellfire Nation: The Politics of Sin in American History* (New Haven, CT: Yale University Press, 2003), 326–327 and passim, chap. 11.

6. On the fall of Prohibition, see Morone, *Hellfire Nation*, chap. 11.

7. Franklin D. Roosevelt. *The Public Papers and Addresses of Franklin D. Roosevelt* (New York: Random House, 1938), 1:647–659. For a newsreel with extended portions of the address, see www.youtube.com/watch?v=-mqWhDwAFmk.

8. "Campaign Address on Progressive Government as the Commonwealth Club," San Francisco, CA, September 23, 1932, Roosevelt, *Public Papers and Addresses*, 1:742–756. For a fine discussion, see Sidney Milkis, *The President and the Parties* (New York: Oxford University Press, 1993), chap. 2–3.

9. Roosevelt, "Address at Oglethorpe University," Atlanta, GA, May 22, 1932, *Public Papers and Addresses*, 1:639–647.

10. For a description see, R. Shep Melnick, *Between the Lines: Interpreting Welfare Rights* (Washington, DC: Brookings, 1994), 68–69.

11. See Robert Lieberman, *Shifting the Color Line* (Cambridge, MA: Harvard University Press, 1998), chap 3; Ira Katznelson, *Fear Itself: The New Deal and the Origins of Our Time* (New York: Liveright, 2013); and Jill Quadagno, *The Color of Welfare: How Racism Undermined the War on Poverty* (New York: Oxford University Press, 1996). On the other side, for skeptics who challenge the centrality of race, see Gareth Davies and Martha Derthick, "Race and Social Welfare Policy: The Social Security Act of 1935," *Political Science Quarterly* 112, no. 2 (Summer 1997): 217–235; and Larry DeWitt, "The Decision to Exclude Agricultural and Domestic Workers from the Social Security Act," *Social Security Bulletin* 70, no. 4 (2010). www.ssa.gov/policy/docs/ssb/v70n4/v70n4p49.html.

12. Eisenhower quoted in Sidney Milkis and Michael Nelson, *The American Presidency* (Washington, DC: CQ Press, 2003), 299. On the Social Security Act more generally, see David Blumenthal and James A. Morone, *The Heart of Power: Health and Politics in the Oval Office* (Berkeley: University of California Press, 2009), chap. 1, 3, and 5.

13. Louis Adamic, "The Collapse of Organized Labor," *Harpers*, January 1932, 167–178. This section draws on James A. Morone, *The Democratic Wish* (New Haven, CT: Yale University Press, 1998), chap. 5.

14. Collins is quoted by Arthur Schlesinger, *The Coming of the New Deal* (Boston: Houghton Mifflin, 1959), 411. For a discussion of ethnic bias in the AFL, see David Kennedy, *Freedom from Fear: The American People in Depression and War: 1929–1945* (New York: Oxford University Press, 1999), 301.

15. Hugh Johnson, *The Blue Eagle: From Egg to Earth* (Garden City, NY: Doubleday, Doren, 1935).

16. See Morone, *Democratic Wish*, 157.

17. Arthur Brisbane, "General Strike Broken!" *San Francisco Chronicle*, July 19, 1934.

18. "Steel, Motor Issues Face Labor Board," *Sunday Daily News (New York)*, August 25, 1935.

19. Rodney Dutcher, syndicated column, "New Deal in Washington: AF of L Determined Not to Miss 'Break in Wagner Act,'" Washington, DC, August 22, 1935; and syndicated column, "New Deal: AF of L Fight Is One of Age Against Youth—Insurgents Say Craft Ideal Has Killed Off Scores of Budding Unions," Washington, DC, November 30, 1935.

20. Jack Vincent, correspondent for I.N. service, "Auto Industry Fears Sharp Letdown Next Year," Detroit, Michigan, December 31, 1937. Lewis quoted in Irving Bernstein, *The Turbulent Years: A History of the American Worker, 1933–1940* (Boston: Houghton Mifflin, 1969), 455.

21. "Riot Causes Still Exist, Jeffries Warns Council," *Detroit Free Press*, July 1, 1943. "Riots to Be Probed by Dies Committee, *Detroit Free Press*, June 24, 1943.

22. William White, *A Man Called White* (New York: Viking Press, 1948), chap. 24. "Negro Leader Assails Criticism by Mayor," *Detroit Free Press*, July 1, 1943.

23. "Two Sides of a Street," *Time*, March 9, 1942, 14.

24. For a discussion of the poverty data, see Robert C. Lieberman, *Shifting the Color Line: Race and the American Welfare State* (Cambridge, MA: Harvard University Press, 1996), 49.

25. For a summary of the shifting black vote, see Nancy Weiss, *Farewell to the Party of Lincoln* (Princeton, NJ: Princeton University Press, 1983), *Chicago Defender* quoted at 17–18.

26. "Negroes Important Factor As Democrats Sweep into Power" and "Negro Vote Not 'On Sale,' Pride Was the Price As Democrats Won Out," *Pittsburgh Courier*, November 12, 1932.

27. W. E. B. Du Bois, "A Negro Nation Within a Nation," *Current History* 42 (June 1935): 265–270.

28. "Democrats Open Negro Vote Drive. Farley Confers with House Member on Campaign for 3,000,000 votes," *Baltimore Sun*, July 30, 1936.

W. E. B. Du Bois, "A Negro Nation Within a Nation," Atlanta, June 26, 1934. Roosevelt, "Address at Howard University," Washington, DC, *Papers and Addresses*, 5:537.

29. "Showdown Planned at Congress Session," *Los Angeles Times*, December 16, 1936. Data on voter identification compiled by Dan Bositis, *Blacks and the 2012 Democratic Convention* (Washington, DC: Joint Center for Political and Economic Studies, 2012). For discussion, see Philip Bump, "When Did Black Americans Start Voting So Democratic?" *Washington Post*, July 7, 2015, www.washingtonpost.com/news/the-fix/wp/2015/07/07/when-did-black-americans-start-voting-so-heavily-democratic/?utm_term=.e9136dc345b2.

30. Frank R. Kent, "Negro Vote Is the Democratic Bogey," syndicated column, *Baltimore Sun*, July 14, 1940.

31. Dorothy Thompson, syndicated column, "On the Record: The Negro Vote," *New York Tribune*, August 11, 1936. Frederickson, *Dixiecrat Revolt*, 19 [buzzing].

32. Sam Lubell, *White and Black: Test of a Nation* (New York: Harper and Row, 1964), 67. John Frederick Martin, *Civil Rights and the Crisis of Liberalism: 1945–1976* (New York: Routledge, 2018), chap. 4.

33. Johnson Kanady, "Senate Hears South Warn of New Deal Bolt," *Chicago Tribune*, December 8, 1943, 1, 6 [honors]. John O'Donnell, "Capital Stuff," *New York Daily News*, December 10, 1943, 5 [Ed Smith]. For a discussion of the early Southern rebellion and why it came up short, see James T. Patterson, "The Failure of Party Realignment in the South 1937–39," *Journal of Politics* 27, no. 3 (August 1965): 606–617, Bailey quoted at 603.

34. Frank Kent, syndicated column, "The Great Game of Politics—Parties and the Poll Tax," *Baltimore Sun*, May 15, 1940.

35. Jay Franklin, "The 10-Point Conservative Manifesto," *Minneapolis Star*, December 27, 1937. On the Liberty League, see Aaron Weinstein, manuscript, *America's Lost Conservatism: The Collected Public Works of the American Liberty League, 1934–1936*.

36. Kent, "The Great Game of Politics."

37. Kennedy, *Freedom from Fear*, 346–350.

38. Schickler, *Racial Realignment*, 183.

39. White, *Man Called White*, 168–170.

40. O'Donnell, "Capital Stuff." For a full description of the soldier voting act, see Katznelson, *Fear Itself*, chap. 6.

41. Industry quotes from David M Kennedy, *Freedom from Fear* (New York: Oxford University Press, 1999), 776. Harold Ickes, *The Secret Diary of Harold Ickes: The Lowering Clouds* (New York: Simon and Schuster, 1954), 3:516.

42. A. Phillip Randolph, "Why Should We March?" *Survey Graphic* 31 (November 1942): 488–89. The meeting is also described in White, *Man Called White*, 190–193.

43. "Race Unites for Drive to Secure Real Democracy" and "What Do You Think of the Double V?" *Pittsburgh Courier*, March 7, 1942. The *Courier* originated the Double V campaign. Like many mainstream black organizations, it had originally been critical of Randolph. On the Packard strike, White, *Man Called White*, 225. For a fine description of these events, see Thomas Sugrue, *Sweet Land of Liberty: The Forgotten Struggle for Civil Rights in the North* (New York, Random House, 2009).

44. Martin Luther King solicited the poem for an event honoring Randolph in 1959 and thanked Hughes by writing, "I cannot say more to express my appreciation . . . than to say it is just what I expected of you." Martin Luther King to Langston Hughes, December 29, 1959, reprinted in Clayborne Carson, Tenisha Armstrong, Susan Carson, Adrienne Clay, and Kieran Taylor, eds. *The Papers of Martin Luther King*, vol. 5 (Berkeley: University of California Press, 2005). Sidney Milkis and Daniel Tichinor discovered the poem in the Randolph archive and begin their fine book by reprinting it. See *Rivalry and Reform: Presidents, Social Movements and the Transformation of American Politics* (Chicago: University of Chicago Press, 2018), 1.

45. The quotes are from Walter George [D-GA], Wilbert O'Daniel [D-TX], Harry Bird [D-VA], and Senator James Eastland [D-MI], all quoted in Katznelson, *Fear Itself*, 188–190, and Governor Frank Dixon [D-AL] and Senator Theodore Bilbo [D-MI], quoted in Frederickson, *Dixiecrat Revolt*, 33–34.

46. "Republican Party Platform of 1944," June 26, 1944, American Presidency Project, www.presidency.ucsb.edu/documents/republican-party-platform-1944. Drew Pearson, syndicated column, "Washington Merry-Go-Round: New Republican Salons Will Be Anti-Labor," Washington, DC, February 9, 1946 [on the midterm results]. Eric Schickler, *Racial Realignment: The Transformation of American Liberalism: 1932–1965* (Princeton, NJ: Princeton University Press, 2016), 243 [Martin].

47. Franklin Roosevelt, Annual Message to the Congress, January 6, 1941, *The Public Papers and Addresses of Franklin D. Roosevelt* (London: Macmillan, 1941), 663–672. Roosevelt's advisor, Sam Rosenman, scrawled a draft of the Four Freedoms on a lined legal pad as FDR dictated it. They labelled it, "peroration"—the rousing conclusion to an oration. Franklin D. Roosevelt Presidential Library, Rosenman Draft of Peroration to Annual Message of Congress, January 6, 1941, President's Master Speech File, Message to Congress Delivered in Person (Box 58).

48. Franklin D. Roosevelt, State of the Union Address, January 11, 1944, Washington, DC.

49. Howard Lancaster, "Zany No More: Martin Dies Grows in U.S. Esteem," release from the Western Newspaper Union, Washington, DC, January 11, 1940 ["scalps"]. Associated Press, "Dies, Wallace Fight over Reds," Washington, DC, March 29, 1942. Frances Perkins, *The Roosevelt I Knew* (New York: Viking, 1946), 315, 320.

50. *Congressional Record*, 77th Congress, Session 2, vol. 88, pt. 6 (September 24, 1942), 7447–7458 [on Randolph]. Martin Dies, *The Trojan Horse in America: A Report to the Nation* (New York: Dodd, Mead, 1940), chap. 9, quoted at 119–120.

51. Franklin, "The 10-Point Conservative Manifesto."

52. Senator Karl Mundt and Representative Clifford Case, "Should the GOP Merge with the Dixiecrats?" *Colliers Weekly*, July 28, 1951, 20–21, 45, 54.

53. See Morone, *Hellfire Nation*, 392–396.

54. The most famous was Louis Hartz, *The Liberal Tradition in America* (New York: Knopf, 1955) and his students. You can see the academic family tree that rose out of his writing in David Erickson and Louisa Green, eds., *The Liberal Tradition in American Politics* (London: Routledge, 1999). Arthur Miller, *The Crucible* (New York: Viking Press, 1953), 132.

55. George Sokolsky, "Trojan Horse Employed in Peace Drive," *Philadelphia Inquirer*, November 18, 1948 [Kaytidid].

56. John Steinbeck, *The Grapes of Wrath* (New York: Viking, 1939), 439.

57. See, for example, White, *Man Called White*, 168-169 (lynching legislation), 182-183 (attacks on her for racial attitudes), and 190-191 (March on Washington); Perkins, *Roosevelt I Knew*, 160, 353-355; Ickes, *Secret Diaries*, 2:289.

58. Suzanne Mettler, *Dividing Citizens: Gender and Federalism in New Deal Public Policy* (Ithaca, NY: Cornell University Press, 1999). Mettler calls it "national citizenship."

59. Norman Cousins, "Will Women Lose Their Jobs?" *Current History and Forum* 41 (September 1939): 14. One of my colleagues graciously read this manuscript and told me that his own parents had hushed up the news of their own marriage—now he knew why.

60. Perkins, *Roosevelt I Knew*, 299.

61. Morone, *Hellfire Nation*, 384–388.

62. "National Affairs: Housing," *Time*, November 19, 1945. For a general description, see Andrew Busch, *Truman's Triumph: The 1948 Election and the Making of Postwar America* (Lawrence: University of Kansas Press, 2002), 7–8.

63. "National Affairs: Wallace on the Way," *Time*, September 23, 1940; and "This Great Endeavor," *Time*, September 30, 1946 (both were cover stories).

64. A. Hagerty, "Wallace Warns of 'Tough' Policy Toward Russia," *New York Times*, September 13, 1946.

65. Americans for Democratic Action, "Henry A. Wallace: The First Three Months," ca. April 1948, Clifford Papers, Subject File: Wallace, Henry, The Harry S. Truman Library [memorabilia re: foreign policy views, resignation, election of 1948].

66. John O'Donnell, "Capital Stuff," *New York Daily News*, July 24, 1948.

67. Charles Wallace Collins, *Wither Solid South? A Study in Politics and Race Relations* (New Orleans: Pelican, 1947).

68. Richard Hofstadter, "From Calhoun to the Dixiecrats," *Social Research: An International Quarterly of Political and Social Science* 16, no. 2 (June 1949): 135–150.

69. Collins, *Wither*, 259.

70. "Anti-Trumanites Win Skirmish, Lose Battle," *New York Times News Service*, July 14, 1948.

71. "Anti-Trumanites Win Skirmish, Lose Battle," *New York Times News Service*. "1948 Democratic Party Platform," American Presidency Project, www.presidency.ucsb.edu/node/273225. You can hear the Humphrey speech at www.youtube.com/watch?v=8nwIdIUVFm4.

72. H. L. Mencken, "Doves for the Victors—Truman and Barkley Erupt Upon the Scene," *Baltimore Sun*, July 15, 1948.

73. "Dixon Speech Warns of Peril," *Birmingham States' Rights*, July 26, 1948 (the speech is included in its entirety).

74. G. C. Long, "Thurmond and Wright Lead 'No Quarter' Fight," *Montgomery Advertiser*, July 18, 1948.

75. Alan Rankin, "Rankin File: At the States Rights Explosion in Birmingham," *Alabama Journal*, July 19, 1948. [No title], *Montgomery Advertiser*, July 19, 1948, 2.

76. Rankin, "Rankin File," *Alabama Journal*.

77. Drew Pearson, syndicated column, "The Washington Merry-Go-Round: Republican National Chair Rebuffed at Convention," Washington, DC, June 23, 1948. George Sokolsky, syndicated column, "These Days: Main G. O. P. Battle Between Taft, Dewey." June 23, 1948. On the handicapping, journalist William Hutchinson had a familiar roundup that more or less reflected the consensus: 288 delegates for Taft, 273 for Dewey (548 to win), "Poll Hints at Early Choice at Convention, No Deadlock," *St. Louis Star and Tribune*, June 14, 1948.

78. Phyllis Schlafly, *A Choice Not an Echo* (Alton, IL: Pere Marquette Press, 1964), chap. 7, quoted at 49. "Civics Lesson," *Time*, April 15, 1946.

79. Andrew Bush, *Truman's Triumphs: The 1948 Election and the Making of Postwar America* (Lawrence: University Press of Kansas, 2012), 46–47 [to dislike him].

80. Jerry Green and Ted Lewis, "Dewey Wins As Rivals Collapse," *New York Daily News*, June 25, 1948, and "Dewey to Give Full Partner's Role to Warren: Halleck Gets the News," June 26, 1948.

81. See Simon Topping, "Never Argue with the Gallup Poll: Thomas Dewey, Civil Rights and the Election of 1948," *Journal of American Studies* 38, no, 2 (August 2004): 179–198.

82. Harry Truman, *Autobiography*, ed. Robert Ferrell (Columbia: University of Missouri, 2002), 82–83 [Prendergast picture]. "National Affairs: After 52 Weeks, A Surer Man," *Newsweek*, April 15, 1946. "The Presidency," *Newsweek*, May 26, 1947.

83. Harry S. Truman, "Special Message to Congress Presenting a 21-Point Program for the Reconversion Period," September 6, 1945, *Public Papers of the Presidents: Harry S. Truman*, 1945 (Washington, DC: US Government Printing Office, 1965), 263ff. William S. White, "Republicans See 1946 Issue Drawn; Truman Plans Drawn 'Out-New Deal; The New Deal' Says Martin," *The New York Times*, September 8, 1945.

84. For discussion, see Blumenthal and Morone, *Heart of Power*, 81–82.

85. The Truman convention speech was the first one to be televised. You can see it at www.c-span.org/video/?3389-1/harry-truman-accepts-1948-democratic-presidential-nomination.

86. "The Election: The Victorious Rebellion of Harry S. Truman," *Newsweek*, October 11, 1948. For a good discussion, see Alonzo Hamby, *Man of the People: A Life of Harry S. Truman* (New York: Oxford University Press, 1995), chap 26.

87. "Campaign Barbs That Won the Votes," *Newsweek*, November 8, 1948.

88. John Kee, letter to President Harry Truman, July 31, 1950, Vertical File, Health Care Policy, 121A, Box 3, File 2, Truman Library. Harry Truman letter to John Kee, August 9, 1950, Vertical File, Health Care Policy, 121A, Box 3, File 2, Truman Library.

89. For a more detailed discussion of the Truman idea, see Blumenthal and Morone, *Heart of Power*, chap. 3. See also, Harry S. Truman, letter to Ben Turoff, April 12, 1949, 286-A; and "Address to Health Assembly," Papers of Harry S. Truman, President's Secretary Files, B File, Folder 12, Truman Library. The notes in the president's hand are far more lively than the rather stiff formal record of the address.

Chapter 7. The Election That Remade American Politics

1. "The Negro in Vietnam: Democracy in the Foxhole," *Time*, Friday, May 26, 1967, http://content.time.com/time/subscriber/article/0,33009,843788,00.html.

2. "Mississippi: Act of Savagery," *Time*, Friday March 10, 1967, http://content.time.com/time/subscriber/article/0,33009,836720,00.html.

3. Phyllis Schlafly, *A Choice Not an Echo* (Alton, IL: Pere Marquette Press, 1963), 6–7. Richard Hofstadter, *The Paranoid Style in American Politics and Other Essays* (New York: Alfred Knopf, 1952), 25.

4. "Transcript of Eisenhower's Speech to the G.O.P. Convention," *New York Times*, July 15, 1964.

5. Belva Davis, *Never in My Wildest Dreams: A Black Woman's Life in Journalism* (Sausalito, CA: PoliPoint Press, 2010), 3–5.

6. Jackie Robinson, "New Breed's Weapons Are Hate, Murder," *Pittsburgh Currier*, July 25, 1964.

7. "Goldwater Show Jolts Negroes, Republicans," *Pittsburgh Currier*, July 25, 1964 [cover story]. "Republicans: The New Thrust," *Time*, July 24, 1964, quoted at 20 [Shelton, segregationist].

8. Richard Rovere, "The Campaign: Goldwater," *New Yorker*, October, 3, 1964 [gold watch]. "Negro Spokesman Bitter on Goldwater Nomination, Saying It Will Aid Racists: Dr. King Assails Senator's Views," *New York Times*, July 17, 1964.

9. Noah Remmick, "The Civil Rights Act: What JFK, LBJ, Martin Luther King and Malcolm X Had to Say," *Los Angeles Times*, June 28, 2014, www.latimes.com/nation/la-oe-civil-rights-quotes-20140629-story.html.

10. Described in Rick Perlstein, *Before the Storm: Barry Goldwater and the Unmaking of the American Consensus* (New York: Nation Books, 2001), 363–366, Goldwater quoted at 364.

11. "The Search" and "This Time, Things Changed," *Time*, July 10, 1964.

12. Walter Lippmann, "The Goldwater Southern Strategy: All White GOP," syndicated column, *Honolulu Advertiser*, September 24, 1964. On liberal bias against Goldwater, see Harry Stein, "The Goldwater Takedown: Media Coverage of the 1964 Presidential Campaign Was a Precursor to Today's Partisan Coverage," *City Journal*, Autumn 2016, www.city-journal.org/html/goldwater-takedown-14787.html.

13. Richard Rovere, "The Campaign: Goldwater," *New Yorker*, September 26, 1964. Kari Frederickson, *The Dixiecrat Revolt and the End of the Solid South: 1932–1968* (Chapel Hill, University of North Carolina Press, 2001), chap. 7.

14. Richard Rovere, "The Campaign: Goldwater."

15. Original Inaugural Address of George C. Wallace, January 14, 1963, Montgomery, Alabama.

16. Dan Block, *From George Wallace to Newt Gingrich* (Baton Rouge: Louisiana State Press, 1996), 2. For my own description, see also James A. Morone, *The Democratic Wish: Political Participation and the Limits of American Democracy* (New Haven, CT: Yale University Press, 1998), chap. 7.

17. Gloria Negri, "Wallace in Stormy Visit," "350 Attend Rights Rally While Wallace Speaks," and "Wallace Broadcasts at Unlistening Yale," *Boston Globe*, November 5, 1963. Zellner story from Dan Block, *The Politics of Rage: George Wallace, the Origins of the New Conservatism and the Transformation of American Politics*, 2nd ed. (Baton Rouge: Louisiana State University Press, 2000), 197.

18. Austin C. Wehrwein, "Midwest Jolted by Wallace Vote," and Earl Mazo, "Wisconsin's Meanings" [hot summer], *New York Times*, April 9, 1964, all quotes at 19.

19. Greg MacGregor, "Reaction Divided on Wallace Vote: Showing Is Discounted in North and Hailed in South"; and Ben A. Franklin, "Brewster Victor, Wallace has 43% in Maryland Vote. Alabaman Does Better Than in Wisconsin and Indiana. Elated at Showing," *New York Times*, May 20, 1964.

20. Abraham Lincoln, *The Collected Works of Abraham Lincoln*, ed. Roy Basler (New Brunswick, NJ: Rutgers University Press, 1953), 2:255–256.

21. "Southerners Pressing Wallace to Withdraw," *New York Times*, July 17, 1964.

22. For a detailed description, along with remarkable quotations from recently released phone logs that reveal Johnson's maneuvering, see David Blumenthal and James A. Morone, *The Heart of Power: Health and Politics in the Oval Office* (Berkeley: University of California Press, 2009), chap. 5, quotes at 183–185.

23. Lyndon B. Johnson, *The Vantage Point: Perspectives of the Presidency, 1963–1969* (New York: Holt, Rinehart and Winston, 1971).

24. Lyndon B. Johnson, "Special Message to the Congress on Immigration," January 13, 1965, www.presidency.ucsb.edu/documents/special -message-the-congress-immigration-0. Hubert Humphrey quoted in Daniel Tichenor, *Dividing Lines: The Politics of Immigration Control in America* (Princeton, NJ: Princeton University Press, 2002), 215.

25. John Avril, "Rusk Hit on Immigration Law Change. Revision of Quota Setup Challenged by Ervin," *Los Angeles Times*, February 25, 1965.

26. "The Central Points," *Time*, March 19, 1965 [cover story].

27. Roy Reed, "Alabama Police Use Gas and Clubs to Rout Negroes; 57 Are Injured in Selma As Troopers Break Up Rights Walk to Montgomery," *New York Times*, March 8, 1965.

28. Reed, "Alabama Police Use Gas," *New York Times*.

29. You can see the stunning footage at www.youtube.com/watch?v=TY tO7zj2zz8; the events are described by Julian E. Zelizer, *The Fierce Urgency of Now: Lyndon Johnson, Congress, and the Battle for the Great Society* (New York: Penguin Books, 2015), 202–220. Nan Robertson, "Johnson Pressed for a Voting Right Law," *New York Times*, March 9, 1965.

30. Lyndon B. Johnson, "Special Message to Congress: The American Promise," March 15, 1965, in *Public Papers of the Presidents of the United States: Lyndon B. Johnson* (Washington, DC: US Government Printing Office, 1965), 1:281–287. You can see the sections of the speech I've quoted at www.youtube.com/watch?v=MxEauRq1WxQ.

31. Tom Wicker, "Johnson Urges Congress at Joint Session to Pass Law Insuring the Negro Vote," *New York Times*, March 16, 1965.

32. Tom Wicker, "Johnson Urges Congress."

33. "Shelby County, Alabama v. Holder, Attorney General," Legal Information Institute, accessed April 4, 2020, www.law.cornell.edu/supreme court/text/12-96. For a systematic study of discriminatory voting measures that followed Shelby County, see "New Voting Restrictions in America," Benner Center for Justice, www.brennancenter.org/new-voting-restrictions -america.

34. Bernard Auer, "A Letter from the Publisher," *Time*, August 20, 1965.

35. *Time*, August 20, 1965, 17.

36. Gerald Horne, *The Fire This Time: The Watt's Uprising and the 1960s* (Charlottesville: University of Virginia Press, 1995), 12. Baldwin was kicking off a panel discussion hosted by Nat Hentoff on New York's WBAI, reprinted in "The Negro in American Culture," *CrossCurrents* 11, no. 3 (Summer 1961): 205.

37. Peter Bart, "Los Angeles Whites Voice Racial Fears . . . Buy Guns As Tension from Riots Spreads," *New York Times*, August 17, 1965.

38. Martin Luther King, *Where Do We Go from Here: Chaos or Community?* (New York: Harper and Row, 1967) [I had preached]. Andrew Kopkind, "Soul Power," *New York Review of Books*, August 24, 1976. Zelizer, *Fierce Urgency*, 230 [never seen].

39. Lawrence Van Gelder, "Martin Luther King Is Slain in Memphis; A White Is Suspected. Dismay in Nation," *New York Times*, April 5, 1968.

40. US Bureau of Economic Analysis, "Real Gross Domestic Product," Federal Reserve Bank of Saint Louis, January 1, 1930, https://fred.stlouis fed.org/series/A191RL1A225NBEA.

Chapter 8. We Win, They Lose

1. Homar Bigart, "3,000 Police Ring Garden as Wallace Stages a Rally," *New York Times*, October 25, 1968. For a good description, see Dan T. Carter, *The Politics of Rage: George Wallace, the Origins of the New Conservatism, and the Transformation of American Politics*, 2nd ed. (Baton Rouge: Louisiana State University Press, 2000), 366–367.

2. "The Fear Campaign," *Time*, October 4, 1968 [cover story]. Homar Bigart, "3,000 Police Ring Garden as Wallace Stages a Rally," *New York Times*, October 25, 1968.

3. Steven V. Roberts, "Wallace Backers Say Why They Are at Rally They Give Voice to Their Dissatisfactions," *New York Times*, October 25, 1968.

4. Franklin Roosevelt, Campaign Address at Madison Square Garden, New York City, October 31, 1936, *The Public Papers and Addresses of Franklin D. Roosevelt* (New York: Random House, 1938), 5:566–573, quoted at 568.

5. Douglas McAdam and Karina Kloos, *Deeply Divided: Racial Politics and Social Movements in Postwar America* (New York: Oxford University Press, 2014).

6. The article was actually written by Patrick Buchanan. Geoffrey Kabaservice, *Rule and Ruin: The Downfall of Moderation and the Destruction of the Republican Party, From Eisenhower to the Tea Party* (New York: Oxford University Press, 2012), 212.

7. "The Fear Campaign," *Time*, October 4, 1968 [cover story]. Phillip Klinkerer and Rogers Smith, *The Unsteady March: The Rise and Decline of Civil Rights in America* (Chicago: University of Chicago Press, 2001), 292 [punch].

8. For a description of the economic data, see Marilyn Geewax, "The Economy and Politics of 1968: Now Playing in Reruns," *NPR*, June 29, 2016, www.npr.org/sections/thetwo-way/2016/07/29/487821128/the -economy-and-politics-of-1968-now-playing-in-reruns.

9. David Halberstam, *The Making of a Quagmire: America and Vietnam During the Kennedy Era* (Lanham, MD: Rowman and Littlefield, 2007), 128.

10. Martin Luther King, "Nobel Peace Prize Acceptance Speech," December 10, 1964, 224–226, and King, "Where Do We Go from Here: Chaos or Community," both in King, *Testament of Hope: The Essential Writings and Speeches of Dr. Martin Luther King* (New York: Harper, 2003).

11. Norman Mailer, *The Armies of the Night: History as Novel and Novel as History* (New York: New American Library, 1968), 224.

12. You can see the execution at www.youtube.com/watch?v=7s3Juw koxZk&has_verified=1.

13. For a description of the Vietnam protests and the new left contribution to American foreign and military policy debates, see James A. Morone, "Hell No! The Anti-War Movement of the 1960s and the New American Partisanship," in *War, Justice, and Peace in American Political Thought*, ed. Bryan-Paul Frost, Paul Carrese, and Stephen Knott (Baltimore, MD: Johns Hopkins Press, forthcoming).

14. See Michael Nelson, *Resilient America: Electing Nixon in 1968, Channeling Dissent, and Dividing Government* (Lawrence: University of Kansas Press, 2014), 110 [Kennedy's chances], 180 [Gallup polls].

15. Kevin Phillips, *The Emerging Republican Majority* (New Rochelle, NY: Arlington House, 1969), quoted at 543.

16. Warren Weaver, review of *The Emerging Republican Majority*, by Kevin P. Phillips, *New York Times*, September 21, 1969.

17. Pat Caddell, memo to Governor Carter, "Additions to December 10 Working Paper," December 21, 1976, Staff Secretary [Presidential Handwriting] File, Box 1, Folder: Cadell, Patrick, 12/76-1/77, Carter Library.

18. *Congressional Record*, House, vol. 110, pt. 2 (February 8, 1964), 2577–2578, 2583. See the description of the law and implementation in James A. Morone, *Hellfire Nation: The Politics of Sin in American History* (New Haven, CT: Yale University Press, 1993).

19. Donald Critchlow, *Phyllis Schlafly and Grassroots Conservatism: A Woman's Crusade* (Princeton, NJ: Princeton University Press, 2005), chap. 9.

20. "What Next for US Women. Houston Produces New Alliances and a Drive for Grass-Roots Power," *Time*, December 5, 1977 [cover story], 24 [loved], 25 [goat].

21. Robert Self, *All in the Family: The Realignment of American Democracy* (New York: Hill and Wang, 2012).

22. James Kirke Paulding, *Slavery in the United States* (New York: Harper and Brothers, 1836), 310 [degraded race]. This argument is developed in Angie Maxwell and Todd Shields, *The Long Southern Strategy: How Chasing White Voters in the South Changed American Politics* (New York: Oxford University Press, 2019).

23. Lewis F. Powell Jr., "Confidential Memorandum: Attack of American Free Enterprise System," August 23, 1971, quoted at 5 [warfare], 26 [unwelcome]. The original memo, written to the Chamber of Commerce and later leaked by columnist Jack Anderson, can be found at www.corporatecrime reporter.com/wp-content/uploads/2012/09/Lewis-Powell-Memo.pdf.

24. Although they are ghost written, Reagan's two autobiographies are charming—and most unusual for presidential political memoirs, usually a deadly dull genre. See Ronald Reagan, *An American Life* (New York: Simon and Schuster, 1990), quoted at 15–16.

25. For a reflection on that "Huck Finn childhood," see James A. Morone, "Huckleberry Finn's Hard Racial Lesson," *The Devils We Know: Us and Them in America's Raucous Political Culture* (Lawrence: University Press of Kansas, 2014), 56–67.

26. Ronald Reagan, with Richard Hubler, *Where's the Rest of Me?* (New York: Karz-Segil, 1965), 66–67. Reagan, *An American Life*, 73.

27. See, for example, John Patrick Diggins, *Ronald Reagan* (New York: Norton, 2007), 68–69; Dinesh D'Souza, *Ronald Reagan: How an Ordinary Man Became an Extraordinary Leader* (New York: Simon and Schuster, 1997), 42.

28. Douglas Kneeland, "Reagan Urges Blacks to Look Past Labels and Vote for Him," *New York Times*, August 6, 1980. See also, Douglas Kneeland, "Reagan Campaigns at Mississippi Fair—Nominee Tells Crowd He Is Backing States' Rights—Attacks Inflation Policy," *New York Times*, August 4, 1980. Ed Magnuson, Christopher Ogden, and Laurence Barrett, "The Mood of the Voter" [cover story], *Time*, September 15, 1980.

29. Andrew Busch, *Reagan's Victory: The Presidential Election of 1980 and the Rise of the Right* (Lawrence: University Press of Kansas 2005), 108–109.

30. On the shooting, see Ronald Reagan, *An American Life* (New York: Simon and Schuster, 1990), chap. 42, and the entry for March 30, 1981, *The Reagan Diaries*, ed. Douglas Brinkley (New York: HarperCollins, 2007). For a description based on interviews with the main characters, see Peggy Noonan, *When Character Was King* (New York: Penguin Books, 2001), 167–179.

31. Ronald Reagan, "Proposal for Economic Recovery: Address to a Joint Session of Congress," Washington, DC, April 28, 1981.

32. David Stockman, *The Triumph of Politics: How the Reagan Revolution Failed* (New York: Harper and Row, 1986). Lou Cannon, *The Role of a Lifetime* (New York: Public Affairs Press, 2000).

33. David Blumenthal and James A. Morone, *The Heart of Power: Health and Politics in the Oval Office* (Berkeley: University of California Press, 2009), 299–315.

34. David Stockman, *The Triumph of Politics*, 8–11. James Reston, "Reagan's Dramatic Success," *New York Times*, January 21, 1981.

35. Reagan, *Diaries*, March 29, 1981.

36. Ronald Reagan, Address to the National Association of Evangelicals ("Evil Empire Speech"), March 3, 1983, Miller Center for Public Affairs, University of Virginia.

37. Stephen Roberts, "Bush Intensified Debate on Pledge, Asking Why It So Upsets Dukakis," *New York Times*, August 25, 1988. Newt Gingrich, *A Nation Like No Other: Why American Exceptionalism Matters* (Washington, DC: Regnery, 2011), 7.

38. Reagan, *An American Life*, 115 [evil]. Peter Robinson, *How Ronald Reagan Changed My Life* (New York: Regan Books, 2003), 69–72.

39. Reagan, *Diaries*, February 16, 1981.

40. Ronald Reagan, Inaugural Address, January 20, 1981, American Presidency Project, www.presidency.ucsb.edu/node/246336.

41. President Ronald Reagan, 38th Press Conference, August 12, 1896, Chicago, Illinois. The full press conference can be seen at www.youtube .com/watch?v=1ySHtDHrLJY.

42. Desmond King, book proposal, *Against the State: How an Idea Transformed American Democracy*, Oxford University Press, August 2019.

43. Kevin Phillips, *The Politics of Rich and Poor: Wealth and the American Electorate in the Reagan Aftermath* (New York: Random House, 1989), 5.

44. William Clinton, Address Before a Joint Session of Congress on the State of the Union, Washington, DC, January 23, 1986.

45. For the Gini index over time, international comparisons, and my analysis of the growing American inequality, See James A. Morone, "The Wages of Inequality," in *The Devils We Know*, chap. 8.

46. E. J. Dionne, *How the Right Went Wrong* (New York: Simon and Schuster, 2016), 242. See also Ezra Klein, *Why We're Polarized* (New York: Avid Reader Press, 2020), chap 6.

47. You get your briefing on the conspiracy here: www.youtube.com/ watch?v=esJY2SK_4tE. Beck quoted at 3:10.

48. Reece Peck, *Fox Populism* (New York: Cambridge University Press, 2019).

49. See Dov Grohsgal and Kevin Kruse, "How the Republican Majority Emerged," *Atlantic*, August 6, 2019.

50. See Sean Theriault, *The Gingrich Senators: The Roots of Partisan Warfare in Congress* (New York: Oxford University Press, 2013), 23.

51. Alison Mitchell, "Gingrich's Views on Slayings Draw Fire," *New York Times*, November 23, 1995. Jack Hitt, "Susan Smith's Judgment Day," *Washington Post*, June 25, 1995.

52. Alison Mitchell, "The Speaker Steps Down: The Career," *New York Times*, November 7, 1988.

53. Hannah Fingerhut, "In Politics, Most Americans Feel They Are on the Losing Side," *Pew Research Center*, November 25, 2015, www.pew research.org/fact-tank/2015/11/25/winners-and-losers-in-politics/.

54. Tanya Broder, Avideh Moussavian, and Jonathan Blazer, "Overview of Immigrant Eligibility for Federal Programs," *National Immigration Law Center*, 2015, www.nilc.org/issues/economic-support/overview-immeligfed programs/.

55. Shankar Prasad, "Red, Brown, and Blue: The Political Behavior of Asian Indian Americans" (PhD diss., Brown University, 2006).

56. Kim Parker, Rich Moran, and Juliana Menasce Horowitz, "Looking to the Future, Americans See Decline on Many Fronts: Views of Demographic Change," Pew Research Center, March 19, 2019, www.pewsocial trends.org/2019/03/21/views-of-demographic-changes-in-america/.

57. John Sides, Michael Tesler, and Lynn Vavreck, *Identity Crisis: The 2016 Presidential Campaign and the Battle for The Meaning of America* (Princeton, NJ: Princeton University Press, 2019).

58. Ben Guarino, "Famously Divisive 'Speak English' Sign Pulled from Philadelphia Cheesesteak Shop," *Washington Post*, October 17, 2016.

59. Amanda Barroso, Kim Parker, and Jesse Bennett, "As Millennials Near 40, They're Approaching Family Life Differently than Previous Generations," Pew Research Center, May 27, 2020. https://www.pewsocial trends.org/2020/05/27/as-millennials-near-40-theyre-approaching-family -life-differently-than-previous-generations/.

Conclusion: What Next?

1. Harold W. Odum, *Race and Rumors of Race: The American South in the Early Forties* (Chapel Hill: University of North Carolina Press, 1943), chap. 9, 12, and 15. Odum, a celebrated sociologist at the University of North Carolina, collected race rumors. For a discussion, see Kari Frederickson, *The Dixiecrat Revolt and the End of the Solid South* (Chapel Hill: University of North Carolina Press, 2001).

2. Drew Englehardt, "White People's Racial Attitudes Are Changing to Match Partisanship," March 21, 2019. Meanwhile, the modal (or most common) Democratic response was all the way at the other end of the scale—least resentment. www.dataforprogress.org/blog/2019/3/20/racial -resentment-is-the-defining-feature-of-american-politics. Marc Hooghe and Ruth Dassonneville, "Explaining the Trump Vote: The Effect of Racist Resentment and Anti-Immigrant Sentiment," *PS: Political Science and Politics* 51, no. 3 (June 2018): 528–534.

3. John Sides, Michael Tesler, and Lynn Vavreck, *Identity Crisis: The 2016 Presidential Campaign and the Battle for the Meaning of America* (Princeton, NJ: Princeton University Press, 2019).

4. For an extend treatment of this topic, see Russell Muirhead, *The Promise of Party in a Polarized Age* (Cambridge, MA: Harvard University Press, 2014), and Nancy L. Rosenblum, *On the Side of the Angels: An Appreciation of Parties and Partisanship* (Princeton, NJ: Princeton University Press, 2008).

5. For the classic analysis of why Americans dislike partisanship, see John R. Hibbing and Elizabeth Theiss Morse, *Stealth Democracy: Americans' Belief About How Government Should Work* (New York: Cambridge University Press, 2002).

6. Congressman John Dingell powerfully makes this point as his first recommendation for fixing American politics. I've paraphrased what he says

in his fascinating story, John Dingell with David Bender, *The Dean: The Best Seat in the House* (New York: Harper Collins, 2018), 39–69. I concluded my first book, *The Democratic Wish*, by criticizing this quote from Dewey. Obviously, I've changed my mind.

7. Jacob Hacker and Paul Pierson, *American Amnesia: How the War on Government Led Us to Forget What Made America Prosper* (New York: Simon and Schuster, 2016) 328-329.

8. I made this case in an op ed one month after the inauguration, urging the administration to toss aside their bipartisan dreams. See James A. Morone, "One Side to Every Story," *New York Times*, February 16, 2009.

9. Associated Press, "Joe the Plumber Becomes Focus of Debate," October 15, 2008, www.youtube.com/watch?v=PUvwKVvp3-o.

10. Barack Obama, Inaugural Address, Washington, DC. January 21, 2009.

11. "Let Us Heed the Lesson," *Wilmington Semi-Weekly Messenger*, August 26, 1898.

12. *Religious Landscape Study*, Pew Research Center, 2019, www.pew forum.org/religious-landscape-study/racial-and-ethnic-composition/.

13. Washington Post Staff, "Full Transcript of President Obama's Speech at the Opening Ceremony of the African American Museum, *Washington Post*, September 24, 2016. www.washingtonpost.com/news/arts-and-enter tainment/wp/2016/09/24/full-transcript-of-president-obamas-speech -at-the-opening-ceremony-of-the-african-american-museum/.

INDEX

Index

Index

Credit: Jeff Woodward

James A. Morone is the John Hazen White professor of political science and public policy at Brown University. He is the author of multiple award-winning books including *Hellfire Nation: The Politics of Sin in American History*, *The Democratic Wish*, and *The Heart of Power*. Two of his works were named notable books by the *New York Times*. He has won university-wide teaching awards five times and been elected to the National Academy of Science, Engineering and Medicine. Jim lives in Nelson, New Hampshire.